For Boyd, Elizabeth, and Greta –
without whom I could not have gotten on

Ways with Words

Language, life, and work
in communities
and classrooms

SHIRLEY BRICE HEATH

Associate Professor of Anthropology and Linguistics
School of Education, Stanford University

CAMBRIDGE UNIVERSITY PRESS
Cambridge
London   New York   New Rochelle
Melbourne   Sydney

Published by the Press Syndicate of the University of Cambridge
The Pitt Building, Trumpington Street, Cambridge CB2 1RP
32 East 57th Street, New York, NY 10022, USA
296 Beaconsfield Parade, Middle Park, Melbourne 3206, Australia

© Cambridge University Press 1983

First published 1983

Printed in Great Britain at The Pitman Press, Bath

Library of Congress catalogue card number: 82-22062

British Library Cataloguing in Publication Data
Heath, Shirley Brice
Ways with words.
1. Teachers – Language 2. Students – Language
I. Title
371.1'02   LB1027

ISBN 0 521 25334 9 hard covers
ISBN 0 521 27319 6 paperback

Contents

Contents

Photographs, Maps, Figures, Tables, Texts

Photographs *between pages 262 and 263*
By Joel H. Nichols, Jr., Winthrop College

A native and longtime resident of the South, Joel H. Nichols, Jr., has been the staff photographer of Winthrop College for the past twenty years. He has followed his father and grandfather into professional photography and has a special interest in depicting lifestyles of the Southeast.

Photographs, Maps, Figures, Tables, Texts

Texts

Acknowledgments

Those to whom the greatest acknowledgment of gratitude is due for help with this book are the community members of Roadville and Trackton, and the school, mill, and business personnel of the Piedmont Carolinas with whom I lived and worked for nearly a decade. They cannot be mentioned by name, but they all know who they are, and they will recognize their contributions to this book. Each will, I hope, enjoy the secret pleasure of knowing his or her particular contribution. Students at Winthrop College, the University of North Carolina at Charlotte, and the University of South Carolina contributed in many ways to both the content of this work and to the interpretations given here of two communities similar to those from which some of them had come.

This book could not have been written except in response to the influence of many professional associates, though I am, as is any scholar-author, solely responsible for any errors of fact or judgment.

Dell H. Hymes is behind this book more than any other single individual. His scholarly concerns are evident throughout. His personal faith in and support of my work, and his patience in waiting for me to decide when this book was ready for publication have been very important. Both his theoretical approach to the study of language in human life and his commitment on a personal level to making anthropology and linguistics relevant to educational practice have influenced the interpretations on nearly every page of this book.

The encouragement and criticism necessary to interpret nearly a decade of data recorded in a sometimes painful and rapidly changing time have come from numerous colleagues. Marjorie Martus was the first of these colleagues to encourage me to bring the data together for a book; throughout the final years of data collection and the months of writing, she kept reminding me of the need to speak to teachers as well as researchers. She repeatedly called for clarification when she felt practitioners would not find the discussion clear. Courtney Cazden was also an early promoter of my attempts to write the stories of Trackton and Roadville for a wide readership, and she responded to early drafts with important questions on both the focus and content of the book. In similar ways, my colleagues at Stanford, Robert Calfee and David Tyack, helped me clarify the goals and the organization of the book. Gordon Wells kindly interpreted the book from the point of view of an outsider to the United States educational system. Tom James and Allison Read deserve special mention for their detailed and repeated readings of the manuscript, and I am especially grateful for their willingness to debate with me in the midst of their own busy months of preparing their dissertation proposals.

Bambi Schieffelin and Elinor Ochs, whose fieldwork in, respectively, a Papua New Guinea and Western Samoan village parallels some of the methods and types of data collected in Roadville and Trackton, offered advice born out of their experience. Numerous discussions with them about the implications of our fieldwork for language learning theories are reflected in many sections of this book. Ann Peters, whose research on units of acquisition informs many portions of the early chapters here, gave valuable comments on several troublesome areas of interpretation. Patricia Causey Nichols, a fellow Carolinian and researcher in her own home territory, has for many years discussed parts of this book with me. Her fieldwork in the Carolinas and her publications complement this study in many ways. Jay Lemke generously gave his advice as a science educator on portions of the second section of the book.

I wish to give special recognition to Charles A. Ferguson who tolerated my challenge of his proposals for universals of child language input. He has encouraged me in the completion of this book, and he has been extremely tolerant of the repeated tales of each child whose story appears here. He has, to my benefit and that of our many common interests in the study of language and culture at micro and macro levels, been a provocative influence.

Joel Nichols of Winthrop College endured numerous sessions with me while he tried to capture in photography what I hoped to capture in text. Amanda Branscombe gave helpful advice in the selection of photographs. Brice Heath and Shannon Heath were over the years partners in this study, for they spent much time in Trackton and Roadville, still maintain associations there, and came to know some of the ways of living of these communities as their own. They were unique research associates since they were able to become a part of the child life of Trackton and Roadville. In more recent years, they have listened to my interpretations from fieldnotes, added their own, and discussed with me the implications of reporting life in Trackton and Roadville. In particular, they have been keenly sensitive to the fear that publication might reveal the identity of their friends in the communities and schools.

I owe a deep debt to Frederick M. Heath, who not only helped stimulate some of the interpretations offered here, but facilitated my work for many years. It was under his tutelage that I first learned the important contribution social history can make to ethnography; as an historian, he first called to my attention the fallacy of the ethnographic present.

Penny Carter, of Cambridge University Press, assumed editorial responsibility for this volume. With her usual thoughtful and concerned handling of details, she contributed in many ways to its final form. I am grateful to her.

Several institutions have facilitated this work. Research for chapter 1 was carried out in the archives of Winthrop College and the Caroliniana Library of the University of South Carolina. Ron Chepesiuk, archivist, and Shirley Tarleton, head librarian, of Winthrop College, took an active interest in this research and went out of their way on numerous occasions to be helpful. Allan Stokes of the Caroliniana Library willingly helped me search out obscure sources and put me in touch with other historians of textile mills in the Piedmont. The Ford Foundation provided a travel-study grant in 1978 which allowed me to begin to organize my fieldnotes and to maintain on-going interactions with teachers in the region. The Department of Linguistics of Monash University in Melbourne, Australia, especially through its chairman, Göran Hammarström, provided a setting in which I could distance myself from the usual responsibilities of teaching and from the field site itself.

In a manner rarely shown an outsider, black churches allowed me the unique privilege of being in their midst as worshiper and as sometime preacher. Their members heard before any others, aside from students in my courses, portions of this book and

Acknowledgments

discussions of its purposes. On occasion, the Biblical text which introduces this book was the stimulus for serious talk about differences in language uses, oral and written, and their meanings in daily life as we compare and measure ourselves against others.

Berlin
November 17, 1982
Buß- und Bettag

For we dare not make ourselves of the number, or compare ourselves with some that commend themselves: but they measuring themselves by themselves, and comparing themselves among themselves, are not wise.

II Corinthians 10:12

Prologue

In the late 1960s, school desegregation in the southern United States became a legislative mandate and a fact of daily life. Academic questions about how children talk when they come to school and what educators should know and do about oral and written language were echoed in practical pleas of teachers who asked: "What do I do in my classroom on Monday morning?"

In the massive reshuffling of students and teachers during desegregation in the South, I became a part of the communities and schools described in this book. I was both ethnographer of communication focusing on child language and teacher-trainer attempting to determine whether or not academic questions could lead to answers appropriate for meeting the needs of children and educators in that regional setting. Described here are two communities – Roadville and Trackton – only a few miles apart in the Piedmont Carolinas. Roadville is a white working-class community of families steeped for four generations in the life of the textile mills. Trackton is a black working-class community whose older generations grew up farming the land, but whose current members work in the mills. Both communities define their lives primarily in terms of their communities and their jobs, yet both are tied in countless ways to the commercial, political, and educational interests of the townspeople – mainstream blacks and whites of the region. The townspeople are school-oriented, and they identify not so much with their immediate neighborhoods as with networks of voluntary associations and institutions whose activities link their common interests across the region.

I was a part-time instructor in anthropology and linguistics at a state university which had an excellent local reputation for teacher-training. Black and white teachers, business leaders, ministers, and mill personnel were in my graduate courses, and with many of them I developed a research-partner relationship. Pressures from desegregation, nationwide condemnation of the Carolinas' low performance in public education, and the general shifting of social and work opportunities for blacks during this period helped create an atmosphere in which individual teachers, businessmen, and mill foremen could initiate changes in their usual practices. Once desegregation began for schools and mills alike, white children went to schools with black teachers and classmates; black teachers faced black and white students; white foremen supervised black mill workers. For the first time, black and white worked side-by-side in the mills, and white foremen, mostly males, worried about ways to instruct black workers, male and female. Communication was a central concern of black and white teachers, parents, and mill personnel who felt the need to know more about how others communicated: why students and teachers often could not understand each other, why questions were sometimes not answered, and why habitual ways of talking and listening did not always seem to work.

In my university courses on anthropology and education and language and culture were teachers, who came to advance their degrees and pay levels, and businessmen and mill personnel, who came either to accompany their teacher-wives or to experience college classroom life again. They brought a central question: What were the effects of preschool home and community environments on the learning of those language structures and uses which were needed in classrooms and job settings? Answers to this question were important for black and white children who were unsuccessful in school, and for their parents who were frustrated in their interactions in credit union agencies (cooperative savings institutions of millworkers), employment offices, and elsewhere as they negotiated for critical goods and services. In my courses, I talked about published research on language differences among black and white children and adults of different socioeconomic classes across the United States. The students in my courses debated the practical applications of this research as well as its appropriateness to the local populations. They pointed out that the vast majority of research on child language had not treated the issue of the community or cultural background of the children studied. In this geographic region, where far more than half of the families qualified for in-state social services on the basis of income, socioeconomic differences among children seemed useless as a variable against which to set their language differences. Ascribing Black, Southern, or Standard English to speakers by racial membership was also not satisfactory to these students, for almost all of them, black and white, could shift among these varieties as occasion demanded. To categorize children and their families on the basis of either socioeconomic class or race and then to link these categories to discrete language differences was to ignore the realities of the communicative patterns of the region.

As long-time residents of the area, the teachers, businessmen, and mill personnel in my classes had observed differences in the language use and general behavior patterns of children and adults from certain communities or cultural groups. They had an endless store of anecdotes about children learning to use language across and within groups of the region, and they asked why researchers did not describe children learning language as they grew up in their own community cultures. Their questions set the stage for me to encourage them to examine their own ways of using language with their children at home and to record language interactions as thoroughly and accurately as possible, without preconceived judgments about what was happening in the exchanges in which they observed and participated. For those members of my classes for whom such descriptions became a serious objective, their initial focus was on their interactions with their own children; subsequently, they gave attention to communicative situations in their classrooms and the textile mills.

It was, however, not enough to enable these townspeople – mainstream blacks and whites – to strive to become objective and accurate recorders of the language habits of their own interactions. Their questions pointed to the need for a full description of the primary face-to-face interactions of children from community cultures other than their own mainstream one. The ways of living, eating, sleeping, worshiping, using space, and filling time which surrounded these language learners would have to be accounted for as part of the milieu in which the processes of language learning took place. Though I did not then set out to do so, my next years were to be spent recording and interpreting the language learning habits of the children of Roadville and Trackton. With these accounts of worlds about which the townspeople actually knew very little, cross-cultural comparisons of the variations of language socialization in the predominant groups of the region would be possible. Using detailed facts on the interactions of the townspeople, and my ethnographies of communication in the communities of Roadville and Trackton, we could then move to answer the central question: For each of these groups, what were the effects of the preschool home and community environment on the learning of those language structures and uses which were needed in classrooms and job settings?

The townspeople in my courses studied their own mainstream ways of teaching, modeling, and using language with their children and with those with whom they worked in classrooms or the mills. They then compared these ways with those described in both the research literature and my accounts of Roadville and Trackton, communities similar to those from which most millworkers and about 70 percent of the students in the local schools came. Mill foremen agreed to teach me about a world of learning very different from that of school classrooms. With their help, I was able to spend part of my time in the textile mills, learning about the varieties of language uses adults from Roadville and Trackton met there, from the weaving rooms to the credit union offices. In addition, teachers welcomed me as teacher-aide or co-teacher in their classrooms. Together, we took fieldnotes, identified patterns of communicative interactions, and delineated what the school and the mill defined as "communication problems." We searched for solutions, wrote curricula, and tried new methods, materials, and motivations to help working-class black and white children learn more effectively than they had in the past. Fifteen of the teachers had preschool children, and this cluster and their families form one portion of the group referred to in this book as the townspeople. This cluster recorded, analyzed, and compared their own habits of interacting with their young children with those of Roadville and Trackton. As associate, colleague, aide, and sometime-co-author of curricular materials, I became a part of the home lives, classrooms, and workplaces of many of the townspeople. They came to recognize that in schools, commercial establishments, and mills, mainstream language values and skills were the expected norm, and individuals from communities such as Roadville and Trackton brought different language values and skills to these situations. The story of these townspeople, especially the teachers, as learning researchers fills the final chapters of this book.

Between communities and classrooms

In the years between 1969 and 1978, I lived, worked, and played with the children and their families and friends in Roadville and Trackton. My entry into these specific communities came through a naturally occurring chain of events. In each case, I knew an old-time resident in the community, and my relationship with that individual opened the community to me. I had grown up in a rural Piedmont area in a neighboring state, so the customs of both communities were very familiar to me though many years had passed since I had been a daily part of such cultural ways. I am white, but while I was growing up, my family's nearest neighbors were black families; the black church was across the road from my house, and the three black school teachers in our area lived just down the road. In our area, both white and black children lived too far from the nearest school to walk, so we took buses to our respective schools, but in the afternoons and the summers, we joined each other for ballgames, bike-riding, and trips to the creek to look for "crawfish." In the summers, we all worked for local tobacco farmers, black and white. These shared experiences and unconscious habits of interaction eased my transition into both Trackton and Roadville.

Over the period of my experiences in the two communities, neither ever had a population exceeding 150, and during some summers, when visits to families in distant locations were frequent, each had as few as 30 residents. There were usually about 40 residents in each community. Most of the households contained one or more members who worked in jobs providing salaries equal to or slightly above that of beginning public school teachers in the Carolinas. They worked in textile mills or construction work, and they farmed or gardened as supplementary activities. Jobs were sometimes seasonal, and work was not always steady. The income levels and occupational lives of adults in the two communities were very similar; one or two families would sometimes make as much as $12,000 in one year; most made between $8,000 and $10,000; and a few had rough years in which disaster struck, and their income went below $3,000. All were accustomed to ups and downs, good times and bad, and most believed good times followed bad.

With the exception of their jobs, life was essentially confined to the home community for adults as well as children. Approximately 80 percent of the occasions when adults went outside the community were work-related. Family trips to town or to the nearby metropolitan center were multi-purpose, major events. Those who came to visit either community knew it by name and knew how to find it. By both geographic location and historical patterns of choice of neighbors and circle of friends, each community tended to be closed, somewhat set apart, with an evolved identity and inner life of its own. Throughout the Piedmont Carolinas, there were many "Roadvilles" and "Tracktons," sometimes "out in the country," sometimes no more than a few blocks from the city hall of a town of 40,000 or more citizens. The youngsters from Roadville and Trackton had much in common with most of the children in the classrooms of the region. Approximately 70 percent of the children in the six counties of the Piedmont region in which I traveled, teaching off-campus courses, visiting homes, and working in schools, came from homes and communities which shared a majority of the features described for Roadville and Trackton.

For my work on children learning language in the two communities, I focused primarily on the face-to-face network in which each child learns the ways of acting, believing, and valuing of those about him. For the children of Roadville and Trackton, their primary community is geographically and socially their immediate neighborhood. Thus, these ethnographies of communication focus on each of the communities in which the children are socialized as talkers, readers, and writers to describe:

> the boundaries of the physical and social community in which communication to or by them is possible;
> the limits and features of the situations in which such communication occurs;
> the what, how, and why of patterns of choice children can exercise in their uses of language, whether in talking, reading, or writing;
> the values or significance these choices of language have for the children's physical and social activities.

Added to all the details of the daily existence of children which the above imply are the history and current ecology of the community. Opportunities, values, motivations, and resources available for communication in each community are influenced by that group's social history as well as by current environmental conditions. Once beyond the preschool years, the children move into school, and descriptions of their language uses there must similarly focus on boundaries, limits, and features of communicative situations, and the significance of choices among language uses. For children in this region in this decade, all these aspects of schooling were in an almost constant state of change.

These ethnographies of communication attempt to let the reader follow the children of Roadville and Trackton from their home and community experiences into their classrooms and schools. The reader will come to know these children and their teachers and will see how both groups retained some of their language and cultural habits and altered others. The influence of these mutual adjustments on an individual level often exceeded that of the major educational policy shifts and reshufflings of teachers and students which marked these times.

Because ethnographic research, especially in education, is currently undertaken by a variety of scholars from a range of disciplines, there is some general sense of a search for a model. This book is not, however, intended as a model for future ethnographic studies of education in and out of schools. To be sure, many features of it could be adapted for use by other anthropologists studying communities and schools, but many could not. The on-going relationship over nearly a decade between anthropologist and communities and institutions studied is not likely to be repeated by another researcher. Conditions of access and accountability for social scientists researching minority communities and schools now largely preclude the open access and cooperation I enjoyed. Furthermore, no deadlines, plans, or demands from an outside funding agency set limits on the time or direction of the cooperative arrangements between teachers and anthropologist. The timing, location, and particular interplay of people and historic and social conditions make this, like every ethnography, a unique piece of social history.

By many standards of judgment, this book also cannot be considered a model piece of educational or child language research. For example, educators should not look here for experiments, controlled conditions, and systematic score-keeping on the academic gains and losses of specific children. Nor should psycholinguists look here for data taped at periodic intervals under similar conditions over a predesignated period of time. What this book does do is record the natural flow of community and classroom life over nearly a decade. The descriptions here of the actual processes, activities, and attitudes involved in the enculturation of children in Roadville and Trackton will allow readers to see these in comparison with those of mainstream homes and institutions.

Often the approaches to research in education have been quantitative, global, sociodemographic, and dependent on large-scale comparisons of many different schools. Terms from business predominate: input, output, accountability, management strategies, etc. Input factors (independent variables) are said to influence, predict, or determine output factors (dependent variables). Pieces of data about social groups, such as number of siblings or time of mother–child interactions in preschool daily experiences, are correlated with the output of students, expressed in terms of test scores, subsequent income, and continued schooling. The effects of formal instruction have been evaluated by correlating these input factors with educational output.

From an ethnographic perspective, the irony of such research is that it ignores the social and cultural context which created the input factors for individuals and groups. Detailed descriptions of what actually happens to children as they learn to use language and form their values about its structures and functions tell us what children do to become and remain acceptable members of their own communities. Throughout the years of this study, parents, children, teachers, and students pursued, to the extent possible in that period of history in that region, their normal priorities of meeting daily needs and sustaining their self-identities. As a matter of policy, I never took into either community objects which were not already familiar to the residents' daily life, and as far as possible I tried not to use any of the items in the communities in ways unfamiliar to them. I spent many hours cooking, chopping wood, gardening, sewing, and minding children by the rules of the communities. For example, in the early years of interaction in the communities, audio and video recorders were unfamiliar to community residents; therefore, I did no taping of any kind then. By the mid-1970s, cassette players were becoming popular gifts, and community members used them to

8

record music, church services, and sometimes special performances in the community. When such recordings became a common
community-initiated practice, I audiotaped, but only in accordance with community practices. Often I was able to write in a field
notebook while minding children, tending food, or watching
television with the families; otherwise, I wrote fieldnotes as soon
as possible afterwards when I left the community on an errand or
to go to school. In the classrooms, I often audiotaped; we
sometimes videotaped; and both the teachers and I took fieldnotes
as a matter of course on many days of each year.

Neither community members and teachers nor I considered that
any special demands of data collection should alter normal habits;
pressures of the changing times, both socially and economically,
made enough demands. The usual tasks expected of a preplanned
"research project" could not have been tolerated by such a large
number of people over such a long period of time. Thus, the
question of how "scientific" this work is will have to depend on
each reader's conceptions of science and valuation of long-term
participation and observation in accounting for the ways of life of
particular groups of people in their communities and schools.

Ethnography and social history

It is important to say something about this book as both ethnography and social history. Anthropologists study social life as and
where it is lived through the medium of a particular social group,
but the ethnographic present never remains as it is described, nor
does description of the current times fully capture the influences
and forces of history on the present. Roadville, Trackton, and the
townspeople of this book are products of the region's history
which determined the times, places, and ways they could interact.
Historians who have studied the Piedmont Carolinas since the
colonial period tell of the relations among these groups and of the
economic forces and political events which provide the legacy of
ideas, values, and actions these groups bear today. The ethnography in these pages tells something of a recent chapter in that
history, the decade between the late 1960s and the end of the
1970s, a time of rapid multi-directional change for blacks and
whites everywhere – especially in the South. Here communities
linked to the textile industry felt the influence of wide-ranging

industrial forces at the same time as they faced extraordinary technical and organizational changes because of foreign competition. The character of the face-to-face network which affected the work settings, schools, and ultimately the home life of Roadville and Trackton shifted throughout the decade. Economic and political forces which originated outside the region greatly influenced the urgency and dedication of the teachers described here.

A natural tendency of readers of this book will be to highlight the different racial memberships of Trackton and Roadville. Some readers will want to explain the differences between the attitudes, events, and patterns of communication of the two communities in terms of race only, overlooking the fact that the blacks and whites who were the townspeople had far more in common with each other than with either Roadville or Trackton. Explanation of social facts is never simple, and the story of language learning in these two communities and all that follows from that is no exception. The various approaches of these communities to acquiring, using, and valuing language are the products of their history and current situation.

It is because one of the communities of focus in this book is black and the other is white that the social history of such communities in the Piedmont region is especially critical to understanding the ethnographic present. For more than two centuries, social and economic factors kept the majority of blacks and whites of this region apart in many ways. People in each group developed a separate set of techniques for adjusting to their physical and social environments. For example, their religious institutions developed along somewhat divergent paths and fostered different types of communication, world views, and patterns of social relations. The Trackton blacks and Roadville whites described in this book have different ways of using language in worship, for social control, and in asserting their sense of identity. They do so, however, because they have had different historical forces shaping these ways. Only in the past few decades have blacks and whites of working-class communities come together in institutions of work, commerce, politics, and schooling where each has met yet a third set of ways of using language to get things done. It is the townspeople – blacks and whites of the mainstream middle class – who have the most familiarity with the communicative habits and preferences of these public institutions. Unlike

Roadville and Trackton people, they have not been tied by historical circumstances so closely to home communities, limited work opportunities, and restricted education.

This book argues that in Roadville and Trackton the different ways children learned to use language were dependent on the ways in which each community structured their families, defined the roles that community members could assume, and played out their concepts of childhood that guided child socialization. In addition, for each group, the place of religious activities was inextricably linked to the valuation of language in determining an individual's access to goods, services, and estimations of position and power in the community. In communities throughout the world, these and other features of the cultural milieu affect the ways in which children learn to use language. The place of language in the cultural life of each social group is interdependent with the habits and values of behaving shared among members of that group. Therefore, any reader who tries to explain the community contrasts in this book on the basis of race will miss the central point of the focus on culture as learned behavior and on language habits as part of that shared learning. Children in Roadville and Trackton came to have different ways of communicating, because their communities had different social legacies and ways of behaving in face-to-face interactions. In other parts of the world, different social legacies and ways of behaving can also be found between villages or communities located only a few miles apart. Members of such social groups may not differ racially, but their respective histories, patterns of face-to-face interactions, and ways of adjusting both to the external environment and to individuals within and outside their groups have shaped their different patterns of using language.

A final note about the audience for whom I wrote this book and how that audience has determined the dual nature of the book. The narrative here tells the story of how children of two culturally different communities in the Piedmont Carolinas of the United States came to use language (Part I – Chapters 1–6), and how their teachers learned to understand their ways and to bring these ways into the classrooms (Part II – Chapters 8, 9). Readers will sense a shift of perspective when the narrative leaves the homes and communities of Roadville and Trackton. These were relatively self-contained worlds in which the residents and I as ethnographer moved in their group-defined ways without intensive normative pressure from outside. When the narrative moves into the towns-people's homes (Chapter 7), the reader will lose the sense of intimacy achieved with the characters of Roadville and Trackton; the townspeople will seem to focus beyond their homes and communities to the larger institutions of the region's society. In part, this effect results from the fact that though this chapter depends on ethnographic data, the details of family daily life and children learning to talk, read, and write (which are given in several chapters for Roadville and Trackton) are here encapsulated in a single chapter. The sociological literature contains many accounts of the family life of mainstream middle-class families across the United States; linguists have focused their language learning research on the children of these families. This chapter does not repeat that material, but verifies the similarities of the lives of townspeople of the Piedmont to those of their counterparts elsewhere. More important, however, Chapter 7 informs the contrast which is the central argument of the book. In Chapter 8, the reader moves with townspeople teachers and Roadville and Trackton children into the Piedmont schools, in which the goal is sociocultural and educational change: teachers are charged to see that all children acquire literacy skills, subject area content knowledge, and school values, such as promptness, politeness, and respect for others' space and property. In the years before desegregation, teachers had viewed these goals as "natural," "necessary," and "expected." With desegregation, the teachers described in this chapter reviewed these goals in the light of their own experience as ethnographers of their interactions and with the ethnographic details of the lives of Trackton and Roadville children. In Chapter 9, these same teachers transmit to their students ways of using ethnography to see themselves and the larger societal contexts in which they must move, not only in school, but also in the commercial, legal, and political realms beyond the school.

In Part I of the book, the reader moves with me, the ethno-grapher, as unobtrusively as possible in the worlds of Trackton and Roadville children. In Part II of the book, my role as ethnographer is intrusive, as I work with teachers to enable them to become participant observers in their own domains and to use the knowledge from the ethnographies of Trackton and Roadville to inform their motivations, practices, and programs of teaching. I as ethnographer have become a major actor in the translation of social reality that occurred in the classrooms described here. From ethnographer *learning*, or coming to "know," I have become ethnographer *doing*. For me, in this particular time and place, this transition was necessary. Trackton and Roadville children had to go to school. I believed teachers could make school a place which allowed these children to capitalize on the skills, values, and knowledge they brought there, and to add on the conceptual structures imparted by the school. Children and teachers across cultural groups, if provided adequate information in suitable forms, could learn to articulate relations between cultural patterns of talking and knowing, and, understanding such relations, to make choices.

The reader should see *Ways with Words* as an unfinished story, in which the characters are real people whose lives go on beyond the decade covered in this book, and for whom we cannot, within these pages, either resolve the plot or complete the story. Through these pages, however, the reader should move very close to a living understanding of the ways of behaving, feeling, believing, and valuing of the children, their community members, and their townspeople teachers. The book is written for what I call "learning researchers," non-academics and academics alike. At the top of the list of such researchers are those teachers at all levels of the curriculum who constantly search out new ways of learning about themselves and their students. Others on the list are those parents and community members concerned about their own gaps in knowledge and the need of children today to learn more, faster than ever before.

Also on the list are academics who concern themselves both with oral and written language and with ways the structures and uses of these are learned. Members of this group may make most use of the notes and citations, which set this book in the context of current research in anthropology, linguistics, and cognitive psychology. These notes and the descriptions and analyses in the body of the book will raise numerous questions for academic researchers. I hope that their questions will be directed not only to the contents of this book, but also to their own disciplines' theories and generalizations about how children learn language.

I have done as much as possible to conceal the real names of all the people and places in this book. All names of people and places are pseudonyms. The sometimes precarious nature of parent–teacher, teacher–student, and teacher–administrator relations has made it especially important that I protect the privacy of all. The special historical situation of the time and place have made disguise difficult and discretion all the more important. Throughout the time I lived and worked among these people in their homes, schools, and communities, I took the responsibility for the influence of my ideas, my presence, and my sometime role as broker between the communities and the townspeople and the outside world. I try to continue to take that same responsibility in this book.

Note on transcriptions

In transcribing the speech of Roadville, Trackton, and the towns-people, I have made no effort to provide an exact phonetic representation. Words are transcribed in an approximation to standard orthography, with as much "eye-dialect" as seems necessary to indicate the varieties of English used. An attempt has been made to transcribe the speech of *all* groups to represent to the layman a feeling for the types of language spoken. There is no intention to stigmatize any variety, and the modified spellings are used in full awareness that all natural English speech differs from what the standard orthography seems to indicate.

Some explanation is needed for what may appear to be inconsistencies. The Roadville and Trackton communities share numerous dialect features, but differ in others; members of each community vary in their occasions for using local dialect forms, and often within the same passage they will use both a Standard English form and a southern white or black dialect form for the same item. Townspeople, black and white, who are teachers, administrators, businessmen, or mill executives with whom Roadville and Trackton residents interact, also use dialect features in their informal speech.

All material in quotation marks or set off from the text is a direct quotation. A few special conventions of notation are used to indicate points of special interest, especially in passages from playsongs, prayer chants, and stories. Exact repetition of words, phrases, intonation, and even sentences appear frequently in these. Patterned repetitions of any of these with some variations – by the same speaker or across speakers – are marked by special spacing of lines and the repeat sign |: .... :| at the beginning and end of the passage. A single line (|) is used to mark off non-repeated material which intervenes between two segments of repeated text.

Data recorded here in texts of more than fifteen lines are identified by community and numbered in order of their appearance in the book to facilitate cross-reference. Texts are also marked to indicate their method of collection. Those marked with an asterisk (*) were tape recorded; those unmarked were usually written down as they were spoken with shorthand transcription for a majority of words, and approximation to standard orthography for dialect items which varied according to style and occasion of speech. Hesitations and nonverbal features of accompanying behavior were recorded opposite the speech transcriptions. Detailing of the situational context of the speech was part of the regular routine of taking fieldnotes. The following transcription conventions are used for passages of texts.

´	Primary stress
`	Secondary stress
:	Vowel elongation
Italics	Heightening of primary stress by vowel-lengthening and raising of pitch
.	Sentence-final falling intonation and a full pause
,	Clause
?	Rising intonation and pause
–	Pause of two seconds or more within an utterance
#	Pause within a playsong or hymn to hold for several meter counts
[	Overlapping utterances (used to mark the point at which an utterance in progress is joined by another interrupting utterance)
=	Contiguous utterances (used when there is no break between adjacent utterances, the second latched to, but not overlapping, the first)

Nonverbal actions of the speaker are indicated within slash lines at the point in the speech at which they begin; those of hearers are on a separate line within double slash lines. Explanations of terms used in speakers' texts are given in brackets within the text.

Part I

Ethnographer Learning

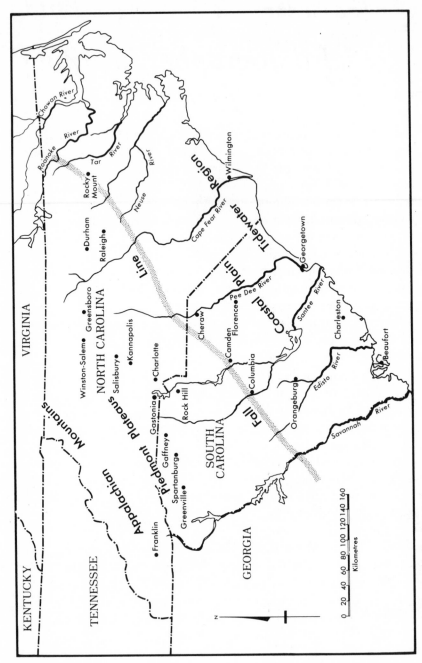

Map 1. The Piedmont Carolinas

I   *The Piedmont: Textile mills and times of change*

A quiet early morning fog shrouds rolling hills blanketed by pine-green stands of timber, patched with fields of red clay. As the sun rises and burns off the fog, the blue sky is feathered with smoke let go from chimney stacks of textile mills: this is the Piedmont of the Carolinas.

The Piedmont, a term used by outsiders and newcomers to the region, but never by local residents, is the "foot of the mountain" which sprawls east of the Appalachians from the southwestern hills of Virginia through North and South Carolina into Georgia and Alabama. Its textile mills are at home along the rivers and railways of the numerous towns and cities which dot the rolling terrain. From Danville, Virginia to Birmingham, Alabama, the Southern Railway cuts through the Piedmont, mingling the smoke of its locomotives with that of the textile mills along its track.

The Piedmont includes the area west of the Atlantic Coastal Plain and east of the Southern Appalachian Mountains. Separating the central Piedmont of the Carolinas from the Coastal Plain is a strip of sand hills with no vegetation except jack pines and scrub oak. Along this strip is a geological fault called the "fall line." River rapids and shoals mark this point at which the rushing waters of rivers falling from the Appalachians across the foothills enter into the Coastal Plain. Above this line is "the up-country," below it the "low-country." Through the Coastal Plain, the rivers slow their pace to meander through pine-dotted valleys to the Atlantic Ocean. Along these rivers, cities such as Columbia and Camden in South Carolina, and Raleigh in North Carolina, mark the historical limits of inland navigation.

Here, in the eighteenth century, slaves, manning barges loaded with goods brought from the coastal port of Charleston, S.C., had to remove the goods for distribution either in these city markets or by wagon through the region above the fall line. In this back country, wagons moved along roads which after a rain could entrap wagon and horses or oxen in a mire of red or grayish clay; rivers too swift to be forded discouraged traveling merchants.

After 1800, more and more families found the Piedmont "easier to settle in than to pass through." White settlers came down from the Middle Colonies and Virginia, and both black and white came up from the Coastal Plain and the Tidewater Region. Yeomen farmers, craftsmen, and merchants of German, English, Welsh, Scottish, French Huguenot, and Scotch-Irish descent came to the back-country to establish schools, churches, and to live decently with hard work. Before 1800, the region was predominantly a non-slaveholding region, but the inland spread of cotton and new people to the back country weakened the yeoman class. Soon some families became personally involved in the slave system and began to provide their families with elements of the low-country plantation life. Called "planters," they managed small plantations with 50–200 slaves, set up dancing schools, and opened such cultural enterprises as opera houses and literary societies. The majority of newcomers, however, had no slaves. They settled on small farms, and in the continuous flow of seasonal tasks, raised corn, cotton, gardens, and kept chickens, hogs, a cow or two, and a horse or mule. They made most of their household items, and craftsmen who settled the region made those items which individual families could not produce at home. The few blacks who had come to the region from the low country worked as blacksmiths, carpenters, and the like, or they hired themselves out as hands on farms owned by whites.[1]

For most households, domestic production became a way of life. Housewives wove woolen cloth at home, and by the third decade of the nineteenth century, textile mills began to supply carded wool and warps for these home shops. Up-country rivers provided the water power for small carding mills and yarn factories. Local farmers supplied the mills with cotton, and white labor was plentiful, since farmers were anxious to supplement their farm incomes with work in these early mills. However, both the individual entrepreneurs who established the mills and those who worked in them went against a regional sentiment which favored farming over manufacturing.

But the Civil War changed this attitude. Intensive cultivation of cotton throughout the century had deplenished the soils, and the devastation to croplands by the war made it clear that the independent spirits of the region had to unite to rebuild. An intense push "to bring the mills to the cotton" developed into the Cotton-Mill Campaign of the 1880s which urged unified support for development of the textile manufacturing industry. Of the two dozen or so mills established in the Piedmont before the Civil War, most had escaped destruction in the war, but many more mills were needed. Within two decades after the end of the war, middle-class merchants, craftsmen, and farmers had begun to enlarge old manufacturing centers and equip them with new machinery. They built new cotton mills which took advantage of the widely available water power and abundant white labor. In South Carolina, the 14 mills in 1880 increased to more than 200 by 1930.[2]

As cotton manufacture established itself firmly in the Piedmont, a pattern of diversified farming also returned, and fields left fallow for years were once again able to support cotton. New mills along the rivers' banks spawned mill villages for white workers, and urban areas expanded around what had formerly been small mill towns. Communities looked upon the mills as community ventures, and together, citizens provided financing, supervisory leadership, and common labor. White families left landless by the war exchanged their tenant farmer status for life in mill villages. Some blacks settled in as tenant farmers on those farms which kept operating after the war. Others bought small pieces of land for themselves. Only an occasional black was hired as a sweeper or janitor in the mills; their lives were otherwise tied to the land.

In mill villages, millowners worked to provide the necessities of community life: houses, a post office, stores, a church, and a school. Leadership in the building of the mills meant responsibility for building and supervising mill and village alike. The young of the founding families of the mills began at an early age to work their way through the mill's structure, sweeping out the clothrooms and taking their turns at tasks such as carding, spinning, and weaving. The ideology of the times presented the mills and their communities as built by and for the folk, and founding families, millworkers, and community as cooperating unit.

By the beginning of the twentieth century, some mills needed more labor than the local area could provide, and they recruited workers from the Southern Appalachian Mountains. Offered a ready-made community, housing, schooling, and cash, the mountaineers came, brought their families, and urged their kinsmen further up the hollows (valleys) to join them. Within the villages, the workers began a new life in their mill houses, gardened on land provided by the company, canned in canneries built alongside the school, and spent their leisure hours in parks, playgrounds, and libraries funded by the mill. Worker and supervisor joined in occasional recreational activities: square-dancing, playing in a country music band, and coaching or joining a baseball team. Worker and supervisor often worshiped together at the community churches built on land provided by millowners, supported largely by mill families, and often named for the mill's founders.[3]

But distinctions and divisions began to grow between millowners and local businessmen and professionals, on the one hand, and wage-earning millworkers, on the other. The former lived in town, and as townspeople, they pursued different values in their homes and held strong attachment to maintenance of what they believed should be regionally accepted moral and religious values. The millworkers, living in company-owned houses in an area set apart from the town and townspeople, were a mixture of farmers, Appalachian migrants, and what the townspeople regarded as "white trash." Townspeople began to characterize mill people as uninterested in schooling, willing to allow and even promote early marriages, and inclined to disrespect both cleanliness and godliness. Initially, townspeople hoped the churches of the mill villages and the recreational activities which provided occasion for mingling of millowners, workers, and townspeople would offer authoritative reminders and appealing models of proper behavior to the millworkers.

Within the first decades of the twentieth century, however, some millowners declared the need for an active reform movement to bring about changes in the millworkers' ways of raising their children and behaving, talking, and establishing values in the mill community. Millowners proposed wide-sweeping social reforms to improve what was often cited in newspaper editorials as the mill people's "mental and moral culture." Townspeople wanted to transmit their own values to the mill people, removing their "country" attitudes, unacceptable speech habits, and slovenly ways. As incentive to the workers, some mill executives suggested that a minimum level of formal schooling be made a prerequisite for obtaining a job in the mills. Gradually, millowners' zeal for reform of the "mill problem" enabled them to support child labor laws and compulsory schooling. North Carolina passed its first compulsory attendance law in 1907; South Carolina followed in 1915. Schools were designated to teach mill children everything from manners to morals; schoolteachers became preachers for the culture of the townspeople. They were charged to teach health and sanitation habits, grammar, self-control, neatness, and obedience. If mill children were to grow up and become voters, they would have to learn to read and write and to reform their "barbaric" "wild" ways.

To the chagrin of the townspeople, however, mill people were scornful of school. One young man, apprehended out of school, indicated his father was the source of his low estimation of schooling: "Pa says tain't nothin' ter it. He says he got 'long 'thout it." Undaunted, millowners increasingly pushed for ways to gain general acknowledgment throughout the Piedmont that schools were needed to reform the "industrial nomads" who had "ceased their wanderings and settled down in the Piedmont Plain and called it home." A surge of enthusiasm for adult education after 1910 derived from a belief on the part of millowners that if schooling for children was to take effect, parents had also to be reformed through some form of education. The first county-wide night school program in South Carolina was organized in 1913. In 1920, the superintendent of education in South Carolina called for a midsummer drive against illiteracy. Teachers were urged to use their summer months to teach illiterate adults who read below the third grade level. The capital's newspaper prepared simply written newspapers for use in such programs during one month of each summer. The focus was on teaching "what the pupils desire. Base all examples on everyday life." In 1921, a program entitled Opportunity School was opened for adult millworkers and farmers.[4]

Some few townspeople decided to become missionaries to the wanderers and, in the face of their resistance to schooling, to give them a chance for both education and work. For example, one preacher/teacher in the Piedmont opened in 1911 what he termed a Textile Industrial Institute for "those on the factory hill who wanted to be somebody." He portrayed millworkers as anxious to be educated, aware of the benefits of education, and clever at finding ways to expose themselves to "larnin'." His school was a "week-about work-study school," established with the blessings of some millowners who agreed that millworkers could study and work in the mill on a weekly alternating basis. Men and women, as well as youngsters, came to the school; the older millworkers often wanted to revive the minimal learning they had accomplished in their early and scant years of schooling. One student begged the school's principal to let him in: "I lived in the country. Moved to the mill and went to work at fifteen year old." Another worker – a master mechanic in a textile mill – wrote from Georgia that he was coming to the Textile Industrial Institute: "I'll be there next Saddy [Saturday], I'll sleep on the flo an eat half rashions ef necessary to git to stay. I need edgercason [education] and mean to have it. Yours truly."

Such talk and habits of writing were often highlighted for reform. Editorial writers, teachers, and businessmen exchanged numerous stories about the "wanderers'" peculiar ways of talking and the dogged pride they took in these ways. If asked "What you got in that bag?", millworkers would retort: "Tain't no bag; hit's a poke. Don't you-uns know er poke?" The principal of the Textile Industrial Institute was keenly aware of the speech which marked town and mill people as distinct from each other. When he moved among the millworkers, he shifted his talk to their ways. He acknowledged a major breakthrough in his relations with millworkers any time one of them commented: "That preacher talks jes like folks, don't he?" Speech forms were only one of the marks of the social line between mill village and town; no social incorporation was possible from either group to the other without some shifts in ways of talking and using talk. Preachers and teachers found it easy to tap into the millworkers' store of proverbs, stories, and ballads to illustrate the point of their messages. Collections of these made during the first decades of the twentieth century found their way into school libraries and preachers' homes, for use by those few who recognized that millworkers' ways with words were more than "country speech."

Contrary to townspeople's view of millworkers as provincials locked in their own language and world view, teachers, preachers, and recreational workers who moved in and out of the daily life of the mill village reported that workers found ways to broaden their world. In the 1920s newspaper circulation increased in Piedmont mill villages, and millworkers, male and female, went to city libraries for novels and adventure and confession magazines. The latter were read in private; other reading materials were shared in reading-aloud sessions in family homes, and in the summertime, the evening paper was the prompter for conversations across porches in the villages.

The decade of the 1920s, however, brought more than new pushes for education. The disaster of the boll weevil forced many white families formerly dependent on the cultivation of cotton to give up their life on the land and move to the mill village. The more fortunate were able to keep their farms by having one or more members of the family work in the mill. Shift work allowed farmers to tend their farms during the day and work the mills on either the second (3 p.m. until 11 p.m.) or third (11 p.m. until 7 a.m.) shift. Many blacks moved north to new jobs in factories desperate for labor because of the curtailment of the immigration of Europeans caused by the onset of World War I. Those who remained behind varied greatly in their control of and access to resources. Some farmed their own land; others were sharecroppers or tenant farmers for white landowners. In many Carolina towns, there were black-owned businesses, ranging from insurance companies to shoe repair shops. Black colleges actively recruited future teachers, and black and white educators alike emphasized home economics and vocational education for blacks.

By the end of the decade, the issue of unionism and the demands for technological changes necessary for the production of man-made fibers forced a cutback for many mills and some shutdowns. Workers began to show signs of an independent and unbiddable spirit when strikes claimed the lives of some of their leaders. From mill homes, some workers' changing view of their relation with the mill was heard in songs which wafted across the evening air in mill communities:

We're gonna have a union all over the South
Where we can wear good clothes and live in a better house.
Now we must stand together and to the boss reply –
We'll never, no, we'll never let our leaders die.

The higher aspirations and reformed ways urged on millworkers through education found their expression in resistance to the status quo by some families.[5]

Other families, however, either ignored the complaints of their fellow workers or resigned themselves to a few more years in the mill just to "tide 'em over" until the farm could once again support the family. For many, a cross-generational relationship with a particular mill continued, and children grew up expecting to work the same machines their mothers or fathers had worked and to enjoy the paternalistic support of the mill company in their adult lives. Young people tolerated school, waiting for the time when they were blessedly old enough or big enough to leave. Some wondered quietly why their parents urged education as a "way to get ahead," when their future was tied to the same machine, the same task, and the familiar mill which had been so much a part of their parents' lives.

Most of those blacks who remained in the Piedmont still seemed inextricably tied to the land. Men tilled the soil, and women hired themselves out as domestics for a few dollars a week. All family members were sometimes called on to pick cotton or hire out for other agricultural jobs. Some heeded the words of local preachers and teachers; they made it through school, got themselves a small business, or went to the black colleges in the South. Some took jobs up-North or in the military service. Many kept their "down-home" ties, however, and tried to come home for funerals, homecoming celebrations at churches, and family reunions. Some sent their children home to the South to stay with kin. A few blacks held menial jobs in the mills.

The Depression broke past patterns of dependency on one specific mill. Mills closed and families pulled up and moved on to other mill towns, hoping the familiar promises of cash, housing, credit, education, and recreation would be met there. A majority were able to relocate in larger mills. They and their children continued a way of life intimately linked to the mill and the families who owned them. But by the late 1940s and early 1950s, the pattern of a total way of life provided by the mill was broken once and for all. Mills in North and South Carolina now produced nearly half the nation's cotton woven goods. Such success brought unexpected changes.

In a majority of mill villages and towns, large northern firms took over the small locally owned and managed mills which could no longer survive in the increasingly competitive national and world market. "Up-North" names – Burlington, Pacific, Celanese,

J. P. Stevens – replaced family names on billboards at the mill gates. These corporations chose not to be landlords or paternal caretakers; they gave up providing housing, offered the mill homes for sale to their occupants, opened federally controlled credit unions for employees, and discontinued support of local educational institutions and churches. For many, the only function held over from earlier days was provision of recreational facilities. More and more workers saw the mill as a place without a heart and began to sing the chorus some of their parents had sung in the 1920s:

We leave our home in the morning
We kiss our children goodby
While we slave for the bosses,
Our children scream and cry.
It is for our little children
That seems to us so dear,
But for us nor them, dear workers,
The bosses do not care.

Discontent was widespread. Yet most of the mills rode out the 1950s without major disturbances from the workers. In the next decades, moreover, changes in the larger society produced a new supply of happier and more willing workers for the mills.

The Civil Rights Movement forced the breaking of the color barrier on hiring, and blacks began to assume production line jobs in the mills. Black males, who had previously been allowed to work only as janitors or maintenance personnel, were now joined by black females and other black males who assumed positions on the production line, in mill laboratories, and in packing rooms. White supervisory personnel, often brought down from "up-North," cared more about meeting production quotas than about the color of a man's skin. Without unionization, the mills paid hourly wages lower than many other hourly-wage occupations, such as plumber and electrician; yet black males and females who no longer wanted to sharecrop or work as hired farm hands or domestics turned eagerly to mill jobs. They moved from the farm into the towns and cities, drawn by new job opportunities and the hope of better schooling for their children.[6]

The rhetoric of the times and desegregation seemed to make high hopes for education realistic. Black teachers from up-North, as well as those who had remained in the South, joined with black preachers and businessmen to urge young people to give their all to schooling. Young black families could, for the first time in the history of the South, start out on their own, without having to depend on the land or domestic jobs in whites' homes. They could model their own futures on the lives of young white families who had gotten ahead working in the mills and were sending their children to schools to prepare to "move ahead" in the next generation.

Meanwhile, some whites, especially the young, began to talk of better pay and working conditions, and a renewal of unionism. Others looked elsewhere for jobs which would insure they might rise above their parents' position in the spinning or weaving room, jobs far away from brown lung disease and threats of shutdowns if the unions should move in. They looked to education for the promises their parents had so often mouthed, and they reaffirmed a faith that schooling ought to make a difference in the job a man or woman could expect.[7]

Black and white communities, tied to the textile mills in different ways, were, in the decades of the 1960s and 1970s, caught between their families and the school, between community and classroom in their urge to be "on the rise." Two such communities are Roadville and Trackton, set in the central area of the Piedmont Carolinas.[8]

Roadville is a white working-class community of families who have been a part of mill life for four generations. Many of the older residents remember life in the Appalachian Mountains and the move in the early decades of the twentieth century to a small mill community in the Piedmont. They speak of these days as the time when their children first began going to school instead of working in the mill. Baseball games, summer canning season, church life, and a general sense of security mark their tales of these times. But the Depression uprooted them from this comfortable life, and oldtimers wistfully recount the trek from the small mill community to mills around Alberta, a major metropolitan center in the Piedmont. They remember their discontent with "city life" even then, and their subsequent search for a smaller town and a mill which seemed to have some of the promises of cash, housing, credit, and recreation they had known in their first move from the mountains. They finally settled in Roadville, a neighborhood of mill houses around Laurence mill, formerly owned by the

Laurence brothers but run since the 1950s by a northern firm. The town of Laurenceville in which Roadville was located seemed small enough that, even without the help of the mill, they could work out credit arrangements, build their church, and spend their leisure time among people who shared their history of experiences as members of mill communities. The younger generations acknowledge, but do not share, their elders' gratitude for and sense of belonging to the mills. Resentment over unionism, health hazards, and blacks in the mills runs high among the young. Now most of the young people in Roadville care little about the mill in their future planning. They are looking to be on their way up and out of the mills.

Trackton is a working-class black community whose older generations have been brought up on the land, either farming their own land or working for other landowners. Old and middle-age residents remember the cotton fields, tenant housing, and long hours of work in those seasons of the year when saving the crop drove landowner and hired hand alike. Fresh in their memory is the move less than two decades ago to Gateway, a mill village in the early 1920s but now a town of nearly 50,000 people. There the big northern-owned mills were hiring blacks; the wages were good and the work was out of the hot sun. There was now a real hope of being on the rise, pulling themselves away from a dependency status on the land and on the landholders' dictation of space, time, and kind of work.

The promise of good living and getting ahead, gaining a new life and expanding the world of their past, helps guide the ways members of both communities organize their daily lives, and especially the ways they condition their children to see school in their future. For Roadville, schooling is something most folks have not gotten enough of, but everybody believes will do something toward helping an individual "get on." In the words of one oldtime resident, "Folks that ain't got no schooling don't get to be nobody nowadays." Trackton adults have had little schooling, but they believe it has made a difference for others, and it will make a difference for them. They tell their children: "Go to school, learn to talk right, to read and write, and you can get on outta here." At home, children in both communities learn language, hear their elders talk about "talkin' and doin' right," and some have come to realize that language, schooling, and learning are critically linked to the ways one gets on at home, school, and work.

2 *"Gettin' on" in two communities*

In Roadville

The neighborhood community of Roadville is located in Laurenceville, a town of about 10,000, which had its beginnings as a mill village in the 1930s. Though no longer indicated on any map as Roadville, the community is known to oldtimers as the early heart of the mill village. A deep gully overgrown with underbrush forms one border of Roadville. On the hill above one side of the gully sits Laurence Mill, its chimneys visible from Mull Road on the hill across the gully. One must turn off Mull Road to go down to the neighborhood community of Roadville. Here and up the hill toward Mull Road, mill houses form three short uneven rows. Though from the crest of Mull Road several streets appear to head down to the gully, only Dura Street goes all the way down to Roadville. It meanders down the hill and parallels the gully before it peters out into a dirt road which eventually connects a couple of miles out of town with the main road to the nearby town of Gateway, a sleepy mill village in the early 1920s now grown to a population of more than 50,000.

Along Dura Street are nine look-alike houses, some set back off the road a bit and others nearer the road. All are frame, painted white, with asbestos roofs; they are set in symmetrically square front yards edged by tired and thin hedgerows with a narrow driveway on one side. A double outline of flowers edges the porches: a row of pots on the porch and marigolds set in the ground across the entire length of the front. In unevenly shaped backyards are gardens, grape arbors, chicken pens, rabbit hutches, and an occasional camper van or boat. An American flag flutters from a high flagpole in the yard of the house nearest the top of the hill.

The screen door on the front porch of this first house on the street opens into a living room filled with showroom-like match-

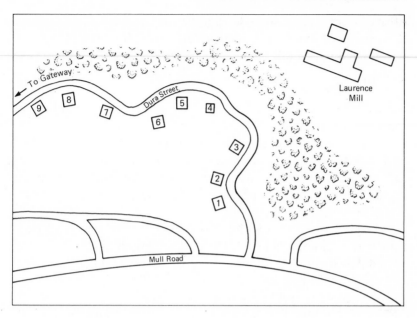

Map 2. Roadville

1 Mrs. Dee and daughter	6 Mrs. Dee's daughter
2 Sue Dobbs and children	and her husband
3 Mrs. Dee's son and	7 Brown family
his wife	8 Mrs. Dee's granddaughter
4 Smith family	and family
5 Macken family	9 Turner family

ing furniture: a suite of sofa and chairs, two end tables, and a coffee table fill the small room as they once did the display window of the furniture store. There have been a few additions: starched stand-up doilies encircle the bases of end table lamps, ashtrays, and vases. Flat crocheted doilies cover the arms of the chairs and sofa and the headrest position of the chairs. A hand-crocheted afghan in the suite's colors is thrown over the back of the sofa. A huge doily of four layers, and a large vase of plastic flowers top the television set. The wooden floor is covered with a large twist rug, and several small matching scatter rugs mark the path to the hall which leads to the bedrooms and kitchen. Off the hall are two bedrooms, a small kitchen and dining area combination, and to the side of the hall is the bathroom. In the bedrooms, floor space is minimal, since dressers and wardrobes take up all available wall space; a double bed fills the center

31

of one room, and twin beds straddle the available floor space in the other bedroom. The double bed is covered by a chenille spread, but a patchwork quilt hangs beneath its edges on one side. In the center of the bed is a doll with a wide skirt made of facial tissues and tied with green yarn. The family Bible on the bedside table is topped by Sunday School lesson books, and crocheted bookmarks mark places in each.

In the kitchen–dining room combination, the table is covered with a red and white checkered cloth, and the sideboard contains salt and pepper shakers in the shape of a dog and a cat, and a catsup-bottle holder which carries the name of a resort knickknack shop just south of a neighboring state's border. The top of the sideboard is loaded with home-canned goods: jars of peaches, tomatoes, pickles, and beans. On the back porch, the freezer is full of similar products, and in the corner, stand buckets, mops, brooms, a kitchen stool, and a utility cart holding a turkey roaster, pressure cooker, and boxes of canning jars.

The widow Mrs. Dee, a plump softly wrinkled woman with fair skin and pale rose-pink fine hair pulled back in a bun, lives in this house with an unmarried daughter. In her eighties, Mrs. Dee works in her flowerbeds, keeps part of the vegetable garden, crochets, and pieces quilts. Her retirement check and her husband's Social Security provide her income. Her son and his wife live two houses down, a daughter and her husband live near the end of Dura Street, and granddaughter Martha and her young family live just before the dirt road leading toward the highway. They all help out in the big garden when they are not working at the mill, and the garden helps feed all four families. Born "away back in the mountains of North Carolina," Mrs. Dee grew up on a farm surrounded by grandparents, aunts, and uncles. Waves of hard living during her upbringing in the mountains had prepared Mrs. Dee to "work all my life."

My daddy was a Baptist preacher and a farmer, and they was seven of us chil'rn – five girls and two boys. And we worked, you know, in the fields in the summertime, just like boys – they wasn't any boys – the boys was the youngest, so the girls had to do the work.*

The children walked three miles to school and attended only four months out of the year. She finished grammar school, met her husband who was a farmer and handyman living near her father's farm, and they married in 1904. They settled in on the rented land they were to farm, and their ten children were born there. But "it was hard to make a livin' and we had so many chil'rn, and he [Mr. Dee] thought if we come to where they could get jobs in the mill . . . they could help, you know, when they wasn't at school." The family moved down to the Piedmont, and lived there for twenty years before the mill shut down during the Depression; none of the nine children who survived to adulthood finished high school. When the mill shut down in the early 1930s, the family moved further south to Roadville, so the children could get jobs in the Laurence Mill, which had opened there a decade earlier. Mrs. Dee, her husband, and three of their children found work in the mill. Seven grandchildren followed them into mill work in either Laurenceville or other towns of the region.

Roadville's community still holds the three children and one of the grandchildren. Mrs. Dee's unmarried daughter worked the same machine her mother used to work, and is now near retirement. She remembers the mountains, living near grand-parents, aunts, and uncles there, moving down from the moun-tains because of "hard times," and facing the changes in the mill in the last twenty years. She no longer works her old machine; she is "too slow now, they say," and she looks forward to retirement. Her younger sister met her husband, a fellow millworker, in the old mill before they moved to Roadville, and she and her husband remember how all six of their children started out in the mill, but soon "got tired of it, and went lookin' for better. They moved away from here." Mrs. Dee's son also met his wife in the mill, and both continue there. One of their three children, Martha, and her husband, are the only third-generation members of the Dee family who continue in the mill, and they're "thinkin' of givin' it up." They talk of this idea with others who live in Roadville.

Of the five other families who live in Roadville, one or more members of each either now works in the mill or has worked in the mill. They all occupy mill houses either they or their parents bought. All these families have children. Adult voices in these households are divided on the place of the mill in their children's future. Between Mrs. Dee and her son lives Sue Dobbs, a widow with three children – teenager Jed, ten-year-old Lisa, and pre-schooler Sally. Sue vows the mill killed her husband: "hard work and that brown lung stuff they talk about," and she intends to raise her children up with a "fittin' education" so they can "do better." Sue, a wiry, jolly-spirited woman with short curly hair, works in the school lunchroom, and Jed, who quit school at sixteen, works in a local garage. He intends to marry Patsy, a fifteen-year-old who lives in Gateway, soon, and Sue hopes he will go back to night school when he "settles down and has a family."

A new family near Sue Dobbs is that of Betty and Doug Smith, who moved into the smallest of the Roadville houses when their first child was expected. They are young; they married when Betty was seventeen and Doug nineteen. Both Betty and Doug have worked in the mill, but Betty did not return to the mill after her child was born, because Doug wanted her to be with the baby. Betty's older sister Peggy and her husband Lee Brown live near the end of the street with their two boys, Martin and Danny. Their baby, Danny, was born just three months before Betty's first baby, and the families share child-care responsibilities. Peggy and Lee both work in the mill, so Betty helps out with Danny. Between Betty and Peggy live Mrs. Dee's daughter and her husband, and Mrs. Macken, a school teacher, and her husband Rob. Everyone always speaks of the two Mackens by naming "Mrs. Macken, the schoolteacher," first. Mrs. Macken is a tall woman with a blonde bouffant hairdo who wears all store-bought clothes. She dislikes the "backwardness" of the mill life and continually tries to pull her husband away from the mill and interest him in other occupations. But he is a loom fixer, has been for fifteen years, and wants no other job. He says he makes good money, "more'n my wife does," and he sees no reason to quit. They have two grown children and one preschooler, Kim, who is looked after by her maternal grandmother in Gateway while Mrs. Macken teaches in a Gateway school.

In the last house is the Turner family, Alice and Jay, and their three teenage children, all of whom are still in school. Both of the Turners work in the mill, but they moved to Roadville only in the late 1960s when the mill in which they worked in another part of the state closed. Mrs. Turner's mother lived in Laurenceville and encouraged them to return. Their three children have had problems in school; their boy wants to quit, and one of their girls is "going steady," and everyone expects her to get married when she "turns sixteen." The boy, however, stays on in high school,

34

because he is a star of the baseball team, and he manages to keep "pretty good grades in math and history." He says he will go to college, maybe "even on a scholarship for baseball," but he hates school now. His sisters expect to go to business college or to nursing school "someday," but they are anxious to get out of Roadville. The town they lived in before was more the size of Alberta – the regional metropolitan center – and Laurenceville is a "hick town" in their view.

When the Turners voice aspirations for their children and distaste for Laurenceville, other Roadville residents, with the exception of Rob Macken, do not argue with them. When Roadville parents talk of their children going on to technical school or college to become secretaries, electricians, doctors, nurses, pilots, and to own their own businesses, Rob scoffs and reminds them "that's further than any of you got." Parents tolerate Rob's general gruff nature and explain they want "better" for their children, and "it's easier now to get ahead." Mrs. Macken urges parents to get books for their children, to read to them when they are "li'l," and when they start school to make certain they attend regularly. She holds herself up as an example of a "millhand's daughter who wanted to be a school teacher and did it through sheer hard work."

Two ways of looking at life cut across Roadville families, and each family has some members who support each perspective. The "oldtimers," who include Mrs. Dee and her children in Roadville, Rob Macken, and the Turners, remember the "hard times" and believe children in those days learned "a lot of lessons school can't teach." They take pride in their years in the mill, and they speak of past days of mill life fondly. A favorite pastime is exchanging stories about the years when the mill was "more like a family."[1] They uphold the mill as a place which gave them work when their large families needed support and the mountains and the farm could not keep their children fed and clothed. Central to their valuing of the mill is the mill's demand for hard work, and the close links which used to exist between the mill and the community in support of work, recreation, and family life. As they watch their children and grandchildren drift away from mill life and Roadville, and newcomers move into Laurenceville, they note the difference in people and the resultant change in life. Mrs. Turner's mother explains:

I don't know the people here now, I might not know four people on Main Street [in Laurenceville] nowadays. The place ain't kep' up the way it was either, but, of course, the young folks don't stay 'round here. Those that live here think they gotta go to Alberta. They just wanna get out on a highway and go. Back in my day, we stayed home, and the mill tried to make ways for us to do things with our chil'rn. But nowadays, that's all gone. Everybody went to church then too. Dinners there'd last all day. Most young folks met at church.

But the oldtimers do not want the young folks to deny themselves the benefits of the modern times. In fact, they themselves have incorporated into their daily living facets of the new times: a liking for travel in campers, a preference for store-bought clothes, and an avid interest in the secular and biracial activities of the Senior Citizens Center. They like to talk about old times but do not spend their days lamenting their passing. Instead they keep busy using the talents and enthusiasm for hard work and family recreation those days fostered in them.

The second perspective on life in Roadville is that identified with the "young folks," meaning, in general, any family who still has young children in school. These families, for example, Martha Dee and her husband, Sue Dobbs, and the Smiths and Browns, seem not to think of the mill as a permanent part of their own life, and they leave it entirely out of consideration for their children's future. They emphasize the success in education they expect their children to have and their assumption that education will carry their children away from the mill. These families talk about leaving the mill and Roadville, and find many of their models for dress, recreation, and aspirations in relatives in the metropolitan center and in key figures of the public media. They themselves had little more than a high school education, if that; yet the women, especially, want more schooling and find ways to mix with those who do have more education, primarily through serving as room mothers or as officers in parent–teacher organizations. The men have less interest in exposing themselves to either the content of schooling or to its personnel. But they follow with keen interest new trends in do-it-yourself projects, camping gear, and hunting and fishing equipment.

The young folks also respect and maintain a need for church life and an independence in providing for oneself. Though they do not talk as freely and as openly about religion as their parents and grandparents, they give the church and religious activities a prominent place in their lives. They also link the ability to do for oneself – to garden, sew, can, do woodworking, and maintain their homes – to moral qualities: thriftiness, industry, independence, and a proper use of God-given talents.

Many of the young folks look to a third group, "those who moved away," as models and sources of information for some aspects of their life in Roadville. Those who moved away have usually tried mill work but have now found other jobs which have taken them to Alberta or other parts of the South. Young folks in Roadville try to incorporate some of what they can learn about life in these places into their aspirations for the future, their home decorations, and preferred toys and activities for their children.

Within both perspectives is an appreciation of what the mill has done for the family. Moreover, the young folks recognize that rural-oriented Roadville offers numerous possibilities of recreation – hunting, fishing, and enjoying a slower pace of life. They all extoll the values of their neighborhood community in Laurenceville, and the way folks there are closer to each other and to the church than people are elsewhere. Yet there is an ambivalence, for Roadville's very restrictions which give privacy, a slow pace, and relative freedom from crime and dirt also keep out some of the ways of living and knowing which might help in getting ahead.

Martha's sister and brother who live in nearby Alberta keep telling her she should quit the mill, go back to school, and get her children out of Roadville so they can get a better education. They tease Martha and her husband and the other young couples in Roadville about being "old-style." They poke fun in a light-hearted way at the "world of difference" between the mill and Roadville and their own lives in plants and offices in Alberta, not more than thirty miles away.

Roadville women wear homemade polyester pants and tops to work; the men wear khaki workpants and cotton shirts. For dress up, the women "sew up" polyester dresses and pantsuits, whose unpressed seams and general unfinished look announce their home-tailoring. When the men get "dressed up," they wear wool and dacron suits, hung back in the closet Sunday after Sunday. Birthdays and Christmas they liven these suits up with new blue, yellow, and pink polyester shirts, fresh ties, and sometimes a striped cotton and dacron shirt with button-down collar. These gifts from their "city-slicker" brothers and sisters bring much jesting, and there is laughter about the new styles of dress those who moved away bring back to their Roadville "country cousins."

Martha's brother in Alberta works as an accountant in a small business machines office. He married an Alberta girl, and they have two children. Martha's sister who now also lives in Alberta married a mill worker at fourteen and had three children. After the children were in school, she attended adult education programs in Gateway for three years to get a high-school diploma, and then had another child. Her husband, whom she met at a local church meeting, worked at the mill, finished high school, and attended a local university extension branch for a year or so while working third shift at the mill. However, shortly after dropping out of the university, he switched jobs and began working for the local electric power company, saying he wanted some control over what he did, "some feeling he could master sump'n," and not be run by a machine or "some boss who ups the quota every week." He condemned the mill for constantly moving people from one job to another in the mill, giving workers no sense of place. He, like other young workers who started out in the mills and moved on to other occupations, compared the way the mills treated them with the way mill supervisors treated their parents, who had been allowed to stay on one machine for years and not be shifted from "their place" by outsiders.

Of Mrs. Dee's daughter's six children who once worked in the mill, all have now found other jobs. Two went back to technical school and have jobs in other towns of the state; three went on to college and have established their own businesses in other parts of the South; one is in seminary, hoping to become a Baptist minister. They all come home to visit often, and Mrs. Dee occasionally goes to visit them. Their reflections on life in the mill are mixed:

It gave me a beginning; I needed to learn hard work; I was a wild 'un, and when mamma and daddy put me in the mill, I had to learn . . .

It's too risky now, 'specially if you're raisin' a family. I'd go in on Monday, and they'd say I could work only 'til Wednesday. We never knew when we'd have a full day's work.

I wanted sump'n better. I hated the dust, the smell, the heat; I even hated that whistle [which signalled shift changes]. I hated to say much against it 'cause I knew mamma and lots of the family had that mill as their life (long pause) but it wasn't for me, and it sure wasn't for my kids. When I met my husband at the tech school in Alberta, we talked about it – his family had been a mill family too – up in Kannapolis, N.C. – we wanted sump'n better for our kids.

When the niggers (pause) uh, the blacks, you know, started comin' in, I knew that wasn't for me. I wasn't ever gonna work for no nigger – my granddaddy'd roll over in his grave if I did. Blacks takin' up the jobs now, ain't no chance for whites to move up, and I gotta have me a feelin' I can be my own boss for some things. I began lookin' for me a way out, and that's when this friend tol' me 'bout the tech school in Alberta.

The homes of the six children, and their aspirations for their children are different than those of Roadville families. Their three-bedroom homes are in suburbs or on small acreages near Southern cities; their children go to big schools and talk as though college were an expected appendage to high school. All the children attend or have attended church nursery schools and they take piano and/or dancing lessons after school. At school, they play in the band, belong to clubs, and work on school newspapers. They spend their vacations at regional beach or mountain resorts. The women's polyester dresses are store bought and the seams are flat-pressed; their bouffant or piled hair styles are beauty-parlor prepared. The men's polyester suits reflect the changing styles from leisure suit to British cut, and the width of their ties expands or contracts with those of the mannequins in the display windows of big-city department stores. They belong to the local country club or the tennis/swimming club which is part of the new suburb in which they live. Their lives and talk are different from those of Roadville's young couples. In Mrs. Dee's words: "Those that have left home here, they talk, uh, I mean, the people here talk different to the people in other places . . . they changed after they moved . . ." Their world is wider, Mrs. Dee sheepishly admits: "Those who live away from here . . . it seem like they (long pause) I enjoy them comin' more than I do the ones that are right around here. It's a difference someway."

At visiting times, those differences are carried into Roadville, and the grandchildren from beyond the mill world share with those of Roadville their clothes and hair styles and talk of what they do in school clubs, at games, and dances. The Roadville young bring their city cousins up-to-date on their latest dance steps, and they exchange the names used for each type of step current at their school dances. Roadville children also recount exploits of their baseball team, and they shock their cousins by telling them of the antics which provoked the last "whupping" from their parents. To the very young, there seems to be little difference between their two worlds; only rarely does talk of working in the mill come up, and then Roadville youngsters go along with their out-of-town cousins who assume that not one of them will go "back into the mill." Mill work is accepted as a regression from the here and now without conscious thought by the third and fourth generations of the Dee family and others of their age in Roadville.

The way ahead

Roadville folks have very definite notions of how to get ahead: there are things for the women to do and things for the men to do. Men are expected to be breadwinners, to work and to provide for their families. Women sometimes work, but they are increasingly not expected to work if they have young children at home. They, on the other hand, have a major responsibility for the household budget, since they are given the bulk of the paycheck to run the household and to pay bills. Men decide on large expenditures for recreation and maintenance of the house; women decide on purchases of furniture and appliances, and are expected to keep the family well-clothed and well-fed.

The expected standard of living in Roadville homes includes a freezer, a sewing machine, garden tools, a power lawnmower, washer and dryer, a car, meat at every meal, and rugs on the floor. Bonuses to which some families aspire are a rototiller plow, an electric saw, and a dishwasher. Every home has a garden in the backyard, and the men plow and plant, keep the garden hoed, and clear it after harvest. Women are expected to pick the produce and can or freeze it. Roadville residents value "hard work," one of the lessons they learned from their parents, and they want their children to grow up "knowing what hard work means." However, families are small and there is no need for large gardens; the homes are not large and therefore require relatively little maintenance. There is not enough work around to satisfy expectations that the young acquire the habit of hard work. Families therefore create household jobs for the young: carrying out the garbage, mowing the lawn, cleaning the front porch, and keeping their own rooms clean. There are more jobs on which they are required to work jointly with their parents: girls help their mothers cook, can, freeze, and take care of younger siblings; boys help in the garden, join their fathers in repairing and painting projects, and help keep the car and camper and/or boat in good repair. Roadville parents do not encourage their children to find outside jobs beyond their school hours, for fear they need the time to study, and working will keep them from maintaining good grades at school.

Paychecks of parents, however, never go far enough, and the women always worry about why all the bills cannot be paid each month. They save at the credit union, "for a rainy day," but they occasionally take money out to help buy large appliances, a car, camper, or boat. Household furnishings, recreation equipment, and lawn mowers, rototillers, etc. are bought on the installment plan and from local dealers, where credit can easily be established but prices are sometimes higher than they are in Alberta. Men and women blame themselves and each other for not working hard enough when there is not enough money. Women find the answer in canning, freezing, and sewing more; men occasionally help each other out with odd jobs on Saturdays, plant bigger gardens, and let house repairs go another few months. For them, work equals money; if one works hard enough, there should be enough money, and if there is not enough money, someone is not working hard enough. Curbing spending by such means as selecting fewer expensive TV-advertised toys is not discussed. Cutting out movies and family trips in the camper is never discussed. Men and women pile jobs on in their hours free from the mill: men agree to haul firewood for sale to the suburbs of Gateway; they commit their Saturday mornings to painting Sunday School rooms when the minister increases talk of giving to the church. Women travel ten miles further to buy a cheaper bushel of peaches for canning; they hang the clothes on the line for several weeks when the dryer breaks down. The work builds up; the leisure time decreases; the camper or boat sits in the backyard several weekends in a row. The resentment and frustration that in all unconsciousness they build for themselves are never expressed in a call for decreased spending, only a push for increased work.

Roadville parents want for their children the best of the old ways *and* the best of the new. From the old ways, they value church-going, respecting authority, the experience of having to work hard, and knowing how to "keep a clean nose" [stay out of trouble]. They expect their children to avoid run-ins with the teachers and other authorities at school; they demand, however, that their young stand up for themselves at school and fight if necessary. But they caution their children not to go "foolin' around with other folks." When blacks began coming to Roadville schools, parents warned their children to "stay away from 'em; leave 'em alone, and they won't bother you. If they do, you gotta stand up for your rights, but the best way to *stay out of* trouble is to *keep out of* trouble." They encourage their children to go to church meetings for young people, and they insist they go to Sunday School and church when they are young. Back-talking, teasing, and challenging the authority of parents are severely punished, by a "strappin'" from the father or their mother's promise that he will give them one. There is to be no doubt about who is boss: old folks know more than young folks, and adults accept no challenges to this premise. The old know more than the young; men know more than women; and in case of a difference in views, the word of the old and the male holds. In the words of one of the Turners' teenagers: "I always ask mom, [if I can do something] 'cause daddy always says 'ask mamma,' but I know I better ask daddy first."

Even young Roadville parents often refer to the "old ways" to explain their behavior, and they frequently express a desire for some means by which to familiarize their children with more of the values from the old days. But they also praise the new, and when they talk of what they like in the new, they speak of things and experiences. They buy their children toys and games advertised on television; they try to get their children in the local church nursery schools at age four; and they take their children to Gateway or Alberta to movies and other forms of entertainment. They encourage their children to join the Scouts and to participate in church activities, such as the choir, which might provide opportunities for travel across the state to other churches. They explain in part their purchase of a camper and/or boat by their desire to have a way to "get out and do things with the kids." Family vacations in the camper take the entire family to regional Disneyland-like entertainment centers or to the beach. On weekends, the fathers go fishing or hunting, mothers insist that the family go to regional flower and home shows in Alberta, and they watch the local paper for news of coming exhibits. Traveling attractions which promote either goods to buy or do-it-yourself activities are far more popular with Roadville parents than are museums, art galleries, and concerts. Roadville people most appreciate recreation and entertainment which lets the observer in on how to be a participant. If it is not something to *do*, Roadville residents – young and old – are not interested. The only exception in concerts are those offered in Alberta by recording stars familiar in country music, the general favorite of Roadville families. Some of the men and young boys, such as Jed, occasionally play instruments in local bands, and all attend country store square-dances.

All in Roadville agree parents have the prime responsibility for raising children, and unless specifically told to do so, neighbors do not punish each other's children. Instead, if a child commits some offense at a neighbor's house, he is verbally scolded and threatened by a reminder that his parents will be told. Some close friends are given a fictive-kin relationship, and they are expressly told by some parents that they can punish their children. Sue looked after Wendy, Martha's preschooler, when Martha went back to the mill on second shift. The non-kin relation was christened with the usual Southern fictive kin term "Aunt," and Martha told Sue to "make Wendy behave." Sue's daughter, Sally, and Wendy were only six months apart in age and grew up as sisters. Neither Aunt Sue nor Martha hesitated to scold either child, both mothers accepting the need to watch carefully over the young. They insisted even the very young show respect and follow orders, and both mothers were firm believers in a "spare the rod and spoil the child" philosophy.

As Lisa, Sue's middle child, neared the pre-teen years, her mother thought she warranted increased scrutiny, since she did not want her to "get in with the bad crowd so sump'n will happen and she'll fool around and get pregnant." Lisa showed some tendency to prefer the company of older girls, and some of her friends had become pregnant at fourteen and fifteen. Once pregnant, they married. Martha's sister, pregnant at fourteen, had married and raised a "fine family," but "it had been hard." The Turner girls were going steady at fourteen, and rumors that they were pregnant flew through the neighborhood periodically. Two teenagers at church became pregnant at fifteen. No one considers abortion or adoption; they just accept early marriage and familihood, set up housekeeping with their husbands, and usually move in initially with one or the other's parents. The young mother assumes immediate and primary responsibility for the baby, and as soon as possible, the young couple and their child move to a small house of their own to start making their way ahead.

Parents fear early boy–girl involvement will deny their children an opportunity to benefit from schooling. Beyond the toddler stage, play and social activities are strictly sex-segregated (and age-graded when possible). Girls who like to play baseball, soccer, and join boys' games sometimes sneak off to do so, but they must watch carefully, so they will not be caught by their mothers or tattled on by other mothers. Only at junior high age (12–15 years) does the church provide coeducational activities, and parents hope their children will make their dating contacts at these functions. They are dismayed that this does not happen now as often as it used to, because the consolidated junior and senior high schools bring together young people from a wide geographical area and range of backgrounds and offer more exciting social activities than the church does. Roadville parents find themselves more and more separated from control over the choices their children make for entertainment and companionship. Some parents respond by creating more and more rules. Others simply despair and ask where they went wrong, as they see their teenager become more interested in their future with one or another boy or girl than in "school" and their future as parents conceive of it.

The role of schooling

Families with teenagers advise those with preschoolers: "Enjoy it while you can, teach 'em all you can now. When they get on up in school, you can't teach 'em anything." Roadville parents of junior and senior high level students therefore both depend on and resent the school; the bringing together of differences in student backgrounds, extracurricular activities, and expectations of behavior have undermined their closed community's control and left them less able to relate to the school of today than to any other institution which touches their lives.

44

They puzzle over the paradox that school, long-familiar in their own lives and the dreams of their parents, is now so changed. They remember their preparations with and their hopes for their preschoolers. When these hopes are clearly not being fulfilled, they blame teachers, school administrators, the blacks, and the federal government. Their children fail to get out of school what education always promised, and they wonder at their children's assertions that they do not need school to get ahead.

Once children begin school, Roadville parents see their responsibilities as restricted to seeing that their children attend regularly, bring their books home, and stay out of trouble. They do not ask about homework, and they offer little help on homework projects. Children rarely ask their parents for assistance, and when projects call for materials or knowledge not available from the classroom, most Roadville students do not complete assignments. They do not bring books home to read for pleasure, and their afternoon activities – beyond the barest attention to mathematics assignments or straightforward fill-in-the-blanks homework – include ballgames, helping around the house, visiting friends, or attending Scout meetings. Roadville parents expect their children to be good students, and they accept C students as good. They do not express dismay when their children get occasional Ds. They praise, admire, and are surprised by their A and B students. Peggy and Lee Brown's older child, Martin, was as a sixth grader an excellent student. Peggy, at any opportunity, expressed their pride in Martin: "He's twelve years old, 'n we're very proud of him, that he's turnin' out to be a *good boy*, an excellent student." Mothers take more interest in their children being good students than do fathers, and mothers are those who brag about their children's grades, while fathers brag about their children's participation in athletic events, cheerleading, and clubs at school.

Adult education classes in Gateway attract Roadville women who quit school to get married and quit the mill to have children. Betty and Peggy both returned to adult education to get their high school diplomas after they were married, and they often spoke of Martha's older sister who did the same. Among the young folks, all the wives have more education than their husbands. The difference between Mrs. Macken's schooling and her husband's is the most marked – and the most talked about by both that family and others. She finished college; he had only a high school

45

education. Martha completed the eleventh grade, her husband quit at the ninth. Betty and Peggy were getting their high school diplomas; their husbands had none. Mrs. Turner had two years of college; her husband finished only high school. Many of the women believe they "know" more than their husbands, but they must keep their knowledge away from their husbands and exert their school knowledge in ways which their husbands will not notice. Mothers serve as Scout "den-mothers" and room mothers for their children's classrooms, and work in the parent–teacher organization in the elementary school. They usually belong to no other organizations, however; those who work in the mill do not have the time, and those who stay home with their children keep busy with gardening and other "hobbies" such as sewing and canning.[2]

In their adult education classes, Roadville women seek out the secrets of the educated middle-class townspeople. They observe and listen to town women talk whenever they can; they want to know how middle-class children succeed in school when their own children do not. However, Roadville women see and hear talk of only some few habits of the townspeople: their purchases, their dress, their travel. In their attempt to "do for their children," Roadville mothers therefore try to sew their clothes in new styles, plan more travel in the camper, and pay more attention to what the public media say one "should" do for children. They take their families to Alberta to the coliseum for flower shows and country-music concerts. No matter that the educated and the school recommend visits to the museum and art shows; the Roadville family as a whole will tolerate only the flower show. There, they can find ideas and tasks to link to home practices and situations.

Their own expectation that hard work brings results, causes them to urge their children to "work hard" in school, and they ask for evidence of such hard work in practices familiar to them: spelling words, "learnin' lessons," and doing homework. Yet on those rare occasions when their children confront them with what they must do at school, they cannot grasp the ultimate purpose of the activities called for; as Lisa put it: "we have to look up definitions all the time, 'n when we have a test, we look up answers to questions in science, 'n such as that." These tasks always seem to point to something else, to suggest that they will have some purpose, some place to be put to use. But neither

Roadville parents nor children see and participate in these ultimate occasions for use. The average, and even the good, students seem to do only minimally what is asked of them to conform. They do not engage themselves creatively in making use of school tasks, in plugging them into some activity where they might make a difference. They see no reason to use the word whose definition was learned in English class last week in either a conversation at home, or in an essay for this week's American History class. Roadville students' social vitality and creativity seem to turn back into their own sense of dress and talk of cars and music. By the time they reach high school, they have written off school as not making any difference for what they want. At their age, they feel sure success in school tasks will threaten their social relations with those whose company they value. The jobs they want seem unrelated to the tasks school sets up for them. They recognize no situational relevance; they do not see that the skills and attitudes their teachers promote make any difference in the jobs they seek: flying, nursing, selling, etc. They want to get out now, or as soon as possible, to get on with the business for which they feel prepared: setting up homes and families, working to make money, and planning to get ahead. Meanwhile, in their own homes with their parents, the good meals and talk of the future go on, the winter gardens grow, mothers attentively sew new dresses for the school dance, and the sun shines on the chimneys of the mill.

In Trackton

About six miles from Laurenceville is Gateway. Mills have come and gone there during the twentieth century; between 1970 and 1980, as many as eight and as few as four operated in Gateway and its immediate environs. Oldtimers still speak of Gateway as a mill center, and people from miles around periodically come there looking for work when the smaller textile mills cut back or shut down. However, since the 1950s Gateway has become attractive to numerous other types of industry, and it has also become a bedroom city for Alberta, the major metropolitan center just across the state line. Business executives from up-North appreciate the lower property taxes in Gateway's state and do not mind the twenty-mile drive to their jobs in Alberta.

Hardly more than a good stone's throw from the renovated

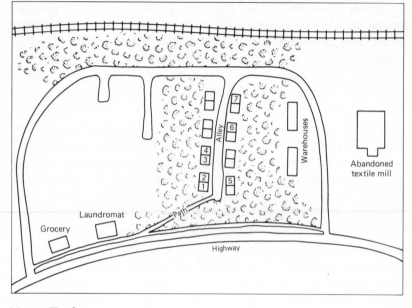

Map 3. Trackton

The "respectables"

1 Allen Young, the "mayor"
2 Ted and Mattie Crawford and family
3 Miss Lula Boyden
4 Lillie Mae Simpson and family

5 Annie Mae Jones and family
6 Mrs. Green and daughters
7 Mr. and Mrs. Smith

downtown center of Gateway is a dirt road which drops sharply off a little-used residential street recently by-passed by the new highway built to lead to the city's center. On one side of the dirt road is a field and an abandoned textile mill. On the other are dilapidated cottonseed warehouses. The road heads straight to the railway track, then turns to the left and follows the track for a mile or so before it connects again with the new highway. Off this railroad lane are several short dead-end dirt alleys creating plaza-like centers around which a few houses cluster. On one of these alleys is Trackton, an all-black neighborhood of eight two-family wooden houses.

Many of Trackton's residents came to Gateway in the late 1950s and early 1960s as young children. Only some remember

48

the rented houses on the cotton farms of white landowners, but all adults recall vividly the wooden shells on the outskirts of Gateway in which they grew up. These wooden shells had no indoor plumbing; water came from spigots set along the dirt road, and toilets were trenches far back in the yard next to the woods. By the time they were young adults, urban redevelopment programs came along, and the city condemned their families' homes and offered housing in one of Gateway's new urban housing units. Trackton families rejected setting up their families in these projects, however, and opted instead for renting in the two-family homes of Trackton. Project rules and regulations, rumored to include restrictions ranging from "immediate family only" to not placing furniture against the walls or letting children open refrigerator doors, scared and angered Trackton people, and they individually chose alternative living arrangements.

For some the choice had been an active one: a firm decision not to have their children grow up in "the project"; for others the decision had been a passive one – filling out forms, proving qualification, and following the processes necessary to be assigned project housing involved too much hassle. Instead, word from a friend about "decent" housing for rent in Trackton or similar neighborhoods close to Gateway's center had provided an option. Though Trackton was not, many of the communities chosen by those who rejected the projects were made up of former mill houses, abandoned by whites who had left the mill for Gateway's suburbs or nearby Alberta. The city now had put the houses up for sale through an arrangement with the mill.

Farthest away from the railroad track on the highest spot off the plaza is the household of Trackton's "mayor," Allen Young. A forty-five-year-old brown-skinned man with "good hair" usually combed with a part, the mayor has a good build, and a steady, self-assured way of carrying himself. His wife is a quiet forty-year-old with "red" skin and long wavy hair. Occasionally, the mayor's mother and one or more grown sons come and stay with the mayor. His mother lives with a daughter in a nearby town; the sons "work construction work" traveling about the region with a large firm centered in another city of the state about eighty miles away.

The self-appointed mayor, from his residence at the highest point in Trackton, "looks out for all the folks." Every Saturday morning, he checks in with those who are up and about outside their homes, seeing how they have been "getting on." Next door to his house, he greets preschoolers Jay, Gary, and Gary B., children of Ted and Mattie Crawford. The boys fight over a tricycle; the mayor watches a few moments, then asks:

TRACKTON TEXT I

You know what you oughta do? Ain't no good fightin' over sump'n you both want, jus' tear it up dat way. Lemme tell you sump'n 'bout dat. One time dere was a real smart man, knew everything, you know, and a woman, uh, two women, brought a child to 'im, each one sayin' it was hers. Dat ol' wise man, he rub his chin jus' so /*putting his hand to his chin*/ (long pause) and you know what he did? /*looking from boy to boy, neither of whom has looked at the mayor during his talk*/ (long pause) He say he gonna chop dat baby in two (pause)
//*both boys look up briefly, then turn back to the tricycle*//
'n give half to each one of dem mammas. Right quick like, one dem mamma say, now you give dat baby to dat woman, don't hurt dat baby. /*looking intently at boys*/ (pause) Now who you think got dat baby? Dat wise man give dat baby to dat mamma what didn't want de baby hurt. Now go 'bout yo' play and don't fight no more, you hear?

Ted, the children's father, a thirty-eight-year-old light-skinned curly-haired man, is sleeping in, because he works late at a feed store on Friday night. His regular job is construction work in the nearby metropolitan center of Alberta, but he sometimes works for the feed store on Thursday and Friday nights to get extra seeds and supplies for his garden. Mattie, the boys' mother, makes no appearance on the porch this morning, because she is busy in the kitchen "fixin' chickens" for Sunday dinner. She is a thirty-year-old dark-skinned woman with hair she straightens and puts on rollers; she has her own two children, Jay and Gary, but she "keeps" Gary B., a child of the same age as her Gary. Gary B.'s mother lives in a town twenty miles away, but she "wasn't fit to be no mamma," and Mattie took the child when he was only a baby. She raised him with her Gary and called him Gary B. He is known to all to be "dull," "not so bright," and Mattie hopes she can get some special help for him at the community child center when he gets a little older.

At the next house, the mayor goes up on the first porch and knocks loudly on the door. Miss Lula Boyden comes shuffling to the door, wiping her hands on her apron. The mayor inquires about her leg, and asks if she has heard from her son. Miss Lula is a stocky woman in her mid-sixties who has heart trouble and is in poor health; her feet and legs swell and she shuffles about most days in bedroom slippers, unable to work and lamenting over the fact that her check never goes far enough. Darett, her twenty-six-year-old son, lives with her; he is brown-skinned with well developed muscles and a propensity to "go out on the town" on weekends. During the week, he swingshifts (alternating shifts from week to week) at one of the local textile mills. Miss Lula's other son is "in the pen," "doing time" for allegedly killing a woman. He's due out "soon," and Miss Lula occasionally hears from him through friends who visit their relatives in a prison in another part of the state.

The mayor's loud knocks have aroused Lillie Mae Simpson in the other half of Miss Lula's house, and she brings the broom to the screen door, announcing "You mighty well-to-do this mornin', mayor." The mayor grins, nods, and inquires after the children: Tony, the eldest, a tall handsome boy in junior high school; Sissy, his sister seven years younger; twins Benjy and Nellie, two years younger than Sissy; and Lem, the baby, who came along two years after the twins. Tony's father is a man who lives across town, and Tony carries his surname, but Lillie Mae is now married to Cuz, a slight, stooped man of thirty with tight curly hair and brown skin. Lillie Mae is warm and self-assured, rail-thin, with a long face, and medium-length curly hair; she is stern with her children and determined to "bring 'em up right."

The mayor looks about the other porches in Trackton and decides he is too early for most folks, and he must be about his other business this Saturday. But across the way from Ted and Mattie's house, Annie Mae Jones, a huge woman with a pear-shaped face and straight brown hair pulled into a bun, hollers "You 'bout to get out, mayor, you givin' me a ride?" Annie Mae always tries to catch the mayor before he leaves for town on Saturday mornings, so she can ride with him to get a few groceries and pay on her layaways (articles reserved by a down payment, paid for in small installments, and claimed only after full payment). It is hot, too hot for the walk to town, and she avoids any exertion on warm days when she must drag her 200+ lb body about. Her husband, Bub, came home last night and brought his check, so

Annie Mae and her pre-teen daughter, Marcy, are heading for town.

The mayor has greeted the "respectables" of the neighborhood, with the exception of "Miz Green" and the Smiths.[3] Miz Green is blind, has severe diabetes, lives with her two pre-teen daughters, and receives a welfare check and help from an older daughter who lives across town. In the last house next to the railroad tracks are the Smiths. Both are in their seventies, and he is on retirement from the railroad; his wife occasionally does day work for a family in whose home she was a maid for fifteen years. The respectables are those who "live right," mind their affairs and their children, and "don't make no trouble" for others. They do for themselves and "don't 'spec nut'n off nobody." They either have regular jobs or receive benefits to which everyone agrees they are entitled because they truly cannot work. They spend their money on their children, household furnishings, food, and they allot a "reasonable amount" for clothes. They intend to buy themselves a house "someday." In the decade between 1970 and 1980, most of the respectables who came to Trackton stayed on, dreaming for a "someday house."

Besides the respectables, there are the transients and the "no-counts" in Trackton. Transients come and go, using the rental properties of Trackton as temporary housing while in town from up North or while waiting to get into the projects. Transients often have the potential of becoming respectables, but they never stay long enough to be accepted by Trackton's own. The no-counts of the neighborhood are usually connected in some way with one or another of the respectable families. Annie Mae, a respectable herself because of her long-time status in the community and her reputation as a decent woman and a good mother, has Bub, a no-count husband whom she and others expect to be gone more often than not and generally to be either drunk or "fresh off another woman" when he comes home. Annie Mae puts up with him because he brings home a check once in a while; she also gets welfare, because the social worker does not think Bub lives in Trackton anymore, and Annie Mae "can't work regular." Cuz, Lillie Mae's husband, is a marginal no-count, because he drinks too much and "fools around" with other women, but he is also seen by Trackton respectables as "sick," because he is often seized by excruciating headaches and is "out" for days. Dovie Lou

Farrell, who lives with her preschool daughter Kim in one of the houses closest to the railroad track, keeps men "coming and going," but the respectables tolerate her, because she is a "fit mamma," takes good care of Kim, and sees to it she goes to kindergarten and dresses neatly. One of Miss Lula's sons is definitely no-count, the other marginal. The one in the pen is unacceptable because he is known to be a troublemaker. The son at home, Darett, "plays it straight" in Trackton, but is known about town as having a "stable" [of prostitutes], and to be in cahoots with taxi drivers who take men out to a motel on the edge of town known to be the black "whorehouse." Ol' Frank Ranker is an old man who often "drinks too much." He lives in the next-to-the-last house before the railroad track and next to Dovie Lou. He has no kin in Trackton, but he was there when many of the resident respectables came. He "gets a check," and his sons and daughters in town come by periodically to look in on him and to clean him and his place up.

Trackton residents are not poor and do not consider themselves so. Most of the respectables have jobs which, though seasonal, provide them with annual earnings of between $8,000 and $10,000, an amount in excess of that earned by beginning public school teachers in the Carolinas in the early 1970s. All are hourly workers, highly vulnerable to both fluctuations in the economy and seasonal changes which affect the availability of work. None can remember a year in which they received a paycheck all year round. Most despise the notion of seeking welfare; some even refuse to apply for unemployment benefits when they are entitled to them. All save through Christmas Clubs and the credit union of their place of employment; these savings are usually used to help pay off accumulated bills and to take care of medical emergencies. All have time payments to make, usually for furniture, a refrigerator, or a television set. During July and August, families use savings to begin putting school clothes on layaway, and in October, they begin paying on Christmas toys for the children. Though they talk of the savings being for the "someday-car or -house," the "li'l things" never seem to get caught up, and there never seems to be enough to go around. For now, they accumulate furniture and household goods.

For those who depend on welfare, retirement checks, or disability, there is the surety that there will not be enough money to go around. They spend their money with painful care, knowing they will have to depend each month on either some outside help from families or on delaying payment of some bills another month. Most of the women want to go to work on the mills' second shift when their youngest child is old enough to be left home with the older children. But to find work and to get to jobs once they are obtained, they must either walk, depend on bus service, or find a ride. In the early 1970s the city discontinued its public bus service. Since then, Trackton women have had to find friends and relatives to help "carry" them places in case of emergency or dire need. Only the mayor and some of the transients own cars. A network of communication keeps Trackton informed about people elsewhere in town who have cars and charge cheap fares for trips to textile mills in the environs. However, such rides are often unreliable, and women who have young children have notorious records for not showing up for employment interviews and for frequently being late or absent from work. Once they have lost a job in one textile mill for excessive absenteeism, they find it hard to get on in any of the local mills again, unless they lie on their application forms about reasons for leaving their past job.

Though Trackton residents are not poor, they live in a run-down neighborhood. There are no front yards; only a few sprigs of grass are able to withstand the constant human and vehicular traffic in the plaza. Furniture delivery trucks; cars of residents, salesmen, and gasmen; children's "hot wheels," bicycles, tricycles, and wagons come and go repeatedly. The houses are run-down, badly in need of paint, and the concrete mold steps are sometimes broken, or the porch has sagged so that one must step down from the top concrete step onto the porch. Rotten timbers support some porches, and there are occasional gaps along the edge of the porches. Behind the houses and all around are thickets of under-brush, broken only by the footpath at the top of the hill which leads to the laundromat and Mr. Dogan's grocery. The under-growth is higher than a man's head, and Trackton residents have no tools suitable for tackling such a thicket. There are no flower beds and only a few flower pots on porches; only Mrs. Smith down by the railroad track manages to get a few flowers to grow along the side of her house. Each half of the two-family units is built on a shotgun model: "stand at the front door and shoot out the back." The porch opens into a living room, the living room into the bedroom (with a bath off to one side), and the bedroom into the kitchen which leads to a small back porch.

The interiors of the houses, however, are usually a sharp contrast to the run-down exteriors. In Mattie's house, for example, the living room is wall-to-wall furniture: two vinyl-covered sofas, two end tables with lamps, a TV, a coffee table, a large lounge chair, and in winter time, a large heater in the middle of the floor. In the one bedroom, there is a double bed, shoved as close to the wall as possible, bunk beds, and a dresser. Nails on the wall above the double bed and hooks on the back of the door substitute for the wardrobe which had to be given up in favor of the bunk beds. There are curtains at all of the windows, and dresser drawers and boxes under the bed are stuffed with blankets, bedspreads, and towels. In the middle of the kitchen floor is a table, with either one or two chairs pulled up to it. A wide variety of plastic containers, aluminum cookware, and dishes and glasses fill the one kitchen cabinet, are on top of the hot water heater, and in boxes stacked on the floor. A refrigerator takes up the wall next to the bedroom, and the gas stove is on the wall at the end of the house. The living room walls are decorated with greeting cards received from out-of-state family members, pictures drawn in school by older neighborhood children, and landscape prints in thin plastic frames. Most households have a double portrait of Coretta and Martin Luther King, often with small school photos of the household's children stuck in the bottom edge of the same frame. There are no toy boxes or cribs, and after a new-born baby is home from the hospital a few weeks, the bassinet box provided by the hospital is thrown out. Children's toys are kept in a bag or box behind or under the sofa; there is no room for them under the beds, for that space is taken with boxes of blankets, sheets, and winter coats, kept from season to season. Half the house seems "packed up," ready for the move which the respectables count on in their daily dreams of someday having their own house. All these linens and winter goods will serve them there, and thus, it is to these things that some of their money goes.

They do not accumulate household and garden tools, stock piles of papergoods and canned foods, or clothes bought ahead. Without ready cash, they have no way of taking advantage of sales or the benefits of on-the-spot cash purchases. They must buy in the season when winter clothes are needed and prices are highest;

there is no room to store clothes bought ahead, even if there were cash to do so. They spend no money on maintenance goods or tools: paint, putty, turpentine, paintbrushes, etc. These are bought in response to a specific need; they are then used and thrown away, for there is no place to store them safely away from children. Moreover, if one has them, neighbors want to borrow, and Trackton folks do not share their goods, their hard-earned purchases, easily with others. Occasionally a hammer, a screwdriver, a cup of sugar, or an axe will be grudgingly lent, but the practice of borrowing is frowned upon, so there can be no exchange of the few goods which do exist in the community. As the mayor put it:

Everybody's gotta make it on his own, you know, you cain't go takin' on other folks' problems. We hep each other, but dere's a límit, and everybody know de other fellow's workin' hárd to get áhead, and he *ought not to pull 'im down.*

His emphasis on this final phrase captures the ambivalence which fosters the community's frequent jealousies and rivalries over the accumulation of new possessions or access to services. When Dovie Lou finds a way to get her daughter Kim enrolled in a morning kindergarten that will send a bus to pick her up, Lillie Mae and Mattie speak ill of her at every chance for several weeks, and Dovie Lou is excluded from front-porch talk sessions among the women. Other children in the neighborhood do not play with Kim, and she spends several weeks entertaining herself in the afternoons alone on her front porch. When Tony is given a new bicycle by Lillie Mae, she insists he keep it locked to the rail on the front porch whenever it is not in use, because "them kids'll steal it or tear it up. You go be havin' sump'n dey don't have, an' dey gonna tear you, or it, down for sure." This attitude toward the mutual struggle and the small signs of success along the way toward getting ahead marks many encounters across all ages in the neighborhood.

Trackton respectables want those they care about who come into their neighborhood to know they "know better," i.e. they know they "ought" to help each other out and fix up the neighborhood. They explain: "Ain't no use fixin' dis place up outside. What I'm gonna do dat for? (pause) Dat ol' nigger [the man who owns the Trackton houses], he won't do nut'n, and I ain't gonna spend mý money on hís house. Save it for my own." Thus Trackton folks explain away the run-down exteriors of their homes. Life goes on day by day as though this were only a transition period, and residents believe "soon we be getting on, movin' to a place our own, 'n be gone from dis run-down place." When the city moved in with bulldozers and cleared the under-growth in the back, some residents followed Ted's earlier example and put in vegetable gardens, and even some flowers. This back area is generally protected from dogs, children, and vehicles, and the gardens can survive without constant policing. Occasionally, Ted, Cuz, or the mayor patch a hole in the porch of their own house or paint a room or put new linoleum down, things the landlord will not do. But, in general, Trackton residents, even the respectables, view their stay in Trackton as temporary and choose not to spend money and effort on their present homes.

Changin' times

Trackton respectables are, in their terms, "risin'," "comin' up in dis world," both because of "changin' times" and because they are willing to work to take advantage of these times. They hold steady jobs, and they push their children to get a good education. Production-line textile mill jobs for males and females and con-struction wages controlled either by unions or minimum wage laws give new chances. Expanded educational opportunities do the same. In the early years of day-care programs sponsored by the city, children whose parents were not on welfare could attend along with those whose were. Head Start was available for many children, and before a change in regulations cut back these services for all but those on welfare and with special needs, Trackton families took advantage of the chance to send their children to school. By the end of the decade, all public schools in Gateway had kindergartens. In addition, neighborhood centers in the projects and black churches ran day-care programs for very low fees. A neighborhood medical clinic allowed families the opportunity to insure that their children had vaccinations and basic health checkups. Blacks no longer had to depend on private doctors for these basics. Some folks said there might even be "good" low-cost housing available for purchase by blacks before the end of the decade, and Trackton respectables hoped, with some skepticism, that this might give them their chance to buy a home.

The mayor's seventy-two-year-old mother, Mrs. Young, in response to Tony's request that she help him with an assignment to collect an oral history, reflects on the "changin' times" which made these hopes possible. She sees schooling and success in school as the way to make these hopes and dreams come to reality.

TRACKTON TEXT II*

Tony: Uh, what role in your pas' would you like to tell us today?
Mrs. Young: It have been a great movement, you know, since my, our, I
          been at my days, because, uh, in our days, uh, de time was
          real hard, don't you know, because we lived on a farm, it
          was, uh, my father 'n my mother 'n uh three brothers 'n
          five sisters. 'n uh it, you know, we didn't get education like
          de chil'rens do at dis day 'n time. Because, uh, mean with a
          large family like dat, it was hard for to get clothes 'n shoes
          'n books you know, for to go to school, 'n, uh, we had to
          work on de farm, which just only lef' us school 'bout three
          months a year. 'n it was hard to even make good grades, at
          dat time. But I think, you know, it have been a great
          improvement since our days. 'n uh, I have work for
          thirty-five cent a day (pause), 'n uh, I don't think not
          anyone 'd work for thirty-five cent, even a hour now, 'n I
          think it's been a great movement, you know, since our
          time. And, uh, I have uh even work for six family at one
          time, 'n I have no, I mean, uh, dey pay, I have *even* iron
          fifteen shirts plus other things, you know, other clothes, 'n
          uh, but we *survive* don't you know, 'n uh, I would advise
          all *young* chil'ren to go to school 'n get an education,
          because it will even better dey life, dey, 'n *too*, education is
          all right, but dey have to take God along wid 'em too.
          /looking at Tony and settling back in her chair/
Tony: Uhh, you stated that it was hard for you all to get good
          grades. Uh, why was it hard for you all to get good
          grades?

                                                  [
Mrs. Young: Because we
          didn't even have (unintelligible), you know, *lights* to even
          study by, don't you know, I mean, líghts even to see how
          to study a li'l bit, because when you come home from

58

school, it wasn't like chil'ren is today, you would had to go
out 'n work.
                    [
Tony: Hm–uh=
Mrs. Young: ='n day be night, you know, when, 'cause you had to walk
             at least seven mile, 'n be night you almost, when you get
             home, yet still you had yo' work to do.
                                    . . .
Tony: What is impor*tant* to you, uh what changes have, have
              made your determination uh better?=
Mrs. Young: =Well, uh because you, I mean, you know, I think you kin
             get better jobs now, 'n den uh you kin better education
             now.
Tony: Uh, you tol' me that you didn't get very much education,
              uh, tell us what, what are you doin' now to uh complete
              yo' education?

                                                         [
Mrs. Young: Well, uh,
             I'm goin' (pauses) well, I'm goin' back to uh adult
             education hu uh school at night, 'n so I'm takin' (unintel-
             ligible) English 'n math, 'n so den I attend de Senior
             Citizen, 'n so I volunteer, 'n I mean do volunteer work, 'n
             so it's improve my education a good bit.

Mrs. Young's responses to Tony's queries stressed the common
experience of hardship and the individual will to survive, plus the
sense of individual accomplishment necessary today to take
advantage of the benefits of the "great improvement."

Mrs. Young, now with two children who are "on the rise," does
not speak of the cooperation of earlier days when the extended
family lived on the farm or in the condemned housing on the edge
of Gateway. These community members depended not so much on
individual enterprise as on joint efforts to survive. In those days,
community members helped each other out, one mother keeping
the children of others while they worked, men helping each other
keep the few cars in the neighborhood running because they were
available to all. Dresses, food, coats, and lunch boxes were shared,
and if one member of a family seemed in greater need than others,
he would receive any temporarily surplus food or clothing. Blood
kin ties were respected, but fictive kin networks whereby an older
man or woman assumed "aunt" or "uncle" status had much the
same functions.

In the days before Lillie Mae moved to Trackton, Aunt Berta Collins, a woman of fifty who lived with her husband, daughter, and two grown sons in one of the condemned houses of the neighborhood filled more of a "big mamma" role for Lillie Mae's children than their real grandmother did. Lillie Mae's children, and her two sisters' children as well, had the benefits of Aunt Berta's care, occasional sharing of necessary items, and advice on what to do in case of sickness. Lillie Mae's mother drank "too much," but was a good friend of Aunt Berta's who was herself highly respectable, and saw to it that her husband and children were respectable. When Aunt Berta saw that one of Lillie Mae's children needed something, she would help out, and Lillie Mae would return the favor usually by sending Tony down to help Aunt Berta carry dirt and water for her flowers. The arrangements for reciprocity were never spelled out; they were simply worked out without conscious articulation. With the move to Trackton and a community dominated by respectables, this sharing gave way to the individual "gettin' even better" which, in her interview with Tony, Mrs. Young spoke of with pride.[4]

The extended families of Trackton respectables who still lived in condemned housing rarely came to Trackton; members who lived in the projects or were, in some cases, landowners in the country-side, came more frequently. Lillie Mae's mother and brother still live with Lillie Mae's sister in the same condemned house Lillie Mae and her family left in the early 1970s. Lillie Mae acknow-ledges they are alcoholics and cannot seem to collect themselves either to move into the project or to find other housing, so they stay on in the condemned shell, getting water from the spigot at the road and using the toilet trench in the backyard. Lillie Mae's sisters have found project housing for themselves and their children, but their stays vary in accordance with their job status, support from their children's fathers, the frequency of their welfare checks, and the intensity of their association with males who are not members of the "immediate family."

Lillie Mae never speaks ill of her mother, brother, or sisters. Occasionally she visits them on a pretty day when she can walk down the railroad track to the old house or the project. Her sister and mother almost never come to visit in Trackton, though the children come occasionally, and once in a while, Lillie Mae will take one of her sisters' children if she feels the child needs special attention. Her extended family can potentially be a drain on her meager resources and a bad influence on her children. They can offer her no advantages or benefits now.

Family members who still own their own "pieces of land" in the country visit more often. Mattie has a brother who has a car and comes several times a year. He brings vegetables, and at hog-killing time, he shares meat and lard with Mattie and her family. Mattie, to reciprocate in a fashion reminiscent of days before Trackton, goes to the country to help at hog-killing time and especially to help make soap and prepare chittlins, a Southern delicacy made from the intestines of hogs. For the most part, however, Trackton families focus on their own.

Church connections are somewhat less frequent and intense than they were in the old communities, for there is often no way to get back to the old country church attended before the move to Gateway and during the days on the outskirts of Gateway. The most necessary occasions for attendance at these home churches are funerals, "preachin' Sundays" (usually every other Sunday or once a month), and "meetin' time," week-long revival meetings held each year in August. On these occasions, family members or friends from the old church come and pick up Trackton residents and take them to church. Sunday services and follow-up socializing may last all day and always provide ready occasions for sharing stories about both old times and current general news about the health and well-being of family and friends. There is little other talk of the here and now.

Some Trackton residents have tried town churches which are populated by "town blacks," mainstream middle-class families. But Trackton residents are too marginal to this culture to feel comfortable in church with mainstreamers. The town blacks live in a suburb of brick houses on one side of town, are school teachers, preachers, and independent businessmen (often retired after twenty years in the army). They serve on the city's human relations council, are elected to city council and the school board, and in the eyes of local white political leaders, they represent "the black community." They all own cars, take vacations out of state, and buy their clothes in Alberta. Trackton folks are not respectable enough for the town blacks and too respectable to reassociate themselves with kin and friends of former days. They do not count, literally or figuratively, in city plans to provide new housing and to clean up condemned housing areas; neither their addresses and jobs nor their language and schooling make them eligible to represent the "black community." They have fallen between the lines of the city welfare and public housing rolls and the lines of the local newspaper proclaiming the election of a new black to the school board.

There is neither time nor tolerance for complaints in Trackton. People look instead to the "great improvement." "Gettin' ahead" and the struggle to do so are positive topics. The old days – the times in the cotton field or in the mills as the lowest-level menial workers – are retold, and the fun and funny things which happened are accented. Their stories tell of the son who stole away and hid under a tree to read instead of picking cotton, the time the son of the white landowner asked the son of the black cotton picker if the black on his skin rubbed off, the church meetings in August with their good music and food. The only exceptions to this response to the "hard ol' times" were the young men who had served in Viet Nam and came home to find "the great improvements" their parents lauded not enough. They found themselves jobs, or, with veterans' benefits, went back to school and on to college, and rented apartments in the new modern complexes on the side of town nearest Alberta. There they set up bachelor quarters, bought new cars and furniture, and "checked in on the ol' folks" very rarely. They offered no help; instead, when they became strapped and needed a "few bucks for a big date," they dropped by in their latest outfits to ask for a "loan."

Though Trackton residents acknowledge the benefits of "the great improvement," they do not themselves take part in any aspect of the political process which town blacks proclaim as a major result of "changin' times." Oblivious to the political decisions made by the city council, apathetic about voting, and unwilling to accept the recommendations of town blacks, Trackton residents live apart from the city's election contests and power plays to gain control of decision-making in urban housing and neighborhood centers. They occasionally condemn town blacks for their snobbish ways, for having forgotten "where they come from," but they never confront them with complaints or use them to obtain inside information about procedures for getting city services or benefits from new federal programs. They keep themselves closed in their respectability within Trackton, and they share themselves most as a closed community, when they share with each other tales of places and times they can all remember.

Miss Lula's sister, Miss Bee, on an extended visit to Trackton, responded at a local Senior Citizens' Center to an oral history interview with some black high school students:

TRACKTON TEXT III*

Miss Bee: In my chil'hood, I kin remember when we live in a li'l log house, in de *pasture* –
|: 'mong de *cows* (laughter)

Interviewers: (laughter)

Miss Bee: *cows* and *hogs* (laughter)
                               (laughter)

Single   You gon' say dat?
interviewer: [

Miss Bee: 'n de cows 'n hogs, in de pasture,:|
li'l log house, 'ere's two li'l windows to it,
|:'n it *rained* in de house,
'n it *snowed* in de house,
'n we could look down through de *crack*,
'n see de *chickens*,
under de house:|
eatin' (laughter)

Interviewers: (laughter)
                [

Interviewers: eatin'
Miss Bee: (laughter) 'n-er-uh,
Single   [
interviewer: All right
Miss Bee: 'n-er-uh (long pause) I know my *mother* (clears throat)
|: had put (pause) paper, magazines,
'n patched *up* de house for us to keep *warm*,
plástered de house all over wid magazines, to keep us warm:|
'n-er-uh (long pause), 'n 'member when
|: we worked in de *fiel'*, she worked in de fiel:|
did, for 'bout (pause) thirty-five cents a day.
'n den (clears throat) (pause) she had to carry her li'l baby out in de fiel' sittin' under de *shade* tree, while we workin' inne *fiel'*.
'n-er-uh den we *move* from dere to a better house.

'n in de *spring*, dey'd uh (pause) wash de *bed* ticks
[mattress coverings]
up off de *beds*, an' empty de *straw* out of 'em
|: 'n pull háy out de fiel'
pull háy out de fiel':|
'n put in dese béd ticks 'n sew 'em back up.
'n dat's what we slép' on.
'n-er-uh we didn't have soap 'n water (unintelligible)
washin' powder, nut'n like dat,
|: dey took sán',
took san' 'n scoúred de house wid it
dey scoured de house wid *san'*:|
ah ash, to clean flo',
'n-er-uh de wáter buckets,
'n tings, dey had wooden water buckets,
|: dey scoured dese water buckets wid ásh,
hung dem out in de sun, let 'em dry,
'n dey scoúred de churn, wid ash (unintelligible) de same
put dém out, let 'em dry,
'n we'd whítewash all 'round de house wid mud get out de
branch,
'n den we whitewash de trées out de yard:| (pause)
Dat's in de spring,
now everything's beáutiful (laughter)

[

Interviewers:	(laughter)
	[
Miss Bee:	Whitewash de fíreplaces
	(laughter)
	[
Interviewers:	(laughter)

Miss Bee: 'n-er-uh
|: we went to *church*,
we *walk* to church,
most de time, had two or three *miles*,
we wálk to church, pull off a shoes
'n carry 'em in a hán' a piece
'n we get to chúrch, dus' off our feet
'n put our shóes on.
'n er-uh when meetin' be goin' on at night,
'n we walk to church,:|
when we get back home,

de chickens be crowin' for daylight.
Done walked all night might nigh home
carryin' a lantern,
see how to walk by.
(long pause) 'n (unintelligible) 'n uh lemme see what else, I
kinda 'member, kinda 'member de first automo*bile* I had
ever saw. 'n hit had spokes in it like a bicycle kinda', like,
now I 'member dat, our bossman, we live on his place,
bought one, 'n we *all* stood 'n watched dat automobile
(unintelligible) automobile (laughter)

	[
Interviewers:	(laughter)
	(unintelligible) (laughter)
Miss Bee:	'n when I first started workin' out, li'l girl, I made one

Miss Bee: 'n when I first started workin' out, li'l girl, I made one
dollar a week, den I went to workin' for a sup'mtendent of
a cotton mill, Reeseville cotton mill, I'z makin' two dollar
'n a half a week (long pause)
'n den, I work dere 'bout twenty-five year, went dere
fo'teen years old.
Den we uh móve, come on up 'ere to uh-er-ah Gateway
(unintelligible)
'n I worked up dere 'bout twenty, some twenty-three year
ironin' (pause) ironin' on de presser
'n uh I made 'bout eight dollars a week,
'n I thought dat was *fine*, hadn't made dat much money
'foh (laughter) . . .

Such public performances, often marked by varied repetitions and
a lilting chant-like quality, brought out laughter about the past.
They also reflected the pride in what had been accomplished, a
sense of acceptance that this was the way things were, and the fact
that there were some good things back then in spite of the
hardships.

Some of this ability to accept carried over into a resistance to
being disturbed by the everyday challenges of current life: a sick
child; a rotting porch; a garden plot too wet to dig for so many
weeks an early garden could not be planted. None of these daily
situations brought a lot of talk about why they happened or what
was needed to set things straight. People just waited quietly or
acted quietly when they saw a chance to change a situation; for a
change to come along, they often had to wait a long time. Aunt
Berta, who had lived in one of the condemned houses in the same

area where Lillie Mae, her mother, brother, and sisters lived, knew she would have to move out of her house. Both her husband and son worked in the textile mills, and she was a domestic who worked for several families, and usually had three to four days of work a week. Her condemned three-room rental house was stuffed with furniture, and, during the winter months, with flower pots as well. In, the front yard sat an abandoned car which needed tires and a battery. She and her family would have to move; they waited months, seemingly without exerting effort toward finding a new place. Aunt Berta knew she was not "goin' into no project:" her family made too much money to qualify and she did not want that life anyway. All these months, Aunt Berta worked on her husband, telling him periodically and quietly he should get something for all his years at the mill, and the credit union might lend them money for a house. Finally, with the help of a family for whom she worked, Aunt Berta found a former mill house, a neat frame house in a recently desegregated neighborhood close to the center of town, and she pushed her husband to get approval from the credit union of the mill.

A bank loan was also necessary, however, and a credit check at the local credit bureau showed that Aunt Berta had a bad credit record. She firmly and quietly stated she had always paid her debts, and she was *not* a bad credit risk. Three items were on the record: a local furniture store showed delinquent payments; a financing company showed delinquent payments for a car loan; and county property taxes had not been paid on the car two years back. The furniture company was shocked to hear that Berta had a bad credit rating:

Berta, huh? You gotta be kiddin', wish all my customers were reliable like her. She don't pay on time, but she always pays. Guess my secretary, got a new one awhile back, just didn't know 'bout Berta, and the way we do business. She must have sent in that bad record.

The problem of the car note was solved when it was discovered that Berta had co-signed a note for her younger son to buy a new car which he had wrecked, and the note had finally been paid off when he collected his insurance. But payment was delayed, and the late payment was shown on the credit record without explanation.

The matter of the property tax on the car her husband had abandoned in the front yard required him to go with a city worker to the county seat to check the records there. He and Berta insisted the bill had been paid, and their quiet firm resolution, plus the righting of the other two accounts, convinced the city worker they were right. Twice, Berta's husband took time off work to go with the city worker to the county seat to clear the record, and on each occasion they were told to come back. On the day appointed for the third visit, he did not show up for the meeting with the city worker. Puzzled, she called Berta at the home where she was working as a domestic. Berta listened to the city worker's complaint, then said quietly "He done been twice, he be workin'." The city worker went to the county seat on her own and found that payment had indeed been made, but records had been misfiled, and a record of no-payment had been sent to the credit union.

Berta and her husband got the credit union loan and the bank loan and moved their accumulated furnishings into their new house. Week after week, Berta returned to the old house to transplant flowers to the yard of the new house. The old car was left behind. The younger son bought another car for which Berta signed another note. In the years after the move to the new house, Berta borrowed money to buy lawn furniture and a freezer, to paint her house, and to replace the old living room suite. Berta's grown son who lived with them paid "some li'l bit of money each week" for food, and when the daughter was old enough to work, she did the same. Berta's money went for the house and groceries, and her husband's check paid the house payment, taxes, and insurance, and occasionally he helped out with groceries or bought something special he wanted her to cook for him. Still, every year, there was the need for short-term loans from the local finance companies, most of which were repaid by Berta at $10 or $20 per month.

In the struggle to get ahead, males and females are sometimes allies, sometimes enemies. Individuals telling stories of the past never recount these stories with a joint *we* of husband and wife, man and woman, but of a collective black experience and individual hardships. Women tell stories of how they kept the children, and worked in the fields or at other low-paying jobs; men tell stories of how they worked in the fields and looked for other kinds of work. Once established in millwork, however, families admit the better earning power of males, and every female expresses a desire for a male to be a part of the family to help

67

secure some income. Females who work as domestics often receive much less than those who find work in the mills. When they begin working in the textile mills on production lines, they are laid off during slow times before the men, and they are often laid off because of excessive absenteeism caused by responsibilities to children or by unreliable transportation to work. Women are also more critical of working conditions in the mills, especially of what they consider unreasonable demands that they lift heavy rolls of fabric or stretch to reach the uppermost parts of the machinery. During periods when the mills are under intensive pressure for higher production at less cost, women feel demands are greater on them, and they refuse to work, for fear they may injure their "female parts." Women, though preferring to be dependent on men for a steady income, are also highly independent of them in decision-making about how the money which comes home will be spent. Most women, when they do get their man's check, have it earmarked for payments on furniture, layaways of clothes for the children, and always for groceries. Men keep out for themselves money for their own clothes, liquor, travel, and payment to any other women for whom they share responsibilities.

Once children are old enough to work, they are expected to share their earnings with "mamma" and thus to pay their share of living expenses in the household. This pattern continues for adult males, many of whom "stay with" [live with on a regular basis] their mothers or occasionally move home for a short stay. For the household budget, they put in a "li'l sump'n" each week and are also expected to provide certain services: to drive their mothers places, to talk to the gas man about putting off the bill until next month, and to fix up the house. But men rarely satisfy the women of the household in the latter's strong desire to enlist them for chores around the house. Men resent the idea of such work: a little gardening and the most dire repairs are the limit. Women, if they really want new linoleum, a room painted, or a piece of furniture thrown out to make room for a new one, must do it themselves with the help of the older children.

The line of allegiance in families is not between male and female as spouses or as parents of children, but rather between parent and child. The link between mother and son lasts the longest and is the strongest. Young men often father and support children who remain with their natural mothers; they wait as long as possible to marry and move in with a wife or steady woman.[5] They prefer to stay on with their own mothers and help them, while at the same time contributing to the support of their children living in other households. Even men who move "up-North" often send money home to their mothers, and if a crisis arises, they will quit a job and come home to help out. If they father children up-North and feel they are not being well-treated, they send the children home to their mother in the South to "keep." Men nearing retirement often live with their mothers, while occasionally visiting the households of their grown children about the area. This bond between "a mamma and her boy" is the strongest kin tie exhibited in Trackton.

The place of children

A good family man takes seriously his responsibilities to his mother first, then those to his children. Little thought is given to his responsibilities to his wife or woman, except that if he maintains a relationship with more than one woman at a time, he is expected to keep his affairs straight, so there will be no trouble between the women. Children are valued as children, not as the offspring of a combination of particular individuals. Sons are most highly valued by both mothers and fathers, for "you gotta always worry 'bout girls gettin' messed up [pregnant]." The pregnancy may be protested but the child is not. The particular father or mother matters little; the neighborhood is glad to have a child. Annie Mae's daughter, Marcy, became pregnant at fifteen after a one-time liaison with Miner Baine, a boy of sixteen. After a month or so of scolding and fussing, Annie Mae declared her acceptance of the child: "It's her baby; she gotta be a woman, but dat's my gran [grandbaby], and it ain't gonna want for nut'n." When the child – a boy – was born, Miner came around to visit infrequently, and brought milk and diapers occasionally in the first few months. Soon after he went into the service and left the area. Miner's family, however, enjoyed the baby, Larry Lee, and they took the child every weekend, and Miner's sister and parents lavished attention on the baby. Annie Mae became the baby's "mamma," taking major responsibility for the child. Larry Lee learned to call his biological mother by her given name, and Annie Mae was "mamma." Marcy, after the birth of the child, went back to school at night, then on to a technical school, working steadily at various jobs and helping her mother pay the expenses for Larry Lee. Mr. and Mrs. Smith, the old couple near the railroad tracks, became co-parents with Annie Mae of Larry Lee, keeping him a good part of the time. At the age of four, he went North with them to visit one of their children, and Miner's family took him to California to visit relatives there. Miner's sister found a nursery school for him in the community when he was four, and somewhat to Annie Mae's chagrin, he began school. She missed him, but had no real control over the decision, and agreed it was probably best nowadays for him to get some "schoolin' 'fore school."

Miz Green, whose diabetic condition grew steadily worse, had three daughters. The middle daughter, Zinnia Mae, a large girl who had social and academic difficulties at school, became pregnant at fourteen. Because her mother could not "see after" her, she had been "messin' around" with some boys and "got herself pregnant." It was agreed by all that Zinnia was too young to take responsibility for the child, and the grandmother could not, so Miz Green's oldest daughter who had lived across town came back to "keep" the child. Shortly thereafter, Zinnia's sister, only a year younger than she, became pregnant, and soon the oldest girl had two babies to take care of. All of Trackton lamented the pregnancies for an unusually long period, primarily because the grandmother could not care for the babies, but once the babies – two boys – arrived, they were immediately accepted in the neighborhood and accorded the same status as all boy children.

In many ways, life during the week in Trackton centers around its children. There are relatively few occasions for leaving the community for any purposes other than work, and visits by mothers to Head Start centers or the medical clinic. Mr. Dogan's neighborhood store, up the path at the top of the plaza, is visited only if supplies are absolutely needed and there is cash which has been hoarded for just such mid-week needs. However, Trackton residents know prices are higher there, and they prefer to buy at the supermarkets at the end of the week. Next to the neighborhood store is a laundromat, and children are sent there during the week with stern warnings to "bring back the change" and not "waste it on Mr. Dogan's high prices."

On Friday afternoon, however, as soon as the children get home from school, the pace in Trackton begins to change. The yards are swept, and riding toys are put on the front porches, as all wait for the paychecks to come home. More often than not, the paycheck has been cashed, and the father or mother will bring goodies to be distributed. Potato chips, light bread (store-bought loaves of sliced white bread), apples or oranges, small plastic toys, and tiny bags of candy or gum are the usual favorites. Distribution focuses on the children in each family with the wage-earner passing out favors and often distributing them unevenly depending on the response he or she gets from particular children. The youngest boys are favored to get the greatest number of treats, and girls and older children stand by and wait, hoping their siblings will share. If it is the man who has brought the check, he will give some to the mother for paying on layaway goods and buying groceries; he will keep a certain amount, and will often leave soon after the distribution.

Radios blare and record players are turned up high as separate or joint family activities center around each porch or living room. Occasional shouts across the plaza punctuate the general excited pace. An unfamiliar car enters the roadway, and the noise subsides, as all watch the stranger get out of the car and be acknowledged by the family on one porch. The noise begins again, as children rip and run about in front of their houses, display their food or new toy, quarrel about suggested trades, or ask questions about the contents of the little paper bags clutched tightly in the hands of other youngsters. There is loud fussing and a general sense of noise, and no one tries to quiet the yells and shouts of the youngsters.

Ol' Frank comes out of his house, relatively sober, and goes about the children teasing them for candy and holding the rope for the school-age girls who have found a level place at the top of the plaza and are beginning a jump-rope round. Darett emerges on his porch and produces shouts of approval from others. He wears a purple silk shirt and black pants with a leather jacket thrown over one shoulder. His expensive black hat with a purple scarf tied around its band is set on one side of his head, and he stops to put it on one of the youngest boys. He talks to each of the smallest boys, engaging them in a repartee about what they can and cannot do, asking each one "What yo' name, huh?" If they respond with the nickname he has given them, he pulls a candy or piece of gum from his pocket or punches them in the stomach. He will then shake a hand, strut to another circle, and make his way down the alley toward the railroad track. Trackton becomes the audience for the joint performances. Soon, Darett claims his hat for a final time, raises it to his mother sitting on her porch, and moves off to meet his buddy who will pick him up at the highway. His friends do not come into Trackton, because either he does not want Trackton to see his big-city buddy's Cadillac, or he knows his buddy's entrance will seem to confirm for Trackton respectables his "wild big-time" life.

Saturdays and Sundays continue the pace begun on Friday afternoons, with the plaza a stage for some performers making entrances and exits, while others are part of the permanent cast. A few children have saved some of their sweets and treats from the night before; others beg from them. Some have not yet had their toys broken or put away by their mothers. Women go off to town, walking in groups, or catching a ride with either the mayor or a friend who drops by. When they return with the groceries, there is a minor replay of the Friday afternoon distribution, but everyone knows this grocery shopping is serious; it must last all week, and there will be little distribution now. Ted works in the garden in back of his house, mending the fence so Tony's dog cannot get in, and repairing his rabbit hutch. The mayor works on his car, and some of the transients wash their cars. Ol' Frank sits on his front porch groaning and holding his head in his hands. Life goes on outside the houses almost all year round. Several scenes go on at the same time, sometimes blending in a scene with the entire cast; at other times, separated into individual sets on the stage. Children move in and out of the different scenes, sparking interactions between sets and ever making known their place in Trackton.[6]

The first year

Babies born to Trackton residents are brought home from the local hospital in the rectangular bassinet box it provides. A small supply of disposable diapers and plastic bottles also comes home with the baby, for Trackton mothers do not expect to nurse their babies, and they depend primarily on disposable diapers, accepting these as necessary since their homes have no laundry facilities. Relatively few provisions are made for the baby beforehand; a few shirts, blankets, and wrappers may be new, and shortly after the arrival home, the father, whether present in the household or not, is expected to send diapers and a supply of milk-formula. He and his family come to visit the child and arrange a time for "keepin' 'im" sometimes every weekend, or a week or so out of each month. If the child is born to a young mother remaining in the home of her family, and the father remains with his family, each family buys independently for the child, especially during the preschool years. The paternal grandparents may buy a snowsuit one week, and the maternal grandparents may buy a heavy sweater the next. The provision of a planned wardrobe to consist of a certain number of particular items is not a goal; the emphasis is on the buying of items for the child. In each household of both the mother's and father's family, the child will have at least a minimal set of provisions kept there at all times.

If the baby is not the child of a young girl whose family will be taking primary responsibility for childcare, the baby does not have the benefits of moving from one home to another. Instead, if the mother has entered a somewhat stable relationship or marriage, usually by her early twenties, the baby is brought into the home of the mother and father. There he enters a household in which any other children born to the mother before this marriage will take some responsibility for the child. The father's family will also contribute, especially if this is either his first child or the first child of this union, but subsequent children of this union may not receive a particularly favored status or spend as much time in the home of the father's family.

Once home, the child is kept in the box bassinet only a few weeks, and is then moved into the bed with parents (or the mother or grandmother if the child is born to a young girl remaining home with her family). If there are not too many older children already sleeping in other beds of the household, the baby is moved into one of their beds by the age of two or three, especially if a new baby is on the way. The baby's clothes are kept in a pile on the foot of the bed, in part of a dresser drawer, or in a box, because there is no space to provide for the separate storage of the new family member's belongings.

The environment of both boy and girl babies during their first year of life is a very human one. They sleep with family members, are held, carried, and cuddled by family members, and by all residents of the community as well. For all community members of Trackton, not only older brothers and sisters, babies are play-things. When they cry, they are fed, tended, held, and fondled by anyone nearby. Since bottle-feeding is the norm, anyone can take on feeding responsibilities. Babies are restrained from exploring beyond the human interactions which surround them. They have little occasion to coo and babble by themselves or in quiet situations where their babbling sounds can be heard above the general talk which seems to go on around them most of the time. They sleep and eat at will; they are fed when they seem hungry if food is available, and they go to sleep whenever or wherever they become sleepy. They are often waked up to be played with when children come home from school or a visitor comes in, and they are often awake late into the night in the living room where a television or record player blares, or loud conversation is going on. Their inclusion as part of the family is continuous. If they fall asleep in the midst of a lively story-telling session or a family argument, they continue to be held until the person holding them needs to move about. Then someone else takes over. The child is almost never alone and very rarely in the company of only one other person.

Encapsulated in an almost totally human world, Trackton babies are in the midst of nearly constant human communication, verbal and nonverbal. They literally feel the body signals of shifts in emotion of those who hold them; they are never excluded from verbal interactions. They are listeners and observers in a stream of communication which flows about them, but is not especially channeled or modified for them. Everyone talks *about* the baby, but rarely *to* the baby. Childtenders direct their talk about the baby to others: "Dis young 'un wet his britches more'n any young 'un I know." "Dis baby ain't actin' right, sump'n wrong wid 'im." Only occasionally do older children talk to the baby while nudging, cuddling, or fondling him.

When the baby is about six months old and responds consistently with smiles and coos, and reaches out to clench a hand, adults and older children begin to engage in face play with the baby, cuddling the baby's cheeks in their lips, nuzzling him about the neck, and manipulating the baby's mouth with their hands. Older women delight in playfully pinching or biting the cheeks of young babies, often making them scream with pain. Babies are always held in a position so they can see the face of their caregiver or the person the caregiver is talking to. They are carried astride the hip or nestled in the cradle of an arm, facing out away from the caregiver's body. There is great joking about those who hold a new baby awkwardly, and men and women demonstrate willingly how to hold a baby as though "he's a part of you."[1]

As children make cooing or babbling sounds, adults talk about the baby's "noise": "he make 'bout as much noise when his belly full as he do when he hungry." When infants begin to utter sounds which can be interpreted as referring to items or events in the environment, these sounds receive no special attention. Trackton adults believe a baby "comes up" as a talker; adults cannot make babies talk: "When a baby have sump'n to say, he'll say it." Adults do not consider a young baby either to be able to or to need to say words. Occasionally school-age children respond to the sounds of the baby as words and may say: "Mamma, you hear? He say 'mamma'." Adults, however, pay no attention to these words; instead they praise the baby's nonverbal responses which seem to them appropriate to the circumstances: a coo and smile for Darett's new hat, and a grasp of Miss Lula's hand when she pokes at the baby. Held in the arms of an adult talking on the phone, a baby may jump up and down, and the adult interprets this as a response to a familiar voice on the phone: "Dis baby know you on de phone, Berta, you better ought to see dis baby." Adults reward these appropriate responses by a squeeze, kiss, face play, or general jostling. Even in contexts where the baby's utterances can be easily linked to objects or events, adults do not acknowledge these utterances as labels. "Mu mu" screamed by a twelve-month-old at the sight of a bottle on the kitchen table is not interpreted as *milk*. The adult, already in the process of getting milk for the bottle, responds: "Okay, I'm lookin', hush yo' mouth all that fuss. Ain't no use in hollerin'." Adults see no need for a baby or child to have to tell them what to do or even what the infant wants. Adults, in their words, "know": "Dat baby don't have to holler out nut'n to me; I *know* when he hungry, he need sump'n."

Adults respond incredulously to queries such as "Did you hear him say *milk*?" They believe they should not have to depend on their babies to tell them what they need or when they are uncomfortable. Adults are the knowing participants; children only "come to know." Thus, if asked, community members explain away their lack of response to children's early utterances; they do not repeat the utterance, announce it as a label for an item or event, or place the "word" in an expanded phrase or sentence.[2] To them, the response carries no meaning which can be directly linked to an object or event; it is just "noise."

As soon as the child can crawl and stand, he is no longer restricted to the laps and arms of those about him. Children at this stage are constantly under the watchful eye of someone in the community. When they approach danger, they are sternly warned: "Get away from dat stove, boy." "Don't you fall off dat porch." They are carefully watched as they explore dangerous situations: the hot food, a cigarette, or the stove, but they are not punished for touching. Adults simply wait to see that they do not go too far and comfort them when they are hurt in exploring. In their shotgun houses, there is relatively little area to explore, and there are no trinkets or breakable items set about on tables. There are few flower pots around unless it is in the midst of winter; therefore, children have relatively few occasions to be restrained.[3]

The toys of children in Trackton are often adaptations of either broken toys (e.g. an old toy truck bed made into a shovel) or household items. Before birth, expectant mothers neither buy nor are given toys and books as gifts. In each interaction, after a baby is old enought to reach and grasp, adults contribute temporary toys – car keys, buttons, earrings, or sunglasses. In the kitchen, a baby may be given a baby food jar top or a spoon to play with, or an older sibling will offer a ball or glove for the baby to handle for a while. During their first year, children are lap sitters, and spend their waking hours in the laps of adults or on the hips of older children; they have no occasions to sit alone and play with baby toys. As children become mobile and move about on their own, they are in demand by older children and adults of the community as toys themselves. They are looked on as entertainers, and all of their waking hours are spent in the company of others. Sometimes an adult will bring toddlers plastic soldiers, trucks, miniature bats and balls, and occasionally doll babies. Toys which have multiple pieces, such as tea sets, doll clothes, or puzzles are not given. Books, puzzles, manipulative toys, and blocks do not exist in the community unless they have been brought in by an outsider.

As children become old enough to demand items they see on television, they want mechanical, electronic, or ride toys: cranes and bulldozers, miniature rockets, Spider Man models and accompanying apparatus, tricycles, and large plastic tractors or scooters. At Christmas, they may get these toys, put on layaway months ahead by their parents. Toys are not exchanged on birthdays, since the birthdays of children are usually not acknowledged except to talk about a child getting older. Christmas is the time for "big presents"; otherwise, children receive very few and very small toys throughout the rest of the year. Visitors and relatives from the local area usually bring the children food, cookies, fruit, gum, potato chips, or candy when they come to visit. Relatives from up-North, or men home from the armed services on furlough occasionally bring a toy on their infrequent visits, but more often they take the children shopping and buy shoes or school clothes for them. Such a visit is a general time of gift-giving, in which the visitor from up-North is expected to share his wealth with the local families, and children and women are the prime recipients of such sharing.

During the first six months or so, and sometimes throughout their entire first year, babies are not addressed directly by adults. An infant is referred to as "the baby," "young'un," and sometimes as "chap." Adults do not address the baby using third person pronouns such as "he," "him," "she," "her," or "it," nor do they refer to themselves by third person expressions, such as kin terms ("mamma," "Aunt Berta") or pronouns.[4] In the hospital, the baby is given a name, often one on which the mother has spent much time and secret deliberation. Family names are rarely chosen, and the most frequent names are those which the mother has only heard, perhaps on television or in a movie, and has never seen written. Therefore, hospital authorities often write the name as they hear it, and not as it would normally be spelled. A mother intending to name her son "Bernard Darrell" might render the name "Bee-nod Terrer," and it would appear on the birth certificate as "Bennett Terry." The birth certificate is often not seen by the family until the child is ready to go to school, and the family has to go to the county seat to pick up the birth certificate to prove the child's age. However, when the mother brings the baby home from the hospital, she proudly announces the baby's name. It is then either given a particular rendering by others of the community or dropped, to be reintroduced only when the child prepares to go to school and needs to know his "real name."

Community and family members usually develop their own names for the baby in their interactive relationships with the child. These names may be diminutives of other names – Richie (Richard), Petey (Peter) – but they need not bear any resemblance to the child's "real name." More often the names characterize the physical or behavioral features the child begins to exhibit consistently by the time of the first birthday. "Monkey" is given to an unusually small and active child; "Frog" to a child who is always squatting to play with toy trucks. Girls are given names for their behavioral characteristics far less frequently than are boys; their nicknames are more often renderings of their "real name" or nicknames referring to features of their appearance ("Red Girl" is the name given to a girl with particularly "red" skin). Older brothers and sisters give their younger siblings names they pick up from books at school or hear among their friends at school. Often by the time a child is three years old, he may be called by as many as half a dozen nicknames, for though one nickname always seems to "stick," and most people use this name as a vocative, there are always alternatives used in particular relationships with certain individuals.[5]

A stage for boys

By the age of twelve to fourteen months, boy babies have a special status. They are then accepted as players on Trackton's stage – the plaza in the midst of their community. It is here that they begin their first explorations beyond the exclusively human environment in which they have developed during their first year. Most of the life of the community goes on outdoors, on the porches and in the plaza, and once boy babies are mobile and fairly steady on their feet, they are put on stage in this public area. Communication is the measure of involvement here. Young boys learn from an early age to handle their roles by getting their cues and lines straight and knowing the right occasions for joining the chorus. They learn to judge audience reaction and response to their performances and to adjust their behaviors in accordance with their need for audience participation and approval. "The measure of a man is his mouth," so males are prepared early by public language input and modeling for stage performances.

Their female counterparts are not excluded from the scene, and they watch and join in the general mood of participation, but they are rarely given parts to play and almost never full-stage performance opportunities. Boy babies toddle about from porch to porch or are "toted" astride the hips of older brothers or sisters. When Ol' Frank challenges Lillie Mae's Lem or Annie Mae's grandbaby, Larry Lee (nicknamed Teegie), "Hey boy, ain't you gonna talk to me? Gimmie dat drink, I like a bottle too, you know," gales of laughter follow as the baby throws the bottle aside and reaches for Frank's nose. Someone in the audience comments: "Dat baby a toughie, you better look out, Frank, he knock you out." Any sign of aggressive play or counter-challenge from the babies is acknowledged verbally by the audience. Especially during the period from twelve to eighteen months of age, boy babies elicit intense involvement from the audience when they respond to adults and others with nonverbal gestures. However, if they scream and cry in response to a poking, pinching, or teasing, no one intervenes to stop the adults' handling of the baby. Adults are given great latitude on these occasions, and many seem to poke or pinch simply to get a response from the child, to engage the child in some sort of active relationship.[6] However, adults scold older children who continue to provoke a crying child.

79

As boy toddlers become a regular part of the outdoor scene, they are teased and challenged verbally and nonverbally by Darett, Ol' Frank, one of the transients, or any of the children home from school. Darett teases Lem about giving up his bottle or cookie, and Lem yanks back his possession, throws it, or punches at Darett. Screaming and crying are not effective, since the aggressor will immediately increase the agitation, scolding all the while: "Boy, you ain't gonna keep that bottle, gimme it." Lem, Teegie, Gary, Jay, and even occasionally boys from the transient families, are put to the test to see if they respond appropriately by counterchallenging their aggressor in what amounts to a mock physical encounter or preferably by combining a verbal and nonverbal put-down. Gary B., judged by the community to be "dull," is rarely challenged, though adults sometimes give him affectionate punches and see that he gets some share in the distribution of Fridays' goodies. Apparently, since successful verbal performance under challenge is thought to be a sign of quickness and intelligence, the community exempts Gary B. from the tests they so continually give to the other young boys.

One warm Saturday in the late spring, Darett spied Teegie, sixteen months old, playing on the porch. Darett went up to the side of the porch, reached through the rails, and began to tug at Teegie's bottle. Teegie pulled back, but Darett soon pulled the bottle away anyway. Teegie stood up, stuck his lips out, made a sucking noise, and "strutted" across the porch, interpreted by the audience as an imitation of Darett's walk. The audience picked up on the ludicrousness of "smart-cat Darett" strutting while sucking a bottle; in the midst of howls of laughter, Teegie turned to Darett and said, "Go on, man." Darett found the performance highly acceptable and gave the bottle back, tickled Teegie, and said, "You gonna be all right, boy, you be just like me."

Between sixteen and twenty-four months, boys develop a special technique for dealing with their accosters. They begin to use first one, then another, utterance for several weeks at a time, varying the intonation, tone, and social function they give it in different interactional situations. These utterances are picked up from older children or adults as whole units. Often, an accoster's teasing jest to a toddler would become the child's new favorite expression.[7] Teegie, at sixteen months, also used his version of "Go on, man" to his mother when she tried to get him to eat something he did not like, or he used it to any of the older children who bothered him. It had a range of meanings of "No," "Give it to me," "Leave me alone" in the two and a half weeks it was his pet expression. He moved from this to "You shut up" for about three weeks, and this too meant "No," "Leave me alone," "Give me that," or "Take it, I don't want it."

Lem used "I dunno" for four weeks, beginning at age sixteen months. If offered a potato chip, he would tuck his head, shake it from side to side and say "I dunno" in a sing-song way, and the meaning would be interpreted as "I want more attention," or "I'm mad about something." The adults' response could range from "Well, see if you get any of my chip" to "What you mad about, boy?" In a week or so, Lem added "I dunno" to mean "No" when he was asked to get a toy for an older sibling, stop standing on a book, or get out of a chair. Within the month, he clearly used "I dunno" in its usual meaning. Darett asked him: "Where yo' mamma?" and Lem responded "I dunno." Darett often rejected this kind of answer (depending on whether or not he had the time to engage Lem in a challenge), and on this occasion he was not satisfied with Lem's literal response, and challenged: "What do you mean, you dunno? You better know sump'n in dat big ol' ugly head. What yo' name?" To this question, Lem was supposed to give Darett the particular name they used in their interactions – "Peanuts." Sometimes Lem gave it right away; at other times, he offered a string of alternatives, teasing Darett into continuing the interaction. In this early stage of language development and in this early period of verbal performance on the public stage, the boys seem to focus on using a single utterance, always a well-formed short sentence, with a variety of semantic values and contexts for interpretation. Thus they learn the variety of meanings a single utterance can have, as they elicit different interactional responses to the variations of intonation, tone, and voice quality they give these favorite expressions.

Feeling and knowing

Teasing through feigned hostility, disrespect, and aggressive behavior marks public occasions for practice in both nonverbal and verbal interactions.[8] In Trackton, the audience demands reciprocity in communicative situations. Children are expected to learn to

pay close attention to nonarticulated signals about the consequences of their behavior and to calculate adjustments in their
own behavior in terms of how those about them may act. Though
ostensibly the center of audience focus on many occasions,
Trackton children, from a very early age, must decenter themselves in their communicative responses, for they must respond in
anticipation of the behavior of those who have the power to give
food, affection, and gifts.[9] Children manage their social interactions, shifting tactics in accordance with their estimation of the
audience's mood. Allowed the widest possible range of interpersonal exploration, young children can take on any role in the
community. They can boss, cuss, beg, cuddle, comfort, tend, and
argue with those about them; they can be old men, old women,
parents, or older children in the ways they communicate. When
Ol' Frank sits on his porch on a Sunday afternoon, holding his
head and groaning, two-year-old Teegie can gently pat him on the
back, fuss at him for his bad behavior, or ignore him. But before
assuming any of these roles, Teegie must judge from Frank's
nonverbal signals what his mood is, and whether or not Frank will
counterchallenge Teegie or simply accept Teegie's role-shifts.
Teegie must so judge the specific contextual cues surrounding
Frank that he will be certain he can mean to Frank what it is he
wants to mean.

In Trackton, this constant sizing up and judging of nonverbal
postures and gestures is prepared for during long sessions in the
laps of those who hold the baby during the entire first year. During
this time, the baby literally feels the nonverbal actions and
reactions of conversationalists and, since Trackton children are
never excluded from any kind of interaction, they have a wide
range of learning opportunities. Once out of the lap and at the
knee or feet of those who are talking, children have hours of
listening and watching; Trackton youngsters often stop their play
on the porches to sit up and watch when adults in their talk begin
to use loud voices or change their pace of speaking. They learn to
associate such verbal changes with what are sometimes rapid shifts
in the behavior or mood of adults. Unprotected on the floor, they
must know when to move quickly to get out of the way of two
older children about to fight or an angry adult walking away from
a challenge. Trackton does not hide its ugly moods, sadness,
gaiety, or passions from the young. Trackton adults also do not try

to be consistent with the young, always punishing them in the same way for particular offenses and repeatedly giving praise for the same responses. Children seem to know they are basically accepted, but that in the daily rounds they must come to expect ups and downs in the displays and routines of this acceptance. One day, a particularly tired young mother will yell and fuss all day at small infractions; on another day, for the same behaviors from her child, she will reward him with play and cuddling. Rewards and punishments come inconsistently, and the cooperation of those poking at or talking to a preschooler is never a sure thing.

Children become intimately involved in the households of several families in Trackton as well as in their parents' families outside Trackton. All of these intimates have similar degrees of power over children, feeding them, giving them affection and punishment, and providing all sorts of goods and services. This wide exposure to many different individuals who have such power over the children provides numerous opportunities and contexts for practicing the interpretation of motives, intentions, and predispositions of individuals and judging the context of reception for any message children communicate.[10] Children must learn to give performances and to play roles to fit the context: to tease, defy, boss, baby, or scold. Though young children often use the same language forms for doing all these things ("I dunno," for example), they and their audience recognize that interpretation of these forms derives from intonation and voice quality and from the interpersonal context, not from the actual words used. Discrepancy between the referential functions of utterances and their intended social function is the norm rather than a stylistic deviation, and all parties are expected to be adept enough in reading their communicative party's nonarticulated signals and fine adjustments to know how to judge and formulate responses.

At one moment, Darett might accept without comment Lem's "no"; on another occasion, he might use it as the stimulus for a long teasing interaction. There are no prescribed or invariant phrases necessary for given occasions which Trackton children must learn or can offer, for which the response will be predictable.[11] If a child says "bye-bye," an adult may respond by a wave and "bye-bye," or he may grab the child roughly and say "You tryin' to make me go home, boy?" The only communicative certainties, once a child is beyond a year old, are high, piercing screams which indicate real pain and bring adult response, or high pitched whines, which bring a scolding or even a smack on the buttocks.

Some residents of Trackton can talk about the fact that daily life in Trackton brings many situations, and yet none can be faced each time with a secure sense that a particular response will bring a specific result. Annie Mae, the community cultural broker, who seems to know *and* be able to explain many of the mainstream cultural practices as well as those of Trackton, sees these shifting sands of reality as good training ground for children. She considers such experiences the only way a child can grow up without being set up to be disappointed in life. Learning language is a critical part of this process of "gettin' on in dis world." She spoke of how she expected her grandchild Teegie to learn to know and talk.

Annie Mae: He gotta learn to *know* 'bout dis world, can't nobody tell 'im. Now just how crazy is dat? White folks uh hear dey kids say sump'n, dey say it back to 'em, dey aks 'em 'gain 'n 'gain 'bout things, like they 'posed to be born knowin'. You think I kin tell Teegie all he gotta know to get along? He just gotta be kéen, keep his eyes open, don't he be sorry. Gotta watch hisself by watchin' other folks. Ain't no use me tellin' 'im: 'Learn dis, learn dat. What's dis? What's dat?' He just gotta léarn, gotta know; he see one thing one place one time, he know how it go, see sump'n like it again, maybe it be de same, maybe it won't. He hafta try it out. If he don't he be in trouble; he get lef' out. Gotta keep yo' eyes open, gotta féel to knów.

Preschoolers, especially boys, are always being presented with situations and being asked "*Now* what you gonna do?" The children must think before they respond, and as Annie Mae realized, must feel the motivations and intentions of other individuals. They are powerless to counter physically; they must outwit, outtalk, or outact their aggressors. Across sets of situations and actors, children learn the domains of applications of a particular word, phrase, or set of actions, and the meanings conveyed across these are often neither literal nor predictable.

Lem and the mayor played a game: the mayor would pull at Lem's bag of candy on Friday afternoons and ask "What you gonna do, I try to take dis? Let me keep it for you. Come on, I just be keepin' it." Lem would yell, clutch the bag, or attack the mayor the first few times this game was played, and the mayor would take the candy and give some to other children, then give the rest back to a tearful Lem. Lem's next tactic was to run to some nearby adults and give them the bag for safekeeping; they often joined the mayor in the game and ate a piece or pretended to do so. One day, when Lem was about two years old, he seemed to have thought ahead on how he would handle the game. When he was given the bag, he watched the mayor, and as soon as the mayor started his challenge, Lem headed for a hole between the boards in the porch and stuck the bag far back in the hole. The hole was too small for the mayor's hand to reach into; thus the candy was safe. The mayor tried the game several more weeks, and Lem each time raced to the hole.

To win the game, Lem had had to size up the possible responses of other adults, to figure out a tactic which made the most of his strengths and caught the mayor in his weaknesses. Their relative size had been the key to the solution; Lem had to find a way to win in which his smallness could defeat the mayor's size and power. Through the process of feedback over the weeks, Lem had been forced to come up with a behavior which could be maintained as a safe way out. He had also had to learn the literal and the conveyed meanings of *keep*. The mayor played on the double meaning of the word – retain indefinitely, and protect. As Lem got older, the mayor would try to reopen his old game with Lem, saying, "Come on, I keep it for you." Lem would retort: "You ain't *keep* nut'n, you eat it."

In this repeated process of challenge, interaction, and unpredictable feedback, little boys have to learn such specific skills as how to handshake with Darett, to calculate the relative timing and height of Darett's thrust of the hand, and to recognize the type of handshake called for by Darett's initial starting position.[12] Darett makes the boys repeat again and again their handshakes until he thinks they have performed a satisfactory one. He does not explain verbally *how* to do it. He says only "Do it like dis," as they repeat the interaction again and again. He sometimes takes their hands and puts them in position for a handshake or a strutting salute. The same type of repetition with urgings to "Do it like dis," "Do it again" are heard from older boys and girls as they model for young ones to learn to take part in playing games, opening candy boxes, or fastening belt buckles. Through all of these learning occasions, watching and feeling how to do something are more important than talking about how to do it.[13] Since almost all interactions of this sort take place on the stage, audience response is an important potential reward. Youngsters know that once they "get it right," someone in the audience will respond, and though they can never be sure certain adults will respond in certain ways, they expect someone in the audience to provide a rewarding response.

Becoming talkers

Trackton adults do not see babies or young children as suitable partners for regular conversation. For an adult to choose a preverbal infant over an adult as a conversational partner would be considered an affront and a strange behavior as well. Adults socialize with one another while the baby is in their laps or nearby, or they talk about the baby or young child. However, unless they wish to issue a warning, give a command, provide a recommendation, or engage the child in a teasing exchange, adults rarely address speech specifically to very young children. Children are not expected to *be* information-givers; they are expected to *become* information-knowers by "being keen," and by taking in the numerous lessons going on in their noisy multi-channeled communicative environments.

When two or more adults or adults and older children are engaged in conversation, children after about the age of twelve months begin to pick up their conversations and use them for practice.[14] The ends of adults' utterances in a discourse are repeated by young children who play or sit on the floor or sofa nearby. The child often plays with a small toy or a piece of food, and is not acknowledged by speakers to be taking part in the conversation. In the following conversation, taped one afternoon on a drive in the car with Lem (age nineteen months), his mother, and older brother and sister (Benjy and Nellie, age four years), Lem picked up pieces of the conversation. The conversation began when Lem's mother was let out of the car to go into a furniture store to make a payment. Lem began crying, and as I drove off, Lem's older brother Benjy asked:

TRACKTON TEXT IV*

A.　1.Benjy:　Miz Hea', where you goin?
　　2.Heath:　I'm goin' 'round de block, waitin' for yo' mamma.
　　3.Nellie:　Why you leáve Lillie Mae?
　　4.Heath:　I'ma pick up Lillie Mae, you see, Lillie Mae come out de sto', when we go 'round de corner again.
　　5.Benjy:　Right down here?
　　6.Heath:　Right down there.
　　7.Nellie:　/pointing to something outside the car/|: What dat thing?
　　8.Lem:　　　　　　　　　　　　　　　　　　　　What dat thing?:|
　　　　　　　　　　　　　　　　　　　　　　　　[
　　9.Benjy:　　　　　　　　　　　　　　　　　　　Miz Hea',
　　　　　　/pointing ahead of the car/dat de block?
　　10.Heath:　Hm?
　　11.Benjy:　Dat's de block, /pointing ahead of the car/ down dere?
　　12.Heath:　The blóck, right there, go /drawing a block in the air/ around like this, one, two, three, four, like a blóck.
　　13.Benjy:　Miz Hea', /pointing to the right in the middle of the block/go right dere.
　　14.Heath:　I can't go dere, no road dere.
　　15.Benjy:　|:You can turn right dere.
　　16.Lem:　　　Can turn right dere.:|
　　17.Nellie:　Miz Hea', *leave* Lillie Mae.
　　18.Lem:　(unintelligible)/standing up to look out the window/De go roun' here, duh, right dere (long pause) a truck
　　19.Nellie:　Ya'll get (unintelligible)
B.　1.Benjy:　Miz Hea', what/pointing to the furniture store/de house, what kinda house dat is.
　　2.Heath:　That's a fúrniture store.
　　3.Lem:　Dat ting.
　　4.Benjy:　What/pointing to a church/kind dat?
　　5.Heath:　|:That's a chúrch, that's a bi::g church.
　　6.Lem:　Dat a church:|
　　7.Benjy:　|:What kinda,/pointing down the road and looking at me for confirmation/kinda truck dat is?
　　8.Heath:　|That truck down there? (pause) That's a Pépsi-cola truck.|
　　9.Lem:　(whine) Kind dat truck:| (unintelligible)
　　10.Nellie:　(unintelligible)
　　　　　　　　[
　　11.Benjy:　What kinda (pause) car dat is?
　　12.Lem:　Color is
　　13.Heath:　That's a greén car.

14.Benjy: What cul' dat truck?
15.Heath: That's a blúe:: truck.
16.Benjy: ‖:What cul' dat town?
                    [
17.Lem: Color dat town:|
18.Benjy: ‖:What cul' dat pólice?
                    [
19.Lem: Cul' dat police:|
20.Benjy: ‖:Cul dat police truck
21.Lem: police truck:|
22.Benjy: What cul' dat police?
23.Heath: That's a whíte car, whíte car, like Benjy's shirt's whíte.
                          [
24.Benjy: |:'n what cul' de mail(pause)
                        what cul' de mailman truck?:|
25.Heath: Blue an' white.
C.   1.Benjy: ‖:Der' go 'nother motorcycle.
     2.Lem: A motorcycle:|
     3.Heath: There goes a motorcycle, see it Lem, there it goes.
     4.Lem: Go, go motorcycle, two boys down de day I was down,
                you play down.
     5.Heath: *Yeah.*
     6.Lem: Uh motorcycle go.
                    [
     7.Benjy: Miz Hea', where you goin'?
     8.Heath: I'm goin' 'round de block till yo' mamma come.
     9.Lem: (unintelligible)
    10.Nellie: (unintelligible)
    11.Benjy: Hey, uh, Miz Hea', where our truck?
    12.Heath: I don't know, where *is* our truck?
    13.Benjy: Dat (unintelligible) truck.
    14.Lem: Tee my truck go, tee my, tee it. (pause)
                (car turns corner, and Lem falls against door)
    15.Heath: Hold on.
    16.Benjy: Miz Hea', turn/*pointing to tape recorder on front seat*/on
                    [dat.
    17.Heath: |:Dat's a truck called a van truck.| A van truck, can
                you say van, look, mail truck's behind us, look Benjy.|
                            [
    18.Lem: (whine) Dat ting, dat's my truck
    19.Nellie: (unintelligible)
                    [
    20.Benjy: Miz Hea', dat ting

21.Heath: Dát's the mail truck.
22.Lem: Dat's my truck:|
23.Benjy: Yonder ya' mail man.
24.Lem: Go 'round (unintelligible)
25.Nellie: (unintelligible) Better move outta way.
26.Lem: (unintelligible) Go de ting.

. . .

In this exchange, Benjy and I maintained the discourse in a series of sequences (A, B, C) of utterances on various topics, most of which were stimulated by the immediate activity – driving around the block while Lillie Mae was in the store – or by objects seen from the car and about which Benjy asked questions. Nellie, Benjy's twin sister, entered the discourse only rarely; Lem hung onto the discourse by picking up pieces of the utterances of the two primary participants. He attempted to join the discourse actively at only one point (line C4) – to comment on his experience with a motorcycle. However, since I did not share the experience to which he referred, the new information which he offered was dropped and was not used to continue the primary discourse. Benjy, on the other hand, drawing on information available to all of us as we looked out of the car window, captured the primary role of setting discourse topics and making certain he had my attention by a series of questions, which at one point (B4–24) became a turn-taking game. Lem got no turn, but interjected his echo after either Benjy's turn or mine. At one point (B11–12), Lem provided the topic for some turns in the questioning routine; he heard "car" as "color," and Benjy, caught up in the process of the game, picked up "color" and carried it through until the end of the game.

During the initial part of the discourse (lines A1–8), Lem was still disturbed that his mother had left the car, and he did not pick up on the conversation. During this time, Benjy began to try to clarify in his own mind what was meant by "going around the block" and asked a series of questions to establish and test a definition for himself. He tried to establish its location first (line A5). A block, in the sense in which it was used here, was something he could not see, and he was trying to reconcile this block with what a block meant to him – blocks of wood, the ends of pieces of lumber used as firewood in Mr. Dogan's store and at home. Once he saw something he thought must be a block

89

(A9,11), he asked for confirmation. I had attempted to explain a block as something with four sides, and Benjy tested this idea by asking me to turn "right dere" (A13) when he saw a passageway between two buildings which could be one of the sides. He was testing the idea of a block having four sides, presumably without a prescribed length for each side. When I asserted that I could not turn, because there was no road there, he reasserted "You can turn right dere" (A15), then dropped his pursuit of finding something analogous in this situation to the block he knew.

Lem picked up once on a question from Nellie (A7) but he consistently hung onto Benjy's utterances. He picked up (A16) Benjy's assertion that I could turn, and in his next line (A18), he echoed in part my earlier explanation (A12) that a block goes around four sides. Benjy, however, shifted topic and began the game of questions about objects outside the car window. This game provided Lem an opportunity to practice restatement and repetition with variation. In line B3, he restated "furniture store" into "dat ting." Lines B6, 9, 17, 19, and 21 are repetitions of the end portions of either Benjy's utterances or mine. At line B23, I broke the pattern of equal turns and ended the game.

The motorcycle seen outside the car a few minutes later switched the discourse topic once again and involved Lem in a role other than restatement or repetition with variation. He tried to tell about his experience with a motorcycle (C4). Neither Benjy nor I took up his topic. At line C6 Lem tried again unsuccessfully. At line C14, Lem took up Benjy's topic of the truck we had seen earlier, and developed his own discourse on "his" truck with the theme of "go" which he had tried to introduce for the motorcycle. He continued to talk about the truck as *his* truck, while Benjy turned his attention to the tape recorder and then to the newly introduced mail truck. In his private discourse, Lem used the topic being pursued by Benjy and me, but he played with his own thematic interpretation of the topic. He both followed our discourse topic and varied it in his own stream of discourse parallel to ours but in no way integrated into it. He did not manage to get the full attention of either of the main speakers, and since nonverbal attention-getting devices (such as tugs or standing in front of the hearer) were unavailable because of the physical restraints of being in a car and having one of the major participants driving, Lem could not gain the floor. But this did not mean he was not attending to the conversation, for unlike Nellie, who participated in the discourse only on topic A, and then only for three intelligible statements, Lem was following the discourse. He was, in fact, having to work hard to do so, because he was both trailing pieces of our discourse through repetition and at the same time attending to ongoing pieces of the discourse.

The patterns Lem illustrates here are very similar to those which are played out day after day for young children in Trackton between the ages of twelve and twenty-four months. They are parties, albeit sometimes passive parties, to the conversations which flow about them. They usually move through the three types of participation illustrated in the passage above in overlapping stages during their second year. In the first stage, which we shall call the REPETITION STAGE, they pick up and repeat chunks (usually the ends) of phrasal and clausal utterances of speakers around them. Here they seemed to be remembering fragments of speech and repeating these without any active production. Lem's utterances in the following passage, noted when he was sixteen months of age, illustrate his repetition of the final chunks of each of Lillie Mae's utterances; in each repetition, Lem imitates the intonation contour as well as the separate and as yet unanalyzed units of the chunk.[15]

Lillie Mae: 'n she be goin' down dere 'bout every week, but I don't
   believe dey|:got no jobs=
Lem: = got no jobs:|
Dovie Lou: Dat woman down dat 'ployment office don't know what
   goin' on, she send Emma up dere to de Holiday Inn two
   time, and dey ain't had|:no job =
Lem: = no job:|
   [
Lillie Mae: She think she |: be he'pin' =
Lem: = be he'pin':|

Here Lem's immediate echoes of the conversation going on about him draw no attention from the adults, and in fact, they sometimes talk while he is repeating.

In the second stage, REPETITION WITH VARIATION, Trackton children manipulate pieces of the conversations they pick up; they continue their own discourse, playing the topic on a particular theme and sometimes creating a monologue parallel to the dialogue or multi-party conversation going on about them. In these cases, they begin to apply productive rules, inserting new nouns for those used by adults in certain language chunks, and/or playing with rhyming patterns and varying intonation contours. At eighteen months, Lem was playing on the porch with a toy truck while his mother and neighbor discussed Miss Lula's recent trip to the doctor.

Lillie Mae: Miz Lula done|:went to de doctor.
Mattie: |Her leg botherin' her?|
Lem: Went to/*rolling his truck and banging it against the board that separates the two halves of the porch*/de dóctor, dóctor leg, Miz Lu Lu Lu,:|rah, rah, rah
                               [

Lillie Mae: I reckon so, she was complainin' yesterday 'bout her feet so swelled she couldn't|: get no shoes on.
Lem: /*swishing his truck through the air*/Shoe, shoe, shoe, went to dóctor in a shoe, doc, doc, duh, duh, duh poo::sh, get no shoe,:|
(sucking his breath in)
      [
Mattie: Somedays she cain't hardly walk.
Lillie Mae: Yea, 'n it ain't gettin' no better.
Lem: /*bouncing truck in a walking-like action on the floor*/|:Walk, walk to de doctor, walk to de sto' [store], git better, walk shoe, walk up, pup, pup, pup, pup:|

Lem here creates a monologue, incorporating the discussion about Miss Lula into his game with the truck. He repeats, without variation, his mother's opening statement, then plays productively with the word "doctor" used as a noun by his mother and the noun "leg" introduced by Mattie. Lem produces "doctor leg," which may be either a repetition of these words as isolated units, or a two-word sentence of uncertain meaning. Lem then goes into sound play, until he picks up the word "shoe" from his mother's statement. He produces a new utterance "went to doctor in a shoe," and surrounds this sequence with word play using words from within the utterance. In the final piece of the conversation given here, he repeats the pattern of his own earlier production with "went," and varies it to "walk to de doctor" and "walk to de sto'," then goes into his monologue accompanying his play with the truck. In this passage, he takes the individual segments of the conversation going on about him, sometimes producing them as repeated chunks, but at other times using them productively to create his own sequences. Once again, the adults pay no attention to his chatter and talk as though he were not there.

The third stage, PARTICIPATION, often overlaps with the second stage, just as the second overlaps with the first. In this third stage, the children become conversationalists. They try to break into adult conversation, making themselves part of the ongoing discourse. They may do so by asking a question, introducing a new topic, commenting on the current topic, or asking for clarification.[16] Such efforts are accompanied by nonverbal gestures and verbal strategies: getting in front of the face of a speaker, tugging at an adult's leg or arm, calling out several times the name of one of the conversationalists, or simply outshouting others in the conversation. Usually adults can understand the child or make enough connection between their comment and the current situation to know what the child means. Adults rarely have difficulty making out what the children, especially boys, say: they can figure out the specific words. However, they more often have difficulty taking up children's comments as a topic of discourse for any sustained sequence. Older children are much better than adults at identifying the younger children's comments and at remembering the situation in which the child first met the topic. One day during a ride in the car, Teegie (at twenty-three months) interrupted his mother's conversation with me to yell: "Dere go Hardee's, dere a bus." His mother stopped talking to me, looked where he pointed, and said: "Dere ain't no bus." However, Tony, who had been in the car with Teegie on a similar ride the week before, said "Yea, but las' week dere was a bus dere, 'n he lookin' for de school bus what was dere las' week."

When adults do not understand what point the young child is trying to make, they often repeat the last portion – or what is usually the predicate verb phrase – of the child's statement. Lem, at twenty months was playing on the porch while his mother and several other women were talking. He had been repeating and varying the ends of their utterances, when suddenly he stopped his play and went to his mother, pulling and tugging at her jeans: "Wanna pop, wanna pop, bump, bump, bump." His mother looked at him and said "Stop it, Lem, you wanna, wanna, wanna, you ain't gettin' nut'n, Darett ain't home. Go ask Miz Lula." The context of Lem's new addition of this discourse topic in the stream of his mother's talk had been set the evening before when Darett had brought Lem a popsicle and had bumped him up and down on his knee as he tried to eat the popsicle. Lem had smeared the ice cream all over his face, much to the delight of the audience, who kept urging Lem to make Darett stop. His mother cued in on "bump," remembering Darett's bumping of Lem the night before; she did not focus on "pop," a local word for soda or soft drink, though it would have been conceivable that Lem was simply telling her he wanted a drink, a pop. She focused on the verbal rendering of the nonverbal cues Lem offered to describe the situation, and she figured out his meaning. Children often give such cues, imitating or describing noises or nonverbal features that took place in connection with the object or event they are trying to introduce as a topic.

When children are not just repeating or repeating with variation, but are participating by trying to add a new discourse topic to an ongoing conversation or to respond to a question directed to them, adults attend to their talk. They do so even when they are simultaneously engaged in another conversation or activity. Adults consistently correct errors of fact or scold for baby talk on such occasions. For example, Teegie, at age twenty-four months, had his first haircut, and when I asked what he did at the barbershop, he answered "I color." His mother, who had been engaged in another conversation, turned to him and said "You *color*, huh, you ain't color, you crý." Teegie then said "I cry." In correcting Teegie, his mother repeated with emphasis *color*. She then explained to me that Teegie had been talking about colors all week, since he had played the week before with some of the schoolchildren's crayons. All week, Teegie in his play had been reciting the names of the colors, picked up from listening to my interactions with older children using the crayons. I suspect that Teegie did not mistakenly say "color" for "cry," but he simply did not attend to my question about the barbershop. Because he knew I had been involved in the coloring last week, he was asking me about coloring again on this day. However, when his mother insisted he answer my question correctly, he did so. Had he said "Me cry," his mother would have scolded him, as she did on those occasions when school-age children used baby talk either to talk to their younger siblings or to try to be cute for adults.[17]

Neither simplifying aspects of baby talk (such as reducing the phonological structure of words, substituting easier sounds for more complex ones, reducing inflections, and using special lexical items) nor clarifying features (such as slowing down speech, using special pitch or intonation patterns, and substituting names for pronouns)[18] are used by Trackton adults, though they recognize them as part of a phenomenon which exists outside their way of bringing up their children. Many Trackton women or their mothers have been maids in the homes of mainstream middle-class families, and there they have noted the use of baby talk. My children and I often slipped into baby talk with infants and young children in Trackton, and the adults made fun of us for doing so. Their toddlers occasionally use a high pitch, a whining tone, or a diminutive (presumedly modeled after the form of some nick-names, such as Froggie, or imitated from schoolchildren's uses), and adults scold them for such usages. Occasionally, older children who have been to school play teacher and use shortened sentences and a slow pace of delivery; if overheard, they too are scolded. Adults in Trackton attend to their children's talk to interpret their additions to ongoing discourse topics, to correct errors of fact, and to scold for features or forms they think too "babyish."

Girl talk

Though families and the community in general consistently state preferences for a boy before a child is born, girl babies are accepted into the community in their first year of life in ways very similar to those of boys. They are fondled, held, tended, pinched, or poked into responding to aggressors, and they are never excluded from the stream of communicative life about them. Once they are old enough to crawl and walk, they play at the feet of adult conversationalists, and they too begin to repeat, and to repeat with variation pieces of the conversations about them. However, girls in Trackton begin participation in the third stage – that of entering conversations and adding new discourse topics – later than the boys. Boys sometimes begin to do this by about fourteen to sixteen months and consistently interrupt adults with these attempts by the age of eighteen months. No girls begin the participatory stage before the age of twenty-two months, and when they do so, they are successful in sustaining conversational

95

roles far less frequently than boys. Adults often do not pick up on
either what the girls mean when they bring up a particular topic or
how that topic relates to the current situation.

When boys make these interruptions, they often refer to events
or objects connected with challenges and ensuing interactions
from the public stage. Girls, however, are restricted from engaging
in such challenges, since these are not issued to them. Thus the
major occasion in which the boys practice nonverbal and verbal
communication with substantial reinforcement is denied to girls.
They are present, hear the exchanges, and sometimes try to
participate, but they are either ignored or told "Go 'way, gal, what
you think you doin'?" Thus, when they try to introduce topics and
to cue adults into their intentions, they have a much smaller store
of experiences from which to draw. Older siblings seem to sense
this relative disadvantage of girls, and they often "work with" girl
preschoolers in quiet sessions offstage or when attention is not
being drawn to them. They ask questions, using books as props,
and they give the children directions "say—, say it like I do."
However, these sessions rarely last longer than a few minutes,
since the younger child quickly loses interest. The older children
often prompt the girls on what to say in their attempts to
participate in conversations. They will tell the younger child to
"tell 'im to leave you alone; tell 'im to go 'way."[19]

By the age of twenty-two months and often continuing beyond
their early school years, however, it is common to see girls setting
up their own practice-interaction sessions. They talk into mirrors,
often taking two sides of conversations. A favorite play toy for
young girls is a mirror, and if they cannot capture one from a
purse, they climb up on a dresser or onto the bathroom sink to see
themselves in the mirror. They, however, do not have to have a
way of seeing themselves to engage in such pretend-play monologues and dialogues. Nellie, at twenty-six months, took a mirror
out of her mother's purse and was in a corner of the room away
from the stream of conversation. The day previously, she had been
at the park with several of the children and me when we had eaten
ice cream and cookies, and in her dialogue she played both her
part (1) and mine (2).

Nellie: part 1: Get some?
       part 2: Yea, get some.

part 1: Dat kinda, duh, hear?
part 2: Dis kinda too.
part 1: Col', huh?

Nellie was replaying a conversation which had gone on between the two of us at the park, when she had watched me serve the ice cream. She had asked for some, I had assured her she would get some, and she had pointed to the strawberry section of the carton. I had given her some of each of the three kinds, but she had not liked the coldness, so had waited to eat her ice cream until it melted. Nellie, in contrast to her twin brother, Benjy, was timid, shy, and characterized in Trackton as "dull." She made few sounds in playing, took any gifts she managed to get and hid them, and generally was very much backstage in any public interactions. Trackton praised her brother, thought him "keen" and blamed her dullness on her small size at birth and severe sickness during her first year. But during gift distributions on Friday afternoons, no special allowances were made for her weaknesses, and she and other girls often received little or nothing in the distribution routine. Girls come to expect the distribution of goods to be unequal, and they rely on their siblings to share, if any sharing takes place at all. Sometimes, the boys' sharing with them is frowned on by adults: "Boy, you give it away, you ain't gonna get no more."

Though girls are not allowed to take an active part in the public-stage challenges given boys, they have two other types of access to participation on this stage: "fussing" and playsong games – the first an activity initiated primarily by women and the second produced only by girls between the ages of six and thirteen years. Fussing is an activity often used to characterize women's talk. During their interactions with others in Trackton, both men and women exchange news, ridicule each other, report on their own activities and those of others, and evaluate the behavior of individuals or the merits of certain events. But fussing episodes, among women and directed by them toward men or children, are uniquely female. They fuss *at* and *with* each other in a series of assertions and counter-assertions related to a specific incident or personality. Fussing exchanges take place between individuals of different age and/or status relations. In these exchanges, either the two parties simultaneously shoot assertions back and forth, or one party makes all the assertions while the lower status or younger individual remains silent.[20] Ol' Frank was a favorite target for Miss Lula's fussing. She and the other older women in the community could fuss at anyone, since their age gave them a status which prevented any response of equal intensity. Younger adults of equal age and status can fuss with each other, but they are not allowed to fuss with older women. They have to take the older women's assertions without responding; if they counterchallenge, the older women attack their "breedin'" or "learnin'" and accuse their mothers of not raising them "proper."

Children are the exceptions to the rules about not fussing with older women or individuals of high status in the community. All children are sometimes the targets in fussing *at* episodes, but they can also fuss *with* anyone in the community. Both boys and girls have this leverage, but girls are particularly encouraged. They fuss at their higher-status male siblings without restraint. They can even fuss at Ol' Frank, their parents, and sometimes Miss Lula (usually on these occasions repeating to her what they have heard other adults say about her when she was not present – "You ought not to eat dat, you gettin' too fat. . ."). The community allows young girls to practice fussing, thus giving them a chance to learn the kinds of counterassertions which are most effective, just as they allow and even encourage young boys to be aggressive in retorts to their challengers. Young boys boast, insult, ridicule, and "put down" nonverbally and verbally all those who challenge them in Trackton's public arena; as older boys and men, they benefit from these practice sessions in peer exchanges, ritual insults, and good story-telling tactics. Similarly, young girls have to learn to be "fussers," because if they do not, they cannot be expected to be good "mammas," able to protect their rights in the neighborhood. When young girls fuss at their brothers or play-mates, they receive comments such as: "Hear dat girl carry on; she gonna be a tough mamma all right." Girls also practice fussing exchanges, fussing at their dolls and at preverbal infants.

Kim (age three):	Girl,/*shaking her doll*/you done eat my dinner.
doll's part:	I ain't, you did.
Kim:	You all time eatin', you took it.
doll's part:	Ain't, I saw you eat it.
Kim:	Set better on me den on you, but I ain't eat it.
doll's part:	You did.

In fussing exchanges, just as in the challenges from Darett and others to preschool boys, the girls are not expected to be submissive or to cry for help from others. They are expected to stand their ground and fuss.

In any exchange between Lem and Nellie, Lem almost always won out, in spite of his younger age. Nellie simply did not fight back, and her lack of skill at fussing or taking part in the games of older girls were examples often given of her "dullness": "She don't stan' up for herself; she don't say nut'n." However, on a few occasions in her preschool years, Nellie came through, to the surprise of all concerned. One day, Lem (twenty-four months) had taken Nellie's tricycle, which he was trying to learn to ride, though Nellie was more than two years older than he and now nearly five years old.

Nellie: Git/*pushing Lem and tugging at the tricycle*/away.
Lem: I'ma ride dis.
Nellie: You ain't, you too li'l.
Lem: I show ya.
Nellie: No you ain't, git off, yo' ol' ugly head don't know how.
Lem: Git outta, outta
      [
Nellie: Ya git, boy, play wif/*pushes Lem off the tricycle*/yo'
                    baby toy.
Lem: (screaming)/*running to the porch*/

To the surprise of all, especially Lem, Nellie had persisted; she had succeeded in making Lem cry, a rare occasion for Lem, who sometimes cried when he thought it might help his case but almost never resorted to crying in any kind of challenge.

The second occasion on which preschool girls are given part of the public stage is in their participation in older girls' playsong games. *Playsongs* include here jump-rope songs, handclap songs, as well as "made-up" playsongs which accompany a wide variety of activities, such as just sitting around, play-dancing, washing dishes, and pretending to be cheerleaders. Older girls perform these frequently in the plaza, often joined by girls from surrounding neighborhoods. They have a repertoire which they use on these occasions, as well as another repertoire used at recess and before and after school. In the home community, they often calculate their performance to entice younger children to participate; adults

99

Table 3.1. *Types of playsongs recorded in Trackton and at schools*

Types	Trackton		Schools	
	n	%	n	%
nonsense word plays	62	28.2	5	2.1
numbers	43	19.5	26	11.0
body parts	38	17.3	11	4.6
mamma and daily life	35	15.9	64	27.0
food	16	7.2	12	5.1
set characters	14	6.4	96	40.5
animals	12	5.5	23	9.7
Total	220		237	

do not participate, though they are usually around, sitting on their porches, washing cars, or coming and going from work when the girls perform. In handclap games, the young girls sit across from each other or in a circle, punctuating what are usually four-pulse unit songs with their claps. Sometimes they stand so they can add stomps to the claps. On occasion, one of the girls comes to the edge of the porch where a preschooler – most often a girl – is playing, picks her up, holds her in the lap while playing, and makes her hands clap on the right occasions.

The jump-rope playsongs are performed with either double or single ropes, with one girl turning at each of the two ends of the rope or ropes, and one or two girls jumping. The usual routines require that a girl jump and carry out actions named in the playsong; when she misses her turn, another girl enters. Determining who turns the ends of the rope is a process which usually includes a fussing exchange and extended power play among the girls.

A major purpose of all types of playsongs in Trackton is the involvement of young children. They are picked up, carried about while the jumping goes on, held in laps, and encouraged to participate nonverbally and verbally. The topics, or major content repetitions, in playsongs performed in Trackton differ markedly from those used at school. The number of topics of all playsongs heard in Trackton and the approximate percentage each of these represented in the total are given in Table 3.1 along with a comparison of those recorded at schools.[21] Those most frequently used at home are those for which an integral audience co-performer is a young child; imitating nonsense word play, learning to count and name body parts, and talking about immediate and important realities, such as family members and food, engage younger and older girls in learning–teaching interactions. At school, on the other hand, characters known to all the girls, black and white, form the basis of the majority of the playsongs. Second in frequency are those which concern events also known to all: marriage, babies, boy–girl affairs, and being sick, seeing a doctor, or going to the store. Though school playsongs are performed by both black and white girls, white girls participate most frequently in jump-rope playsongs and not in handclap games or made-up playsongs. Their presence and that of the teacher or other school personnel, no doubt, have a strong influence on topics chosen for school playsong performances. Yet another factor seems certainly to be the absence of young children who could participate with the girls in nonsense word plays, number-counting actions, and naming body parts.

These are common topics of teaching-type interactions in mainstream middle-class homes where they take the form of nursery rhymes, pat-a-cake, and question–answer sessions ("Where is your nose?", etc.). In Trackton, playsongs of school-age girls take on some of this teaching role. Adults do not engage in such interactions with young children. They do not name portions of the anatomy and point them out; they use such terms in talking with children or about children, but they do not teach them as labels. Similarly, they do not teach the numbers, engaging the children in counting their fingers or toes, pieces of food, etc. But young girls in their handclap and jump-rope playsongs focus on some of these activities, and though the particular name of a part of the body is often buried in the text of the playsong, it is pointed out by a particular activity – foot by stomping, hip by bumping hips, etc.

> Grámpa, grámpa, yóu ain't sée
> All you néed is a híck'ry stíck
> Let's gét togéther with uh # díng-dòng
> Let's gét togéther with uh # díng-dòng
> Let's gét togéther with uh cláp/*clap, clap*/
> Let's gét togéther with uh cláp/*clap, clap*/
> Let's gét togéther with uh foót/*stomp, stomp*/
> Let's gét togéther with uh foót/ *stomp, stomp*/

Let's gét togéther with uh híp/*bump hips*/hí dáll
Let's gét togéther with uh híp/*bump hips*/hí dáll
Let's gét togéther with éverythíng/*general body shake*/
Díng-dòng#hót dóg

The girls often make up playsongs on certain topics. One afternoon, several young children were on their porches, and the usual Saturday afternoon crowd was highly engaged in talk and play. Some girls had been performing handclap "exercises," but stopped and withdrew to the steps of one of the porches. Soon they moved to a new performing spot, the mayor's front steps. They began their playsong quietly at first, tentatively, and gradually repeating their new song again and again. Nellie, who was then a toddler playing on the next porch, stopped playing and watched. On the fifth time through, she began imitating the older girls, repeating their nonsense words and clapping her hands. One of the older girls came over, put her astride her hip and took her to the porch steps where the other girls were performing. The rhyme sounded like gibberish, play with isolated words later incorporated into nonsense sentences.

Sú/*clap, clap, clap*/Mi::sú/*clap, clap, clap*/
Mísú aróund de bámmer
Lét's gó mú::bé
Chiga bóo, chiga bóo, chiga bóo, boo, bóo
Mámma got méat, dáddy got sóup
Héy, nów, I eát yóu

Once Nellie joined the game, on the last line above, the girl carrying her pretended to eat her under the chin, providing some indication the playsong had been made with just such an activity in mind. The girls continued the song:

Héy, Sá-ah [Sarah], my cúd'n [cousin's] náme
Héy, Sá-ah, mámma wánt some télephone
'n ít áin't my méat, 'cause I áin't húngry (long pause)
Péel like a 'táter, péel like a 'táter
Dó like I sáy ta, wáitin' on a pláy ta::
Bóo ke-ta páh, bóo ke-ta páh
Gó bóo::m

On the final line of the song, the older girl holding Nellie pretended to drop her. Other young children took their turns in the new playsong, and it went on for an hour or more. Though many of its words were from a well-known playsong, "Miss Sue from Alabama," this performance was unique.[22] I had never heard it before nor did I hear it in exactly the same form again after that afternoon in Trackton. Other new inventions, similar in style and purpose, took its place. Some lasted; others, like this one, served their purpose in one particular form on only one occasion, and then were dropped or modified. Those which are most likely to last are those which involve set characters, for example, Ronald MacDonald, a character used to advertise a major chain of roadside hamburger restaurants. But these often have different versions, one which carries heavy connotations of sex and death for performance in the community, and a cleaned-up version for the schoolyard.

In other activities, the girls sometimes incorporate features of their playsong performances. When they read books to their younger siblings, which they do only rarely, they almost never read the text as it appears in the book. They choose alphabet books or nursery rhyme books which lend themselves to sing-song performance, and they dress up the reading by giving the lines a definite pulse and by adding sing-song-like portions or a chorus at the end of the reading. They rarely (unless they are "playing school") ask the younger children questions about these or other performances, and adults rarely comment verbally on what the girls do either on stage or in their other playsong-like interactions with very young children.

Making connections

Children do not expect adults to ask them questions, for, in Trackton, children are not seen as information-givers or question-answerers. This is especially true of questions for which adults already have an answer. Since adults do not consider children appropriate conversational partners to the exclusion of other people who are around, they do not construct questions especially for children, nor do they use questions to give the young an opportunity to show off their knowledge about the world.[23] The questions they ask preschool children are of five types, as illustrated in Table 3.2. Crucial to an understanding of the uses of these questions in Trackton is their embeddedness in interactional contexts. Questions are especially useful for testing what a child

Table 3.2. *Types of questions asked of preschool children in Trackton (listed in approximate order of frequency)*

Type	Response called for	Examples	
		Question	Response
Analogy	Nonspecific comparison of one item, event, or person with another	What's that like? (referring to a flat tire on a neighbor's car)	Doug's car, never fixed.
Story-starter	Question which asks for explanation of events leading to first questioner's question	Did you see Maggie's dog yesterday?	What happened to Maggie's dog?
Accusation	Either nonverbal response and a lowered head or a story creative enough to take the questioner's attention away from the original infraction	What's that all over your face?	You know about that big mud puddle . . .
A-I (Answerer has information)	Specific information known to addressee, but not to questioner	What do you want?	Some juice
Q-I (Questioner has information)	Specific piece of information known to both questioner and addressee	What's your name, huh?	Peanuts

knows about what a particular utterance means to the speaker and what the speaker intends the hearer to interpret. As Annie Mae commented: "Ain't no use me tellin' 'im: 'Learn dis, learn dat, what's dis? what's dat?' He just gotta learn, gotta know; *he see one thing one place one time, he know how it go, see sump'n like it again, maybe it be de same, maybe it won't*" (my emphasis). Annie Mae here indicates how Trackton children are expected to recognize that the same form of language – or anything else – is not expected to carry the same meaning at all times. Instead, children are expected to learn how to know when meanings are not literal, but conveyed meanings. To do this, they continually have to draw analogies from one situational context to another, and to determine how the situational context gives the form its particular meaning at that point.

The most prevalent kind of question asked of preschoolers in Trackton is the ANALOGY QUESTION, which calls for an open-ended answer which draws from the child's experiences. Analogy questions test children's abilities to see things which are similar in their environment, and the prevalence of these questions in adult–child interactions may perhaps point to the importance Trackton adults give to this ability. They ask their young "What's dat like?" "What you think you are?" (said, for example, to a child who is hopping about, dragging himself on his stomach, or crawling under a piece of furniture). When adults talk among themselves, they frequently use metaphors and similes in their conversations:

Mayor: What you know 'bout him [a new black man in the area running for public office]? How do he take on [what is he like]?

Transient: He nut'n but a low-down polecat, you know what he did to his own folks? Lemme tell ya, he so low he cain't git under dat rock yonder.

Some of these comparisons are stock formulae applied to different situations: "low-down polecat," "She got eyes like a hawk." Others are comparisons that build on these stock phrases and exaggerate the feature highlighted in the comparison: "He so low he cain't git under dat rock." However metaphors and similes are also used instead of detailed descriptions as illustrated in the

passage below. A transient has a new car; Cuz has seen it and Ted
has not.

Ted: I hear Doug got hisself a new car.
Cuz: Yea, he total his las' one.
Ted: What'd he git dis time.
Cuz: Ya· know Robert's car?/*looking at Ted*/
//*Ted gives an affirmative nod*//
It's like dat, 'cept red.

Young children hear comparisons used continuously in the conversations about them. Their own behaviors are often responded
to by comments comparing them to something else: "You act like
some monkey." Children are often given names referring to
features seen as analogous to something else, as when a child who
hops about is nicknamed "Frog" by a member of the community.
Therefore, preschoolers have to begin to develop ways of seeing
the world about them in terms of comparisons in order to make
sense out of much of the conversation that goes on around them,
including references to them and their behavior.[24]

Even as infants, children notice likenesses between objects;
preverbal but mobile children, upon seeing a new object, often go
and get another which is similar. They match up shoes, lids and
pans, and stack spoons inside each other without adult encouragement. From about the age of two years, children seem to remember the details of objects and to call attention to them; they
comment on the world in terms of how one thing is like another.
For example, on rides in the car, they often pointed out "Robert's
car," a car just like Robert's, or called attention to "'nother
Hardee's" [a chain of fast food restaurants], as they saw the
restaurant in a new area of town and remembered this Hardee's
was like one in another section of town. They announce similarities of situations, scenes, personalities, and objects, which reflect
not only a gestalt-like sense of whole scenes, but also a recognition
of minute details as well. Lem, on a car ride announced "dere go a
fire truck." No fire truck was visible, yet the fire truck had been
parked in the restaurant's parking lot the week before. He
recognized the scene, remembered the fire truck, and called
attention to it, though it was not currently there. Out of the entire
scene, he had not missed this detail. Coming again on a scene

which had somehow changed, he tried to re-establish the missing items by verbal declaration.

A focus on details without naming them was illustrated in the children's responses to "games" we played. I once brought a set of thin wooden pieces to a park where I took several Trackton preschoolers to play. I spread the blocks on the picnic table and asked each child individually to come sit with me and to put together those pieces which were alike. Each child (ages two to four years) sorted out those pieces which had slight bits of glue stuck on them (from having been used as parts of an art project) and placed these in one pile; each then sorted the remaining clean blocks into another pile. When asked to make more piles, they sorted out those which had both glue and a darker or lighter grain of wood from those which had no glue and were either darker or lighter grained. They persisted in their attention to the fine details of bits of glue and wood grains and did not attend to the global characteristics of shape in their sorting. Several of the children asked if my children had played with these blocks; repeatedly they asked questions in which they tried to establish for themselves the context out of which the blocks had come: "Dese Shannon's blocks?" "You buy dese?" "Can I keep dese?" "What you do wid 'em?" "How'd dat git dere/*pointing to the glue*/?"

Establishing the context of any newly introduced item – where it came from, whose it is, and how it is used – is often the purpose of Trackton children's questions. When introduced to a new item which is called by a name they use for reference to a different object, they try to test the extent of similarities between the old and the new. For example, in Trackton Text IV, Benjy, hearing "block" used to refer to something unfamiliar to him, tested his own definition of block in an operational way. He did not know a city block, but he did know the term *block* as referring to scraps of lumber. When I used the term *block* to mean city block, he issued a series of questions and challenges to establish how similar the new referent was to that one which he knew.

Trackton children, however, never volunteer to list the attributes which are similar in two objects and add up to make one thing like another. They seem, instead, to have a gestalt, a highly contextualized view, of objects which they compare without sorting out the particular single features of the object itself. They seem to become sensitive to the shape of arrays of stimuli in a scene, but not to how individual discrete elements in the scene contribute to making two wholes alike. If asked why or how one thing is like another, they do not answer; similarly, they do not respond appropriately to tasks in which they are asked to distinguish one thing as different from another. For example, on our trips to parks, I often brought along "jobs" I had to do while they played, and I would ask individual children to help me with these jobs. They sometimes involved sorting tasks, and I varied the directions I gave the children (ages two to four years) about the tasks. On one occasion, I brought plastic forks of different sizes and asked the children to take out all those which were different from (or not alike) one which I held up as the model: "I want all the forks which are not like this one to go into this box." The children invariably did one of the following:

1. They scattered the forks over the table and lost interest in my "job."
2. They picked up the model fork and placed it on those which they seemed to visualize as like it but for which they needed the model to test the match. They then picked out those which were like the model and placed them in the box.
3. They focused on some distinguishing feature of the model fork, such as a slight bluish tint in the color of the handle, and pulled out all those which had similar coloring and put these in the box.

None of the children seemed to hold constant the model of the fork I had shown them and to pick out those which differed from that one. Instead they picked out those which were like the model on some indistinct and unnamed feature (such as a bluish tint or a blemished end of a prong) and placed those in the box.

When I asked them how they chose the forks they had put in the box, they gave answers such as "Dis one go wid dat one." "Dese all go together." "You kin make dese like dis/*laying the forks on their sides and nesting them one against the other*/." Occasionally, they would pick up a fork of the wrong size – i.e. a different one – and try to nest it with the others, but they would reject it and put it back into the scattered pile when it did not fit the game they had set for themselves. They often took my jobs and made them into games of their own. When I protested that we had to do my "job," they asked "Why?" "Who make you do dis?" When I asked them *why* or *how* questions about their sorting procedures or games, they usually answered "I dunno." Trackton children have almost no practice in having *why* questions addressed to them, and when adults use *why* questions among themselves, there are often no clues in the situation to the referents of answers: "Why she don't throw dat man out?" "Why every time I wanna go downtown, she gotta go too?"[25] Furthermore, since Trackton adults do not engage their children in dialogues in which they specifically monitor questions and answers for them, the children have no experience with answering *why* questions. Trackton preschoolers ask *why* questions, but they do not answer them with substantive responses.

Trackton adults recognize that they do not talk about the bits and pieces of the world and that their general way of introducing their young to "knowing" differs from that of the mainstream middle class, which many of the women come to know intimately from service as domestics in their homes. On numerous occasions, the women of Trackton would watch Shannon, my daughter, playing with their children and would laugh and comment on the ways in which Shannon played with toys and talked about them. When Shannon would try to read with the preschoolers or sort out puzzle pieces or parts of toys, Lem's mother often tried to explain to her that "Lem don't know how to play like you." Once Lem's older brother Tony showed the same type of awareness, when Lem, at twenty-eight months, had broken a model of a motorcycle Tony had made. When we were driving in the car, Lem asked: "Dat like Tony cycle?" His brother did not reply to him, but turned to me and volunteered: "He know dat like my cycle what he broke. He don't ask whát dat is." On another occasion, a Trackton grandmother commented to me: "We don't talk to our chil'rn like you folks do. We don't ask 'em 'bout colors, names, 'n things." Instead, they use among themselves and direct to their children analogy questions, requests for nonspecific comparisons of one time, event, or person with another.

STORY-STARTERS, the type of question second in frequency to analogy questions in Trackton, elicit from the listener a question that asks the speaker for a description of a scene or event. Older children and adults address these questions to the oldest preschoolers as well as to each other. Questions of this type are used by a speaker to elicit a request for a story from the addressee, and though the question seems to be a request for information, the questioner expects the addressee to understand that this is not what is meant. "Didja hear 'bout Willie's accident?" "Didja see Kim cryin'?" A simple *yes* or *no* is not an appropriate response to such questions. Instead the addressee is expected to say, "No, what happened?" and thus to ask for the recounting of a narrative.[26]

From a very early age, Trackton children, especially boys on-stage, have to learn to handle yet another type of question: the ACCUSATION. On occasions when these are used, they are addressed by adults to children either in a teasing exchange or to initiate a fussing routine. The adults ask questions such as: "What you tryin' to do, rush me off?" after a child waves "bye-bye" to a guest. A child with muddy shoes is asked "What'd you do wid dose shoes?" A youngster found wandering in the plaza when adults are not around is accosted with a question such as "Who tol' you to leave dat porch?" On such occasions, children can bow their heads, say nothing, and wait for the fussing which is sure to come. Or, they can respond verbally with a story or some other type of verbal rejoinder clever enough to draw the adult's attention away from their misdeeds and to deflect the expected scolding. It is on these occasions that children most often shift roles, becoming less child-like and taking on roles which seem to challenge adults in their authority. On one occasion, Lillie Mae, exasperated with Lem for taking off his shoes, asked him what he had done with his shoes and suggested: "You want me ta tie you up, put you on de railroad track?" Lem hesitated a moment and responded:

> Railroad track
> Train all big 'n black
> On dat track, on dat track, on dat track
> Ain't no way I can't get back
> Back from dat track
> Back from dat train
> Big 'n black, I be back

Everyone laughed uproariously, and Lillie Mae did not pursue any further the matter of Lem's removing his shoes. Older children use such responses to accusation questions from low-status adults, other children, and occasionally their parents. Complete freedom to switch roles and challenge adult authority is limited to pre-schoolers. Once children begin to go to school, they are not expected to challenge their parents or community adults of high status with playful language; instead, they are expected to bow the head, say nothing, and take the scolding.

Questions for which the addressee has the information (A-I QUESTIONS), when addressed to preschoolers, usually relate to their state of being or feeling: "Where are you?" "What do you want?" Sometimes these are clarification questions, asked when adults attempt to meet what they conceive of as the need of a child, but the child seems dissatisfied.[27] One day Gary had come in, holding a skinned knee and crying to Mattie, his mother. She washed the knee and tended it, but he still cried. She asked "What de matter wid you, boy?" and discovered that Gary B. had taken his truck. Loss of the truck was the real source of crying, not the wounded knee.

Questions for which the questioner has the specific information necessary for the answer (Q-I QUESTIONS) are very rare in Track-ton. They often occur when adults ask older children to give certain politeness formulae. An outsider visiting in the community who offers a gift might provide an occasion in which a parent will say "What do you say?" to the child who has received the gift. However, among community members and especially in teasing interactions, questions which seem to have set answers are often used to challenge young children: "What's my name?" "What's your name?" "Who gave you dat?" To these, children are not expected to respond with literal accurate answers, but to provide answers appropriate to the relationship and to show that they recognize the use of such questions as a request for confirmation of the special relationship they have with the questioner. For example, Darett asks Lem his name to elicit "Peanuts," the name only Darett uses with the child in their teasing. To other people, a response of *Lem*, or any of a variety of nicknames certain individuals used with him, is appropriate.

Flexibility and adaptability are the most important characteristics of learning to be and to talk in Trackton. Children learn to shift roles, to adapt their language, and to interpret different meanings of language according to varying situations. In the elementary school grades, children take this ability into their "mamma" games, in which they exchange insults, usually including references to "yo' mamma". As teenagers, they have to adapt their responses in repartee between males and females and in boasting and toasting exchanges.[28] As adults in their own community interactions, they have to be able to maintain their status by playing different roles with language and by offering challenges with language. They shift roles and language, in accord with the needs of the situation. Lillie Mae, in fussing at Dovie Lou, can be an aggressive matriarch, but in taking Aunt Berta's fussing, she is a submissive girl. This shifting is a necessary form of protection for one's own status and for the maintenance of status relations within the closed community. The ability to shift roles in accord with expectations of outsiders also serves as protection. Children learning language in Trackton have to come to know when to switch roles and how to use language appropriate for each of these role shifts. In doing so, they focus on interpersonal relationships, as well as links between things, and across scenes and places. Annie Mae, watching her grandson play with kitchenware and make roads of knives and bridges of forks, commented:

Our children learn how it all means, un-er-ah, I guess what it all means, you'd say. They gotta know what works and what don't, you sit in a chair, but if you hafta, you can sit on other things too – a stool, a trunk, a step, a bucket. Whatcha *call* it ain't so important as whatcha *do* with it. That's what things 'n people are for, ain't it?

When the baby comes

The coming of a baby is a big social event for the women of Roadville. When the expectant mother is in her sixth or seventh month of pregnancy, the neighborhood and church women, plus those who work on her shift in her section of the mill, plan "stork showers." These are parties to which only women are invited and to which they are expected to bring a gift for the new baby. These showers are usually held in the evening in the home of one of the women sponsoring the shower or in the church recreation hall. First babies always receive several showers, but subsequent babies, at least through the second and third child, generally receive only one small shower.

In contrast to their grandparents and parents, Roadville women now prefer small families. They recognize that, for their grandparents especially, a large family was an economic necessity. Some children worked on the farm, and others in the mills to help their parents make ends meet; few got an education. But now Roadville children have to be educated, and because education "takes time and money," parents see a large family as an economic liability. Families pride themselves on "doing well by" just two or three children. Having only one child is, however, frowned on, for an "only child" is pitied, sure to be "spoiled rotten," and to suffer from being deprived of the fun of brothers and sisters.

Stork showers are planned to provide the expectant mother with the necessary clothing, supplies, and equipment. If several showers are given, the sponsors plan carefully, so that the baby receives clothes at one shower, and supplies and items of equipment at others. For the more expensive items, such as a plastic infant seat, several women join together and buy cooperatively. Basic items considered necessary for every household with a new baby are:

playpen – a wooden or metal and netting square enclosure used for babies between the ages of six and eighteen months;

high chair – a raised metal or wooden chair in which the baby sits to be fed or to eat his food from a tray attached to the chair;
stroller – a low-wheeled carriage in which the baby sits for excursions out of doors;
bassinet – a basket-like bed in which a newborn infant is placed; usually used for only two or three months;
infant seat – a plastic seat in which a young baby may be placed in a partially reclining position;
car seat – a padded seat which attaches to the seat of an automobile and into which the baby is strapped for car rides.

The baby's family is expected to provide, by either buying or borrowing, a crib, chest of drawers, and rocking chair for the baby. Some of these items may be borrowed from other families to be returned at the time the child outgrows the need for them. If a family buys these items, they are expected to lend them to others when they are no longer needed. Several Roadville families have cribs and rocking chairs which have been passed down from their grandparents.

At the stork shower, the cake is usually decorated in pale green and yellow, and mints of pastel colors are offered with coffee, tea, or punch. Gifts are usually given in whites, yellows, and greens, but some women give outfits in either blue "for boys" or pink "for girls," with much joking between the mother-to-be and gift-giver about what will be done if the child is the "wrong sex" for the gift. If the gift-giver is of child-bearing age, she offers to take her gift back for use with her own next child. If the gift-giver is beyond child-bearing age, she offers to keep the gift for "some young mother who comes along." Blue gifts are given more frequently than pink gifts, and showers are occasions which bring forth general comments such as "Boys are just easier." "You don't have so many worries with boys." "My boys always help me out; I wouldn't take nut'n for my three boys."

At each shower, there are some toys for the new baby and items to decorate the baby's room or the portion of a room which will be given over to the baby. Rattles, in blue or pink, stuffed animals, "busy boxes" (long plastic boxes which attach to the side of the crib and have knobs and levers for the baby to play with), mobiles, and wall plaques on a religious theme or illustrating nursery rhymes are favorite items. Some women attach cloth books to the outside wrapping of their gifts of clothing. All new babies receive some handknitted items, usually sweaters, caps, booties, and a baby blanket or quilt. They also receive some "store-bought" shirts, several one-piece stretch knit outfits, and blankets or zippered blanket wrappers. The handknit items and most expensive pieces of clothing are passed from family to family or from child to child within the same family. Some families have sweaters, booties, blankets, and quilts which have been handed down over three generations.

At the shower, women play bingo-like games, do worksheets or puzzles which have scrambled words related to child care (such as *burp, bottle, diaper, colic, pacifier*). They also have team races which involve each team in fastening and unfastening safety pins, snapping babies' clothing, and getting tops on bottles. There is much laughter and gaiety, and much teasing of the young mother-to-be. All talk of what she will name the baby, and there may be games which allow the women to list their favorite names. During refreshments, the women exchange beliefs about whether or not they could tell the sex of their child before its birth, tell tales of their own behavior quirks during pregnancy, and share general beliefs they and their families hold about pregnancy and child care. The stork shower is a conservative rite of passage which has been consistently maintained in the mill community over the past half century, while many other social activities have changed form and function.[1] This rite brings the young mother-to-be firmly into the circle of motherhood and womanliness in the mill community, and provides an occasion when all other mothers intensify their own status as mothers and as women.

If the young couple is still living with one or the other of their parents, a portion of their bedroom will be planned as "the baby's corner." Usually, however, the young couple try to have a rented place or their own home before the birth of the first child, and they therefore have a "baby's room." Much planning and attention go into the preparation of this room, and neighbors and family members come by in the last few months before the birth to inspect the room and to give suggestions. The room usually includes a crib, bassinet, book shelves, chest of drawers, toy box, scatter rug, and curtains of a fabric which illustrates a nursery rhyme or commercial representation of a children's motif. The young mother-to-be is expected to "sew up" these things on her

115

own and to use this occasion before the birth of the child to show her expertise in decorating her baby's room properly. On the book shelf are diapers and basic childcare needs, plus the cloth books, rattles, and stuffed toys received at showers. A mobile over the crib is a popular decoration, and it may carry nursery rhyme themes or be made of brightly colored plastic birds or other animals. Some of these contain music boxes which play lullabies or simple children's songs. Covers for the crib are often homemade patchwork quilts, made of polyester and cotton fabric. The room is neatly arranged with rectangular items, and every piece of furniture except the bassinet and rocking chair is set parallel to a wall. As soon as the baby is old enough to be placed in the crib, the bassinet will be removed, returned to its owner, and replaced within a few months by a playpen. When the baby begins to crawl and toddle about, the rocking chair will be moved to another part of the house where its rockers will not endanger an unsteady toddler. Often the baby's chest of drawers and toy box are bought unfinished and painted by the father-to-be and stenciled with nursery-rhyme motifs. Plaques on the wall may carry out the same themes – Hickory Dickory Dock, Little Boy Blue, Little Bo Peep, etc. Printed prayers and simple Bible verses are often embroidered and framed for hanging on the walls.

After the baby is brought home from the hospital to this room laid out in such a linear arrangement, he spends most of his first year within this world of colorful, mechanical, musical, and literacy-based stimuli. He hears the nursery rhymes recited and referred to, and he is expected to come to know their association with characters, rhymes, and pictures in books. The things of his environment promote exploration of colors, shapes, and textures. He is fed in an infant seat with a row of colored balls across the front. His car seat has a mock steering wheel covered with vinyl or terry cloth. In his crib, he plays with a stuffed ball with sections of fabrics of different colors and textures, and his stuffed animals vary in texture, size, and shape.

Neighbors, church people, and relatives come to visit the new mother and baby; they exclaim over his size and general appearance and the details of his room. Female relatives of the new mother are in charge of visitors, and they usher visitors in to see the sleeping baby and allow some close relatives to hold the baby for a feeding or while the bottle is being prepared. Roadville mothers do not nurse their children. Those who are going back to work need to get the baby on a bottle and a schedule as soon as possible, and those who are not returning to the mill just "don't wanna nurse." Within the first three months, mothers place great emphasis on keeping the baby to a schedule and seeing to it that they work the baby as quickly as possible into a routine of eating only at certain times of day, sleeping through the night, and taking a morning and afternoon nap. Questions asked about the child during these first few months center around whether or not he is keeping to schedule, has developed colic or any food allergies, and is sleeping well.

"Kin folks" have special privileges with the baby, and ideally the young mother arranges for a female relative who is no longer working in the mill to take care of her baby when she returns to work. Occasionally, if her husband really objects, she stays out of work to take care of the child herself. Connections with kin are carefully drawn and much talked about, and if the child has cousins, they are allowed to visit the baby and are given a sense of proprietary interest in the new baby, because they will become "like brothers and sisters." A big-family atmosphere for every child – lots of children to play with and to grow up with – is still highly valued, and since each nuclear family is small by past standards, parents place much emphasis on cousins as substitutes for brothers and sisters. When new family members come visiting, they are introduced to the baby as "Aunt Sue," "Cousin Bill," "Uncle Harry," etc., and special friends are described as "not your *real* aunt (or cousin) but we'll call her 'Auntie'."

As soon as the baby is brought home, he is referred to by his given name. Before the birth, the mother and father usually study books of baby names, and the family suggests numerous names. The young couple often choose two names, one for a boy and another for a girl, before the mother goes to the hospital, but they do not tell anyone the names they have chosen. Often family names are chosen, but the association between a child and the specific relative bearing the same name is rarely noted once the baby is born. The parents usually choose a nickname for the baby as well as a "real name," or sometimes they decide they do not want the baby to have a nickname, but want instead for the full name to be used at all times. Certain names and nicknames are especially popular: Robert, Bob; David, Davie; Matthew, Mat;

Douglas, Doug; Margaret, Peggy; Elizabeth, Betty; Patricia, Patty. Since there are many men and women with these names, there is little point in indicating that a baby is "named for" someone once the child is born.

Betty Smith, age nineteen when her first baby, Bobby, was born, brought him home after four days in the hospital. Betty's husband, Doug, had decided he did not want her to go back to work in the mill but to stay home with the baby. Her neighbor, Aunt Sue, and her older sister, Peggy, were to help her out in her role as a new mother. They gave their advice directly and indirectly and made themselves available for consultation when needed. One day, a month or so after Bobby's birth, Aunt Sue came to visit. Immediately she went into the baby's room and picked up Bobby, who had been whining and crying as she came in. She changed him, all the while talking to him and casting a secondary message at Bobby's mother:

Wha's a matter, Bobby, yo' widdle tum-tum all empty? Here you are, a growin' boy, and dese folks won't feed you. You tell dese folks they gotta feed you. You tell 'em, they can't just let you cry, not while Aunt Sue is 'round.

Betty went to the kitchen to prepare the bottle, and Aunt Sue followed, continuing her talk to Bobby.

You're a-gonna be a big bóy, just like your daddy. Mamma gonna hafta get you some new rompers soon. What's this size, /*looking at tag in neck of his outfit*/ hmm, Betty, this is gonna be too small for him soon, he's stout about the neck.
//*Bobby begins to cry*//
Okay, Okay, lóok, lóok, there's mamma, she's cómin', she gonna get dat bottle ríght now and get it ready for you. /*taking the bottle from Betty*/ It's a hungry boy, it is.

Aunt Sue took the bottle from Betty and went into the living room to sit down and feed the baby.

In the first few months, close female relatives and friends take it upon themselves on their visits to the young mother to give her pointers on how to take care of her baby. They often do as Aunt Sue did and cast their advice in baby talk directed to the child. Young mothers who follow instructions are described as "catchin' on fast" and "gettin' to be a good li'l mother soon." If the baby's father works at night at the mill and needs to sleep during the day, the young mother often takes the baby "over to mamma's" or to a relative's house each day for fear its crying will disturb her husband. There she has an opportunity to take an apprentice-like role and to talk about any feeding problems or difficulties she is having in getting the child adjusted to a schedule.

There she also has the opportunity to hear and to practice "baby talk" with her new baby. Aunt Sue's "conversation" with Bobby illustrates the predominant characteristics of baby talk used in Roadville.

Wha's a matter, Bobby, yo' widdle tum-tum all empty?

Aunt Sue here asks a question, addressing the baby by name, and she then proposes an answer to her question in another question. She drops the endings of some words (what → wha), substitutes the semi-vowel /w/ for the liquid /l/, and uses a special lexical item *tum-tum* for stomach. The word *all* is used as a modifier in a phrase which parallels another baby talk item commonly used – *all gone*. She continues by telling Bobby what to say to his mother and all "dese folks." She includes herself in the generalized "other" Bobby is to address, but she refers to herself and to the baby's mother by name rather than with pronouns. Aunt Sue here uses *dese* for *these* and later in the passage *dat* for *that*; these are pronunciations which she commonly uses only in informal speech situations and especially with her own family. The passage in the middle ("Betty, this is gonna be too small for him soon, he's stout about the neck") is clearly directed to Betty and is not baby talk. Aunt Sue marks this message as intended for Bobby's mother in several ways: she uses the vocative *Betty*, the *th* in *this* is retained, and the sentences are full, with no ellipsis of words or sounds (such as that found in the sentence "Mamma gonna hafta . . ."). When Bobby begins to cry and squirm, she addresses him.

Okay, Okay, lóok, lóok, there's mamma, she's cómin', she gonna get dat bottle ríght now and get it ready for you. It's a hungry boy, it is.

She repeats "look, look," a simple directive, and calls attention to "mamma" again by her name before she uses a pronoun to refer to her. When Aunt Sue gets the bottle in hand and starts to feed Bobby, she refers to him by the third person singular pronoun *it*.

Throughout those portions of the passage addressed to Bobby, Aunt Sue has spoken more slowly than usual, directed her talk to

Bobby's face or to the objects to which she directed his attention (mamma and the bottle), the pitch of her voice has been abnormally high, and the intonation somewhat sing-song. This passage, however, carries a double purpose – baby talk to Bobby, plus a lengthy content message to his mother. Therefore, it is more complex in structure than are those passages addressed only to babies when there is no adult around to receive a secondary message.

Betty, after visiting her sister one day when Bobby was about eight months old, returned home with a tired and fussy Bobby. As she opened the back door to the kitchen, she said:

Don't fuss, don't fuss, we're home now. We put Bobby, go all-night-night. Mommy get his bottle.

Here, Betty uses the first person plural pronoun *we* in addressing Bobby, refers to herself as "mommy" and uses *his* instead of *your* to refer to Bobby's bottle. The expression "go all-night-night" is a common one used by Betty when she prepares Bobby for bed. In this passage, Betty uses very short sentences, omits auxiliary verbs, and keeps her talk much simpler in message content than in those passages designed to carry a secondary message to another adult present.

The first words

Relatives especially caution young mothers not to spoil their babies by picking them up and holding them too much, yet they are also not to let their babies lie and cry. A distinction of noises from the baby is the guideline for when the baby should be picked up. If he is "jus' makin' noise, talkin' to himself," he should be left alone; if, on the other hand, he is "cryin' a li'l bit," he is to be listened to, but not picked up. Only to a loud cry sustained for several moments is the mother to respond by picking up the baby. Those giving advice to young mothers urge that a baby be left to himself some, to explore, to move about, to make noise.[2] The babbling and cooing of babies before and after they go to sleep is recognized as part of this exploring, and mothers happily report to their female relatives when their babies begin to coo, smile, and babble. Young mothers often take the first "da, da, da, da" sounds from the crib as "daddy" and report the "word" proudly to the father. Whenever the baby is then picked up by the father or by anyone to whom the story had been reported, "daddy" becomes a favorite word for use in talking to the baby.

Young mothers home alone, with their first child in particular, often have many hours with no one around to talk to. They talk to their babies, strapped in an infant seat after a feeding, and placed on the kitchen table while the mother sews or irons. When her hands are not busy with household chores, she carries the baby about, telling him to "see" certain things, such as his own image in the mirror or the nursery rhyme plaques on his room's walls, or to touch the family pet. As soon as babies begin to smile, mothers impute motives to the smile: "You like that, don't you?" "You're all happy today, 'cause you know we're goin' for a ride." Young mothers often take their babies out in the stroller to visit relatives or friends or to walk downtown. Adults and older children along the way stop and stoop down to talk to the baby. They tickle toes or "tummy," hold a hand, or straighten a cap while addressing the child. For a woman friend not to stop and talk to a baby is considered the gravest of rebuffs. Men acquaintances who do not do so are considered awkward or "ignorant 'bout babies." Young boys are the only ones who rarely stop to talk to babies. Young girls ask to hold the baby, and once the baby begins being taken to church, young girls take the baby around and show him off. All those who talk to babies and toddlers use baby talk; especially short, simplified sentences, special lexical items, a high pitch and exaggerated intonation, and a punctuation of talk with tickling, manipulation of the baby's chin, and most often with direct face-to-face contact. If a baby is sleepy and closes its eyes while someone is talking to him, the speaker stops talking. If the baby does not seem sleepy but is, for example, being held so the sun is in his eyes and he is squinting, the talker suggests turning the baby to get the sun out of his eyes and then begins talking again once the baby's eyes are open. Baby talk during the first two years of a Roadville child's life is a normal part of the baby's daily interactions.[3]

Alone during the day, each young mother uses the reporting of her child's new accomplishments as an excuse for visiting with neighbor women either in person or by phone. When, by the age of seven or eight months, babies vigorously avoid certain foods by turning their heads away from a proffered spoon or by lashing at the air with their arms, the mother reports to a neighbor: "He doesn't like that new cereal, and he knows how to tell me so." Eye movements to follow mobiles, family pets, or siblings are noted and reported, and mothers comment on these movements and their "meanings" to the baby and to any other available audience.

When the baby begins to respond verbally, to make sounds which adults can link to items in the environment, questions and statements are addressed to the baby, repeating or incorporating his "word." This practice is carried out with not only first children, but also subsequent children, and when adults are not around to do it, older children take up the game of repeating children's sounds as words and pointing out new items in the environment and asking babies to "say —." When Sally, Aunt Sue's youngest child, began saying "ju, ju, ju" from her infant seat and high chair, Lisa, her older sister, said "Juice, juice, mamma, she wants some of my juice, can I give it to her?" Lisa also named other items for Sally: "Milk, say milk," and when Sally discovered a sesame seed on the tray of her high chair and tried to pick it up, Lisa said "Seed, see:d, that's a seed, can you say see::d?" There is verbal reinforcement and smiles and cuddling when the baby repeats.

If the baby renders the "word" with a peculiar pronunciation or over-extends its meaning, the family may even take up the baby's version. For several weeks, after Lisa introduced Sally to "tissue" at age twenty months, Sally called everything that was soft and crushable in her hand and could be used to wipe her face a "tita." The family began to use "tita" occasionally as the conventional signal for not only tissues, but also diapers, baby wash-cloths, and Sally's bib. *Tita* for *tissue, diaper* or *bib* was used on occasion by all the family members for a period of three months. Sally, after a month or so, began using *tiza* for all soft cuddly things made of fabric: her stuffed lamb, tissues, diapers, towels, etc., and then began sorting out terms for each of these. Only gradually did the original term *tita* pass out of use for other members of the family. Sally's game of picking up cuddly things and wiping them across her face or the tray of her high chair was replaced by other games exploring how her communicative behavior could produce adult reactions and participatory responses.

Certain lexical items referring to excrement develop in each household and tend to continue throughout the preschool period for use by all the young children of the family. Bobby, at fourteen months, was playing with Danny, his cousin, whose mother, Peggy, had put him in Bobby's playpen while she visited with Betty. Danny dirtied his diapers, and when his mother picked him up, saying "Poooo, you stink, boy." Danny responded "Poo, kee, poo, kee." Later in the afternoon, the boys managed to puncture a jelly-filled teething ring in the playpen, and the thick peculiar-smelling substance oozed out on the plastic pad covering the playpen floor, Bobby got his fingers in it, and Danny began sliding toys through it, squealing "Poo::kee, poo::kee." Both boys continued their play until Danny's mother came in to find the mess. A day or so later, Bobby was given a new food for lunch, and after the first approach of the spoon, he drew away and said "poo:kee." His mother, unfamiliar with the use of the word in connection with something which had an unusual smell, reported the incident as one which had produced a new word referring to the specific food item. She persisted in trying to get Bobby to eat the food, but he slapped at the spoon, getting the food on his hand and smearing it on the highchair tray. Later, that afternoon when Bobby woke from a nap and had a particularly messy and smelly diaper, he monologued in his crib: "Poo kee, noo kee, nee, nee, nee, poo kee, nee, neekeenee, neemee, neemee, mama, mama." His mother came in to hear this and as she changed the diaper, said "You're pookee yourself." Bobby laughed, and his mother repeated the word, making contorted faces, laughing, and squeezing Bobby's chubby legs. Thereafter, *pookee* became generalized as a family word to refer to a general category of smelly, messy substances, and its meaning was extended to refer to having a bowel movement. During Bobby's toilet training period, his mother would ask "Let's go pookee now." Once when Danny and Bobby were playing, when both were beyond two years of age, Bobby began saying "Pookee, pookee" to Danny. Bobby's mother shushed him, scolding, saying "No, Bobby, we don't use that word, that's not nice," and giving them both a cookie to stop the language play with that word.

Children's language play alone or with siblings or other play-mates is encouraged, and adults often intervene to offer reinforcement unless the words are dirty or the children are making too much "racket."[4] When children are left to play in their rooms, parents put records on for them or turn on their music boxes or toys that talk. Martha's daughter, Wendy, at thirty-two months was playing with Kim Macken (thirty-six months); the girls were setting up a "tea party," and their mothers were having iced tea at the kitchen table nearby. As the girls prepared tea and handed each other cups and "cookies," Wendy handed a cookie to Kim saying "here." Wendy's mother broke in and said, "Wendy, that's no way to talk, 'Have a cookie.' Now say it right." Kim held the cookie and waited. Wendy repeated "Have a cookie," and Kim began munching happily. Mrs. Macken said, "Kim, what do you say?" Kim responded "It's good, good." Her mother said "No uh yes, it's good, but how about 'Thank you'?" Kim said "Thank you, good."

A baby will often repeat parts of a mother–child dialogue in monologue when he is alone. If his mother overhears him, she repeats and extends these phrases as she changes and feeds him. Bobby at eighteen months often talked to himself in his crib before and after a nap:

wanna, wanna a cookie wanna a cookcook now? cook, cook, book, book ah, ah a a a ta ta [thank you] ta ta cook cook nudder cook book cookbook, book cook cook, all gone.

This monologue contains parts of a dialogue he and his mother had carried out earlier in the afternoon, when after lunch, she had offered Bobby a cookie, forced him to say "ta ta," and after he had done so and eaten the first cookie, she had offered him another cookie. Children who are too young to engage in cooperative play are often put together in playpens, and there they babble and monologue to themselves in parallel play. Their mothers often intervene and try to get the two children to talk to each other, for example, to talk about the sharing of a toy rather than to squeal and tug.

When Roadville children begin combining words, usually between the ages of eighteen and twenty-two months, adults respond by expansions, that is, by repeating the combined items in a well-formed adult utterance which reflects the adult interpretation of what the child has said. Sally, banging on the backdoor, screamed "Go kool," and Aunt Sue responded "No, Sally, you can't go to *school* yet, Lisa will be back, come on, help mamma put the pans away." Aunt Sue assumed Sally both wanted to *go to school* and was commenting on the fact that Lisa had just *gone to school*. This phenomenon of expansions, taking a minimal phrase

such as "Go kool" and interpreting and expanding it, characterizes much of the talk adults address to young children. Adults seize
upon a noun used by the child, adopt this as a topic, and build a
discourse around it. The topic is then accepted as known to the
child, and the adult utterances which follow use definite articles,
deictic pronouns (those which locate something in space and time,
such as *this* and *that*) and anaphoric pronouns (those which
substitute for an expression already used by either the child and/or
the adult). The habit of picking up a topic from a noun used by a
child either in a spontaneous utterance or in response to an adult's
question which asks for the name of something is illustrated in the
following exchange.

Mrs. Macken and two-year-old Kim were making cookies in the
kitchen. They were using cookie cutters in the shape of Christmas
items. Kim especially liked the snowman, and she was allowed to
put the "red hots" (small pieces of red candy) on the cookies to
mark the snowman's nose. Kim picked up a freshly baked
snowman and bit the head off, saying "'noman all gone." Mrs.
Macken, in the next three minutes, used eleven utterances which
either restated the label *snowman* or assumed it as a given topic in
the discourse. Talk about the snowman continued in spite of the
fact that Kim and her mother were using cookie cutters in the
shape of a Christmas tree, a reindeer, a Santa, and a bell – and not
the snowman cutter – as they talked.

Did you eat the snowman? Do you want to give daddy a snowman? That
snowman's smile is all gone. He's lost an eye. He has a nose too. Did the
snowman fill you up? We can make some more like him. 'member the
snowman song? Can we build one? There's a snowman in your book. We
can take Gran'ma one.

Kim did not collaborate with her mother on the snowman topic,
but went on chattering about the red hots, the green sugar for the
Christmas trees, and the broken cookie in the shape of a bell.
Mother and daughter seemingly engaged in parallel talk, and not a
cooperative dialogue, once Kim introduced the topic of *snowman*
for her mother. Mrs. Macken talked on about the snowman, as
though she thought Kim had intended this as the topic of
discussion.

The use of a child's label for an item, as the topic of an extended
dialogue constructed primarily by adults, is a habit which is

especially evident on certain occasions. When a child and adult interact over a book, or on occasions when the child has himself shown an interest in some item or event in which the adult wishes him to maintain an interest, adults almost always adopt the label as the focus of the dialogue. Wendy and her mother Martha were looking through Wendy's baby book one day when Wendy was just over two years old. Wendy had been sick, and the doctor had told Martha to keep her quiet for twenty-four hours, so the uninterrupted exchange between mother and child over a specific item was particularly extended. Martha had explained to Wendy that she had to be "doctored" for awhile, and that meant she had to stay in bed and be quiet. Martha was trying to keep Wendy entertained until she fell asleep. An excerpt from the ten-minute exchange follows.

ROADVILLE TEXT I

Martha: /pointing to a picture of Wendy's dog in the baby book/ Who's that?
Wendy: Nuf [the dog's name was Snuffy]
Martha: Let's see if we can find another picture of Nuffie.
//Wendy points to the same picture//
/pointing to another picture/ Here he is, he's had a bath with daddy. There he is, this is Nuffie.
Wendy: All wet.
Martha: Nuffie got daddy all wet too.
Wendy: Where's daddy?
Martha: Daddy's gone to work. /seeing Wendy look at the picture/ Oh, he's not in the picture.
Wendy: Where Nuf
Martha: Nuffie's over to gran'ma's, he dug under the fence again.
Wendy: Bad dog, Nuf, bad dog.
Martha: That's right, Nuffie *is* a bad dog, now let's find another picture of Nuffie /turns pages of book/
Wendy: Nana, nana /pointing to a picture of Mrs. Dee/
Martha: Yes, that's nana, where's Nuffie?
Wendy: I don't wanna /pushes book away/
Martha: But, look, there's daddy fixin' to give Nuffie a bath.
Wendy: No. /trying to get down off her bed/
Martha: No, let's stay up here, /holding Wendy around her waist/ we'll find another Nuffie.
See, look here, who's thát with Núffie?
//Wendy struggles and begins to cry//

Here, Martha, in spite of Wendy's wandering interest and struggles to change first the topic and then the activity, persists in looking for pictures of Snuffy. Once Wendy responded to her request for that label, Martha continued it as the topic, and did not take up Wendy's possible suggestion of Nana (or the finding of pictures of other persons) as new topic. Thus throughout the conversation, Nuffie is the topic, both with reference to the pictures in the book and to the here and now. Martha lets the topic drop only once – when Wendy asks the question "Where's daddy?" Initially, Martha thinks Wendy is referring to daddy's whereabouts at the present moment, but she then realizes Wendy is referring to the fact that daddy is not in the photograph they have been discussing. Martha remembered the incident surrounding the picture, but daddy's getting wet was not recorded in the picture, and Wendy called attention to the dissonance between what Martha said was in the picture and what was actually in the photograph.

Adults help children focus their attention on the names and features of particular items or events. They believe that if adults teach children to "pay attention, listen, and behave," children learn not only how to talk, but also how to learn.[5] Roadville adults believe young children have two major types of communicative abilities to develop during their preschool years. First, they must learn to communicate their own needs and desires, so that if mothers stay attuned to children's communications, they can determine what these are. Secondly, children must learn to be communicative partners in a certain mold. Preschool children do not go to playschool or nursery schools before the age of four; thus they must play alone much of the time. Parents believe that the mother must therefore talk to her child and give him adequate opportunities to communicate. As adults talk to their children, they teach them how to talk and how to learn about the world. They sort out parts of the world for them, calling attention to these, and focusing the children's attention. Children learn the names of things; they then learn to talk about these "right." Peggy, describing her own thoughts about how Danny learned to talk, said:

I figure it's up to me to give 'im a good start. I reckon there's just some things I know he's gotta learn, you know, what things are, and all that. 'n you just don't happen onto doin' all that right. Now, you take Danny 'n Bobby, we, Betty 'n me, we talk to them kids all the time, like they was grown-up or something, 'n we try to tell 'em 'bout things, 'n books, 'n we buy those educational toys for 'em.

Peggy acknowledges here her feeling that her guidance is necessary for Danny to learn what to say, how to say it, and what to know.

This guidance comes through conversations in which adults force children to accept the role of both information-giver and information-receiver. Adults ask for the names of items; if the child gives an unsuitable name, the adult proposes another and then follows with a series of questions to test the child's reception of this term. On future occasions, adults use the same term again and again, making a conscious effort to be consistent in the information they give, and often one member of the family insists that his term for an item or for an animal sound be used with the child and not an alternative term.

Sally had a woolly lamb which she kept in her crib and later in her playpen. Her family heard her begin to associate her sound of "wa wa" with the lamb, but rejected this as the "right" label and began asking Sally "What does the lamb say?", and answering their own question with "The lamb says baaaa." This sequence for giving an item the "right" name is continued and elaborated on as adults read early picture books to the preschoolers. Adults point to the item on the page, name it, provide a simple sentence such as "That's a lamb." "Sally's got a lamb like that." "What does the lamb say?" "Where's Sally's lamb?" Sally was asked to point to the lamb in the earliest stage of "book-reading," and later to answer questions such as "What's that?"[6]

Children are believed to progress in stages – to crawl, take their first step, walk, and run, to respond nonverbally; to babble, to say words, to put them together, and then to ask and answer questions. Mothers keep "baby books" on their children's progress, and such records are kept not only for the first child, but often for the second and third child as well. Mothers with children of the same age compare their developmental stages: "Is he walking yet?" "How many words does he say?", and they report and evaluate their children's behavior in accordance with what they believe to be the ideal stages. The particular time schedules and co-occurrences of action in these sequences are, however, highly varied; some mothers believe a child always talks before he walks; others believe a child does not talk until he can walk. Therefore, though there is a general consensus on the fact that children follow a sequence of behaviors and certain activities occur with others, there is no consensus on when the sequence begins or which stage in the sequence follows another stage.

Adults see themselves as the child's teacher at the preschool stage, and teachers ask and answer questions. Aunt Sue described herself: "I'd have been a good teacher, if I could have got some real school education. I can make children listen, an' I'm all time askin' questions and thinkin' up things they oughta know. I ask Sally all kindsa questions, so she'll learn about this world." Questions were of the types indicated in Table 4.1.

QUESTION-STATEMENTS are used predominantly with children in the first eight months and often carry a message not to the baby, but to others present. Young mothers and the older female relatives or friends most intimately involved with the baby begin asking questions of babies within their first few weeks home from the hospital. As noted earlier, older women often do this to give an indirect message to the young mother, saying to the baby, "You're too warm, aren't you?" "That shirt's too big for you, isn't it?" These question-statements serve another function, however; they often express the needs and desires of the child. Adults speak for the child, and since adults believe that the first type of communicative ability children must develop is the expression of their needs, they perhaps unwittingly model this function of communication in the earliest stage of the baby's development. They make statements about the baby's state of affairs, wants, likes, dislikes, etc. The high pitch, marked intonation, slow pace, and direct face-to-face contact with the baby mark this as baby talk though it does not consistently have all the simplifying and clarifying features of talk addressed solely to the baby. Because the message serves the secondary purpose of telling the young mother what the baby needs, there are often fully formed adult sentences in the midst of this talk to babies.

Young mothers themselves begin to use question-statements in their talk with their baby, usually within the first month for the first child and almost immediately with subsequent children. Betty, within the first month of bringing Bobby home from the

Table 4.1. *Types of questions asked of preschool children in Roadville*

Type	Response called for	Examples	
		Question	Response
Question-statement	No verbal response. Used primarily in baby talk addressed to young infants; carries a content message to nearby adult listener who is expected to interpret the message as a mild directive or as a statement about the baby	Mamma's got to get some softer bedsheets, don't she? Bobby's gettin' a rash	(None)
Q-I (Questioner has information)	Specific piece of information known to both questioner and addressee. Used often to initiate ritualistic rote performances	What's that? (pointing to a picture in a book)	Nuffie
Question-directive	Realignment of behavior and/or utterance of a politeness formula. Often carries secondary message to listeners other than the child	Don't you know I just wiped that off? (said to a child dropping crumbs on the table)	I'm sorry (brushing crumbs off)
A-I (Answerer has information)	Specific information known to addressee, but not to questioner	Do you want chocolate or vanilla?	'nilla

Note. These types are *not* listed in approximate order of frequency, because the frequency of each varies greatly in accordance with the age of the children and who is around as audience.

hospital, commented on her own uneasiness with the practice, seemingly so easily engaged in by older women:

I guess hit's 'cause I'm here by myself so much. I talk to this baby all the time. I feel foolish, but Aunt Sue says, talkin' like that's only natural, and it shows I care, uh, I guess I mean, it shows I'm payin' attention to Bobby. 'Bout the only time I don't talk to 'im is when my soaps [television soap operas] are on, and even then, I find myself, oh, well, ya know.

Questions in which the questioner knows the answer (Q-I), indeed often has a specific answer in mind, are frequent throughout the preschool years, but are most frequent when the child is between two and four years of age. When Bobby was twenty-eight months old and again when he was forty-three months old, Betty taped her talk with Bobby every day for a week in the period before his morning nap (about two hours each day). The tapes indicated that out of an average daily total of 110 sentence-like utterances directed to Bobby, 54 percent were in question form in his second year and only 32 percent in his fourth year. In his second year, most of the questions were in ritualistic attention-focusing routines such as those discussed earlier in this chapter. In the fourth year, Bobby not only talked more (of a total of 230 utterances, only 90 were made by Bobby's mother), but a high percentage (56 percent) of *his* talk was given over to questions. Though Betty was exasperated by his questions to her (she now had a newborn baby to care for), she looked on his talkativeness and curiosity as signs that he would "run the teacher crazy," and bragged about the child's inquisitiveness, which she believed would have good positive transfer to school.

In their earliest talk to babies, Roadville parents use QUESTION-DIRECTIVES, utterances in the form of questions which function as directives or commands: "What'd you do that for?" "Oh, Bobby, won't you ever sit still?" They use many of these in the presence of others to exclaim over their own dismay at a disobedient child or the general fatigue they feel in dealing with a child. Betty, pregnant with her second child by the time Bobby was three, often asked such questions of Bobby in the presence of her husband and relatives who she thought might help her out. Bobby was a very active and persistent child, and Betty easily became exasperated with his antics which others tended to think cute. One Sunday afternoon, several family members were sitting in the backyard visiting, and Bobby had disappeared around the house. He came out the back door, carrying a sand bucket full of water. Betty looked up and yelled at him "Bobby, what are you doing?" Everyone stopped talking and laughed as they watched Bobby carefully walk down the back steps, while explaining he was "makin' cookies." Betty, in her sixth month of pregnancy, got up to go in the house to survey the damage and found sand tracked from the front door across the living room and into the bathroom, where a trail of water began and led out the back door. Betty began a series of scolding questions, designed as much to inform the adults and elicit a response from them as to scold Bobby: "Will you look at this mess?" "Bobby, won't you ever learn?" "Why on earth did you do that?" "Don't you know I just mopped this floor? What am I going to do with you?"

These questions are used as scoldings and as directives. Betty's "What are you doing?" was intended to be interpreted as "Don't do that" as well as an exclamation over Bobby's unusual action of going through the house to get water for sandbox play. Other questions used as directives are those issued by parents requesting a specific politeness formula or the recounting of a previous scolding or a story (see Chapter 5). As early as six months, children are asked "Can you wave bye-bye?" as their hands are manipulated for them in a suitable gesture. The pattern of "Can you say ——?" continues through the preschool years requesting children to say "ta-ta [thank you]," "more, please," and on through a hierarchy of politeness formulae ranging from these baby talk items to such responses as "Pleased to meet you" on being introduced to someone and "Come again" to guests as they prepare to leave. Such occasions are prefaced by a particular look in the child's direction from a parent or intimate relative, and if the child does not respond to the nonverbal cue, the parent asks: "Can you say ——?" or "What do you say?" or "Don't you have anything to say?"

Other types of questions addressed by adults to Roadville children are those which ask them about their state of affairs, or their feelings and desires (A-I). These questions often ask children their food preferences when choices are feasible. Children are also asked to explain where they hurt and how they feel when they seem feverish, cry, or are whiny. When they are toddlers and have occasions to play with other children, they are often asked to give an accounting of what led to a sand-throwing, wet clothes, or broken toy.

Play, toys, and games

Once beyond the age of two, Roadville boys and girls do not play together, but are sex-segregated if there are playmates of the appropriate sex and age available. Friendships tend to develop between young mothers who have girls or boys of the right age to play together. Roadville divides its behaviors sharply into male and female, and this division begins for toddlers.[7] Beyond rattles, stuffed animals, early ABC books, and books on basic objects, toys and games are sharply differentiated for boys and girls. Preschool girls are given Raggedy Ann dolls; boys are given Raggedy Andy. Girls are given metal tea sets; boys, plastic soldiers. Girls are given dollhouses and doll furniture; boys are given toy trucks, tractors, campers, and jeeps. Girls are given books about little girls, babies, and baby animals living in a human family-like setting; boys are given books about trucks, ballgames, and boys and their animals.

Both boys and girls receive educational toys, and with the exception of certain elementary toys, such as a teeter pole onto which rings in basic colors and of diminishing sizes fit, these toys too are distinguished by sex. Girls are given educational toys which stress girls' and women's activities; boys are given those which emphasize the activities of boys and men. For their first birthday and on the Christmas closest to their first birthday, Roadville children receive numerous educational toys, since they are not yet old enough to have riding toys, to play ball, or to take care of mechanical toys or games which have multiple pieces. Favorite toys for one-year-olds emphasize matching colors, sizes, and shapes through specific activities: putting rings on a teeter pole in the right order, fitting tools into their proper holes in a toy wooden work-bench, and fitting blocks of different shapes into a toy mailbox.

Many of these toys and the pull toys given children during their second year have a book-related theme and make sense only in terms of one's knowledge of the story to which they refer. For example, one popular toy is a house on wheels. The house has a large keyhole in the roof and a large key on the end of the string by which the toy is pulled. The chimney atop the house is too small for the key to fit into, but the four small stylized figures inside the house can be put into the house either through the chimney or through holes in one half of the roof which match the shapes of the bottom portion of the figures. Three figures are bears, the fourth is a blond-haired girl with pigtails. Inside the house, visible when one side of the roof is lifted up, there is a table with three chairs around it. The chairs are painted on the floor of the house in shapes and colors to match the bottom portions of the bear figures. When the toy is pulled, the house on wheels makes a clinking sound and two "eyes" in the front of the house blink. Children can relate the toy to its book source of "Goldilocks and the Three Bears," only if they both know the story and recognize that there are components and features of the house (the blinking eyes, wheels, keyhole in roof, lift-up roof, etc.) which bear no relationship to the story.

Other popular toys are those which feature campers, boats, and houses with figures which fit inside. TV characters, especially those from "Sesame Street," are also popular, since as soon as children begin to protest staying in their playpens, Roadville mothers invite, and in fact encourage, them to watch TV, especially "Sesame Street" and cartoons. Books and records produced in connection with the "Sesame Street" program are also popular gifts for preschoolers.

Parents and other adults who play with babies and preschoolers use toys as props in a majority of their games. The exceptions are peek-a-boo games, pat-a-cake and knee-riding games. Peek-a-boo games usually begin when the child is about six months old, and mothers most often play the game when they are changing the child's diaper and wish to distract him from crying and wiggling. A diaper or other soft item around the crib is the cover-up screen behind which the mother hides the child's face first, and in later versions of the game, her own face. The usual pattern is for the mother to pull the shirt part way over the head of the child and say "Where's ―― [baby's name]?" and then to pull the shirt down quickly and repeat "There's ―― [baby's name]." While changing a diaper, mothers often take a second diaper and put it on the child's chest, and then while actually pinning the diaper, place this second diaper over the child's face and say "Where's ―― [baby's name]?" and wait for the child to grab the diaper off his face. In peek-a-boo games played with children who are beginning to crawl, parents hide their own faces behind a large cereal box, tea towel, or sweater, etc. The mother covers only her face and says "Where's mamma?" and waits for the child to react by a shriek of joy and by grabbing at the screening object. Fathers play peek-a-boo games which are more mobile, and they very rarely play peek-a-boo games which do not involve mobility of both child and parent. Once children are crawling or walking, fathers hide behind a newspaper or a door, call out to the child, and wait to be found. Sometimes the child reverses the game and begins to hide and call out. The father pretends an inability to find the child, asking "Where's —— [child's name]?" "Mamma, have you seen —— [child's name]? I can't find him anywhere." The usual pattern is for the child to hide quietly for approximately thirty seconds and then to rush out from his hiding place once his father's back is turned. Children maintain in this way one of the major rules of the game – the surprise element; they will not come out of their hiding place when their parent is facing in their direction. They reappear only when they can do so without revealing their hiding place.

Older children playing with babies beginning to crawl often take a toy and hide it either along with themselves or by itself. Parents often scold for the latter game, since the baby often cries when he is unable to find the toy or has found the older child, but not the toy. Parents seem to view the hiding from the baby acceptable only if a large portion of the item being hidden remains in the baby's field of vision.[8] Parents play this game with their children "'cause it's something we can do together at this stage," and "'cause it keeps 'im happy and makes 'im laugh." Above all, the game is social, and parents do not think of this game as educational as they do their play with the specific toys they buy for their children.

Other social games played without special props are pat-a-cake games involving clapping or patting motions, played as early as five months with some children. During the sixth to twelfth months, these become bouncing games accompanied by a song which ends in a mock fall-through of the baby from the adult's knees to the floor. "Ride-a-cock-horse" is an especially favorite song mothers sing or chant to accompany this game; males rarely chant this, but more often just bounce the baby, then wait for an unsuspecting moment to pretend to let the baby fall. Thus when mothers play the game, they provide both verbal and nonverbal cues to indicate when the mock fall will come. Fathers provide only nonverbal cues. Relatively short chase games and hide-and-seek games are also played between adults and toddlers, and these are usually done by fathers who tend the child while the mother prepares dinner or readies the child's bed for putting him down for the night.

Beyond these games, however, adults and older children require a toy, book, or ball to "play" with preschoolers.[9] If a preschooler approaches them to try to gain attention, adults respond by saying "Go get you ——— [name of a toy, book, wooden puzzle, etc.]." Adults play with one-year-olds by taking all the rings off a teeter pole and beginning to replace them, sometimes in the right order to show the child how. Later, however, once the child can put the rings on in the correct order, the adult places the rings in an incorrect order to elicit correction from the child. Often adults play for a little while and then draw away, preferring the child to play alone once he has given his attention to the object and not to the social interaction with the adult. A purpose of adult play with children's toys seems to be to draw the attention of children to toys (or other stimuli) and to encourage the child to practice by himself the skills called for in play with the particular object, e.g. matching colors, shapes, sizes, etc. Parents have visited local nursery schools and voice their choice and use of toys at the preschool stage in terms of their "educational value." Peggy explained her selection of first- and second-year birthday gifts for Danny: "While he's this young, *I* can pick his toys, and Fisher-Price [brand name of educational toys] toys always seem to teach kids something. I figure if he plays with these now, by himself, he'll be ready for nursery school. Besides, some of 'em are kinda fun for us too."

The practice element of play with toys by adults and preschoolers contains a strong emphasis on language interaction as well as manual manipulation. While playing with a teeter pole and rings, adults ask questions of the Q-I type: "Where does this go?" "Can I put this one here?" Of parts of toys and pictures in books, they ask children to recite their names, attributes, and to repeat certain associated sounds. A popular toy for boys is a workbench into which a hammer, screwdriver, and other simple tools fit. Fathers play with this with their young sons, saying, "This is a hammer, see, I'm gonna hammer Bobby's shoe. Hammer goes bang bang."

Bobby is then asked "What's this, Bobby?" "Where does it go?" "How does the hammer go [what sound does it make]?" Young children are expected to learn to repeat these formulaic responses exactly as they have heard them. Later as they are told stories in connection with the use of certain items and given directives about how to use certain toys and where to keep them, parents ask on the occasion of later infractions, "What did I tell you about ——?" Children are then expected to repeat the story and its moral. Such morals pertain to how to use certain items ("Don't stick the screwdriver into the electric socket hole." "Don't bang on mommy's table with the hammer"); when to use them ("Not now, Sally, we're trying to talk, and that's too loud"); as well as where items "belong," i.e. where they should be kept.

From the earliest months of the child's life, the ideal goal of the household is to keep "baby's things in baby's room." Within that room, items come to have their own place, and though they are not always kept there, the expressed ideal of doing so is often repeated. As new toys are acquired, and as the toddler begins to move about the house, the ideal is frequently repeated that his toys are to be kept in his room in their appointed place. Before company is coming, or even before Daddy is coming home from work, toddlers hear their mothers say: "Let's clean up." "Let's put this away." Hearing such statements, they see their mothers pick up and return objects to their intended place in the baby's room. Roadville parents want their children to grow up with a strict sense of everything having its place, and adults often quote their own version of Scriptural confirmation of the value of space-function and time ties: "to everything under heaven there is a time and place." Though the Biblical verse (Ecclesiastes 3:1) mentions only time, the Roadville version adds place to make the verse fit their own sense of values and needs. Their homes are small, and Roadville adults feel there are too many people and too many things going on inside their homes; therefore everything has its own place. All the women sew, and they have their sewing baskets and sewing corners organized to be whipped out in the shortest possible time. During certain seasons of the year, Roadville women can and freeze large quantities of food, and they now have to do this in their own homes, because most of the canneries operated by the mills closed over a decade ago. Thus, they must store jars, large pressure cookers, and other bulky equipment used only on these occasions. Year after year, when canning season is over, this equipment is returned to its place on the back porch, or in the back of a cabinet.

As children grow old enough to play outdoor games, they carry with them the notion of spaces having definite purposes. Certain parts of the yard or the neighborhood are designated for certain games, and children are strictly admonished to play only in certain ways and in these designated areas. Their riding toys, miniature balls and bats, and footballs are meant to be put away when they are not being used, and children are punished for not keeping things "in their place."

The emphasis on educational toys and playing with children with these toys begins to fall away as youngsters approach age four. By this age, fathers take their sons into the yard to teach them how to play ball; they dress them in football jerseys and encourage in numerous ways their sons' futures as football or baseball players. Fathers tussle with their sons, emphasize their toughness, and urge them to be able to stand on their own and fight. Little girls are increasingly left to their tea sets, dolls, and doll houses, and they begin to ask for "little-girl" toys and games advertised on television. Adults no longer play question-games and read books with their children with any regularity. The nightly going-to-bed routine which lent itself to reading books and playing games is abandoned, as children stay up later and later and go to bed without special routines. Many of the children are placed in church nursery schools for either a morning or an afternoon session at the age of four, and parents seem at this point to abdicate their responsibility for continuing play with educational toys, book-reading-and-naming games and extended question-asking sessions. They turn their attention instead to providing equipment and occasions to model their children's behavior according to appropriate sex roles. They believe that in the child's earliest years, they have taught them "right" and helped set them on the road to school, which they must now travel on their own.

The rightness of the Word

The grandparents and parents of the present generation of parents in Roadville often speak of what they did in their childrearing practices by asserting it was "right." The rightness of their behaviors and beliefs is, in their minds, in line with their religious teachings and the precepts of the Bible. They often quote such simple admonitions as "Honor thy father and thy mother" and other rulings on parent–child relations from the Bible. Most Roadville residents regularly attend Protestant churches, many of which are termed "fundamentalist" by town middle-class residents. There they often hear their ministers preach on relationships between children and parents, and the duty of parents to be strict and to raise children in the right way.

Though not all members of the current generation of parents either attend church as regularly or talk as openly about their belief in the Bible and the church as their elders do, they recognize that their parents' links between Christianity and good parenthood have influenced their own behaviors as parents. Mrs. Dee said of her minister and the Bible: "He taught us ta, ya know, ta read duh Bible and to believe it all, 'n I still do . . . I, I think it is very important." Her daughter said of her own belief that what the preacher spoke was "the truth" and that the Bible was "important"; she remembered her grandfather's strictness and his ability "to live by the Bible." Mrs. Dee's granddaughter echoed the view that the preacher spoke the truth and the Bible was very important, and she commented that she attended the same church her grandparents had begun attending when they first moved to Roadville.

Church activities reinforce the links between church teachings and behaviors as parents. Parents and children attend the Sunday School before the church service on Sunday. The regular Sunday morning service has a special children's sermon, and children remain in the sanctuary through this sermon before going again to Sunday School rooms for "little church." There they are allowed some mobility, but the teachers attempt to give them activities and stories that relate to the lesson of the day being used in the preacher's sermon. There are Sunday evening meetings for young people above junior high age (fifteen years), and there are several married couples' classes, which periodically focus on the study of the Bible and its precepts for childrearing.

The link between religious practice and childrearing is not only in the influence of the precepts of the one on the other, but also in the striking similarities of the teaching methods used in church and home. At church and in church-related activities, children are asked to answer questions with prescribed routines. The minister and the people hold "the Word," the Bible, up as "the absolute." Religious knowledge in the church and church-related activities is fixed, and the emphasis in all transmission activities is conservational, relying on the finite nature of religious knowledge. Within the church, the minister and the people believe that the compass of study of religious matters should be narrow, confined for the most part to the Bible, and the minister is believed the one most able to make any explicit explanations of the Bible for teaching purposes. Any informal attempts to draw away from the Bible and to offer alternative materials for study which might carry complementary or corollary messages are considered inappropriate. The measure of a child's understanding of the Bible, following from these adult beliefs about the nature of "the Word," is then very explicit: recitation of specific passages, memorization of the books of the Bible, and answers to specific Bible quizzes, covering names of characters, places, and historical periods.

Children learn from very early ages simple verses, such as the shortest verse in the Bible, John 11:35 ("Jesus wept."), and later more complicated verses, such as John 3:16, and particular passages or chapters (such as 1 Corinthians 13). These memorizing tasks are graded in difficulty, so that the youngest children learn the names of Bible characters, words of songs such as "Jesus loves me," and move on to short verses, books of the Bible, short passages, and whole chapters or psalms by the time they reach junior high age. There is an orderly progression in what is learned and how it is learned. Families are expected to reinforce these practices from the church in home lessons, which take a verse a day with brief explanation, and to ask children to prepare for Sunday School lessons. They rarely do this, but all regard this practice as an ideal. The family is believed to be integrally involved in the preparation of children for "knowing religion." Recitation of the proper verse for the appropriate occasion or comment on daily life is appreciated and expected of some adults, such as teachers in Sunday School. The church judges such recitations highly important for leading church men and women.[10]

The religious experience at church and in church-related affairs thus reinforces the home emphasis on the teaching of fixed and memorizable statements and labels. Recitation in both church activities and the home calls for bounded knowledge which is exhibited in the repetition of memorized words exactly as they have been taught. Evenings at home with children before they go to bed are similar to the lesson circles used in the church: parents ask children to repeat names and to recite knowledge they have learned during the day or in connection with certain events. Children have to repeat information as precisely as possible on these occasions, and if they do not do so, they are corrected. Occasionally, if an object can have two names, and the child uses the name which is least expected or which the parent has not had in mind as the answer, the parent corrects the child. Rarely are explanations offered for the fact that an item can have two names. Common nouns are asked for most frequently in these lesson circles, next attributes of items or actions, then phrases and sentences which relate to particular items or events, and stories which have been told the child about these phenomena or situations.

When Sally was just a little over two years old, and canning season had come, Aunt Sue was peeling tomatoes and preparing them. She was trying to get Sally to say *tomato*, but each time Aunt Sue asked "What is that?" and pointed to the tomato, Sally would answer "red." Aunt Sue kept insisting "Yes, it's red, but it's a *tomáto*." "You like *tomatoes*, don't you?" Repeatedly parents reject children's descriptions of things by their attributes before they have learned to respond with the *name* of the item. When adults misunderstand or mishear a child's statement, they ask for clarification most frequently by saying "A what?" "You want a what?" requesting a noun or noun phrase rather than a repetition of the entire statement or another part of the sentence. Children are expected to learn through incrementally acquiring knowledge which includes names, attributes, phrases, and stories. Children have little choice in what they recite to parents or the ways they show off to visitors. They are expected to perform as asked and to recite the "pieces" called for. Adults often refer to their own experiences as youngsters of having to learn "pieces" to recite in church, at home, and at school.

Roadville adults, when asked how they learned language, recall bits and pieces of their own experiences, but they have consistent general impressions of the effect of their experiences in learning to "say the right thing." Peggy and Danny had one day been visiting

Mrs. Dee, and Danny knocked over a potted plant on the front porch. Danny did not stop his play, but went on charging around with his GI Joe toy. Peggy, in horror, asked "Danny, what do you sáy?" Danny looked at his mother, paused for what seemed an endless interlude, and said "I don't know." Peggy apologized repeatedly to Mrs. Dee, and left in great remorse and dismay that Danny had not produced the expected "I'm sorry." After Danny had been berated and put in his room, Peggy and I sat down for a glass of iced tea. She said: "He talks all the time, why can't he learn to say the *right* thing?" I asked if she remembered how she had learned to talk and to talk "right."

ROADVILLE TEXT II

Mamma and daddy just tálked to me and made me talk to them. They'd ask me questions; it was then that I began to learn how to talk to other folks. They'd uh, ask me over and over again, to tell my aunts and uncles things, and I'd know they wanted me to say it right. They taught us children to be polite too, to talk right when other folks were around. Mamma would always say: "What do you sáy?" "Did you forget your manners?" If I didn't say something when I was supposed to, they'd fuss at me for not *acting* right, not *doing right* by other folks. Saying "I'm sorry," "excuse me," and "thank you" were important, showed the kind of person you were. If you couldn't learn to say the right things, seems like they thought you couldn't learn nothing right. They always taught us to respect the preacher, the teacher, and older folks. They taught us to believe that what they said was right, and we ought to learn what they said. When we had done something wrong, mamma and daddy didn't want no excuse. They wanted us to be sorry we hadn't done what we might oughta have done. We grew up with a lot of *should*s in our house, "You *oughta* do so and so," "You *should* say 'thank you,' 'I'm sorry,' " "You *should* write a thank you note." Uh, I 'member whenever I, uh when I first learned that "I'm sorry" could take care of most anything. My brother and me had been playing ball alongside my house. One of us hit a ball went right through the window of Mrs. Bell's house. We knew we hadn't oughta been playing there, and we knew we'd get in trouble, for sure if we ran, 'n somebody told on us, so we went to Mrs. Bell, and told her how *sorry* we were, and we wouldn't do it again no more. For a long time after, she told folks how we had "done the right thing," come to her and said we was *sorry*. We learned to do that at school, too. Most anything you did, if you talked right afterwards, and said what the principal and teachers wanted to hear, you'd be O.K. (pause) You know I think that's one of the reasons so many of our teachers hated the nigger kids so, they never would say they was sorry. They'd lie, give excuses, say nut'n, but they'd never say they's sorry, or anything like that. They just didn't seem to have manners like our folks brought us up with.

Other young parents recall similar experiences and invariably linked their parents' insistence on "saying it right" with moral dictates from the church. Betty said of her parents:

ROADVILLE TEXT III

We learned at church and at home too that things were either *right* or *wrong*; you did things the *right* way and you were *right*; you did wrong or said wrong and everybody *knew* it was wrong. Most everybody accepted that; those that didn't just didn't fit in at all. I guess they became what you might call the black sheep. I used to think it was funny that other folks' mammas had some of the same sayings about right and wrong,
    "Pretty is as pretty does."
    "A job well done is twice done."
    "Haste makes waste."
We, uh mamma used to talk about how we [in the mill community] was cut from the same pattern. We all knowed what to expect. We had certain expected uh, you know we, almost like a muscle reflex, we knew to give. We also knew when we'd done bad, and we wanted to make our folks proud of us, and we didn't want to cause 'em no trouble at church either. When we was teenagers that was hard sometimes, on account of we wanted to go our own way, and some of us stirred up a lot of trouble, especially the boys. But you look around now, and you see most of us have settled down, except the real black sheep, and most of them moved away. I'd say most of us are trying to teach our kids to do right, to talk right, to do good in school, to get ahead. We might not wanna live just like mamma and daddy did, they come through some hard times, and there's more chances now. You don't hafta work in the mill anymore. But I'd say most folks wouldn't want to throw away those ways of talking, thinking, and doing our folks taught us neither.

Peggy and Betty indicate in their comments their own sense of the close connections between religious knowledge and practices of learning, and those ideally promoted by parents teaching their children to have appropriate and acceptable language performance. For many of the practices and precepts the church holds for language, a parallel ideal is expressed by parents. The church insists on verbatim performance as a prime way of showing off knowledge; parents demand verbatim performance from their children at home as a way of showing they are learning. The church imposes memorization tasks from simplest to most difficult; parents buy educational toys according to their graded difficulty and introduce these to their preschoolers with demonstration and question-and-answer drills.

The patterns of teaching language in Roadville homes are consistent with those of the church. At both individual and group levels, the belief in and practice of using "the right word" help structure the cognitive patterns which children draw of the world, i.e. what they come to know, and their notion of how to show what they know. Rigidly prescribed oral performance (based on many occasions on a written source, most often the Bible) is the way to prove learning. Children come to know they must be careful about following directions on the links between words and behavior; if they "say it right," they show they've "got it right," and they themselves are, in turn, "right." Such expectations discourage the potential recognition of alternatives – both alternative choices of what it is one is to learn and alternative ways of saying what one has learned. In Roadville the expectations which surround the fixed uses of language and practices of teaching language generate and regenerate support for a fixed set of roles and view of the world, and provide a continual test of commitment to existing modes and values of social institutions and relationships.

Contrasts between learning and teaching

In both Roadville and Trackton, all physiologically normal children learn to talk; yet the social and linguistic environments which surround young children as they grow into their language competence differ strikingly in a number of features. These include: the boundaries of the physical and social communities in which communication to and by children is possible; the limits and features of the situations in which talk occurs; the what, how and why of patterns of choice which children can exercise in their uses of language, and the values these choices of language have for the children in their communities and beyond.

In Trackton, adults talk of children "comin' up"; in Roadville, adults speak of "bringin' up" their children. In Trackton, all babies spend the first year of their lives swathed in human touch and verbal interactions; their lives flow with few spatial and time barriers imposed by their caregivers. In Roadville, infants live within predictable physical and time limits, which their families watch over as they narrate to them the objects and events to which they should attend. The two communities hold different concepts of childhood; each carves out roles for adults and children which fit their notions of who can and should teach children to listen, talk, read, and write. In each community, by the time they go to school, the children know the sounds, words, and grammatical systems of the language spoken around them. They have learned their community's ways of using language to get along with the people and to accomplish their social goals. They have learned to use language to acquire the knowledge their community has judged they should know at their age, and they have learned appropriate ways of expressing that knowledge. Yet their caregivers' uses of space and time, as well as their talk and games, differ greatly. For both communities, the church and its precepts and practices surrounding talk have reinforced what goes on in families and the neighborhoods.

Roadville parents see themselves as responsible for "training" their preschool children, and they plan ways and means to provide what they regard as appropriate experiences before their children go to school. Both mothers and fathers have critical roles to play, and the functions of these roles are differently distributed between the two parents. Provision of financial means rests primarily with the father, while the mother is responsible for nurturing and meeting the daily physical needs of children. Ideally, mothers spend most of their time with their preschool children, and they are thus expected to provide emotional support and appropriate friends, places, books, and activities for their youngsters. Together, both parents expect to instill in their children a desire to work hard, "grow up right," and "be good." The entire family, on holidays and weekends, works at finding times and ways to "play" together – fishing, traveling, visiting, watching television, or going to movies or do-it-yourself exhibits.

Critical to Roadville parents' playing out their role appropriately is the "proper" use of space and time in the children's environment. As tiny individuals, children "should" have some space and time of their own for their possessions – toys, books, clothes, and for their activities – sleeping, eating, and playing. Taught to respect the uses of these spaces and times their parents model and prescribe, Roadville children learn to interpret, and often to tell others, the rules they live by. For Roadville parents, there is no substitute for their role; children need parents to train them. Extended family and trusted friends may reinforce the teachings of parents, but the critical functions rest with parents. Older siblings and peers of the child must be enlisted to help and not to undermine the teachings of the parents.

Any baby born into Trackton is born not to a family, but to the community. Parents – especially the mother and her family – are expected to meet the physical needs of the child; the father and his family should help out. Integration of the infant as a social member of the community is taken over by all; older siblings or children in the neighborhood carry the baby about and introduce the infant to their games and other social interactions. Immersed in a constant, complex stream of multi-party communication, the child comes to define himself as a speaker. Nicknames, plaza-center roles, playsongs, and frequent teasing help each child learn how to act to enlist the greatest number of supporters in the crowd and thus to insure emotional and social support. Time and space have few restraints in the community; their only limits are interactional. Trackton parents and community members see in each child "the makin's of sump'n," but the way the child comes up and uses these "makin's" depends on the child. Parents and other adults have limited influence and power over any child: "children will turn out the way they turn out."

These concepts of childhood and parenthood determine the kinds of talk and play adults provide Roadville and Trackton children. Roadville parents talk to their babies, modifying their speech in ways they believe appropriate for speaking to children. Seen as conversational partners, children are expected to answer questions, read books cooperatively, and learn to label and name the attributes of real-world and book objects. Encouraged to engage in adult-like activities such as fishing, cooking, and caring for babies, Roadville youngsters have both toys and times for role-playing their parents. Moreover, they are brought into tasks, asked to try activities, and supported and corrected in their efforts. Parents read to and play with their preschool children, hoping to foster their ability to carry out both activities eventually on their own. In multiple, redundant, and repeated ways, the children of Roadville hear their parents' high hopes for their futures, and for their abilities to participate in and talk about what they learn from a gradually expanding world beyond the mill community.

From their earliest days in the arms or on the hips of community members, Trackton children hear talk about themselves; their behaviors are described to others, their physical features encapsulated in nicknames, and their moods and manners mocked and narrated. As they come to talk, they repeat, vary the language about them, and eventually use their language to work their way into the streams of speech about them. Boys especially are challenged to show their nonverbal and verbal skills for interacting before the audience of the community; girls are invited to perform with older girls in playsongs, spontaneous games, and role-playing. Once old enough to be accepted in ongoing talk, children are expected to answer questions comparing items, events, and persons in their world, to respond creatively to question challenges, and to report their own feelings, desires, and experiences. Without specific explication, they must learn to see one thing in terms of another, to make metaphors of the world about them.

For both Roadville and Trackton, the church is a key institution helping to provide occasions and rationale for their approaches to being parents and to enabling their young to use language. Young and old of both communities participate in the church; Trackton youngsters sit with their families through services which may last for hours. Their participation, verbal and nonverbal, is cause for comment and reinforcement by their elders. At home, they hear little more than a few stories, wafts of songs, or Biblical quotations to remind them of church teachings, but many of their celebrations share the spirit of group participation and construction of meaning they have felt in worship services. Roadville churches provide special materials, places, and occasions for the participation of the young; in their Sunday School classes, they are read to, asked to remember characters and events, and to begin an initial linkage of these to the Bible. At home, their books, blessings before meals, and often the proverbs and admonishments regarding their behavior remind them that they and their parents have a commitment to a force beyond the immediate. The preacher's message for

Trackton folks is one which stresses feeling and being, as well as living one's life with a spirit of acceptance of what cannot be helped, joy over blessings of the past and present, and great hopes and responsibilities for the future. In the churches Roadville families attend, they are told to know their weaknesses, to struggle to acquire more strengths, to rejoice over their blessings, and to keep striving to be worthy of the gifts of grace.

5 Oral traditions

In Roadville

A piece of truth

Roadville residents worry about many things. Yet no Roadville home is a somber place where folks spend all their time worrying about money, their children's futures, and their fate at the hands of the mill. They create numerous occasions for celebration, most often with family members and church friends. On these occasions, they regale each other with "stories." To an outsider, these stories seem as though they should be embarrassing, even insulting to people present. It is difficult for the outsider to learn when to laugh, for Roadville people seem to laugh at the story's central character, usually the story-teller or someone else who is present.

A "story" in Roadville is "something you tell on yourself, or on your buddy, you know, it's all in good fun, and a li'l something to laugh about." Though this definition was given by a male, women define their stories in similar ways, stressing they are "good fun," and "don't mean no harm." Stories recount an actual event either witnessed by others or previously told in the presence of others and declared by them "a good story." Roadville residents recognize the purpose of the stories is to make people laugh by making fun of either the story-teller or a close friend in sharing an event and the particular actions of individuals within that event. However, stories "told on" someone other than the story-teller are never told unless the central character or someone who is clearly designated his representative is present. The Dee children sometimes tell stories on their father who died shortly after the family moved to Roadville, but they do so only in Mrs. Dee's presence with numerous positive adjectives describing their father's gruff nature. Rob Macken, on occasion, is the dominant character in stories which make fun of his ever-present willingness to point out where other folks are wrong. But Rob is always present on these occasions, and he is clearly included in the telling ("Ain't that right, Rob?" "Now you know that's the truth, hain't it?"), as story-tellers cautiously move through their tale about him, gauging how far to go by his response to the story.

Outside close family groups, stories are told only in sex-segregated groups. Women invite stories of other women, men regale each other with tales of their escapades on hunting and fishing trips, or their run-ins (quarrels) with their wives and children. Topics for women's stories are exploits in cooking, shopping, adventures at the beauty shop, bingo games, the local amusement park, their gardens, and sometimes events in their children's lives. Topics for men are big-fishing expeditions, escapades of their hunting dogs, times they have made fools of themselves, and exploits in particular areas of their expertise (gardening and raising a 90-lb pumpkin, a 30-lb cabbage, etc.). If a story is told to an initial audience and declared a good story on that occasion, this audience (or others who hear about the story) can then invite the story-teller to retell the story to yet other audiences. Thus, an invitation to tell a story is usually necessary. Stories are often requested with a question: "Has Betty burned any biscuits lately?" "Brought any possums home lately?" Marked behavior – transgressions from the behavioral norm generally expected of a "good hunter," "good cook," "good handyman," or a "good Christian" – is the usual focus of the story. The foolishness in the tale is a piece of truth about everyone present, and all join in a mutual laugh at not only the story's central character, but at themselves as well. One story triggers another, as person after person reaffirms a familiarity with the kind of experience just recounted. Such stories test publicly the strength of relationships and openly declare bonds of kinship and friendship. When the social bond is currently strong, such stories can be told with no "hard feelings." Only rarely, and then generally under the influence of alcohol or the strain of a test in the relationship from another source (job competition, an unpaid loan), does a story-telling become the occasion for an open expression of hostility.

Common experience in events similar to those of the story becomes an expression of social unity, a commitment to maintenance of the norms of the church and of the roles within the mill community's life. In telling a story, an individual shows that he belongs to the group: he knows about either himself or the subject of the story, and he understands the norms which were broken by the story's central character. Oldtimers, especially those who came to Roadville in the 1930s, frequently assert their long familiarity with certain norms as they tell stories on the young folks and on those members of their own family who moved away. There is always an unspoken understanding that some experiences common to the oldtimers can never be known by the young folks, yet they have benefited from the lessons and values these experiences enabled their parents to pass on to them.

In any social gathering, either the story-teller who himself announces he has a story or the individual who invites another to tell a story is, for the moment, in control of the entire group. He manages the flow of talk, the staging of the story, and dictates the topic to which all will adhere in at least those portions of their discourse which immediately follow the story-telling. At a church circle meeting, many of the neighborhood women had gathered, and Mrs. Macken was responsible for refreshments on this occasion. The business and lesson of the circle had ended, and she was preparing the refreshments, while the women milled about waiting for her to signal she was ready for them. Mrs. Macken looked up from arranging cookies on a plate and announced Sue had a story to tell. This was something she could not normally have done, since as a relative newcomer, a schoolteacher, and a known malcontent in Roadville, her status was not high enough to allow her to announce a story for someone who was as much of an oldtimer as Sue. However, as the hostess of the circle, she had some temporary rank.

ROADVILLE TEXT IV

Mrs. Macken: Sue, you oughta tell about those rolls you made the other day, make folks glad you didn't try to serve fancy rolls today.
Mrs. Dee: Sue, what'd you do, do you have a new recipe?
Mrs. Macken: You might call it that
                                     [
Sue: I, hh wanna=
Martha: =Now Millie [Mrs. Macken], you hush and let Sue give us *her* story.
Sue: Well, as a matter of fact, I did have this new recipe, one I got out of *Better Homes and Gardens*, and I thought I'd

try it, uh, you see, it called for scalded milk, and I had just started the milk when the telephone rang, and I went to get it. It was Leona /*casting her eyes at Mrs. Macken*/. I thought I turned the stove off, and when I came back, the burner was off, uh, so I didn't think anything about it, poured the milk in on the yeast, and went to kneading. Felt a little hot. Well, anyway, put the stuff out to rise, and came back, and it looked almost like Stone Mountain, thought that's a strange recipe, so I kneaded it again, and set it out in rolls. This time I had rocks, uh, sorta like 'em, the kind that roll up all smooth at the beach. Well, I wasn't gonna throw that stuff all out, so I cooked it. Turned out even harder than those rocks, if that's possible, and nobody would eat 'em, couldn't even soften 'em in buttermilk. I was trying to explain how the recipe was so funny, you know, see, how I didn't know what I did wrong, and Sally piped up and said 'Like yeah, when you was on the phone, I came in, saw this white stuff a-boiling, and I turned it off.' (pause). Then I knew, you know, that milk was too hot, killed the yeast /*looking around at the women*/. Guess I'll learn to keep my mind on my own business and off other folks'.

The story was punctuated by gestures of kneading, turns of the head in puzzlement, and looks at the audience to see if they acknowledged understanding of the metaphors and similes. Stone Mountain is a campground in the region which everyone at the circle meeting had visited; it rises out of the ground like a giant smooth-backed whale. The beach is a favorite summer vacation spot for Roadville families, and the women often collect the smooth rocks from the beach to put on top of the dirt in their flower pots.

Several conventions of stories and story-telling in Roadville stand out in this incident. The highest status members present, Mrs. Dee and her granddaughter Martha, reannounce Sue's story and subtly convey that Mrs. Macken stepped out of line by asking Sue to tell a story on this occasion. Within her narrative, Sue follows a major requirement of a "good story": it must be factual, and any exaggeration or hyperbole must be so qualified as to let the audience know the story-teller does not accept such descriptions as literally true. Sue qualifies her Stone Mountain description with "almost," her equation of the rolls with rocks by "sorta like 'em," and her final comparison of the rolls to rocks with "if that's possible." She attempts to stick strictly to the truth and exaggerates only with hedges and qualifications.

Perhaps the most obligatory convention Sue follows is that which requires a Roadville story to have a moral or summary message which highlights the weakness admitted in the tale. "Stories" in these settings are similar to testimonials given at revival meetings and prayer sessions.[1] On these occasions, individuals are invited to give a testimonial or to "tell your story." These narratives are characterized by a factual detailing of temporal and spatial descriptions and recounting of conversations by direct quotation ("Then the Lord said to me:"). Such testimonials frequently have to do with "bringing a young man to his senses" and having received answers to specific prayers. The detailing of the actual event is often finished off with Scriptural quotation, making it clear that the story bears out the promise of "the Word." Sue's story is confession-like, and its summing up carries a double meaning, both a literal one ("on my own business" = cooking) and a figurative one ("on my own business" = general affairs). Any woman in the group can quote Scripture describing the sins of which the tongue is capable (for example, James 3:6 which likens the tongue to a fire which spreads evil).

Unspoken here is the sin of Sue and Leona – gossip – the recounting and evaluating of the activities and personalities of others.[2] Gossip is a frequent sermon topic and a behavior looked upon as a characteristic female weakness. Leona, who is not present at the circle meeting, is a known gossip, who occasionally telephones several of the women to fill them in on news in the neighborhood. All of the women know, but none says explicitly, that any phone call with Leona is likely to bring trouble, both to those who are the topics of her phone conversation and to those who are weak enough to listen to her. The story, told at the end of a church circle meeting, appears to be an innocent piece of female chatter, but it carries a message to all present which reminds them of their own weakness in listening to Leona. All the women have gossiped, and all have given in to listening to Leona at one time or another. Yet on this public occasion, all avoid direct negative talk about either Leona or anyone else, since engaging in this censured activity in such a public setting where more than two individuals are present would be foolish. Instead Sue's story is an occasion in which all recognize their common, but unspoken, Christian ideal of disciplined tongue. The major understandings and background knowledge on which a full interpretation of the story depends are unarticulated.

Sue's story carries subtle messages about the values and practices of the culture out of which the story comes. She reaffirms that the most frequent gossip in Roadville takes place between only two people, with an unstated and often unfulfilled agreement that neither will reveal her participation to others; breaches of such trust are frequent causes of female disagreement. Moreover, Sue asserts her maintenance of certain community norms for homemakers: she makes her bread "from scratch" instead of buying store goods; she is unwilling to throw out food; she has obviously trained Sally, her daughter, to be attentive to kitchen matters. Picking up, or recognizing all of this information depends on the familiarity with Roadville's norms and daily customs which the women of the church circle share.

In several ways, stories such as Sue's are similar to Biblical parables, a frequent source for sermons and Bible lessons, and a literary source familiar to all. Parables told by Jesus recount daily experiences common to the people of his day. Often parables end with a summary statement which is both a condemnation of one or more of the story's characters and a warning to those who would hear and understand the parable for its relevance to their own lives. In a parable, two items or events are placed side by side for comparison.[3] The details of the story bring out its principal point or primary meaning, but there is little or no emotional expressiveness within the story evaluating the actions of the characters. The action is named and detailed, but its meaning to the characters is not set forth in exposition or through a report of the emotions of those involved. Biblical parables often open with formulas such as "The Kingdom of heaven is like unto this . . ." (Matthew 13:24, 13:31, 13:33, 13:44, 13:45, 20:1, 25:1), or admonitions to listen: "Listen then if you have ears" (Matthew 13:9) and "Listen and understand" (Matthew 15:10). Roadville's parable-like stories often open with announcement of the comparison of the events of the story to another situation: "That's like what happened to me . . ." Both men and women often open their stories with the simple comment "They say . . ." or a metaphor such as "We've got another bulldog on our hands" (referring to a fighting personality who is the central character in an upcoming story). In ways similar to Biblical parables, Roadville folks share with their listeners experiences which provide a lesson with a meaning for the life of all. The story is told using direct discourse whenever possible: "And he goes 'Now, you look out.'" or "Like yeah when you was on the phone . . ."

For the best of the parable-like stories, that is, those which are told repeatedly or are handed down in families over generations, the retelling of the entire story is often not necessary. Only its summary point need be repeated to remind listeners of the lesson behind the story. Proverbs or well-known sayings also carry lessons stating the general will of the community and ideals of Roadville families. Understanding of these depends, as do parable-like stories, on comparing one thing to another, for example, seeing similarities across nature.

A whistlin' girl and a crowin' hen will come to no good end.
A rollin' stone gathers no moss.
A stitch in time saves nine.
Rain before seven, clear by eleven.

For those activities which are traditionally part of the daily routine of mill families' lives – agriculture, weather, male–female relations, pregnancy and childbirth – proverbial guides to behavior abound. Proverbs help determine when certain crops are planted and harvested, predict rain, sunshine, good fishing or bad, link personality traits to physical features, and dictate behaviors of mothers-to-be. The anonymous and collective voices of those who have abided by these lessons in their experiences remind Roadville residents of behavioral norms and reinforce expectations of predictable actions and attitudes among community members.[4]

The Bible's parables and proverbs are sometimes quite consciously used as a written model for Roadville's oral stories and proverbs. However, few written sources, other than the Bible, seem to influence either the content or the structure of oral stories in Roadville. Access to written stories, other than those in the Bible, is relatively rare. Women buy home and garden magazines and read their stories of successful remodeling or sewing projects – testimonials on the merits of budget shopping, thriftiness, and tenacity in do-it-yourself projects. Some women buy "True Story" magazines and publications which feature the personal stories of movie and television personalities, but they do not usually read these publicly. Some women occasionally buy paperback novels, and when asked about their hobbies, they often include reading, but then add comments such as "There's no time for it, for reading, you know, for pleasure or anything like that."

In church-related activities, they not only use stories from the Bible, but they occasionally hear certain other types of content-related stories. The circle meeting at which Sue was asked to tell her story is an example of one such activity. In such meetings, women share study of a designated Bible passage or a book of the Bible. The leader often reads from other short story-like materials to illustrate the need to follow the precepts covered in the Biblical passage. Throughout the discussion, however, there are numerous references to "our own stories [the experiences of those present]" which better relate to the Bible message than do the printed materials supplied for Bible study. Men's and women's Bible study groups prefer that a pastor or an elder lead them. The pastor sometimes suggests to lay leaders that they use a book of exposition of the Scriptures (especially when the Bible study focuses on a particular book of the Bible, such as Revelation). Some members of the Bible study group may be assigned portions of supplementary materials to read and discuss at the next Bible study. However, such efforts usually fail miserably. Roadville men and women do not like to read in public and do not wish to admit their lack of understanding of expository materials. They state strong preferences that, if any written materials are used to expand on Biblical passages, the pastor, and not they, should do it. As Mrs. Turner's mother explained. "I believe what the preacher speaks to be the truth, because I feel he is our leader, and I don't feel, well, I feel like *he* is tellin' us the right thing."

Thus, in interpreting the Bible, church members prefer either their own stories or Biblical accounts to written stories – whether factual expositions or tales of the lives of other modern-day Christians. Their own stories are often modeled on Biblical parables, but they are also personal accounts of what God's Word has meant to them. They reject depersonalized written accounts which come from unfamiliar sources. They use their own stories told on themselves and their friends to entertain and instruct, as they highlight personal and communal weaknesses and their struggles either to overcome them or to live with them.

Children's stories

Preschool children of Roadville first meet stories as their parents read to them from books. A majority of these books are not sustained chronological narratives on a central character or event, but are nursery rhymes, alphabet books, and collections of one- and two-line descriptions of animals and familiar objects. Some few are, however, sustained narratives such as "Goldilocks and the Three Bears," tales of a boy and his pets on a farm, or simplified stories from the Bible.

In Sunday School each Sunday and in Vacation Bible School (a week-long Bible study and camp-like activity held each summer), the children are given printed materials prepared by the national association of their church's particular denomination. Some stories in these booklets are Bible stories (such as Daniel in the lions' den, or Miriam placing the baby Moses in the reeds, etc.) rewritten in contemporary English. Others, however, especially since the mid 1970s, are stories about boys and girls of today meeting temptations and overcoming them through remembering and living according to Biblical precepts. The end of the story always contains the moral and the Bible verse most relevant to the story's conflict resolution. Children talk about these stories with their Sunday School teachers and are encouraged to tell about similar incidents in their own lives: "Were you ever asked to do something you didn't think you could do, and God gave you the strength to do it?" When children do not offer such incidents, teachers provide examples which revolve around their membership in families and their activities with their playmates. Occasionally children are asked to give the moral of such stories, but they are discouraged from introducing situational ethics – "what if . . .?" "but maybe he . . ." – and they are admonished to "pay attention to what the story says, how it goes, and don't go wandering off somewhere and making up things." Children are called upon to use their rote memorization of Bible verses to suggest appropriate verses for morals to the stories they volunteer or their teachers provide about their transgressions. At home, parents continue the practice of asking children for stories about their weaknesses and

157

providing morals for these stories. Adults, however, rarely tell stories focusing on their own behavior in front of their children. The only exception is the occasional story an adult may tell of his own childhood, and the moral of such stories usually carries the message "Don't do what I did." Older members of the community sometimes tell young people stories they remember about their children as they were "comin' up," but these stories also carry heavy didactic messages.

Children in Roadville are not allowed to tell stories, unless an adult announces that something which happened to a child makes a good story and invites a retelling. When children are asked to retell such events, they are expected to tell non-fictive stories which "stick to the truth." Adults listen carefully and correct children if their facts are not as the adult remembers them. In contrast, fictive stories which are exaggerations of real-life events, modeled on plots or characters children meet in story-books, are not accepted as stories, but as "lies," without "a piece of truth." Children grow up being taught to tell *true* stories on themselves:

ROADVILLE TEXT V

Sue: Tell yo' mamma where we went today.
Wendy (at five years): Mamma took me 'n Sally to the Mall. Bugs Bunny was=
Sue: =No, who was that, that wasn't Bugs Bunny.
Wendy: Uh, I mean, Peter, no, uh a big Easter bunny was there, 'n we, he, mamma got us some eggs=
Sue: ='n then what happened?
Wendy: /*turning her head to one side*/ I don't 'member.
Sue: Yes, you do, what happened on the climbing=
Wendy: =me 'n Sally tried to climb on this thing, 'n we dropped, I dropped, my eggs, some of 'em.
Sue: Why did you drop your eggs? What did Aunt Sue tell you 'bout climbin' on that thing?
Wendy: We better be careful.
Sue: No, 'bout the eggs 'n climbing?
Wendy: We better not climb with our eggs, else 'n we'd drop 'em.

Throughout the story (told when Martha came to pick up Wendy from Sue's house), Aunt Sue calls for strict chronicity ("'n then what happened?" "What happened on the climbing?") and adherence to the correct facts of the story. She has given an open-ended directive: "Tell yo' mamma where we went today," which Wendy could take as an invitation to tell about the grocery store, service station, or department store in Laurenceville, other places they also went that day. But Aunt Sue is after a particular story, and using questions which ask for information already conceived in the head of the questioner, she probes until Wendy produces the particular story in Aunt Sue's mind. Furthermore, the story which Sue wants Wendy to tell is one which has the same conventions as those told by adults: Wendy is to detail her foolishness, and to give a summary moral or a repetition of the moral – the lesson – of the story at its closing.[5]

Repeatedly, Roadville children are prompted to tell such stories on themselves, and they are prodded until they construct the story along the model of adult stories. Here Wendy wants to tell about what she saw – Bugs Bunny and other characters; she does not want to retell the conflict, but Aunt Sue insists, and Wendy, with considerable coaching, finally constructs the story as her aunt had decided it should be before the telling.

Wendy is asked to recapitulate both the story and the adult's warning in this episode. Often adults admonish children through the use of a saying or proverb, which at one time accompanied a particular story, but used alone thereafter serves to remind children of the message and moral of the story. For example, Mrs. Dee told a story of a grandmother who had money enough to take only one of her two granddaughters on a trip; the grandmother debated numerous ways to decide which child should go. She finally chose the "wait-a-minute" test. She called each girl to her. One answered "Wait a minute" and the other came at once. The granddaughter who came at once was chosen to go on the trip. Mrs. Dee recounts this story whenever a young child does not come immediately upon being called. However, if the child knows her story, she admonishes a child who is slow to come with only the question "A little Mr./Miss wait-a-minute, huh?" and the child is expected to register remorse and to apologize for his or her misbehavior. Often a proverb or a summary moral from Biblical parables is used to stimulate a child to recall the entire story to which the moral belongs and to remind him of his failure to conform to expected norms. Parents ask "How does *that* story go?" Children's recall of a particular story as the context of a statement or moral dictate is a highly valued and frequently practiced method of social control. On such occasions, children are expected to repeat in just the way they have been told both the story and its moral. They are not expected to evaluate the actions of the story or to punctuate their retelling with expressions about how they or other story figures feel. They may introduce no fanciful or fictive characters for a bit of levity or reduction of tension.

Thus there is not a chance that in the exchange between Wendy and Aunt Sue noted above, Wendy could tell a story in which she joined with Bugs Bunny or any other fanciful character to participate in fictive antics. To do so would shock the adults and cause them to accuse her of "tellin' a story," i.e. changing a real incident to make it a lie. In general, only children and the worst scoundrels are ever accused of lying. "Thou shalt not lie" is an adage on the tip of everyone's tongue, and the community is on the lookout for offenders. "Don't you tell me a story" means "Don't tell me a lie." Young children caught doing wrong and tempted to tell stories to get themselves off the hook or to exaggerate the responsibility of others are quickly and severely admonished.

Danny and Bobby, at age four, played in the backyard of the church one afternoon while their mothers attended a meeting. The boys had begun a sand-throwing contest when their mothers emerged from the church to catch the game in full swing. They stopped the battle, and each child began to blame the other. Each mother had seen her own child throw sand, and neither was willing to accept her child's blaming the other. Both children were scolded, first and foremost for blaming the other, and secondarily for throwing the sand. Later, on the way home in the car, Bobby was carrying a small toy truck. Betty noticed it and asked where it came from. Bobby answered: "Found it in the sandbox, 'n some lady said I could have it." Betty hesitated a moment, looked at Bobby, and said, "Don't you tell me a story! Now where did you get that truck?" Bobby hesitated again and said: "Danny made it. He got a big truck, it makes lotsa li'l trucks, 'n I got this one." Betty stared in amazement: "Don't you *ever* tell me a story!" Bobby looked remorseful and whined: "Digger Dan talks." Betty seemed not to hear this comment, took the toy away from the child and demanded "Where *did* you get this truck?" Bobby answered: "I took it outta the sandbox." Betty's worst fears had been confirmed: Bobby had taken the truck from the church and he had lied.

The background of Bobby's story and follow-up comment ("Digger Dan talks") begins with the afternoon nursery school provided by some local women in the social hall of one of the churches. There the church women had collected many books for the children, and among the books was one which featured Digger Dan, a mechanical crane which performed magnificent feats in building skyscrapers, befriending little boys, and treating small trucks kindly. Digger Dan had animated features, talked, and did many other things unlikely in the behavior of mechanical cranes. Bobby was especially fond of playing with trucks, cars, and road equipment toys, and was always fascinated by the Digger Dan story. Bobby's follow-up to his story of where he had gotten the truck seems an attempt to say to his mother that his story was no wilder than those of the books at his school; if cranes could talk, then big trucks could make little trucks. In nursery school, Bobby played with trucks, big and little, and entertained his friends at play time with stories of fantasy about the escapades of his trucks, many of them fashioned after Digger Dan. At both nursery school and in play, Bobby could suspend reality and create trucks that flew, talked, and produced other trucks.

Before they enter nursery school (usually at age four), Roadville children have had relatively little exposure to extended prose fictive or fanciful stories, either told or read to them. They have also not been allowed to tell stories, except those which they recite in accordance with adult coaching. The nursery school, however, provides a wide variety of books about fanciful characters doing preposterous deeds, and the children themselves are often asked to tell stories. Nursery school teachers do not follow the story-telling norms of the Roadville community, but instead they begin rehears-ing the preschoolers for the book-reading and story-telling experi-ences of the school. As nursery school teachers read from books, they guide the children through the story: "Who is this (pointing to a picture of the main character)?" "What do you think is going to happen?"[6] Questions, gestures, announcements of links be-tween text and illustrations in the book, and reinforcement of teachers' story-reading with TV programs, records, or songs repeatedly present the children with fictive characters whose behaviors do not follow real-world constraints.

Yet when the children are asked to tell stories, they do not volunteer tales of fictive characters doing fanciful deeds. Only if a certain frame for asserting a departure from reality is introduced do the children move into creative fictive stories. Children build such a frame for these stories either by announcing "Let's pretend" or "Let's make-believe," or by establishing what they are saying as part of *play*. Only in situations where they have released themselves from the need to stick to the facts and to tell the truth do preschool Roadville children tell fictive stories, exaggerate real-life events, draw in TV characters or events, and create their own combinations of events, objects, and causes and effects.

As long as children do not hit, throw sand, cause excessive noise, or destroy property, Roadville adults usually do not intervene in their play; thus even at home, children get away with using fanciful stories in their play. Flights of fantasy in play often occur in their role-playing of adults; therefore, such stories may more appropriately be viewed as sociodramas than as stories.[7] They are punctuated with props, exaggerated gestures, facial expressions, and usually take place in settings children have transformed by announcing them as something or somewhere else. Boys play in sandboxes or in other backyard locations declared by them to be specific settings; in these appropriately named scenes, they play at being fishermen, mechanics, heavy equipment drivers, firemen, policemen, etc. They also play at being monsters, flying saucers, and Buck Rogers. Girls designate areas of the yard or their room to be kitchens, churches, stores, bedrooms, etc., and in these places, they pretend to be mothers, babies, church leaders, "fancy ladies," and experts in other female-dominated activities. They also play at being monsters, Wonder Woman, and wild animals, but their extreme flights into fantasy are less frequent and boisterous than those of the boys.

In their play, the children tell stories to each other or they monologue their creations. They frame parts of the whole drama of adulthood in sandboxes, corners of the playroom, or the play yard. But there they also declare themselves members of the world of children and members of a community which does not let its members ever go too far or too long away from the constraints of reality. For example, four-year-old Danny in the sandbox behind the church played out the following sociodrama during nursery school. Friends who were playing about him paid no attention to his monologue until he drew them all into a shared real-world experience.

> This my bi:g truck /*displays truck to all around him, circling it through the air*/
> It go all up, up, up /*makes upward swing with truck in air, then down in corner of sandbox*/
> Then down, down, down /*digs truck into sand*/
> |:My truck lose a tire
>   My truck lose a tire:|
> Jimmy come on his dozer /*reaches with one hand over to bulldozer in far corner of sandbox*/
> All the little ones help /*pulls bulldozer up to truck, now buried in corner of sandbox*/
> And they all fly away /*takes his truck up in air in swinging motion*/ Way up in the sky, sky
> Get oil, cookies, bird feathers, and (pause) (giggles and laughs) do-do-do
> //*Some other children nearby stop and listen*//
> Jimmy, Jimmy, Jimmy, Jimmy, bird do-do on Jimmy, do-do-do-do (other children begin to laugh)

In this story–sociodrama Danny sometimes forced the players (the truck and the bulldozer) to do as the story said; he and Jimmy became truck drivers who fixed flat tires, and when the truck needed help, the bulldozer came. In other portions of the story, he ignored reality constraints and let the words of the story transform the truck into a flying vehicle. In the final portion of the story, he had the truck in the air, mentioned bird feathers, seemed to think then of bird droppings, and began to giggle and laugh. Others stopped their play to listen and laugh. Here Danny not only used a taboo word, *do-do*, but he also told about a real event, one in which they had all participated. Jimmy was not around today, but earlier in the week, he had been playing outside with a blue jacket on, and a bird had flown over, leaving droppings on his jacket. This was cause for greater glee among the children when one of them discovered it, and Danny's fanciful story ends when he takes his truck into the air, thinks of meeting birds, and remembers Jimmy's episode earlier in the week.

The mixture of fictive and nonfictive in stories associated with play is also illustrated in the following story told by four-year-old

Sally. She was fingering a flat smooth rock from a pile of stones in the nature corner, when her nursery school teacher asked her to tell her a story. Sally lowered her head and said nothing. She fidgeted, obviously uncomfortable, and continued fingering the rock. The teacher asked if she would like to draw a face on the rock. Sally looked relieved for the change of focus, and registered keen interest. Once the teacher had drawn a smiling face and big ears on the rock, Sally picked it up and began playing with it, talking as she moved away from the teacher.

Bump, bump, bump /*making rock hop along the book counter*/
Eeeeeee, a bug, /*putting rock down, twisting it, lifting it, and looking unpleasant*/
All pooo /*making a face as though sight under rock was unpleasant*/
Mamma /*holding rock suspended*/
Gotta ant, ant, /*putting rock back on counter ahead of imaginary ugly spot*/ skeeee
Bump, bump, /*making rock hop along book counter*/ bump
Bump, bump, bump
Can at you house? [Do you have a spraycan at your house?] /*looking toward teacher*/
Go happy, my rock meet a friend,
Ice cream, candy, red shoe, (pause) didja ever have ants?

A few days earlier, there had been a trail of ants in Sally's yard, and her mother had sprayed them with poison from a spray can. Sally, in the story-sociodrama produced once she had a prop in hand, gave the rock a bumping action which re-enacted her own efforts to stomp on the ants. She combined the fictive and the real, equating the rock's bumping up and down with her own foot stomping, but also making the rock a caricature of someone who had friends, ice cream, candy, and red shoes. When the teacher did not answer Sally's question about having a (spray)can at her house, Sally returned to the topic of ants and ended her story–sociodrama a few lines later.

The constraints of reality enter into the play which accompanies these story-sociodramas in yet other ways. Once the children have announced a suspension of reality by declaring a sandbox a city, a rock a little girl, or a playroom corner a kitchen, they paradoxically more often than not insist on a strict adherence to certain details of real-life behavior. In playing with doll babies, girls insist they are not dressed unless a diaper is pinned about them. Children in a play kitchen will break their routine of washing dishes by reaching over to shake a frying pan or to stir the contents of a pot on the stove. When asked why they do this, they reply "Hit'll burn." The insistence on adherence to reality occurs most frequently in those activities in which the children – especially girls – have taken part in real-life: helping with baby brothers or sisters, standing on a stool and helping wash dishes or cook, or helping put a wriggling worm on a fishing line.

The demand for reality (in the form of consistency in presentations) occurs also when children hear retellings of stories which have been read to them in nursery school. Dialogue must be reported exactly as it has been read repeatedly from the book or produced on the commercial recording of the story. A nursery school teacher telling the story of "The Three Little Bears" changed the wording of the bears' complaints about Goldilocks in one retelling, and a chorus of children stopped her to provide the complaints as they were usually given in the story. Similarly, items or events, once named in the nursery school routine, must retain this label consistently. If a substitute teacher invites the children to come "play with clay" when they are accustomed to having an invitation to "work with playdough" they correct the newcomer. Even among themselves, children often disagree about whether someone has said something one way or another.

Thus into their play, Roadville children carry their parents' requirements for using language: report exactly how something is said, maintain a single consistent label for items and events, and render stories in absolute chronological order with direct discourse. They even sometimes correct their parents when they think they have not observed these requirements. Their own preschool years are filled with constant reminders of the need to attend to auditory details and to imitate these. For children, the learning to detail names and features of the environment and to recapitulate accurately past events is marked by boundaries and limits their parents establish very firmly in their preschool years. These aspects of language learning and story-telling in particular are reinforced in many of the community's church-related practices and on other occasions when adults tell stories on themselves or each other. In other words, the expectations of children's stories and story-telling interactions continue to be called for in the adult world of the community. Yet practices and values at nursery school differ greatly from those learned in the preschool experiences. Though the nursery school is usually held in community churches and taught by some community women, the materials and methods of handling stories at school do not fit with those of the home. Roadville parents and teachers appear to see no conflict between the expectations of the home and church and those of the nursery school and the formal education system ahead. It is as though the school is not expected to link with or reinforce the norms of story-telling in the home, church, and community.

In Trackton

Talkin' junk

Trackton folks see the truth and the facts in stories in ways which differ greatly from those of Roadville. Good story-tellers in Trackton may base their stories on an actual event, but they creatively fictionalize the details surrounding the real event, and the outcome of the story may not even resemble what indeed happened. The best stories are "junk," and anyone who can "talk junk" is a good story-teller. Talkin' junk includes laying on highly exaggerated compliments and making wildly exaggerated comparisons as well as telling narratives. Straightforward factual accounts are relatively rare in Trackton and are usually told only on serious occasions: to give a specific piece of information to someone who has requested it, to provide an account of the troubles of a highly respected individual, or to exchange information about daily rounds of activities when neither party wishes to intensify the interaction or draw it out. Trackton's "stories," on the other hand, are intended to intensify social interactions and to give all parties an opportunity to share in not only the unity of the common experience on which the story may be based, but also in the humor of the wide-ranging language play and imagination which embellish the narrative.

From a very early age, Trackton children learn to appreciate the value of a good story for capturing an audience's attention or winning favors. Boys, especially on those occasions when they are teased or challenged in the plaza, hear their antics become the basis of exaggerated tales told by adults and older children to those not present at the time of the challenge. Children hear themselves made into characters in stories told again and again. They hear adults use stories from the Bible or from their youth to scold or warn against misbehavior. The mayor captures the boys' conflict in the story of King Solomon which features a chain of events and resolution of a conflict similar to that in which they are currently engaged (see Trackton Text 1). Children's misdeeds provoke the punchline or summing up of a story which they are not told, but are left to imagine: "Dat póliceman'll come 'n git you, like he did Frog." The story behind this summary is never told, but is held out as something to be recreated anew in the imagination of every child who hears this threat.

Trackton children can create and tell stories about themselves, but they must be clever if they are to hold the audience's attention and to maintain any extended conversational space in an on-going discourse. Young children repeatedly try to break into adult discourse with a story, but if they do not succeed in relating the first few lines of their story to the on-going topic or otherwise exciting the listeners' interests, they are ignored. An adult's accusation, on the other hand, gives children an open stage for creating a story, but this one must also be "good," i.e. highly exaggerated, skillful in language play, and full of satisfactory comparisons to redirect the adult's attention from the infraction provoking the accusation.

Adults and older siblings do not make up sustained chronological narratives specially for young children, and adults do not read to young children. The flow of time in Trackton, which admits few scheduled blocks of time for routinized activities, does not lend itself to a bedtime schedule of reading a story. The homes provide barely enough space for the necessary activities of family living, and there is no separate room, book corner, or even outdoor seat where a child and parent can read together out of the constant flow of human interactions. The stage of the plaza almost always offers live action and is tough competition for book-reading. Stories exchanged among adults do not carry moral summaries or admonitions about behavior; instead they focus on detailing of events and personalities, and they stress conflict and resolution or attempts at resolution. Thus adults see no reason to direct these stories to children for teaching purposes. When stories are told among adults, young children are not excluded from the audience, even if the content refers to adult affairs, sexual exploits, crooked politicians, drunk ministers, or wayward choirleaders. If children respond to such stories with laughter or verbal comments, they are simply warned to "keep it to yo'self." Some adult stories are told only in sex-segregated situations. Men recount to their buddies stories they would not want their wives or the womenfolk to know about; women share with each other stories of quarrels with their menfolk or other women. Many men know about formulaic toasts (long epic-like accounts of either individual exploits or struggles of black people) from visitors from up-North or men returned from the armed services, but these are clearly external to the Trackton man's repertoire, and they do not come up in their social gatherings.[8] Instead, Trackton men and their friends focus on stories which tell of their own current adventures or recount fairly recent adventures of particular personalities known to all present. All of these are highly self-assertive or extol the strength and cleverness of specific individuals.

Women choose similar topics for their stories: events which have happened to them, things they have seen, or events they have heard about. Considerable license is taken with these stories, however, and each individual is expected to tell the story, not as she has heard it, but with her own particular style. Women tell stories of their exploits at the employment office, adventures at work in the mill, or episodes in the lives of friends, husbands, or mutual acquaintances. Laced through with evaluative comments ("Didja ever hear of such a thing?" "You know how he ak [act] when he drunk." "You been like dat."), the stories invite parti-cipation from listeners. In fact, such participation is necessary reinforcement for the story-teller. Perhaps the most characteristic feature of story-telling by adults is the dramatic use of dialogue. Dovie Lou told the following story one afternoon to a group of six women sitting on the porch of Lillie Mae's house. The Henning family was transient and had been in Trackton only a few weeks.

TRACKTON TEXT V

Now you know me – I'm Dovie Lou, and you may think I'ma put up wid that stuff off Hennin's ol' lady, right? Who, who, after all, gives a hoot about her – or him, for dat matter? I been here quite a while – gonna be here a time yet too. She holler off her porch "Yo man, he over in Darby Sat'day nite." I say "Shit, what you know 'bout my man? My man." It was a rainy night, you know ain't no use gettin' fussied up to go out on a night like dat. Tessie 'n I go play bingo. But dat ol' woman, she ak like she some Channel Two reporter or sump'n:

"P.B. Evans was seen today on the corner of Center and Main Street. He hadda bottle in each hip pocket, and one under his Lóndon Fóg hat. Sadie Lou [a well-known stripper in a local topless bar] was helpin' him across the street, holin' her white mink in front of him to keep his shíny shoes from gettin' wet. The weather tomorrow promises to be cloudy for some."

What she think she doin', tellin' *me/looks around to audience/*'bout my ol' man? Sayin' "He lookin' mighty fine, yes sireeeeee." (long pause) She betta keep/*casting a sharp look in the direction of the Hennings' house/*her big mouf 'n stay shut up in dat house.

Throughout the story, the audience laughed, nodded, and provided "yeah," "you right," "you know it." Dovie Lou's shift to the exaggerated Standard English of the Channel Two reporter brought gales of laughter from the audience.

Numerous cultural assertions are made in the story. The evaluative introduction establishes Dovie Lou as an oldtimer, a fixture in the neighborhood, and Henning and his old lady as relative newcomers. Dovie Lou announces herself a victor before the story begins. Later, she makes it clear that she knew her man, P. B. Evans, was out that night, and that she had had a chance to go out with him, but had decided it was not worth getting "fussied up" to go out in the rain. Instead, she and a girlfriend had gone to play bingo. She uses the TV report to show exaggeration, to report her man out with a famous stripper, and also to brag about the fancy dress of her man who wears name-brand clothes and has a reputation for keeping himself "fine." The final point of the story asserts that her animosity to the Henning woman is not over. Dovie Lou warns that the newcomer should stay inside and not join the neighborhood women on their porches. Once Dovie Lou's anger wears off or she is reunited with her man publicly, she can fend off Henning's wife's stories. Dovie Lou's story is based on fact: Henning's wife had said something to Dovie Lou about her man being out with another woman. But beyond this basis in fact, Dovie Lou's story is highly creative, and she ranges far from the true facts to tell a story which extols her strengths and announces her faith in her ultimate victory over both her wayward man and her "big-mouth" neighbor.

Children telling stories to community audiences follow many of the same patterns as those used by Dovie Lou. They may base their stories on rivalry over objects or people, but their primary messages are of accomplishments, victories over adversity, or cleverness in the face of a mutually recognized enemy. Many of the children's stories include the same stylistic devices Dovie Lou used. For example, they may incorporate a television character adapted to fit the story's needs. Sometimes such characters comment on or evaluate the story's action, as the Channel Two reporter did in Dovie Lou's story; at other times, fantasy characters, such as Spider Man or Bat Man, may actually come to the rescue of the story's hero. Children's stories, like Dovie Lou's, are based on a real-life event, but they report the event with exaggeration, a twist of results, and free expression of their feelings about the story's events.

Between the ages of two and four years, Trackton children, in a monologue-like fashion, tell stories about things in their lives, events they see and hear, and situations in which they have been involved. They produce these spontaneously during play with other children or in the presence of an adult. Sometimes they make an effort to attract the attention of listeners before they begin the story, but often they do not. Lem, playing off the edge of the porch, when he was about two and a half years of age, heard a bell in the distance. He stopped, looked at Nellie and Benjy who were nearby and said:

Way
|:Far
Now|
It a church bell
Ringin'
Dey singing'
    ringin'
You hear it?
I hear it|
Far
Now:|

Lem had been taken to church the previous Sunday and had been much impressed by the church bell. He had sat on Lillie Mae's lap and joined in the singing, rocking to and fro on her lap, and clapping his hands. His story, which is poem-like in form, is in response to the stimulus of a distant bell.[9] This kind of story-poem, in which children describe an event or item in a series of verse-like utterances, is characteristic of Trackton's preschoolers. On this occasion, Nellie and Benjy stopped and listened to Lem's story and returned to their play with no comment.

This story, somewhat longer than those usually reported from other social groups for children as young as Lem,[10] has some features which have come to characterize fully developed narratives or stories. It recapitulates in its verbal outline the sequence of events being recalled by the story-teller.[11] At church, the bell rang while the people sang. In the line "It a church bell," Lem provides his story's topic, and a brief summary of what is to come. This line serves a function similar to the formula often used by older children to open a story: "This is a story about [a church bell]." Lem gives only the slightest hint of story setting or orientation to the listener; where and when the story took place are encapsulated in "Way. Far." Preschoolers in Trackton almost never hear "Once upon a time there was a—" stories, and they rarely provide definitive orientations for their stories. They seem to assume listeners "know" the situation in which the narrative takes place. Similarly, preschoolers in Trackton do not close off their stories with formulaic endings. Lem poetically balances his opening and closing in an *inclusio*, beginning "Way/ Far/ Now/" and ending "Far/ Now/" The effect is one of closure, but there is no clear-cut announcement of closure. Throughout the presentation of action and result of action in their stories, Trackton preschoolers invite the audience to respond or evaluate the story's actions. Lem asks "You hear it?" which may refer either to the current stimulus or to yesterday's bell, since Lem does not productively use past tense endings for any verbs at this stage in his language development.

Preschool story-tellers have several ways of inviting audience evaluation and interest. They may themselves express an emotional response to the story's actions; they may have another character or narrator in the story do so, often using alliterative language play; or they may detail actions and results through direct discourse or sound effects and gestures. Trackton children particularly use the latter means to insure that their story-performance attracts attention on the plaza stage. All these methods of calling attention to the story and its telling distinguish the speech event as a story, an occasion for audience and story-teller to interact pleasantly, and not simply to hear an ordinary recounting of events or actions.

Teegie, at about two years of age, illustrated some of these features of story-telling in the following story-poem. He had not seen me in a few days, and he recounted a story of a big event in his life which had occurred the previous Friday during the exchange of gifts.

Up /*pointing high up*/	Orientation	by	gesture
Way up dere	Evaluation	by	detailing of attributes
All time up			
Tony	Actor		
Choogie got it	Actor + Action		
|:All up dere/*spinning around with his arms high up in the air*/	Evaluation/Result	by	gesture + detailing of attributes
All up dere:|	Result/Coda	by	repetition and poetic balance to opening

The situation being recounted is Tony's taking away a container of potato chips from Teegie. In the Friday gift distribution, Teegie had gotten the container, but he refused to share. Tony (nicknamed Choogie by Teegie) took the chips and held them above Teegie's head so he could not get them. Finally, Teegie's mother intervened and put the container on top of the stove, "way up," the place in the house where all forbidden things were kept, since it was the only area inaccessible to small children. The meaning of the story-poem is not immediately evident to someone unfamiliar with the Friday gift distribution, Teegie's fondness for potato chips, the ambiguous norms of sharing, and the rarity of occasions when adults put things out of the reach of children. Once these pieces of background knowledge are known, Teegie does provide an orientation to the story by pointing out that the result of the action was to have the potato chips put up, away from him. He evaluates this action by "Way up dere. All time up." He then names the actor and major action. He finishes off his story-poem by varying his opening lines in a twice-repeated utterance. Throughout the story, Teegie's gestures add meaning to the story and enable him to re-enact parts of the event being recounted.

Lem, a better story-teller than Teegie on most occasions, uses alliterative narrator-type comments in his story-poems, plus gestures, sound effects, and emotional evaluations. A favorite topic of his stories is the train which passes the end of the plaza numerous times each day. There are no longer any passenger trains on the line, only freight trains, and they are often long and loaded with a wide variety of items. Young children are forbidden to go near the end of the plaza toward the tracks, but from the midst of the plaza, they can see the train go by. The older children often walk up and down the tracks in going back and forth to the city center. One warm sunny afternoon, Lem (aged three) was playing in the center of the plaza as a train came by. He stopped playing, watched the train, then turned to a group of adults and children who were nearby.

Track?
Can't go to |:de track
                dat track
        to   dat train track:|
|:Big train on de track
  Tony down by de track:|
  Mamma git 'im
|:Track
  Train track:|
  He come back.

Tony had been at the track the day before and Lem had tried to follow. When he was scolded, he had become highly indignant that he was not allowed to follow his older brother. When Lem told the story, he was given little attention by any of those in the group he approached. Though highly alliterative and filled with repetitions of variations of "train track," the story-poem was said in a pouting manner, with little of Lem's usual animation. This was atypical of the story-poems of good verbal performers such as Lem and older preschoolers, for they had usually learned that verbal elaboration and exaggeration of detail plus nonverbal embellishments could win over an audience. For example, Benjy was generally a highly successful story-teller who made use of all these strategies. The occasion of Teegie's getting a new "bicycle" (a big-wheeled tricycle) and his attempts to learn to control it brought forth several good story performances from Benjy (aged five). One of these follows:

Zoom,/*racing part-way down the hill of the plaza, and then falling down*/zoom, zoom, zoom, zoom, zoom, zoom, zoom, zoom, zoom, zoom

Ethnographer learning

Hi ay,/*walking back up the hill, as though he were on a tottering bicycle*/hi ay, ay, ay, ay, ay, ay, ay
Teegie got/*continuing to trudge up the hill with exaggerated motions of a tired old man*/
|:a bike
 a new bike
 a bike to ride:|
See Teegie bike?

Benjy then repeated the entire story-poem, complete with all gestures and movements, this time reversing the opening lines:

Hi ay,/*tottering part-way down the hill*/hi ay, ay, ay, ay, ay, ay, ay
Zoom,/*racing the rest of the way down the hill*/zoom, zoom, zoom, zoom, zoom, zoom, zoom, zoom, zoom, zoom, zoom
Teegie got/*walking proud and high back up the hill*/|: a bike
                                                        a new bike
                                                        a bike to ride,
                                                        ride, ride:|

Benjy was, in the opening section, imitating Teegie trying to race down the hill, turning over, then getting up and trying the bike more slowly. Teegie walked his bike back up the plaza hill, tried it again, this time slowly at first, and ended in a victorious flourish of a zooming motorcycle. The repetition with variation of "a bike, a new bike, a bike to ride" is reminiscent of the patterning used in the early stages of combining words and is also similar to variations found in the playsongs and stories of older children.

Learning how to talk junk

The stories of young children and the insults and playsongs of older children are similar in several ways. The structuring of repetitions with variations in both of these resembles patterns in adults' narratives (see Trackton Text II, for example). To understand any of these, one must have some prior knowledge of the situation being recounted and must accept the ritualized routine of the performance as having meaning in the context of community life. Descriptions of ritualized insults, such as playing the dozens, sounding and riddling, among black children have emphasized that listeners make sense of these only by knowing both background meanings and intentions.[12] These elaborate word games, played by older children, parallel the type of verbal play, social interactional style, and treatment of themes which children who become successful story-tellers in Trackton learn to use.

On the plaza, school-age boys and girls model a wide range of methods of verbal play, imaginative exaggeration, and ways to vary treatment of themes in their exchanges of insults and playsongs. When a ballgame or other play breaks into an altercation, the children either fuss or shout playsong-like insults at each other. Most of these include "mamma" or other members of the family and focus on personal characteristics or behaviors. Some are chanted in a sing-song pattern; others are simply shouted. Those which are chanted have a four-beat rhythm.[13]

TRACKTON TEXT VI* (boys and girls 9–12)

> Yó' má, yó má
> Yo' gréasy gréasy grán' má
> Got skínny légs 'n fát behín'
> Enúf to scáre ol' Fránkenstéin
>
> Yóu gót a úgly héad
> Yóu néed sóme cornbréad
>
> Yóu kin róll yó' éyes
> But you cáin't contról yó' síze
>
> Shé so méan,
> Shé like Méan Jóe Gréen [a football player for a national team]

Both two-liners and four-line verses often have either internal or end rhyme, and spontaneous creations which have such rhyme are most likely to be picked up and used again and again by other children. When preschoolers first begin to mock verbally the behavior of their aggressors, there is great audience mirth, and enthusiastic response. They soon begin mocking their challengers by repeating the insults they hear older children use to each other. Young children, because of the extraordinary latitude they have in taking on varying roles and related language uses, can toss these insults out to community members, old and young. Thus they have numerous occasions for testing the degrees of approval insults of different form and content receive. Clever language play (rhyme, alliteration, etc.) plus skillful manipulation of content score the highest response from the audience.

Children experiment with these insults, usually by the age of three years. Sometimes they are successful, sometimes not. Benjy was especially persistent in trying his own versions of insults; but he was late in grasping the fact that some characteristics of individuals were appropriate for mocking, and others were not.

Yo' daddy have false teef. (3 years, 6 months)
Yo' daddy name Brer. (3 years, 8 months)
Yo' daddy mamma eat po'k 'n beans. (4 years)
Yo' mamma wear combat boots. (4 years, 2 months)
Yo' mamma wear army drawers. (4 years, 8 months)
Yo' mamma wear a batman cape. (5 years)
Yo' mamma name Frankenstein. (5 years, 2 months)

Only gradually did Benjy come to recognize which characteristics would be incongruous or appropriate for a ritualized, not a personal, insult to a mamma or daddy. False teeth and adult nicknames such as Brer were neither uncommon nor incongruous; mammas wearing combat boots and named Frankenstein were both.[14] Benjy, by the age of four, was consistently able to choose the correct content for the ridicule in his one-liners.

Before they go to school, children rarely create two-liners. The following from Benjy (5 years, 6 months) is a rare example, but it shows his level of control of both content and end-rhyme.

> Yóu, snággle-toof mónster, yóu,
> Becáuse you éat a rótten shóe. (said in a sing-song chant)

Benjy seemingly forces an effect on the verse, however, because he simply says the first line, almost as a one-liner, and then chants the second line. Though shoes are not often described as rotten in the community, Benjy has captured the insult power of accusing someone of eating rotten food (suggesting he is so poor he has nothing else), and he has made a causal connection between eating shoes and being snaggle-toothed.

At school, children hear many two-line insults, and boys especially acquire very quickly a much more extensive repertoire of these than they have in Trackton. Soon after they are settled in school, they begin bringing home their own two-liners. These always contain some rhyme, but they do not always successfully create a sense of the ridiculous or nonsensical. The rhyming requirements of two-liners seem to be learned earlier in the primary school years than are appropriate patterns of content for insults.[15] By the second grade, Benjy brought home the following couplets. No doubt, he had heard them at school, and he had mixed several to make some of his own creations. The following were, however, all newly introduced to Trackton by Benjy.

> Nóbody fíddle
> Wid de óreo míddle. [a well-known school adaptation of a
> television commercial]

> Héy fiddle díddle, de mán in de míddle
> Wid de twó chéeks ón de síde. [portions of several insult verses
> combined]

> Shít, Gód damn
> Git off yó' áss 'n jám. [a "classic" among older primary-school
> children]

> You ríde my áss [probably a line out of an older student's
> conversation Benjy adopted]
> I stéal yo' páss.

These last verses illustrate Benjy's efforts to incorporate "dirty words," taboo terms, into his verbal play. The one-liners below were among his earliest efforts; these were all brought home within the first school term.

My mámma ain't fúck Móther Góose.
Yó' mamma gót a bíg áss.

Within the community, these do not receive particular reinforcement from adults. By the time they begin school, children are challenged for verbal dueling much less frequently by community adults than they are in their preschool years. Preschool occasions for verbal play and witty lighthearted exchanges between child and adult become more and more rare as children get older. Once a child begins school, adults lose interest in him as a partner for verbal challenge, and preschoolers coming along behind him in the community take his place on the plaza's stage.

School-age peers become the reinforcers for the use of these insults, and they acclaim and denounce certain types of insults in a developmental sequence of acceptability. In the earliest school years, children laugh, giggle, and act appropriately mock-shocked at any one-liner with taboo words. One-liners receive little reinforcement without these taboo words. Two-liners or four-line verses with rhyme, but with little punch in terms of insult, usually bring approval; those with both rhyme and insult are sure to win a direct announcement or gesture of praise if directed to a child higher in peer ranking, and an abdication by silent retreat if directed to a peer of equal or lesser rank. Boys engage in these verbal challenges at the bus stop, on the bus, and in the playground at school when they are certain they cannot be heard by school authorities. The use of these insults becomes most intense in the upper primary grades and junior high school (12–15 years). By the time the boys reach high school (15–18 years), they rarely use verbal challenges to establish and maintain status relations. Instead they use sports, direct challenges to a particular display of skill (for example, in a pool game), or direct physical confrontation. Verbal play appears to be viewed as the game of young boys, those who have neither the freedom of access to places suitable for direct challenges of skill or physical prowess nor the courage for them.

Among girls, many features found in boys' insults appear in their assertions of challenge and mockery in both insults and playsongs. During the early primary grades, girls rarely engage in insults through one-liners, couplets, or verses. Instead, they become apprentices of a sort to girls in the older grades who teach them playsongs which contain many linguistic and social features of insults. At school, certain groups of black girls, aged nine to twelve years, become known as performers, and at every possible opportunity, they segregate themselves to use their playsongs in jump-rope or hand-clap games. These playsongs carry generalized messages of mockery and assertion and tell of experiences the girls seem to see as their own. White girls or mixed groups never sing playsongs of the following type; these are performed only in all-black groups. They are chanted with a clear, four-beat rhythm.

TRACKTON TEXT VII*

> Sar dínes, wóo, 'n po'k 'n béans, wóo
> Sar dínes, wóo, 'n po'k 'n béans, wóo
> I kin téll by yo' héad
> Dat ya éat cornbréad

Sar dínes, wóo, 'n po'k 'n béans, wóo
Sar dínes, wóo, 'n po'k 'n béans, wóo
I kin téll by yo' híp
Dat you eat potáto chíp
Sar dínes, wóo, 'n po'k 'n béans, wóo
Sar dínes, wóo, 'n po'k 'n béans, wóo
I got stéak in my pláte
'n I júst cain't wáit
I got bóogers in my éyes
'n I don't táke no jíve
Sar dínes, wóo, 'n po'k 'n béans, wóo
Sar dínes, wóo, 'n po'k 'n béans, wóo

Several chunks of the language often included in insults (cf. Benjy's one-liner "Yo' mamma eat po'k 'n beans," and the couplet rhyming "head" and "cornbread") also appear in the playsongs. Throughout this playsong, foods associated with poverty – sardines, pork and beans, and cornbread – carry a message of what may be taken as mockery and ridicule from the speaker: you eat cornbread; sardines and pork and beans are pervasive in your life; I eat steak, and "I don't take no jive." The message is twofold: insult to listener and assertion of speaker's strength. Telling experiences – the eating of certain foods, participation in getting the spirit at church, having babies, playing the fool, and overcoming obstacles – appear again and again in these playsongs.

Girls usually come to use pieces of the language of playsongs in their one-liners, couplets, or verses by the time they are in the upper primary grades. However, in any serious challenge of peer relations, especially between girls from different communities, a physical confrontation is preferred over verbal challenges. The latter are usually reserved for challenges between friends or between girls for whom there is no serious confrontation in status relations. By the junior high school years, the girls stop performing the playsongs entirely. They seem to be regarded as child's play, and the older girls will participate in them only occasionally when they correct or comment on the performance of younger girls in their own community. However, at the junior and senior high levels, the girls transfer the skills they used in the playsongs and insults to cheers they make up for their school teams. The desegregation of schools and the closing of all-black schools cut off the major opportunity for the creation and performance of these cheers, though occasionally they can still be heard in all-black neighborhood functions. A few have been transferred into use by mixed cheerleading squads in the desegregated junior and senior high schools. Occasionally, a group of black cheerleaders from the mixed squad will perform one of the cheers formerly used in the all-black schools. These cheers are accompanied by more and different kinds of steps and hand-clapping routines than are the cheers performed by the entire squad. Often only black students in the crowd respond to these cheers.

> Óne, twó, three, four, fíve
> Hárlem Héights don't táke no jíve
> Síx séven, eight, nine tén
> Táke it úp 'n dó it agáin

> Say héy, hey, héy, héy, hey, héy
> Whát y gót-ta-say, whát ya gót-ta-say
> Whát ya gót-ta-say, whát ya gót-ta-say
> Sáy [name of school] (drawn out over three beats)
> Dey are súper (drawn out over three beats)*

Immediately following *super*, a complicated clap and kick routine begins which continues for almost a minute. The entire cheer is repeated twice. The clapped ending the second time is the same as the first, with the exception of the final two measures, which provide a coda-type ending and final flourish. The following cheer has a similar pattern.

> Thúnder, thúnder, thúnderátion
> Wé de dévil's délegátion
> Wé de ríght cómbinátion
> Wé creáte a sénsátion
> Thúnder, thúnder, thúnderátion*

In this cheer, the five-line stanza given is punctuated by a syncopation of hand-clap and stomp which reinforces the four-beat measure of each line. The stanza given above is repeated three times; the final repetition ends with a giant jump and a shout to *THUNDER*.[16]

Within these cheers, the strategies of insult, mockery, and assertion children use in insults and playsongs appear. The central message is one of victory, overcoming the adversary. Though these insults, playsongs, and cheers are not stories, they do provide opportunities for both boys and girls to practice the strategies and performance skills which good story-tellers must have in Trackton. These include:

word play (including rhyming, alliteration);
gestures and sound effects;
extensive use of metaphors and similes;
suggestion of behavioral and social attributes through re-peated use of a single lexical item (po'k 'n beans = poverty);
involvement of public media figures (such as Spider Man).

"Sayin' it short" or wrapping description in lively but pithy statements characterizes good insults, playsongs, and "talkin' junk" in Trackton. Just as insults, playsongs, and cheers report strength in conflict, facility in struggle, and an ability to vary ways of defeating one's adversaries, so do good stories. In many ways, stories in both their form and content reflect the linguistic and role-playing lessons learned from an early age on the stage of Trackton's plaza.

Once they are in school, both boys and girls bring together the play with language and the experiences of knowing and feeling their preschool language learning has taught them. They continue to practice these skills and strategies in their peer language play. Twelve-year-old Terry, the son of one of Trackton's transients, told the following story to a group of boys after his first week in a new school.

TRACKTON TEXT VIII

You don't know me, but you will. I'm Terry Moore. You might think I look sissy, sittin' in dat class ackin' like I'm working, you know. But I'm de tough one around here, and I done been down to Mr. — office more'n you can count. You know, I'm de onliest one what can stand up to dat paddle of his. He burn me up. I'ma tell you 'bout dat (pause). One day I was walkin' down de hall, now you ain't 'posed to do dat, 'less'n you got a pass, and I ain't had no pass on my ass. And all of a sudden I hear somebody comin', and dere was a feelin' like my ass was caught for sure. And it was Mr. —, and he come roun' de corner like he knowed I was dere. I took out runnin' (pause) now don't ever run 'less'n you know you don't hafta stop. Dat was my mistake. It was good while it lasted. I run all the way down Main, but my feet 'n legs start hurtin' and then I got me a strain, but den a power like Spider Man, and I look back, and dis web fall all over Mr. —, and he struggle (pause), and he struggle (pause), and he struggle. 'n den dis big old roach [cockroach] come outta de walls of dem ol' buildings on Main, and that roach start eatin' his head (pause), his fingers (pause), 'n his toes (pause) 'n he holler, 'n he holler, 'n I come to de end of Main, and I stop to watch.

"Hey Terry lis'n, hep me."

"Yea, I hep you, you gonna do what I say?"

"I do it, I do it. Just get me óutta here."

I just hold my sides laughing, and him getting madder and madder. So after I had me a good laugh, I go,

"You gonna burn dat paddle úp?"

He go,

"You can háve it, you can háve it."

So I let 'im up, and call off dat roach and dat spider web, and we went back to school. But he didn't do what he say. He git me, 'n he took dat paddle to me, and to' [tore] me up (long pause). But somewhere out dere, old Spider Man, he know I'm takin' it for him, and he hep me out next time.

In this story, Terry has shown that he learned to "talk junk" well.

His story contains some internal rhyme (*pass, ass, Main, strain*), taboo words, similes, items associated with poverty (roach), and involvement of an outside agent of assistance – Spider Man. Terry suggests that the principal, once out of his own territory and onto Main (one of the most run-down sections of town), has no strength to overcome the forces there. The roach attacks, and the principal becomes Terry's victim, begging for help. Terry extols his own virtues – strength, wit, and wisdom. He offers some direct advice from a newcomer, showing he knows the school rules:

you have to have a pass in the school hall;
don't run away unless you are sure you can outrun your pursuer.

He also offers more subtle messages, showing he knows some rules which are not often explicitly stated: kids almost always get caught, and when a kid gets caught, he takes it like a man. Terry makes clear his undaunted spirit in spite of what may sound like defeat at the hands of the principal and abandonment by Spider Man.

Terry's story includes two double entendres. The first is in the principal's response "You can have it," and Terry does "get it" in the end. The second is his own in the question "You gonna burn dat paddle up?" The principal does "let him have it" and does "burn dat paddle up," but at Terry's expense. As children, especially boys, get older, their insults, playsongs, and stories carry numerous examples of double entendre: harmless references on the surface, but heavily suggestive – often of sexual references. Boys delight in watching listeners to see if they catch both the literal and suggested meanings of certain expressions. Teachers and other authority figures are usually helpless either to respond to or to punish for these.

Terry's tale illustrates a type of story in which boys especially excel – the performance of a "true story" in which they "talk junk." In these, the story-teller is usually the star, and he gives highly detailed exaggerated accounts of his adventure. He gestures wildly, contorts his face, grunts, groans, and offers other dramatizations of the story's actions. The story may highlight the ridiculous, but it often also provides illustration of the hard lessons of life the story-teller and the audience share. Terry remains undaunted in spite of the unhappy ending to his story, and he shows, both through his story and presumably in his real struggles in the new school, that he knows the principal will have to continue to believe he, not Terry, is the winner.

Many of these true stories are cooperative stories, told with the help of the audience or with two or more participants in an event sharing the recounting. Tony and Terry, several weeks after Terry moved into the neighborhood, cooperatively built the following story, which Terry opened with a story-starter question.

TRACKTON TEXT IX

Terry: Didja hear 'bout Aunt Bess' cat las' night?
Tony: No, what 'bout dat ol' cat?
Terry: Dat cat get in a fight.
Tony: A fíght?
Terry: Yea, it kilt a dog.
Tony: Ain't no cat can kill no dog.
Terry: Dís cat, he kilt a big dog, dat ol' German shepherd stay down by ol' man Oak's place.
Tony: What'd you do?
Terry: Me? I kilt a horse.
Tony: You áint kilt no horse, (pause) more'n likely a móuse. Where?

Terry: On Main Street. Yesterday.

Tony: And you kílt one, for sure?

Terry: Yea, me 'n dat ol' cat, we built a big fire, stirred it aroun',
threw oil in it, got it goin' good, and I rod dat horse right
in.

Tony: Ya did?

Terry: Yup=

Tony: =I know, it took a while to git de cat outta de fire, 'bout
(pause) maybe a week or so, 'n Mr. Rowe [who owns a
bicycle shop on Main Street] give us a bicycle, 'n we|:ríde
de horse, 'n my friend, Steve, he ríde de hórse, too:| 'n we
come back and foun' dat ol' cát done kilt dat big dóg.

Terry: Why?

Tony: 'Cause dat cát say "Wow, I'm de greates', ain't no dog kin
git me," (pause) like ain't no fire gonna git *me* (pause) 'n
my horse (pause) 'n my bicycle.

Terry starts the story, Tony continues it with his questions, and
about two-thirds through the story, Tony takes over and reverses
leadership positions in the telling. The cue to Terry that he has lost
the primary story-telling role comes when Tony interrupts with "I
know," and continues, developing Tony's plot and theme, but
adding a variation that includes him and his buddy, Steve, as
heroes. Terry is a newcomer, and Tony builds the story's ending to
remind Terry that the oldtimers in Trackton have adventures and
win victories too.

The traditions of story-telling

People in both Trackton and Roadville spend a lot of time telling
stories. Yet the form, occasions, content, and functions of their
stories differ greatly. They structure their stories differently; they
hold different scales of features on which stories are recognized as
stories and judged as good or bad. The patterns of interaction
surrounding the actual telling of a story vary considerably from
Roadville to Trackton. One community allows only stories which
are factual and have little exaggeration; the other uses reality
only as the germ of a highly creative fictionalized account. One
uses stories to reaffirm group membership and behavioral norms,
the other to assert individual strengths and powers. Children in the
two communities hear different kinds of stories, they develop
competence in telling stories in highly contrasting ways.

Roadville story-tellers use formulaic openings: a statement of a comparison or a question asked either by the story-teller or by the individual who has invited the telling of the story. Their stories maintain a strict chronicity, with direct discourse reported, and no explicit exposition of meaning or direct expression of evaluation of the behavior of the main character allowed. Stories end with a summary statement of a moral or a proverb, or a Biblical quotation. Trackton story-tellers use few formulaic openings, except the story-teller's own introduction of himself. Frequently, an abstract begins the story, asserting that the point of the story is to parade the strengths and victories of the story-teller. Stories maintain little chronicity; they move from event to event with numerous interspersions of evaluation of the behaviors of story characters and reiterations of the point of the story. Stories have no formulaic closing, but may have a reassertion of the strengths of the main character, which may be only the opening to yet another tale of adventure.

In Roadville, a story must be invited or announced by someone other than the story-teller. Only certain community members are designated good story-tellers. A story is recognized by the group as an assertion of community membership and agreement on behavioral norms. The marked behavior of the story-teller and audience alike is seen as exemplifying the weaknesses of all and the need for persistence in overcoming such weaknesses. Trackton story-tellers, from a young age, must be aggressive in inserting their stories into an on-going stream of discourse. Story-telling is highly competitive. Everyone in a conversation may want to tell a story, so only the most aggressive wins out. The stress is on the strengths of the individual who is the story's main character, and the story is not likely to unify listeners in any sort of agreement, but to provoke challenges and counterchallenges to the character's ways of overcoming an adversary. The "best stories" often call forth highly diverse additional stories, all designed not to unify the group, but to set out the individual merits of each member of the group.

Roadville members reaffirm their commitment to community and church values by giving factual accounts of their own weaknesses and the lessons learned in overcoming these. Trackton members announce boldly their individual strength in having been creative, persistent, and undaunted in the face of conflict. In

Roadville, the sources of stories are personal experience and a familiarity with Biblical parables, church-related stories of Christian life, and testimonials given in church and home lesson-circles. Their stories are tales of transgressions which make the point of reiterating the expected norms of behavior of man, woman, hunter, fisherman, worker, and Christian. The stories of Roadville are true to the facts of an event; they qualify exaggeration and hedge if they might seem to be veering from an accurate reporting of events.

The content of Trackton's stories, on the other hand, ranges widely, and there is "truth" only in the universals of human strength and persistence praised and illustrated in the tale. Fact is often hard to find, though it is usually the seed of the story. Playsongs, ritual insults, cheers, and stories are assertions of the strong over the weak, of the power of the person featured in the story. Anyone other than the story-teller/main character may be subjected to mockery, ridicule, and challenges to show he is not weak, poor, or ugly.

In both communities, stories entertain; they provide fun, laughter, and frames for other speech events which provide a lesson or a witty display of verbal skill. In Roadville, a proverb, witty saying, or Scriptural quotation inserted into a story adds to both the entertainment value of the story and to its unifying role. Group knowledge of a proverb or saying, or approval of Scriptural quotation reinforces the communal experience which forms the basis of Roadville's stories. In Trackton, various types of language play, imitations of other community members or TV personalities, dramatic gestures and shifts of voice quality, and rhetorical questions and expressions of emotional evaluations add humor and draw out the interaction of story-teller and audience. Though both communities use their stories to entertain, Roadville adults see their stories as didactic: the purpose of a story is to make a point – a point about the conventions of behavior. Audience and story-teller are drawn together in a common bond through acceptance of the merits of the story's point for all. In Trackton, stories often have no point; they may go on as long as the audience enjoys the story-teller's entertainment. Thus a story-teller may intend on his first entry into a stream of discourse to tell only one story, but he may find the audience reception such that he can move from the first story into another, and yet another. Trackton audiences are unified by the story only in that they recognize the entertainment value of the story, and they approve stories which extol the virtues of an individual. Stories do not teach lessons about proper behavior; they tell of individuals who excel by outwitting the rules of conventional behavior.

Children's stories and their story-telling opportunities are radically different in the two communities. Roadville parents provide their children with books; they read to them and ask questions about the books' contents. They choose books which emphasize nursery rhymes, alphabet learning, animals, and simplified Bible stories, and they require their children to repeat from these books, and to answer formulaic questions about their contents. Roadville adults similarly ask questions about oral stories which have a point relevant to some marked behavior of a child. They use proverbs and summary statements to remind their children of stories and to call on them for comparisons of the stories' contents to their own situations. Roadville parents coach children in their telling of stories, forcing them to tell a story of an incident as it has been precomposed in the head of the adult.

Trackton children tell story-poems from the age of two, and they embellish these with gestures, *inclusios*, questions asked of the audience, and repetitions with variations. They only gradually learn to work their way into any on-going discourse with their stories, and when they do, they are not asked questions about their stories, nor are they asked to repeat them. They must, however, be highly creative and entertaining to win a way into an on-going conversation. They practice the skills which they must learn in order to do so through ritualized insults, playsongs, and of course, continued attempts at telling stories to their peers.

In Roadville, children come to know a story as either a retold account from a book, or a factual account of a real event in which some type of marked behavior occurred, and there is a lesson to be learned. There are Bible stories, testimonials, sermons, and accounts of hunting, fishing, cooking, working, or other daily events. Any fictionalized account of a real event is viewed as a lie; reality is better than fiction. Roadville's church and community life admit no story other than that which meets the definition internal to the group.

The one kind of story Trackton prides itself on is the "true story," one in which the basis of the plot is a real event, but the details and even the outcome are exaggerated to such an extent that the story is ultimately anything but true to the facts. Boys excel in telling these stories and use them to establish and maintain status relations once they reach school age, and particularly during the preadolescent years. To Trackton people, the "true story" is the only narrative they term a "story," and the purpose of such stories is to entertain and to establish the story-teller's intimate knowledge of truths about life larger than the factual details of real events.

Three other types of stories are not termed such in Trackton: these are the retold story, the formulaic story, and the straight-forward report or factual story. Girls, by the second or third grade (7–8 years), excel in telling stories they have them-selves read or had read to them. They retell these stories, bringing every detail to life with exaggerated gestures, a sing-song intona-tion, and often an additional embellishment to the ending. They usually announce themselves before they begin the story: "I'm Zinnia, 'n I'm 'onna tell y'all sump'n." Girls particularly enjoy retelling tales in which there is a great deal of dialogue, for they play out the talking parts of characters with great relish. "Goldi-locks and the Three Bears," "Billy Goat Gruff," and other stories in which animals engage in highly personalized styles of talking are favorites of the youngest school-age girls.

In formulaic stories large chunks of an oral story are retold in a frame which varies slightly from telling to telling. Both boys and girls tell these stories, as do adults in Trackton on occasion. The most common of these are stories based on Bible stories (cf. the mayor's tale of King Solomon to the quarreling boys) and ghost tales. Portions of these formulaic stories remain the same across generations, but the framework into which the chunks of dialogue, description of the ghost, or detailing of the murder victim's wounds is placed is adapted in accordance with the situation which provoked the story. Often such stories are used as a form of social control by adults. If they do not want their children in a certain section of town, they tell ghost stories about things which happened there. Often the central character is not a ghost, but simply a scary figure who has taken on supernatural qualities and does not want his territory invaded.[17] Respectables, when asked about these stories, link them to superstitions and to old-timey ways. They feel they are "not real stories, just ol' folks trying' to scare the young'uns."

The fourth type of story is simply a straightforward reporting of events. This is sometimes actually referred to as a "story" by Trackton children after they have begun attending school. Both boys and girls in school respond with this type of real-life report when asked to tell or write a story. They hear the primary school social studies lesson on Abraham Lincoln introduced as a story about his life, and they see that the lesson is a recounting of factual events in his life. They hear the term "story" used repeatedly in school to mean a factual reporting of what has happened or is happening, and they seem to adopt this definition for most of their in-school performances.

The classification of true, retold, formulaic, and factual stories is based only on the source of the stories, and is not one which would be regarded as making sense to the Trackton residents. For them, a "true story" calls for "talkin' junk," and only after one has learned to talk junk can one be a good story-teller. Trackton people admit, however, that children hear and read stories from books at school, and they themselves listen to "stories" [soap operas] on television. They also understand that people outside Trackton often mean a factual summary of an event when they ask Trackton folks to tell their "story" or "side of the story." But in Trackton, there is only the "true story," which would be to a Roadville resident anything but true. In contrast, neither Roadville's factual accounts nor tales from the Bible would be termed stories in Trackton. Since Trackton parents do not read books with their children and do not include these in their gifts to preschoolers, they have no occasion to talk of the stories in books. In short, for Roadville, Trackton's stories would be lies; for Trackton, Roadville's stories would not even count as stories.

6   *Literate traditions*

In Trackton

Concepts of print

Newspapers, car brochures, advertisements, church materials, and homework and official information from school come into Trackton every day. In addition, there are numerous other rather more permanent reading materials in the community: boxes and cans of food products, house numbers, car names and license numbers, calendars and telephone dials, written messages on television, and name brands which are part of refrigerators, stoves, bicycles, and tools. There are few magazines, except those borrowed from the church, no books except school books, the Bible, and Sunday School lesson books, and a photograph album. Just as Trackton parents do not buy special toys for their young children, they do not buy books for them either; adults do not create reading and writing tasks for the young, nor do they consciously model or demonstrate reading and writing behaviors for them. In the home, on the plaza, and in the neighborhood, children are left to find their own reading and writing tasks: distinguishing one television channel from another, knowing the name brands of cars, motorcycles and bicycles, choosing one or another can of soup or cereal, reading price tags at Mr. Dogan's store to be sure they do not pay more than they would at the supermarket. The receipt of mail in Trackton is a big event, and since several houses are residences for transients the postman does not know, the children sometimes take the mail and give it to the appropriate person. Reading names and addresses and return addresses becomes a game-like challenge among all the children, as the school-age try to show the preschoolers how they know "what dat says."

Preschool and school-age children alike frequently ask what something "says," or how it "goes," and adults respond to their queries, making their instructions fit the requirements of the tasks. Sometimes they help with especially hard or unexpected items, and they always correct errors of fact if they hear them. When Lem, Teegie, and other children in Trackton were about two years of age, I initiated the game of reading traffic signs when we were out in the car. Lillie Mae seemed to pay little attention to this game, until one of the children made an error. If Lem termed a "Yield" sign "Stop," she corrected him, saying, "Dat ain't no stop, dat say yield; you have to give the other fellow the right of way." Often the children would read names of fastfood chains as we drove by. Once when one had changed name, and Teegie read the old name, Tony corrected him: "It ain't Chicken Delight no more; it Famous Recipe now." When the children were preparing to go to school, they chose book bags, tee shirts, and stickers for their notebooks which carried messages. Almost all the older boys and girls in the community wore tee shirts with writings scrawled across the front, and the children talked about what these said and vied to have the most original and sometimes the most suggestive.

Reading was a public group affair for almost all members of Trackton from the youngest to the oldest. Miss Lula sometimes read her Bible alone, and Annie Mae would sometimes quietly read magazines she brought home, but to read alone was frowned upon, and individuals who did so were accused of being anti-social. Aunt Berta had a son who as a child used to slip away from the cotton field and read under a tree. He is now a grown man with children, and he has obtained a college degree, but the community still tells tales about his peculiar boyhood habits of wanting to go off and read alone. In general, reading alone, unless one is very old and religious, marks an individual as someone who cannot make it socially.

Jointly or in group affairs, the children of Trackton *read to learn* before they go to school to *learn to read*. The modification of old or broken toys and their incorporation with other items to create a new toy is a common event. One mastermind, usually Tony, announces the idea, and all the children help collect items and contribute ideas. On some of these occasions, such as when one of the boys wants to modify his bicycle for a unique effect, he has to read selectively portions of brochures on bicycles and instructions for tool sets. Reading is almost always set within a context of immediate action: one needs to read a letter's address to prove to the mailman that one should be given the envelope; one must read the price of a bag of coal at Mr. Dogan's store to make the decision to purchase or not. Trackton children are sent to the store almost as soon as they can walk, and since they are told to "watch out for Mr. Dogan's prices," they must learn to read price changes there from week to week for commonly purchased items and remember them for comparisons with prices in the supermarket. As early as age four, Teegie, Lem, Gary, and Gary B. could scan the price tag, which might contain several separate pieces of information, on familiar items and pick out the price. The decimal point and the predictability of the number of numerals which would be included in the price were clues which helped the children search each tag for only those portions meaningful to their decision-making.

Children remember and reassociate the contexts of print. When they see a brand name, particular sets of numbers, or a particular logo, they often recall when and with whom they first saw it, or they call attention to how the occasion for this new appearance is not like the previous one. Slight shifts in print styles, and decorations of mascots used to advertise products, or alterations of written slogans are noticed by Trackton children. Once they have been in a supermarket to buy a loaf of bread, they remember on subsequent trips the location of the bread section and the placement of the kind of "light bread" their family eats. They seem to remember the scene and staging of print, so that upon recalling print they visualize the physical context in which it occurred and the reasons for reading it: that is, what it was they wanted to learn from reading a certain item or series of items. They are not tutored in these skills by adults of the community, but they are given numerous graded tasks from a very early age and are provided with older children who have learned to read to perform the tasks their daily life requires. Young children watch others read and write for a variety of purposes, and they have numerous opportunities for practice under the indirect supervision of older children, so that they come to use print independently and to be able to model appropriate behaviors for younger children coming up behind them.

The dependence on a strong sense of visual imagery often prevented efficient transfer of skills learned in one context to another. All of the toddlers knew the name brands and names of cereals as they appeared on the boxes or in advertisements. Kellogg's was always written in script – the name of the cereal (raisin bran, etc.) in all capital letters. On Nabisco products, Nabisco was written in small capitals and the cereal name in capital letters as well. I was curious to know whether or not the children "read" the names or whether they recognized the shapes of the boxes and the artwork on the boxes when they correctly identified the cereals. I cut out the name brands and cereal names and put them on plain cardboard of different sizes, and asked the children to read the names. After an initial period of hesitation, most of the children could read the newly placed names. All of the children could do so by age three. When they were between three and four, I cut out the printed letters from the cereal names to spell Kellogg's in small capitals and otherwise arranged the information on the plain cardboard as it appeared on the cereal boxes. The children volunteered the name of the cereal, but did not immediately read Kellogg's now that it was no longer in the familiar script. When I asked them to read it, they looked puzzled, said it looked "funny," and they were not sure what it was. When I pointed out to them that the print small-capital K was another way of writing the script K, they watched with interest as I did the same for the rest of the letters. They were dubious about the script e and the print E being "the same," but they became willing to accept that what configured on the box also configured on the paper, though in some different ways.

Gradually we developed a game of "rewriting" the words they could read, shifting from script to all capitals, and from all capitals to initial capitals and subsequent small letters for individual words. It was always necessary to do this by moving from the known mental picture and "reading" of the terms (i.e. the script Kellogg's) to the unknown or unfamiliar (rendering of Kellogg's in small print capitals). Once shown they already "knew" the item, they accepted that they could "know" these items in new contexts and shapes. We continued this type of game with many of the items from their daily life they already knew how to read. When I first wrote house numbers just as they appeared on the house on a piece of notebook paper, the three- and four-year-olds said they could not read it; if I varied slightly the shape of the numerals on the notebook paper, they also did not read the numbers. Once comparisons and differences were pointed out, they recognized that they already "knew" how to read what had seemed like strange information to them on the notebook paper. Using the "real" print and my re-created print in a metaphorical way provided a bridge from the known to the unknown which allowed the children to use their familiar rules for recognition of print. They transferred their own daily operations as successful readers in an interactive way to pencil-and-paper tasks which were not immediately relevant in the community context.[1]

Their strong tendency to visualize how print looked in its surrounding context was revealed when I asked the three- and four-year-old children to "draw" house doors, newspapers, soup cans, and a letter they would write to someone. Figure 6.1 illustrates how Gary's representation of a newspaper shows that he knew the letters of headlines were bigger than what came below, and that what was below was organized in straight lines. Moreover, the "headline" near the bottom of the page is smaller than that at the top. Mel writes a "letter" which includes the date, salutation, body, closing, and signature. His "letter" is somewhat atypical, but, since Mel's mother, a transient, wrote frequently to her family up-North, he had numerous opportunities to see letters. None of the other preschoolers provided any of the components of a letter other than body and signature. Mel, however, not only indicates several parts, but also scatters some alphabet letters through the body, and signs his name. Mel also "drew" a soup can, making its name brand biggest, and schematically representing the product information and even what I take to be the vertical pricing and inventory information for computerized checking at the bottom of the can. When asked to "read" what they had written, some giggled, others asked older brothers and sisters to do it and some "read" their writing, explaining its context. Mel's reading of his letter was prefaced by "Now I send you dis letter." Then he read "Dear Miz Hea, bring me a truck we go to Hardee's, Mel." Everyone giggled with Mel who enjoyed the joke of having written what he so often said orally to me. His rendering contained only the primary message, not the date or his letter's closing. It is doubtful that Mel knew what went in these slots, since when I asked him if he had read those parts to me, he shrugged his shoulders and said "I dunno." Trackton children had learned before school that they could read to learn, and they had developed expectancies of print. The graphic and everyday-

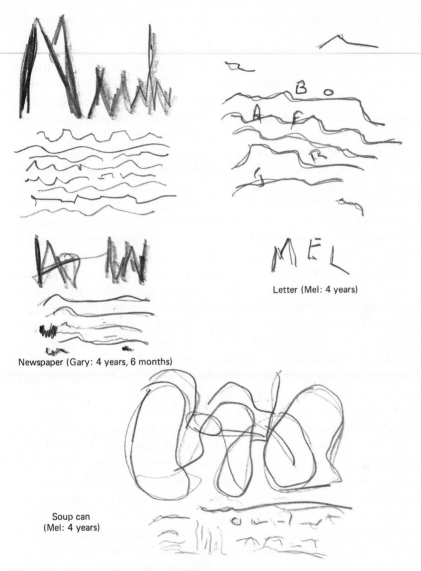

Letter (Mel: 4 years)

Newspaper (Gary: 4 years, 6 months)

Soup can
(Mel: 4 years)

Figure 6.1. Preschool concepts of print

life contexts of writing were often critical to their interpretation of the meaning of print, for print to them was not isolated bits and pieces of lines and circles, but messages with varying internal structures, purposes, and uses. For most of these, oral communication surrounded the print.

Ethnographer learning

"Talk is the thing"

In almost every situation in Trackton in which a piece of writing is integral to the nature of the participants' interactions and their interpretations of meaning, talk is a necessary component.[2] Knowing which box of cereal is Kellogg's raisin bran does little good without announcing that choice to older brothers and sisters helping pour the cereal. Knowing the kind of bicycle tire and tube on one's old bike is translated into action only at Mr. Green's bicycle shop or with a friend who has an old bike he is not using. Certain types of talk describe, repeat, reinforce, frame, expand, and even contradict written materials, and children in Trackton learn not only how to read print, but also when and how to surround the print in their lives with appropriate talk. For them there are far more occasions in the community which call for appropriate knowledge of forms and uses of talk around or about writing, than there are actual occasions for reading and writing extended connected discourse.

For Trackton adults, reading is a social activity; when something is read in Trackton, it almost always provokes narratives, jokes, sidetracking talk, and active negotiation of the meaning of written texts among the listeners. Authority in the written word does not rest in the words themselves, but in the meanings which are negotiated through the experiences of the group. The evening newspaper is read on the front porch for most months of the year. The obituaries on the back page are usually read first, followed by employment listings, advertisements for grocery and department store sales, and captions beneath pictures and headlines. An obituary is read for some trace of acquaintance with either the deceased, his relatives, place of birth, church, or school; active discussion follows about who the individual was and who he might have known. Circulars or letters to individuals regarding the neighborhood center and its recreational or medical services are read aloud and their meanings jointly negotiated by those who have had experience with such activities or know about the forms to be filled out to be eligible for such services. Neighbors share stories of what they did or what happened to them in similar circumstances. One day when Lillie Mae had received a letter about a daycare program, several neighbors were sitting on porches, working on cars nearby, or sweeping their front yards.

Lillie Mae came out on her front porch, read the first paragraph of a letter, and announced:

TRACKTON TEXT X

Lillie Mae:	You hear this, it says Lem [then two years old] might can get into Ridgeway [a local neighborhood center daycare program], but I hafta have the papers ready and apply by next Friday.
Visiting friend:	You ever been to Kent to get his birth certificate? [friend is mother of three children already in school]
Mattie Crawford:	But what hours that program gonna be? You may not can get him there.
Lillie Mae:	They want the birth certificate? I got his vaccination papers.
Annie Mae:	Sometimes they take that, 'cause they can 'bout tell the age from those early shots.
Visiting friend:	But you better get it, 'cause you gotta have it when he go to school anyway.
Lillie Mae:	But it says here they don't know what hours yet. How am I gonna get over to Kent? How much does it cost? Lemme see if the program costs anything. (She reads aloud part of the letter.)

Conversation on various parts of the letter continued for nearly an hour, while neighbors and Lillie Mae pooled their knowledge of the pros and cons of such programs. They discussed ways of getting rides to Kent, the county seat thirty miles away, to which all mothers had to go to get their children's birth certificates to prove their age at school entrance. The question "What does this mean?" was answered not only from the information in print, but from the group's joint bringing of experience to the text. Lillie Mae, reading aloud, decoded the written text, but her friends and neighbors interpreted the text's meaning through their own experiences. The experience of any one individual had to become common to the group, however, and that was done through the recounting of members' experiences. Such recounting re-created scenes, embellished the truth, illustrated the character of the individuals involved, and to the greatest extent possible brought the audience into the experience itself. Beyond these recountings of episodes (such as one mother's efforts to get her doctor to give her "papers" to verify her son's age), there was a reintegration of these

Table 6.1. *Types of uses of reading in Trackton*

INSTRUMENTAL:	Reading to accomplish practical goals of daily life (price tags, checks, bills, telephone dials, clocks, street signs, house numbers).
SOCIAL-INTERACTIONAL/RECREATIONAL:	Reading to maintain social relationships, make plans, and introduce topics for discussion and story-telling (greeting cards, cartoons, letters, newspaper features, political flyers, announcements of community meetings).
NEWS-RELATED:	Reading to learn about third parties or distant events (local news items, circulars from the community center or school).
CONFIRMATIONAL:	Reading to gain support for attitudes or beliefs already held (Bible, brochures on cars, loan notes, bills).

Note. Listed in relative order of frequency of occasions when time on these types of tasks exceeded five minutes per day.

now commonly shared experiences with the text itself. After the reading episode, Lillie Mae had to relate the text's meaning to the experiences she had heard shared, and she checked out this final synthesis of meaning for her with some of the group. Some members did not care about this final synthesis and had wandered off, satisfied to have told their stories, but others commented that they thought her chosen course of action the right one, and her understanding of the letter to fit their interpretations.[3]

About the only material not delivered for group negotiation is that which involves private finances or information which members feel might somehow give them an opportunity their neighbors do not have. A postcard from a local mill announcing days on which the mill will be accepting new employment applications will not be shared aloud, but kept secret because of the competition for jobs. On the other hand, a newspaper story about the expansion of the mill will be read aloud, and all will pool information in general terms.

Tables 6.1 and 6.2 show that the uses of writing and reading in the community are multiple, though there are few occasions for reading of extended connected discourse and almost no occasions for writing such material, except by those school children who diligently try to complete their homework assignments. Foremost among the types of uses of reading and writing are those which are

Table 6.2 *Types of uses of writing in Trackton*

MEMORY AIDS: (primarily used by women)	Writing to serve as a reminder for the writer and, only occasionally, others (telephone numbers, notes on calendars).
SUBSTITUTES FOR ORAL MESSAGES: (primarily used by women)	Writing used when direct oral communication was not possible or would prove embarrassing (notes for tardiness or absence from school, greeting cards, letters).
FINANCIAL:	Writing to record numerals and to write out amounts and accompanying notes (signatures on checks and public forms, figures and notes for income tax preparation).
PUBLIC RECORDS: (church only)	Writing to announce the order of the church services and forthcoming events and to record financial and policy decisions (church bulletins, reports of the church building fund committee).

Note. Listed in relative order of frequency of occasions when time on these types of tasks exceeded five minutes per day.

instrumental. Adults and children read what they have to read to solve practical problems of daily life: price tags, traffic signs, house numbers, bills, checks. Other uses are perhaps not as critical to problem-solving, but *social-interactional* uses give information relevant to social relations and contacts with persons not in Trackton's primary group. Some write letters; many send greeting cards; almost all read bumper stickers, newspaper obituaries and features, and church news bulletins. Other types of reading and writing are *news-related.* From the local newspaper, political flyers, memos from the city offices, and circulars from the neighborhood center, Trackton residents learn information about local and distant events. They rarely read much more than headlines about distant events, since the evening news programs on television give them the same national or metropolitan news. Stories about the local towns are, however, read, because there is often no other source of information on happenings there. Some individuals in Trackton read for *confirmation* – to seek support for beliefs or ideas they already hold. Miss Lula reads the Bible. When the mayor maintains that one kind of car gets better mileage than another, and others disagree, he has to produce a brochure from a car dealer to prove his point. Children who become involved in boasts often called on written proof to confirm their lofty accounts of themselves or others. Every home has some permanent records – loan notes, tax forms, birth certificates – which families keep, but can rarely find when they are needed. However, if they can be found and are read, they can confirm an oral statement.

The most frequent occasions for writing are those when Trackton family members say they cannot trust their memory (*memory-supportive*), or they have to write to *substitute for an oral message*. Beside the telephone, women write frequently called numbers and addresses; they tack calendars on the kitchen wall and add notes reminding them of dates for their children's vaccinations and the school holidays, etc. Some few women in the community write letters. Lillie Mae often writes relatives up-North to invite them to come home and to thank them for bringing presents. Women sometimes have to write notes to school about children's absences or tardiness or to request a local merchant to extend credit a few weeks longer. Men almost never write except to sign their paychecks, public forms, and to collect information for income tax preparation. One exception in Track-ton is the mayor who meets once a month with a group of other church members to prepare Sunday church bulletins as well as to handle business related to the building fund or to plan for revival meetings. These written materials are negotiated cooperatively at the meetings; no individual takes sole responsibility.[4]

Community literacy activities are public and social. Written information almost never stands alone in Trackton. It is reshaped and reworded into an oral mode by adults and children who incorporate chunks of the written text in their talk. They often reflect their own awareness that print imposes a different kind of organization on written materials than talk does. Literacy events in Trackton which bring the written word into a central focus in interactions and interpretations have their rules of occurrence and appropriateness, just as talking junk, fussing, or performing a playsong do. The group activities of reading the newspaper across porches, debating the power of a new car, or discussing the city's plans to bring in earthmoving equipment to clear lots behind the community, produce more speaking than reading, more group than individual effort. There are repeated metaphors, comparisons, and fast-paced, overlapping language as Trackton residents move from print to what it means in their lives. On some occasions, they attend to the text itself; on others, they use it only as a starting point for wide-ranging talk. On all occasions, they bring in knowledge related to the text and interpret beyond the text for their own context; in so doing, they achieve a new synthesis of information from the text and the joint experiences of community members.

A special case

In attempting to understand the unconscious rules members of a group follow in their lives, we often look for patterns and themes of behavior which are carried from the home life into other institutions community members themselves control. The churches attended by Trackton families and their friends were such institutions. Most went to country churches for Sunday services, usually held twice a month. In these churches, the pastor serves not one, but several churches, and he often also holds one or two other jobs during the week. The pastor, often called "reverend," is always a male. Few have had formal training at a theological seminary. Many are known to have lived "sinful" lives in their younger days and to have "come to the Lord" after recognizing the evil of their ways. Their training has usually been in one of the black colleges of the South, where they have majored or taken courses in religion, and they have supplemented this training with additional work at summer programs, through correspondence courses, or in graduate programs at nearby integrated state schools.[5]

Most of the country churches in the area were built in the late nineteenth or early twentieth century. They are wooden structures, placed on foundations of rocks gathered from nearby creek beds. The pulpit and choir loft are in the front of the church, and a small space separates the raised pulpit from the congregational pews. Some have an organ; most have only a piano. The churches are small, usually seating less than one hundred worshipers. The Piedmont countryside is dotted with these churches, but nowadays, almost all have a new counterpart set beside them – a low one-story brick church. Raising the money for a new church is a slow process, so the congregation continues to worship in the old church, while building the new. Once the new is complete, the old church is left standing either to deteriorate naturally or to be used occasionally for congregational meetings or Sunday School classes. These country churches bring together the black families who still live in the countryside as well as their former neighbors who have moved to Gateway and other Piedmont towns. The churches Trackton families go to are also attended by school teachers, domestic workers, clerks in local retail businesses, farmers, sharecroppers, hospital staff members, and retired military personnel who have come home to the South to live. Levels of formal education vary greatly. Many of the elderly have had only a few years of grammar school, and some are now returning to schooling through senior citizen projects (see Miss Bee's account in Trackton Text II). Others such as the minister, retired military personnel, and school administrators, have had graduate-level education.

Yet the habits of communal worship level all distinctions among the congregation's members, and literature and oral traditions established long ago continue in these churches. Many believe these ways of "praising God" have persisted since the early worship services held during slavery. Yet preaching, singing, and praying often depend on formal reading and writing, which coexist with a wide range of types of oral performance. Formal reading and writing are increasingly in evidence as the churches acquire hymnals, and put hymn boards at the front of the church announcing the numbers of the hymns. A congregation member is always asked two weeks ahead to read the Bible the next preaching Sunday, and the Sunday School Superintendent reads his report during the worship service.[6] All adults are expected to bring their Bibles to church and to follow along as the reader reads from the Bible. Many churches provide bulletins each Sunday, which give not only the order of service, but also announcements of the building fund's programs, forthcoming circle meetings, the pastor's activities, forthcoming congregation meetings and revivals, and regional and state-wide denominational events. Funeral services, or celebrations of life for still-living but elderly members of the church, are the occasions for brochures of several pages, containing pictures of the individual, an account of his life, list of family members, details of the service, favorite sayings of the individual, and testimonials from friends and family members.[7]

The Sunday service as a whole is a harmonious blend of uses of highly formal written materials, lists of items and informally written announcements, oral performances which draw from the written words, and spontaneous oral performances which take the formulae of either written or oral expressions and expand these. Hymns, prayers, and sermon are intertwined in patterns which defy analytic description by their complication in overlapping and simultaneous pieces. Outsiders, unfamiliar with the routines of the service and the norms of participation by members of the congregation, cannot understand the service in many parts, and often report their feeling that "too much is going on at the same time." A personal testimony provokes a spontaneous response in song, which ends abruptly as a prayer begins; throughout the prayer, as many as three different songs may be hummed or sung; as the prayer ends, the sermon may begin, the preacher speaking slowly and deliberately at first, and only gradually moving into a series of chants, each with its own crescendo, punctuated by spontaneous bursts of song, prayers, or verbal expressions of agreement from the congregation.

Almost all parts of the service – hymns, prayers, and sermon – have in their background written sources. There are hymn books, and the hymn board at the front of the church gives the hymn numbers, as does the bulletin. Those who are called on by the minister to pray have always been asked to prepare in advance, and most bring a card or small piece of paper with their prayer written out on it. The sermon is based on a Biblical text, and the pastor always writes out portions of the sermons in preparation for Sunday services and revival meetings. Yet in each of these parts of the service, there is a pattern of movement away from the form and formality of the written sources. For example, most of the country churches still "raise" their hymns, though they have hymn books with prepared words. In raising a hymn, the choir leader may begin the hymn by announcing the hymn number from the book, then reading the first verse of the hymn, slowly and dramatically, pausing often to look at the congregation. The congregation then begins singing and may continue through the entire first verse before a member of the choir or congregation breaks in with new words which may be a phrase or set of phrases from an earlier prayer, the hymn, or one of several formulaic phrases that may raise a hymn. The congregation is quiet while the new self-appointed leader raises a set of phrases, and they then join in repeating it, then pause for another leader to offer another set. This pattern of alternation continues until the hymn ends, seemingly as if by prearranged agreement; there are no rough edges, but a smooth simultaneous end. A variation on this pattern may occur when someone begins a testimony or prayer instead of raising a new set of sung phrases; on these occasions, the music usually subsides into background humming until someone in the congregation picks up a phrase either given or related to the theme of the testimony or prayer, and the congregation raises a new hymn.

The sermon begins slowly and deliberately with low pitch, and there is no distinctive recitation pattern for the first few minutes of the sermon. However, soon the preacher introduces a question or a phrase, which is taken up as a chant either by him or members of the congregation, and from that point on, the performance is joint – pastor and congregation. The congregation takes many parts; different leaders hum portions of songs, raise hymns, or give verbal approval through comments such as "Amen," "Yes, Lord," "That's right."[8] As the sermon reaches its climax, the piano may begin playing, there will be humming from the choir, and a solo by a member of the choir. The minister gives the "call," urging members to come forward to accept salvation. Members of the congregation add praises or expressions of agreement, but during the call from the minister for "sinners" to come forward, no hymns are raised. When it is clear that the call is over, the choir leader signals the choir and congregation to begin singing again. This initial post-sermon hymn is broken into repeatedly by testimonies and prayers until the service ends, seemingly by unexpressed mutual consent. To the outsider, there are no signals that the service has ended, just as there is no overt signal that a hymn has ended and another activity is about to begin.

Throughout the raised hymns, there is an in-and-out pattern of verbal response from the congregation, offering hymns, prayers, and testimonies. The phrases offered by the leader who raises a hymn may become a formula which subsequent sets of phrases modify or play with, or the initial sets of phrases may only introduce a theme (e.g. gratitude for salvation) which other leaders comment on and vary throughout the raised hymn. Thus, what may seem like set formulae are changed, and new formulae are produced as different individuals lead the congregation in expanding a particular theme picked up from either the sermon, a prayer, or a testimonial. Every performance of a raised hymn is different, and though individual choir leaders have the reputation of having different styles of raising hymns, each interaction between leader and congregation is unique, for not only are the members of congregations different, but leadership from within the congregation varies from Sunday to Sunday. Indeed, these unique combinations out of the familiar gathering of the congregation make it possible for each member of the congregation to be at once creator and performer.[9]

The following illustration of a raised hymn occurred at a point in the church service when a member of the congregation – a hospital orderly – recounted an experience he had faced in his work the past week. He told of his own sense of emptiness as he tried to help a dying patient. The choir leader continued after the story by saying "After all, I'm gonna tell ya, there are some times. . ."

TRACKTON TEXT XI*

A single voice on the other side of the church repeated in a chant, slowly rising in pitch –

> There are some times

The choir leader picked up as his chant died, and chanted –

> When things be rough.

The congregation then began humming the tune to Kumbaya, a familiar song often heard in popular recordings of Afro-American music. A portion of the congregation then repeated with the new melody –

> There are some times

The choir leader introduced in chant –

> When there is no other help.

The congregation had by this point joined together to sing –

> There are sometimes, yea Lord
> There are sometimes, yea Lord

Ethnographer learning

Another leader added in chant —

> Yea, oh Lord, yea sometimes

The choir leader then chanted while the congregation hummed —

> When we be back at twelve o'clock [a metaphorical expression for birth and death, the beginning and the end].

While the congregation returned to humming, another single male voice raised from the congregation —

> We need ya, Lord

The choir leader added in chant —

> Sometimes, yea

The single male voice which had emerged as the lead voice in the congregation then chanted —

> So, come by here, Lord

and the congregation immediately sang the phrases —

> Come by here
> Come by here
> Yea Lord.

The congregational leader then chanted —

> Somebody needs ya, Lord.

The congregation sang —

> Somebody need ya, Lord
> Somebody yea
> Somebody need ya Lord
> Come by here.

Another congregational member chanted —

> Aye, aye, come by here
> Come by here
> Yea, somebody need ya, Lord
> Come by here.

Two sharp claps came from the congregation, there was a momentary pause, and the choir leader chanted softly —

> Somebody's waitin', Lord.

The congregation sang –

> Come by here
> Somebody's waitin', Lord
> Come by here.

A congregational leader shouted shrilly –

> Somebody's waitin', Lord.

The congregation sang quietly –

> Come by here.

The choir leader chanted slowly and with crescendo –

> My Jesus, come by here, Lord
> Yea, come by here
> Yea, Lord, come by here
> Come by here.
> *Yea, Lord, come by: here.*

The congregation sang softly –

> Oh, Lord, come by here
> Yea, Lord, come by here
> Come by here, Lord
> Come by here.

As the congregation finished, the leader chanted with a falling cadence –

> Yea, Lord, come by here.[10]

Following this hymn, simpler by far than most performed in the church because the melody and word patterns were somewhat predictable, there was quiet for slightly over one minute before a female voice in the back of the church raised a shrill crying chant –

> Oh my Lord, which way to go?

Only the women in the congregation picked up this phrase and sang to a melody different from that of the last hymn –

> Which way, Oh Lord?

Another female added in a chant –

> I feel so alone, Lord.

These and subsequent words of this hymn were all contributed by women, though near its end, men joined in the humming, and at one point, the choir leader shouted "Sing it, sing it," and added "I'll be somewhere with Him."

It is important to remember that this singing, punctuated by claps and foot stomping on the second and fourth beats, and shouts of praise are participated in by educated and uneducated, literate and illiterate alike in the church. When I asked those in the church who had had formal training in music or graduate-level training in education how they had learned to raise hymns, they answered my questions as follows:

> Well, you just begin singing and the others join in.

I asked: "But how do they know when and what to sing?"

> Well, they sing the words.

I persisted: "Which words?"

> The ones they hear and the ones that belong.

I tried a different avenue of questioning: "But when?"

> When they feel it's right.

This type of questioning about a practice apparently so unsuitable for analyzing step-by-step in terms of the respective bits and pieces and the particular cues for different roles was fruitless. I asked the same questions of members of the congregation who had no education, and the answers were similar. Neither formal music training nor a college education in which one learns to analyze some parts of the world about one seems to carry over to hymns on Sunday morning. As one leader chanted to the congregation –

> Yea, yea, now Christian friends
> Now, I'm gonna say it
> I know dat I feel good
> I know dat I know de Lord
> 'n I'm gonna tell sump'n
> If ya'll don't feel good
> It's sump'n wrong.

The congregation responded:

> Yea, yea sump'n.

It is a "sump'n" which allows the raising of hymns that leaders and congregation compose during, in, and for the performance. It is a "sump'n," which cannot be articulated by the members that accounts for the process and force by which they sing, tell a tale, compose a story, or pray a prayer.

The following prayer illustrates a pattern of theme adoption and subsequent adaptation, as well as the pattern of using the written word yet moving away from it, which permeates the service. The prayer was given orally by a forty-five-year-old female school teacher who had been asked two weeks before to pray at the next preaching Sunday. She had written out a text beforehand on a card which she held in her hand during the prayer:

> Kind heavenly Father, we thank thee for watching over us through the night.
> We thank thee for thy guidance, kind heavenly Father, for your strong protection.
> We pray that you will be with us, Lord, be with our families, young and old, near and far.
> Lead us not into temptation, Lord. Make us strong and ever mindful of your gifts to us all. Amen.

Her oral version went as follows, however, and was full of shifts of prosody, melodic strains, and changes in pace. The intonation pattern for the first few lines was that of a slowly deliberately spoken prayer, but by the end of line 10, she broke into actual melody, and the remainder of the prayer was chanted. Throughout the prayer, there were sharp pitch modulations, and on one occasion (end of line 35), a member of the congregation broke in with a supporting bar of melody, lasting only 3.5 seconds. All of the vocatives, direct addresses, to God after line 6 were marked by a lilting high-rise–mid-fall contour.

TRACKTON TEXT XII*

1 We thank thee for watchin' over us, kind heavenly Father
2 Through the night.
3 We thank thee, Oh Lord.
4 For leadin' 'n guidin' us.
5 We thank thee, kind heavenly Father.
6 For your strong-arm protection around us.
7 O Lord, don't leave us alone.
8 We feel this evenin', kind heavenly Father, if you leave us

9 We are the least ones of all.
10 Now Lord, I ask thee, kind heavenly Father,
11 to go 'long with my family,
12 I ask thee, kind heavenly Father, to throw your strong-arm protectors around.
13 Oh Lord, I ask thee, oh Lord,
14 to take care of my childrens, Lord, wherever they may be.
15 Oh Lord, don't leave us, Jesus.
16 I feel this morning, kind heavenly Father, if you leave me,
17 Oh, Lord, please, Lord, don't leave me.
18 In the hands of the wicked man.
19 Oh Lord, I thank thee kind heavenly Father,
20 for what you have done for me.
21 Oh Lord, I thank thee, kind heavenly Father
22 Where you have brought me from.
23 Oh Lord, I wonder sometime if I didn't have Jesus on my side,
24 Lord, have mercy now.
25 What would I do, oh Lord?
26 Have mercy, Jesus.
27 I can call on 'im in the midnight hour,
28 I can call on 'im, Lord, in the noontime, oh Lord,
29 I can call on 'im anytime o' day, oh Lord.
30 He'p me, Jesus,
31 Oh Lord, make me strong.
32 Oh Lord, have mercy on us, Father,
33 When we have done all that you have 'signed our hands to do, Lord,
34 Have mercy, Lord,
35 I want you to give me a home beyond the shinin' river, oh Lord,
36 Where won't be no sorrowness,
37 Won't be no shame and tears, oh Lord.
38 It won't be nothing, Lord, but glory, alleluia.
39 When we have done all that you 'signed our hands to do, kind heavenly Father,
40 And we cain't do no mo',
41 We want you to give us a home in thy kingdom, oh Lord.
42 For thy Christ's sake. Amen.

The prayer is personal, and several features make it seem so and link it in many ways to the vocative shouts and personal pleas used in the raised hymns. She often uses "Oh Lord," "kind heavenly Father," and "Jesus," after she has left her printed text. All sentences of the written text contain such a vocative, but in the oral text, there are often two per sentence. The woman personal-izes her prayer by shifting from the *we* of the written text to a singular plea in line 10, where she is speaking as the "weak sinner," the easily tempted, and she prays for continued strength and readiness to being helped by her Lord. At line 20, she stops using *thee, thy,* and *thou,* archaic personal pronouns, and shifts to the second person singular *you.* The sentence structures of the oral version are far more complex than the simple sentences of the written prayer, and numerous informal and vernacular forms come into the oral prayer. The first suggestion of informality comes with the "dropping of the g" in line 4, but as the prayer progresses, several other informal forms and features associated with the Black English vernacular are used.[11]

Throughout the sermons, prayers, and raised hymns of the church, there appears a familiar pattern which marks many other features of Trackton life: the learning of language, telling of stories, and composing of hand-clap and jump-rope songs. Throughout these habits and the shifts from oral to written language, there is an oral performance pattern of building a text which uses themes and repetitions with variations on these themes. The young children follow this pattern in practicing and playing in their language learning; older siblings use it when they entertain the community with their songs and games; it permeates greetings, and leavings, and parts of stories. Often a formulaic phrase expresses an essential idea, but this phrase is for building from, and as such is continually subject to change as individuals perform and create simultaneously.

In Roadville

Staying in touch

Mrs. Macken, while kneading bread, kept one eye on Kim, who was studying a single sheet of lined stationery at the kitchen table. Kim twisted and turned, chewing on the pencil, while Mrs. Macken said, "Just ask how they are, and tell them what you've been doing. Then tell them 'thank you' for the nice birthday present." Kim wrote slowly and laboriously using her best second-grade writing for several lines, carefully forming the letters, and then asked, "How do you spell *basket?*" Mrs. Macken lifted her hands out of the dough, dusted them off and walked to the table to look over Kim's shoulder: "Why do you want that word?" "I wanted to tell 'em what I made at Bible School." Mrs. Macken smiled and said, "That's not necessary; just say you went to Bible School. That's enough, and don't forget to thank them." Kim erased the last line she had written, wrote "Thank you for the present.", and signed her full name with a flourish of triumph as her pencil point broke. Mrs. Macken reminded her to add "Love," above her signature and released Kim to go outdoors to play.

In Roadville, this kind of note-writing takes place in connection with holidays, family celebrations, and crises in personal lives, such as sickness and death. From Valentine's Day through Christmas, holidays are occasions for greeting cards, usually with a personal note and some family photos included. Following those holidays or celebration days when gifts are exchanged, children and adults alike write thank you notes. The children labor over the lined stationery they usually receive as a birthday or Christmas gift from their families, and the adults use small single-folded note-paper decorated with a silver- or gold-scripted "thank you" on the outside fold. Get-well or sympathy cards are made personal by a "Thinking of you," scrawled before the closing and the signature. Roadville residents refer to these written exchanges as ways of "staying in touch."

Apart from these notes added to commercial messages or the "thank you's" written after celebrations and holiday gift exchanges, there are few letters. The Roadville women in Mrs. Dee's family sometimes write letters to their sisters who have moved away, because their husbands resent the phone bills when the sisters talk on the phone. Mrs. Dee will often ask Martha to write for her to one of her children to arrange a visit or to ask them to bring a specific item the next time they visit Roadville. These letters are brief, devoid of unpredictable topics, marked with a proper and formal air about them, and always in accord with a general outline. They open with a salutation of "Dear —," and the first paragraph invariably contains the greeting "How are you?" What follows is only somewhat less invariable: "Fine, I hope. We are all fine." or "We are fine, and hope you are too." If there has been a serious recent illness or accident in the family, the addressee of the letter is never informed about it through a personal letter, but by telephone. Thus, any comments on an individual's state of health merely up-date the knowledge the addressee has previously received by phone: "Mama is doing better and eating better. She walked out on the porch this week."

The next topic is almost always the weather; severe heat or drought, heavy rains, a snowstorm, big hail, or a destructive thunderstorm are the major topics of early paragraphs of those Roadville letters written in the few weeks following their occurrence. If the intent of the letter is to make a request or to inquire about an impending visit, this topic follows next. Often no specific or immediate purposes motivate the letters written between the women of Roadville and their out-of-town female relatives. Thus, after the greeting and paragraph on the weather, the writer moves on to "news," which may include her latest sewing projects, progress of the children in extracurricular or church activities, and perhaps a tidbit of gossip ("I hear Jed Dodd is doing real good at the garage, and he told one of the Turner girls he wasn't coming back to school. Poor Sue."). The closing of letters is always apologetic. "Well, I got to get to that ironing. I have to close for now. Write soon and let me know how you are." Following the final note of "Love," there is almost always a P.S., which often seems to exceed in importance all else in the letter: "P.S. If you come for Thanksgiving, we need to plan. Will you?"

Roadville letters are conversations written down. The writer sometimes supplies both parts of the conversation, as in the greeting. The opening "How are you?", usually responded to in oral conversation by "Fine," is filled in by the writer ("Fine, I hope"), who then immediately responds to the unstated second-party question of "And how are you?" Other portions of the letter are more one-sided conversations in which the writer chooses to take up one or more of those topics acceptable in personal letters: daily activities, general news of family life and children's activities, and news of groups or individuals already known to the addressee. Questions are asked, but there is no specific request for a reply: "Did you see the May issue of *Better Homes*?" "Is Jimmy playing football?" Often the P.S. contains a question, a response to which could be taken as the reason for an answer to the letter.

Roadville women who write letters seem to assume they will be understood, and they make no effort to imagine the recipient of their letter trying to make meaning out of it. Every letter-writer is part of a familiar unbroken chain of linkages between relatives and/or friends. Martha said of her infrequent letters to her aunts who lived out of town: "I oughta write more, just to stay in touch, you know, but I don't have the time. When I do write, though, I don't have to think much about what I'm gonna say. We know each other so well, and after all, they lived here for a long time, so they know about life here. I don't have to tell 'em, and they know all the folks I'd mention, so I don't have to say who they are. They'd be able to (pause), well, I guess, *see* it when I tell 'em 'bout things." Roadville writers assume a shared background of knowledge and do not provide background information or spell out presuppositions behind their statements or queries. They write on notebook paper or stationery, in either pencil or pen, and if they are in a hurry, they may address the envelope in pencil.

Roadville residents talk about letters as though they are parts of oral conversations, using terms such as "say," "tell," and "answer" just as they would in referring to talk. They report: "She said she was coming [referring to a response written in a letter]." "She tells [wrote] me he's playing the piano." "I gotta answer Margie [write a letter in response to one received from Margie]." "I owe Wilma an answer [letter]." Roadville women especially see letter-writing as a one-to-one affair which must remain balanced: each letter from one party is an answer to a recent letter from the other party, and no one ever writes two letters consecutively. Letters often contain answers to specific questions without designation of the query being answered: "No, I didn't see it. Was it good?" "Jimmy decided to play soccer instead of football this year. The outfits cost less, so I'm glad. Do you have soccer yet?" "If we come for Thanksgiving, we'll have to come Thursday morning. Is there room for all of us to eat at Mamma's house? Maybe we could split between hers and Sue's." The conversational nature of the sequence of letters between two individuals forms a conversational chain. Each letter is a link in this chain, and interpretation of its meaning depends on remembering the initiation of topics or even specific sentences of the previous letter. Senders and receivers of letters develop a two-sided relationship in which they maintain a closed conversation on paper. Any single letter in this dyadic linkage makes little sense to an outsider, and even members of the twosome themselves sometimes laugh at their own loss of a train of thought from one letter to the next. Since each writer keeps no copy of her letter, it is possible, especially if a long period of time has passed between letters, for the receiver to be unable to link a specific answer in a letter to a topic, or to recall the question which had provoked the answer. For example, the reason for asking about the May issue of a magazine may have slipped from the memory of the writer who posed the original question, and she may have to write back: "Now I can't even remember what I said that made you tell me you didn't see it. Seems like I'm losing my mind. Ha! Ha!" Writers, adults and children alike, often mark such expressions in their letters with exclamation points, or words such as *Ha Ha*, *Tee hee*, or even *sigh*. They also add symbols such as a string of Xs or Os for kisses and hugs, or a smiling face at the bottom of the letter.

Such conversational chains in writing are relatively rare in Roadville. Over a period of twelve months, women average writing less than one letter per month. Some women occasionally express the ideal that they "should" write more letters, just as they "should" read more, but childcare and household responsibilities take "too much time." As the young women of Roadville get older, they write letters less and less frequently, saying that they have no quiet time to themselves, and to write a letter when others are around would be considered "rude." The greeting cards and thank you notes continue, however, for these are strongly tied to courtesy and "good breeding." The brief notes on these carry little news though, and their only conversational gambit is the "how are you?" opener which is answered and closed off by the writer. The remainder of the message is without conversational character and carries a minimum of content.

Receipt of greeting cards, thank you notes, and letters is orally acknowledged and shared in each household, especially between women and children. Arriving home from school, children in Roadville often hear: "We got a letter from Aunt Margie today; let me read it to you" or "There's a birthday card for you from your cousins." Telephone calls between some family members occur frequently, and the letters or cards are often referred to in these calls. Reserved for relaying news of crises, impending events, or discussing serious family or business affairs, phone calls do not overlap in content with letters. Only rarely is an intervening phone call mentioned in subsequent letters. For some families, phone calls parallel greeting cards: distant relatives, especially the elderly, receive birthday cards *and* a phone call on their birthday. On these occasions children, as well as adults, speak briefly on the phone to the honored party.

When asked what kinds of writing they do, Roadville residents first name *letters* and *notes*. The latter are distinguished from the former by their brevity, range of purposes, possible transmittal by means other than the official mail service, and by the fact that they do not contain all the parts normally included in a letter (such as date, salutation, closing, etc.). Roadville residents include as *notes* they write (as opposed to *notes* in general) their additions to commercial greeting cards, messages to teachers sent through students, reminders to children or others of duties or requests, jottings made while reading, reminders put in lunch boxes or attached to the refrigerator with a magnet, and the troublesome missives sent back and forth between children in school. Teachers write notes on students' work, and parents are often asked to respond; parents have to send notes to ask for excused absences for their children or to ask for appointments with the teacher. The most frequent type of note to school – that explaining an absence – contains no salutation, usually no date, and is highly formulaic: "Please excuse Bobby's absence because he was sick [had to go to the doctor, had a fever, etc.]." There is usually no closing before the signature. Far more wide-ranging in content and form are notes written to children and left to remind them of chores or to tell them the whereabouts of parents who are not in when they come home from school. "Dear Bobby – Do your homework. Don't turn on the TV. I'll be home by 5:00. Mamma." A note to the mailman who has left a postage-due request might read: "I didn't have change. Can you change the dollar? Sorry. Mrs. Jay Turner."

When given tasks for Sunday School class or for Women's Circle, Roadville residents often make notes on materials they have to read or jot down points they want to make. They "borrow" notebook paper from the schoolchildren in the family, usually fold the sheet in half, and write partial sentences. For example, preparatory notes for a circle meeting might read as follows:

Rita to lead prayer
Betty – lesson – Genesis 16–23
Questions after lesson

Sarah's qualities, trials, help to Abraham
Her child
Sarah's age
Closing prayer – Sue

Slips of paper will be placed in the Bible to mark passages to be read, location of maps, or useful commentaries. Both men and women dislike reading aloud in public or having to speak formally. When they have control over activities in their clubs and church circles, they keep reading aloud to a minimum, ask individuals ahead of time if they will lead in prayer and no one ever seems to think these occasions call for the writing-out of a full text beforehand. Prayers are brief, simple, formulaic, and often said quietly so that only those closest to the person "leading" the prayer hear the actual words said aloud. A public prayer is not an occasion for performance. Notes for such occasions seem to be primarily a reminder of the sequence and participants in events and major points to be covered.

These varieties of notes and the letters of Roadville women are the longest connected texts written by adult community members. Almost all other types of writing in the community are disconnected texts, made up of isolated words, brief and often incomplete sentences, and short notations of explanation to accompany numerals. Just as women write more letters and notes than men, so they write more of these disconnected texts than men. They make grocery lists, write checks, fill out church envelopes for their tithes to the church, write labels in their baby books and fill in the blanks beside statements such as "I first smiled at —." "I walked at age —." Certain times of the year call for more writing than others. In October, many Roadville women order some of their Christmas gifts from mail-order catalogues; during canning and freezing season, all jars and packages are labeled and dated. School forms have to be filled out each September. Men only rarely write lists, sometimes write checks, and often make notes when getting together information for "the income tax man." Some men order items from sporting goods magazines, but they often ask their wives to fill out the forms, write the check, and address the envelope. Table 6.3 indicates the types of uses of writing in Roadville homes and the general categories of purposes these writing tasks serve.[12]

Table 6.3 *Types of uses of writing in Roadville*

MEMORY AIDS:	Writing to serve as a memory aid for both the writer and others (grocery lists, labels in baby books, outlines of sequence and content of circle meetings, frequently called telephone numbers jotted in front of phonebook).
SUBSTITUTES FOR OR REAFFIRMATION OF ORAL MESSAGES:	Writing used when direct oral communication was not possible or to follow up on oral exchanges (notes for tardiness and absence from school, assignments following class discussions, messages left by adults for children coming home before parent).
FINANCIAL:	Writing to record numerals and to write out amounts and purposes of expenditures and for signatures (checks, signing forms, filling out church, school, and mail-order forms).
SOCIAL-INTERACTIONAL:	Writing to give information and extend courtesies and greetings pertinent for maintaining social linkages (letters, notes on commercial greeting cards, thank you notes).

Note. Listed in relative order of frequency of occasions when time on these types of tasks exceeded five minutes per day.

The types and uses of writing by children in Roadville are far more restricted than those of adults. Their occasions and tasks for writing are largely motivated by others – parents forcing them to write thank you notes, teachers giving assignments, and coaches asking them to sign pledges of good behavior. There are few opportunities for children themselves to decide on occasions for their writing: making their Christmas gift lists, filling out order forms for items from sports magazines, and sending notes back and forth in classrooms. Girls do more of the latter than boys, and the number of such notes decreases as the children move through the grades in school. Mothers, especially, often scold their children for not recognizing when they need to do some writing. For example, children who leave the house while their parents are out are told to leave a note telling where they are, but instead children usually just tell a neighbor and count on the fact their parents will check with the neighbors when they wonder about their children's whereabouts.

In Roadville writing is an individual choice, not a group activity or even a group-sanctioned event. Those who write share their writing uneasily with anyone outside their familiar dyads for letter-writing or note-exchanges. They refer to their notes for circle meetings or their grocery lists or memos on the phonebook cover as "jottings," or "chicken-scratchings." Writing is private, done only when necessary, and as such, it occupies only a small part of daily life in Roadville. Most residents would agree with Rob Macken who said: "I don't write much, don't see a need to, what with the telephone and all. I can when I have to, but that's about it." Only Mrs. Macken expressed the view that if children saw and did more writing at home, their schoolwork would improve, but her own writing habits did not differ markedly from those of other Roadville women, and her average number of letters written during a year was about that of the rest of the Roadville women. Writing is not a high priority among the "shoulds" of community members, and there is little interest in extending their writing habits or improving their children's except insofar as writing relates to specific school tasks.

A useful habit and "a good one besides"

Talk about reading differs in tenor and content from talk about writing. Talk about writing seems pointless to Roadville residents, and they find little to say about it. But they readily talk about reading, naming it as a "should" of high priority for them and for their children. The church values reading; the school depends on it; all should do it "for their own good." Reading can be done in groups and by individuals; reading is a way "to help not only yourself, but others." Parents should read to their children: "by reading, you learn things you can share with others"; "through reading you learn to *do* things." Reading is enthusiastically endorsed by all of Roadville, and there is an abundance of reading materials around community members. They subscribe to magazines: *Better Homes and Gardens, McCalls, Popular Mechanics, People,* and *Time* are the favorites along with denominational magazines that come as a result of their church membership. They have the local paper delivered every evening, and some few families also receive the regional paper each morning. They buy *National Enquirer, Family Circle,* and other reading materials available at the grocery store or drug store. In addition, there are numerous advertisements and catalogues which come through the mail. Roadville residents also have numerous types of reading they

Table 6.4 *Types of uses of reading in Roadville*

INSTRUMENTAL:	Reading to gain information for practical needs of daily life (telephone dials, clocks, bills and checks, labels on products, reminder notes, school messages, patterns for dress-making).
NEWS-RELATED:	Reading to gain information about third parties or distant events (newspaper items, church denominational magazines, memos from the mill on the union, health and safety, etc.).
CONFIRMATIONAL:	Reading to check, confirm, or announce facts or beliefs (the Bible, Sunday School materials, camper or sports magazines, newspaper stories, appliance warranties and directions).
SOCIAL-INTERACTIONAL: (primarily used by women and children)	Reading to gain information pertinent to social linkages and forthcoming activities (church newsletters, greeting cards, letters, newspaper features – especially on sports page).
RECREATIONAL/ EDUCATIONAL:	Reading for temporary entertainment or planning a recreational event ("funny papers" or comics in newspapers; brochures on campgrounds; advertisements for home shows, movies, or musical programs; ball game schedules, scores, and line-ups; bedtime stories to preschoolers).

Note. Listed in relative order of frequency of occasions when time on these types of tasks exceeded five minutes per day.

save – some, such as the church bulletin, for only a week; some, such as programs of football games in which their children played, for years, tucked away in scrapbooks. There are other materials certain authority figures tell them to read: the Bible, Sunday School lessons, warranties, circulars on union movements in the regional textile mills, directions for putting together Christmas toys or playing new games.

Two features stand out in the observation of reading habits in Roadville: everyone talks about reading, but few people do it; and of those who do read, few follow through on any action which might be suggested in the reading material. Table 6.4 indicates the types of actual uses of reading in Roadville homes and the general functions reading serves.[13] It is important to note that some of these uses included here occur only rarely for most individuals, though the sources and the belief in their value exist in every Roadville home. For example, Jay Turner is one of those who praise reading. He subscribes to three magazines – one on camps and camper life, another on mechanics, and another on sports. He faithfully brings home the church bulletin, Sunday School books, and notices from the mill about new health and safety regulations, visits from a union representative, or changes in credit union practices. Night after night, he sits in his big chair after dinner and watches television. The piles of magazines grow higher and higher in the large basket beside his chair, until Alice declares a general house-cleaning and throws them out or moves them to the garage. Mrs. Dee and her daughter say children today cannot read as well as "they used to," and they often ask the neighborhood children to read to them or to tell them a "piece" they learned in school. They receive several publications through the church, and they also subscribe to *Southern Living*, a magazine distributed primarily in the South, and several needlework catalogues arrive each month. These decorate the bottom shelf of two tables in Mrs. Dee's living room, and when asked about them, Mrs. Dee confesses she has looked at the pictures, picked a recipe or two from *Southern Living*, and she plans to get back to the magazines "later."

No one is more adamant about proclaiming the values of reading than the young mothers in Roadville – Betty, Peggy, and Martha. They themselves subscribe to one or another of the magazines from companies which supply patterns for sewing, and they either buy on the newsstand or subscribe to one or more of the home decorating magazines. Occasionally one of them will buy a romance magazine and read it in private, being careful to discard it quickly, so it will not be discovered. They also occasionally buy or borrow a novel or nonfiction book from a visiting relative from Alberta. But they, like their elders, praise reading more than they practice it. They carefully save the magazines and may even clip recipes, room plans, or do-it-yourself ideas they talk about with their husbands over dinner or during a weekend camping trip. They will clip obituaries, features about friends, recipes, or decorating schemes from the local newspaper and save these as well, stuffing checkered notebooks or desk drawers with these clippings and their good intentions to read and reread these materials "someday."

Ethnographer learning

Clipped recipes and home decorating ideas, notices of home shows (convention-hall exhibitions of gardening and home decoration projects) in Alberta, or sales at local stores are not enough to prompt Roadville family members to action. If they see the recipe demonstrated on a television cooking program, hear and see an announcement of the home show on radio and television, or talk to someone who has gone to the sale, they may take some action. But there are no possible secondary reinforcements to help them take the steps from actually possessing many of the reading materials that are in their homes, to reading them, to following up the written messages. Notices sent home from school are read, but not acted upon without some prompting from the children. Directions to home appliances are saved, but not read except when something goes wrong. Home decorating schemes are read and often discussed, but only rarely do either husband or wife follow them through. The only exception to the general failure to follow through on the message of written materials is pattern instructions for dressmaking. Betty, Peggy, and Martha sew for themselves and their children, and though their mothers say they used to sew without dress patterns, they all buy and use dress patterns now. They follow these instructions more closely in the sewing of the garment than the cutting, for they have been taught by their mothers or older relatives how to lay out the pattern on the fabric more economically than indicated by the pattern instructions. When Betty and Peggy started their homemaking, they reported that they had to read basic cookbooks to learn how to do "the simplest things." They had grown up in homes where most of the vegetables were provided from a garden and then canned or frozen, but they often did not know how to recognize different cuts of meat in the supermarket or how to cook vegetables, such as broccoli, which were not homegrown.

Bedtime stories

Roadville wives and mothers buy books for their children and bring home from church special Sunday School materials supplied for the young. Before their babies are six months old, Roadville mothers read simple books, usually featuring a single object on each page, to their children. Later they choose books which tell simplified Bible stories; introduce the alphabet, numbers, or nursery rhymes; or contain "real-life" stories about boys and girls, usually taking care of their pets either at home or on a farm. When their children begin to watch "Sesame Street" and "Electric Company" on television, they buy books, games, and toys derived from these shows. They read the advertisements for other games and toys that appear on boxes the play things come in, and as their children get older, they advise them to do the same.

Within Roadville, the most predictable reading activity in those homes with preschoolers is the bedtime story. Before taking a nap and before going to bed at night, children are read to from their books. If the baby is fussy and hungry, the father will try reading to the child while dinner is prepared. But usually, mothers do the bedtime reading. Mothers rarely sustain book-reading with a child of less than one year of age for more than a few minutes. Mothers and fathers may try, by naming the item on the page of the cloth book, letting the baby handle the book, pointing to the item, and generally trying to maintain the child's interest by talking about the item, but if the baby seems fussy or restless, the mother, father, or other family member puts down the book and tries gentle jostling, patting on the back, or diversions with pets, older siblings, or nearby lights or noise.

Shortly after one year of age, however, most children tolerate being read to by adults. Before bedtime, Peggy would initially choose a book for Danny, but as he grew older, she would let him choose a book from his bookshelf for her to read. For new books, Peggy would talk the story through before reading the actual words: "This is a book about a little boy. He has a dog. See, there's his dog. He takes care of his dog. Let's read the book now and see what else he does." Throughout the reading of the text, Peggy would ask questions about the boy and his dog, often answering her own questions if Danny did not respond. When reading the alphabet or number books as Danny got older, Peggy would ask him to read or to point to the letter or numeral on the page. Danny loved blocks and block-building, and one set of his blocks was marked with letters of the alphabet. A familiar routine of trying to find the block to match the letter in the alphabet book developed when Danny was about two years of age. Though the game never lasted for more than seven letters of the book, Danny found the linking of letter on the block to letter in the book a game which held his attention. Simplified Bible stories are told or read to the children, and they are asked to name characters (the baby Jesus, Mary). Adults repeatedly ask children to name the animals and other objects in the pictures; they are also asked to imitate the sound the animal makes or to tell the name of the animal or object in a familiar story. The earliest stage of reading emphasizes labels and answers to questions like "What is it?" "Who is it?" "Where is it?" and other questions which can be answered from immediate attention to the text and its pictures. Some few formulaic questions move away from the text of the storybook itself and draw on the child's real-world knowledge or information learned in other contexts. Immediate and tangible links between book materials and real life are occasionally called for by adults or volunteered by the children; some of these depend upon attention to subtle features of illustrations or events in the book. If the child has just bought cowboy boots, the mother may ask what the boy in the book's pictures is wearing. The boots may not have been mentioned anywhere in the story, nor have they ever been discussed before this occasion. Yet now the child is asked to link his own new boots to those on the boy in the book.

All the preschoolers of Roadville participate vigorously in bedtime story reading. Danny was continuously active, bouncing in and out of his mother's lap, interrupting, or announcing his intention to end the episode. Bobby was more tolerant if the book's subject interested him, and he was fascinated by animals. He liked to name them, touch them in the books, ask his own questions about them, and imitate their sounds and actions. Kim, Sally, and Wendy were also tolerant during these early stages of book-reading. Kim was offered the widest choice of books, because her mother as a teacher could bring books home from the school library; Kim's selection of books was not limited to simply real-life stories or nursery rhymes. Her mother introduced her to some books by the best-known current writers and illustrators of children's books. All of the children could, before they were three years of age, pretend to "read" certain books, holding the book before them correctly, and reciting some passages from the page. They "titled" books according to their major topic. *Apples* was the name of the book about a kitten of that name, but the alphabet book which began with a picture of an apple was also often termed *Apple* by Bobby.

Parents extend their efforts with reading at home to certain domains outside the home. Preschoolers are kept entertained at the dentist's or doctor's office with magazines and books, and if none is available, adults name the items in the office and describe their features to the children: "Look, that's a goldfish. This one is striped. You don't have one like that, do you?" Sometimes in the car, they will name traffic signs, stores, churches, or parks as they drive past; and visits to the grocery store also occasion numerous reinforcements of overgeneralized terms to a variety of items. All the children associated some favorite items with print by the end of their first year. For Wendy, it was animal cracker boxes; for Danny, it was boxes of Bugles, a type of snackfood made of corn. Both would yell when they saw these in the grocery: "cook-cook" for animal crackers, and "booga" for Bugles. When they overextended the meanings of these to similarly shaped boxes, as Danny (18 months) did one day to a box of pretzels, their parents did not correct them. Danny's father took a pretzel from the box and gave it to Danny, but did not offer a new name initially. After Danny had tasted the pretzel, he smacked his lips and rubbed the salt on the remaining portion of the pretzel. His daddy then said, "Salty, that's probably too salty for you." Thereafter, when Danny saw pretzel boxes, he could distinguish them from Bugle boxes, and he called them "sot" on a few occasions, then went back to calling them "booga" when his parents did not understand his reference to pretzels as "sot." Sometimes parents said they did not correct overgeneralizations, because they thought the correct word "too hard" for the child.

On the way to the grocery, Wendy (3 years, 18 months) saw a sign and yelled out "Stop." Martha agreed, "Yes, that's a stop sign." Wendy had, however, misread a *yield* sign as *stop*, and her mother offered no explanation of what the actual message on the sign was or why she did not actually stop at this sign on all occasions. I asked Martha later why she had not told Wendy the word read *yield* and not *stop*. Martha said she thought *yield* was too hard for Wendy, and she would not understand its meaning because "it's not a word we use like *stop*."

When Roadville children pass their third birthdays, both parents and Sunday School teachers expect them to be able to sit and listen to a story and not to participate – either verbally or physically – during the story. Bedtime stories at this age become something of a struggle of wills, since mothers want to read longer stories and have their children sit and "learn to listen" passively. The children, many of whom have come to enjoy and relish active verbal and physical participation in the stories, find this shift to a new learning experience troublesome, and the story time is often cut short. The same pattern is followed at church, where children are age-segregated between "the little ones" and the three- and four-year-olds. The "little ones" bound about the playroom engaged with toys and only periodically give overt attention to the teacher, who may be reading a storybook and asking questions, or demonstrating differences and likenesses between the trucks (or dogs, firemen, etc.) of the story and those of the Sunday School playroom. Three- and four-year-olds are usually in a room of their own, without as many toys for riding or blocks for building. The teachers read stories to the children and ask them to listen to the story and then answer questions. In smaller churches, five-year-olds are placed with this group, and their listening passively and responding with the right answers is pointed out as model behavior for the younger children to follow.

Within this passive "listen and learn and repeat" period (which is usually established by the age of four), the Sunday School teacher gives the children Bible story pictures to color and lets the children draw pictures for their mothers on Mother's Day.[14] They are also given the opportunity to draw on a large wall mural "things I am thankful for." Teachers add to children's drawings magazine pictures of mothers in the kitchen, sunsets, houses, etc., but the children are encouraged to draw flowers, their pets, the sun, raindrops, and other items familiar to them from their environment. At home, the children are given coloring books illustrating television characters, the alphabet and numbers, Bible stories, and farm animals – books which repeat the themes of the earliest storybooks the children had read to them. During the preparation of dinner, Mrs. Macken frequently asked four-year-old Kim to get her coloring book of animals and sit at the kitchen table and color. She pointed out places where Kim must stay in the lines and advised choices of colors. Of all the children in Roadville, Kim was the most advanced in this task and the most tolerant of parental influence on her choice of colors. Danny, at about age four, was also a great fan of coloring books, but he was less inclined to choose the colors his mother suggested. Children never initiated these coloring, connect-the-dot, or punch-out-and-paste tasks themselves. An adult was always present, asking questions such as "What is it?" "What color will you color it?" "Who's that?" and giving directions and advice.

In Roadville, there is a concerted effort on the part of adults to initiate their children both into pre-scripted discourse around printed material and into passive listening behavior, and they believe book-reading to be both recreational and educational for children. Both mothers and fathers expect their children to answer questions they ask about books, but they also expect them to listen quietly when someone is reading from a book. The questions asked are almost always requests for *what*-explanations, and there is a set answer decided upon in the mind of the adult before the child answers. A dog in a book is a *dog* – not a mutt, a hound dog, or Blackie – unless the parent has established one of these terms as the answer to the question "What's that?" Just as children are expected to answer questions about objects around them with the "right" answer, they are to give the "right" answer to queries about books. Adults believe that the proper use of words and understanding of the meaning of written words are important for their children's educational and religious success.

For Roadville children, there are three overlapping stages of their experiences with print before school. In the earliest stage, they are introduced to discrete bits and pieces of books – alphabet letters, simple shapes, basic colors, and commonly represented items in books for children (apple, ball, baby, clown, etc.). Since few of the books bought for them when they are very young have a story-line, usually items pictured are neither illustrated in their ordinary context nor placed in the make-believe context of a fictional story. They are often represented in two-dimensional, flat-line drawings. Parents ask simple questions and expect their children to be predictable information-givers, repeating the specific and discrete bits of information the adults have preformulated as the answer. During this period, there is an on-going pre-scripted participation by adult and child, in which parents ask questions, and children also sometimes pose questions and take turns pretending they are reading to adults.

In the second stage, adults expect children to recognize the power of print to instruct, inform, and entertain. Adults or older children perform for the benefit of young children: they read to them, and in return, the children sit passively and listen and learn in order to participate in follow-up questions. Instead of alphabet and farm animals books, adults usually choose books with a story; old familiars such as "The Three Bears" and some tales of "Sesame Street" characters. They do not like to be interrrupted until the tale is finished, and they may then ask questions about the story and offer a moral about the misbehavior of Goldilocks, Ernie, or the Cookie Monster.

As children approach the age for kindergarten, the third stage begins. They are given workbooks and encouraged to write their names, draw straight lines, color in the lines, follow the numbers and dots and push out and paste shapes and letters. These adult-supervised experiences reinforce repeatedly that the written word can be taken apart into small pieces and one item linked to another by following certain rules. Children gain manipulative experience in the linear sequential nature of books. Parents tell them to follow simple rules: stay in the lines, write answers on the lines, begin at the beginning, match the cutouts of letters and shapes to the corresponding diagrams. Adults and children repeatedly link these behaviors to school. Adults tell their children they will need to learn to do all these things before they go to school; five-year-olds proudly announce to visitors they have "school books" as they show off their coloring books.[15]

Bedtime stories and sessions of coloring and cutting and pasting in books at the kitchen table come to an end when children go to school. Instead of practicing cooperative questions and answers, passively listening to stories, or working in workbooks, children in the kindergarten and first grade bring home their schoolwork and display it proudly. Mothers admonish the children for not staying in the lines and agree with the teacher's marks showing the need for more care, better printing, etc. Increasingly as the children move through the grades, there may continue to be some display of schoolwork, but adults offer no comments on the content or specific form of such work, other than to say "It looks nice," "It's messy," or "Does she let you write in pencil?" The age for any bedtime routine has passed, and there is no established time for reading together between adults and children. The family watches television together, when there is agreement on the programs to watch, and there is talk of when and where the family will go camping next. Fathers sometimes ask their sons to look at a brochure for a new camper van or a new piece of equipment for the truck. Fathers and sons talk about the football and baseball scores, and fathers sometimes announce the averages while reading the evening newspaper.

Occasionally, especially immediately after a birthday or Christmas, the family will play a new game together or join in putting together a toy or piece of mechanical equipment which has been given the children. Choice of such toys usually depends upon the stated preference of a child, who has become familiar with the game at a friend's house or by watching television. Thus, there is usually no question of having to read directions, since the children usually know how the game is to be played, or how the remote control race car goes together. If in doubt, some parents read the directions, but they then turn to putting together the item by "common sense." Fathers and their children usually work in silence, with an occasional protest from the child to say "That doesn't look right." No talk of sequencing the steps, deciding on the location of all parts before assembly, or considering the consequences of assembling pieces in the wrong order goes along with the task. The same silent demonstration of how-to-do-it occurs when children learn to hold a bat, wear a catcher's mitt, make jello, sew a doll's dress, or plant a watermelon seed. Adults say "Do it this way," without detailing the steps or components of "this way." Mothers watch and encourage their daughters' efforts at sewing, gardening, and cooking; children are often told "That's good," or "That looks right." If they do something wrong, they are scolded with general admonitions, such as "Next time be more careful," "Put it away [in its usual place]," "If you don't know how to do it right, you shouldn't be doing it," or "Put it up [in its usual place]; you know that's not the way to do it." Explanations which move beyond warnings or general statements of encouragement are rarely offered by adults, but they encourage and invite children to practice skills frequently. Help in the garden or kitchen during canning season, and in the preparation of the camper for a family trip is welcomed, and children are almost always willing to help, since all the children of Roadville take part in such activities, and to have to do so is not considered "sissy" or unusual in any way. If, during these tasks, children do not understand an order, they keep trying, and may ask a question such as "You want me to do this? [demonstrating their current efforts]," or "Is this right?" There is no talk of school habits and how they might help in home tasks. Occasionally, a parent will say to a child who has just done a stupid thing "Can't you read? What are you going to school for, anyway?" In general, however, the domains of school and home are kept separate by both child and parent once the child starts to school and certainly by the end of the primary years. Adults expect the school to teach, and the child to learn.

A question of degree and kind

Both Trackton and Roadville are literate communities and each has its own traditions for structuring, using, and assessing reading and writing. The residents of each community are able to read printed and written materials in their daily lives and, on occasion, they produce written messages as part of the total pattern of communication in the community. In both communities, the residents turn from spoken to written uses of language and vice versa as the occasion demands, and the two modes of expression serve to supplement and reinforce each other. Yet, in terms of the usual distinctions made between oral and literate traditions, neither community may be simply classified as either "oral" or "literate."

Many authors have painted the contrast between "oral" and "literate" traditions in strong terms, emphasizing important differences in attitudes and behaviors. Most of these accounts, and many images in the mind of the general public, categorize communities as *either* literate *or* oral. Oral traditions are often considered as essentially the same, with only minor cultural differences, wherever they are said to characterize a society. Many accounts also tend to consider the forms and functions of literacy in a "literate" community as having certain universal characteristics. For example, many analysts of the social and individual functions of literacy limit their analyses essentially to the development of expository prose and closely related phenomena, or those literacy requirements most valued in the school and often automatically associated with the workplace. In Trackton and Roadville, there are multiple uses of written and oral language, and members have access to and use both. Spontaneous oral adjustments of written material often result in longer, more complex sentences with accompanying shifts in style from the formal to the more informal. Talk around and about written material incorporates personal or group experience; the highly personalized first person singular of the oral mode replaces the more formal, distant third person. Using the instructions to put together a toy or reading a letter from a daycare agency can provoke recitation of personal experiences or evaluations based on what one has seen, done, or been told by friends. What is written – whether it be obituary, recipe, or letter – calls up multiple specific cases, from which Roadville and Trackton members move to make generalizations and – sometimes – to decide on their own course of action. In each community, there are established patterns of language use around the written word: types of questions to be asked, listening behaviors to be observed, and types of talk by individuals or groups about reading and writing. It is impossible to characterize Trackton and Roadville with existing descriptions of either the oral or literate traditions: they are neither and they are both. Yet the forms, occasions, content, and functions of their reading and writing differ greatly from each other, and each varies in degree and kind from patterns followed by the townspeople.

Roadville residents use writing only when they have to, and view it as an occasional necessary tool – to aid their memory, to help them buy and sell things, and sometimes to help keep them in touch with family and friends. Few write letters; those who do, see them as conversations between parties who know each other well and need no background information. The content and form of their letters are predictable. They do not use letters to complain about faulty products, to advise their politicians, or to provide extended narratives for photographs in their baby books. They prefer direct face-to-face contact to transmit or obtain information. They telephone distant relatives to advise them of family crises. They confront the local hardware man when the small appliance they bought there breaks on its first use. When he maintains the faulty product is the company's fault, and that they should write to the company, Roadville families denounce the businessman to their neighbors and vow never to buy there again. With one exception – Lillie Mae – Trackton women write few letters but send greeting cards. Most men write only for financial affairs; women jog their memory with written notes and send occasional brief notes to school or the local merchant.

Reading in Roadville is a frequently praised ideal. In Trackton, almost no one talks about reading as an activity unto itself.

Ethnographer learning

Trackton residents read aloud to anyone who wants to listen on the plaza, report what they have read, ask for interpretations of written materials by the group, and enjoy the stories which invariably ensue from a report of something read. Roadville family members consciously collect reading materials for themselves and for their young children; they often talk about how they are going to learn how to do something by reading, but the steps of reading the materials and translating knowledge from the written word into action are often not taken. Women read and follow carefully directions for sewing from dressmaking patterns; men sometimes read sports articles, announcements, vacation and camper information, the headlines, and advertising materials; but do-it-yourself projects and plans, old magazines, and brochures often simply accumulate in the garage, kitchen, and beside the "reading chair." Trackton residents have no such accumulation of reading materials; whatever comes into the community is usually either read, then burned or used for other purposes, or immediately discarded. There is no space or time assigned for reading; its occurrences follow the flow of daily social interactions and decision-making in the community. The meaning of whatever is read is interpreted jointly and socially: "What does it mean?" becomes "What does it say about me, or someone or something I know, and what do I do?" But such meaning is not built individually, except in financial matters, because the community members share their experiences to build interpretive bridges from print to practice.

Children in Roadville grow up surrounded by print: their room decorations, homemade alphabet quilts, books, toys, and church experiences give them an abundance of reading materials. Adults consider these materials and their uses important for every child's development – intellectually and spiritually. Mothers and fathers read to their children, focus their attention on illustrations, question them closely about items and events in the text, ask them to recite nursery rhymes, and buy them storybooks and coloring or punch-out books about television characters. They play with their children, telling them to pay attention to keeping the parts of games with the instructions in the "right" game box, and saying they should read the directions for their mechanical toys. They guide their children to understand baseball scores, line-ups, and averages by frequent talk about these, and they model and demonstrate with encouragement their children's efforts at ball-playing, piano-playing, and putting a new fishing pole together.

Trackton children have no books, and they find their reading in tasks which evolve for them in the house, the plaza, and at the neighborhood store. They learn to vie with each other in reading when reading is a game of challenge or competition for a favor. They remember print from re-creating its scene and its use. For them there seems a holistic coherency about print which does not depend on its discrete elements, and they find it puzzling to shift the context or alter the manner of presentation of print. Each new appearance of the same words seems at first a new reading task, because it does not cohere as the same whole read earlier. Buried in the on-going stream of eating, buying, and playing, reading for Trackton children is reading to learn what they need to know before they go to school to be successful in their community. They and their parents at home and in church take written materials and build from these, creating sets of phrases, and varying repetitions of these phrases in raised hymns, prayers, sermons, playsongs, and "junk talk." Words are action, and a creative oral rendering of a message can move an audience to action. Preachers, men of music, and the best playsong performers claim they cannot stick to written text. Seemingly thoughts which were once shaped into words on paper become recomposed in each time and space. Abiding by the written word limits one's performance from being created anew with each audience and setting. To be sure, some of the meaning in the written text remains stable, but as one preacher put it, "the Words must live," and performer and audience alike must therefore integrate the words into their personal experience and express their meaning for them.

Beyond their home and community life, Roadville and Trackton residents have few occasions for reading or writing on the job. For those working in the textile mills, in years past, they had to fill in the blanks on the employment application, but in the past decade, potential employees are interviewed, and the personnel officer fills in the application. The employee is asked only to sign the application. Once on the job, occasions for writing and reading vary. Those who operate machines in the weaving or spinning rooms, for example, simply record numerals and sometimes abbreviations for technical terms used to refer to aspects of the process. At those times of the year (July 4 and Christmas) when a mill party is planned, employees may be asked to sign up and note times of attendance. In some of the smaller mills, when an employee is ill, someone will put a greeting card on the bulletin board and ask others to sign it. Those who hold more specialized jobs, such as loom fixer, occasionally have to write out orders for parts, brief reports on repairs or defective parts, but this writing is usually prescribed in content, length, and placement on a form. Numerous abbreviations are used to refer to parts, since those receiving the written order know the terminology well. Those who work in the laboratory of the mill label containers, write brief reports or notes, using abbreviations and terms familiar to those in the laboratory, and occasionally fill out order forms for equipment or chemical supplies. For most employees, reading material in the mill, beyond section names and signs marking restrooms, lunch-room, trash cans, soft drink machines, etc., is limited to information on the bulletin boards. There are posted notices of health and safety rulings, opportunities with the credit union, and newspaper clippings featuring the marriage, death, or recent family reunion of an employee of that section of the mill. There is, in short, no need or direct incentive in mill jobs to make Trackton and Roadville adults feel they should read and write more than they already do.

Roadville and Trackton residents have a variety of literate traditions, and in each community these are interwoven in different ways with oral uses of language, ways of negotiating meaning, deciding on action, and achieving status. Patterns of using reading and writing in each community are interdependent with ways of using space (having bookshelves, decorating walls, displaying telephone numbers), and using time (bedtime, meal hours, and homework sessions). Habits of using the written word also develop as they help individuals fulfill self-perceived roles of caregiving and preparing children for school. Roadville parents believe it their task to praise and practice reading with their young children; Trackton adults believe the young have to learn to be and do, and if reading is necessary for this learning, that will come. In both communities, women write and read more than men; and there are patterns of certain types of reading and writing tasks only members of one or the other sex or individuals of a certain age are expected to do. In Roadville, the absoluteness of ways of talking about what is written fits church ways of talking about what is written. Behind the written word is an authority, and the text is a message which can be taken apart only insofar as its analysis does not extend too far beyond the text and commonly agreed upon experiences. New syntheses and multiple interpretations create alternatives which challenge fixed roles, rules, and "rightness." In Trackton, the written word is for negotiation and manipulation – both serious and playful. Changing and changeable, words are the tools performers use to create images of themselves and the world they see. For Roadville, the written word limits alternatives of expression; in Trackton, it opens alternatives. Neither community's ways with the written word prepares it for the school's ways.

7 *The townspeople*

The way to be

When Annie Mae says, "They've come up with some new rules to make 'em feel important," she is referring to the townspeople – teachers, preachers, politicians, and "all the 'big heads.'" The townspeople are blacks and whites[1] whose names and influence waft in and out of Trackton and Roadville through newspaper articles about the city council's debate on city buses, permission forms for school field trips, and invitations to a "community" meeting to talk about new urban housing. Townspeople not known by name can be identified immediately by Roadville and Trackton residents: clothes, bearing, speech, and habits of talking from or with pieces of paper mark them. Even preachers, black and white, who have churches in town and have become identified with Gateway's city projects such as daycare programs, neighborhood centres, the human relations council, and housing projects are "town folks." Only those preachers who remain "in the country" are not automatically counted as "big heads" – "folks that have forgotten where they come from or what it's like to have to keep up with all those rules."

The townspeople, black and white, are *mainstreamers*,[2] people who see themselves as being in "the main stream of things." They look beyond the Piedmont for rules and guidance in ways of dressing, entertaining themselves, decorating their homes, and decision-making in their jobs. Though for some of the oldtime families, their core values may be regional, many of their norms of conduct and bases for forming judgments about their own and others' behaviors have much in common with the national mainstream middle class generally presented in the public media as the American client or customer. Townspeople are strongly school-oriented, believing success in school, academically and socially, is a prerequisite for being successful as an adult. For them, school is an institution which helps instill values such as respectability, responsibility, and an acceptance of hard work. Early achievement within an institution that rewards adherence to norms of conduct reflecting these values is necessary for success in the workplace, whether as a businessperson, lawyer, politician, doctor, or teacher. Beyond these easily expressed ideals of mainstream behavior in school and workplaces, townspeople exhibit but can rarely articulate other mainstream norms of conduct. They respond to linearity as a criterion of organization: to be neat and orderly is to be in line; to be well-arranged, pieces of furniture are set parallel to the wall or at right angles to each other; to be properly landscaped, yards are marked off by straight hedgerows and flowerborders. Secondary sources, not the face-to-face network, are usually authoritative for mainstreamers. They choose their movies on the advice of the critics; they select their automobile tires on the recommendations of consumers' guides; they seek out professional advice for marital problems, and for interior decorating and landscaping ideas. An individual's assertion of formal credentials – either university degrees or public awards and distinction – makes him an authority. They formalize or "spell out in writing" rules for group activities, such as neighborhood tennis clubs, ladies' auxiliary clubs of the church, meetings of the human relations council, and graduation events at the senior high school.

The townspeople fall into two groups – oldtimers and new-comers. White oldtimers have long-standing family ties which link them to nearby farmlands; local businesses – hardware stores, department stores, etc.; or legal, medical, clerical, or educational roles in the region. Some are from the old textile families who founded the mills earlier in the century and still carry strong political influence across the state. The oldtime black townspeople are descendants of the free, propertied blacks who have remained in the region since the antebellum period, received their education in black colleges of the South, and have established business or farming reputations. White newcomers have come to the region through relocation by Northern industries, and they now consider the South their long-term future home. Black townspeople considered newcomers are from families whose ancestors had moved North in the 1920s and 1930s, achieved economic success, and now prefer to live in the South; they have returned to set up businesses, teach school, or farm and work in local industries. It is the rare newcomer who becomes actively involved in leadership in city politics, churches, or even the schools, since oldtimers look on newcomers in these positions with considerable caution.

Oldtimers are careful, however, not to appear to fear the changes newcomers might bring to the region. In many areas of the region's life, oldtimers say they welcome "new blood" and new ideas, but they want any change which comes to follow directions they define and to come with as little disruption to local habits and institutions as possible. Since Northern firms now control the textile mills, oldtimers and newcomers now work side by side in the mills' executive offices, and long-established families have become accustomed to passing their worship and leisure time shoulder-to-shoulder with newcomers in city churches and in the swimming and tennis clubs of their housing subdivisions. The newer families can be found in all the churches of town, even those Presbyterian and Baptist churches considered the oldest and most traditionally linked to the long-time elite families of the region.

Only among themselves do oldtimers recognize and talk about their long-standing family ties to the region or their forefathers' role in building the textile mills and the surrounding communities. With newcomers, they talk openly only of certain old allegiances: their ties to regional colleges and their preferences for one or the other of the region's professional football teams. For many of the oldtime families, the parents of young children today are the second generation to have represented their family at a regional college; their babies wear toy-sized bibs and sweat shirts announcing their membership in a future class of the same college or university. There is much good-natured rivalry as newcomers hear passionate arguments on the relative merits of these institutions of higher education.

In general, oldtimers are careful to present themselves as relatively free from old allegiances and open to new ideas and opinions. They say loudly they do not oppose change: they are in favor of bettering education, building a new pool at the Young Men's Christian Association, improving the downtown business district, allowing soccer in the public schools, changing zoning laws to allow multiple family housing, and supporting a halfway house for delinquent girls. They see themselves as modern-thinking, and they have no intention of allowing newcomers to think of them as backward, too conservative or religious, or unwilling to move the Piedmont ahead. They believe their forward thinking has made the quality of life the Piedmont offers superior to that of many other parts of the nation. Calm city politics, safe and clean streets, adequate recreational facilities, and interstate highways to major metropolitan centers announce the good life in the region.

White townspeople are particularly verbal about the need to include good schools as part of this quality package. The few private schools in the area argue that they offer solid academic standards, good discipline, and a Christian environment. They invite all who qualify to apply. Most oldtimers know, however, that to attract more industry to the region and to prove the quality of life is all that it should be, the *public* schools must be good. Therefore, many men and women among the oldtimers read carefully the relative ratings of school districts in the region and wait anxiously for the yearly reports on Scholastic Aptitude Test scores of students of high schools across the Piedmont. These are the scores that now count. Old scores, such as the relative percentage of black and white teachers and students in the schools, or the successes of the athletics teams and cheerleading squads, do not count nearly as much. By the end of the 1970s, there are very few who express resentment of black representation on the city council or the school board; they simply weigh the relative merits of the ideas and manner of presentation of black as well as white members. Busing as a major issue has passed for this area; academic standards, school discipline, teacher qualifications, uses of Federal funds, and the effects of low-achieving black and white students on the general academic reputation of the local high schools have increasingly become recurrent topics of concern and debate. Many of the oldtimers have at least one member of the family teaching in the local public schools, so there is a constant flow of specific incidents to feed the general trends reported in the local paper. In many of these families, school teaching has been in the family for three generations, and there is a sense that the family experiences across the years qualify oldtimers to evaluate and recommend changes in school practices.

Black townspeople also believe family experiences qualify them to place a high value on schools, but theirs is a more recent and perhaps a more cautious view. Several local black families have been in the region for years, having come there as free blacks and having established in the early twentieth century the few local black-owned businesses – shoe shops, laundromats, groceries, print shop, and trophy center, for example. Some have owned small plots of land for decades. Though they may have left to work up-North temporarily or to serve their twenty years in the service, they have now retired to the region to build a new house on the old farmland and to set up a business in town. Other black towns-people are the children of teachers who taught in the black schools. They have high hopes for education and a long-standing commitment to the view that schooling does make a difference. They are graduates of the region's black colleges and universities, and though they may have spent periods of their life out of the area, they are now back to stay, to build, and to show their children the advantages of the South as home. Some have built brick homes in the black suburbs of the region's towns, or they live in Alberta in integrated condominia or apartment complexes. Local, state, and regional sorority activities keep many of the women involved: planning scholarship drives for black students, scheduling regional conferences, or planning the food and decorations for the next reception for new members and installation of officers. They also give their time as church deaconesses or as members of the church ladies' auxiliary or choir. Both men and women financially support their college alma mater, and homecoming (an annual football game which all alumni are encouraged to attend) and other athletics events bring together alumni from all over the region. Though many of their children will not go to black colleges but rather to regional universities or state colleges, parents do not forget their own allegiance to their alma mater.

Within the black suburbs, many of the men are active in voluntary coaching of the community-center soccer or baseball team; their teams train regularly and seriously. They play to win, and many have brought home state trophies to the local neighborhood center, formerly the black high school. The older men, in particular, often with long-established roles in the black high school, serve on the human relations council or the school board. Their time is taken up by numerous committee meetings connected with that work, and they are frequently called on by local colleges and high schools to appear at public events, to speak on black heritage, or to judge the Miss Black Gateway contest.

For both black and white mainstream families, social interactions center not on their immediate neighborhoods, but on voluntary associations across the city and the region. Around Gateway, for example, some white mainstreamers live in the half dozen or so suburbs scattered on the outer edges of two sides of the city. The major black suburb of ranch-style brick homes is on another side of the city. A few white mainstreamers, especially those from up-North, have found some of the older downtown homes suitable for restoration, and these families remain near the city center, but they have generally chosen to restore only homes on the same side of the city center as the white suburbs. White and black mainstream families also locate themselves within a fifteen-mile radius of the city on pieces of land which have been in the family for decades. Few farm the land; they have small gardens, sometimes a horse or pony, and many have built a new brick ranch-style home a few miles from the rapidly deteriorating, now-abandoned, old frame family home. Younger black and white mainstream couples who do not yet have children often reject all of these local living options and choose instead apartments or condominia in Alberta, which offers far more entertainment possibilities than surrounding towns.

Thus it is not possible to speak of a centrally located mainstream community in either Gateway or any of the towns in the region. In all of these, mainstreamers, black and white, spread themselves out from the city center through expanding circles of suburbs around the town or city, and even to the big-city-like apartments and condominia of Alberta. From all of these locations, mainstream adults and children cluster their activities around voluntary associations, such as the Elks Club, Masonic Lodge, Young Men's Christian Association, Junior League, church activities, tennis and swimming clubs and work-related recreational occasions. Amidst the diverse student populations of integrated schools, mainstream children continue friendships initiated within their parents' network of friends. Hence in both in-school and out-of-school activities, the mainstream young choose as friends the children of those adults with whom their parents interact in specific clusters of voluntary associations. In school, rivalries among these mainstream groups of friends do not surface as group rivalries, but as competition among individuals. Leadership in student government and extracurricular clubs is said to be determined not by race, clique membership, or social status, but by the abilities and personality of individual students, black or white. This sense of competition among individuals striving to win by personality is linked to an air of entitlement which mainstream children develop through their continuous preschool and out-of-school opportunities. For most of them, activities out of school are as rigorously planned and scheduled as their participation in daily school classes. In the extracurricular lives their parents plan for them, they learn appropriate ways of getting ahead and displaying individual prowess and accomplishment. These ways of improving practice and performance are mingled with opportunities for learning what it means to be a member of a group and to choose, work with, and strive to be a group leader among those with whom one has voluntarily associated oneself.

Though accepted and expected by townspeople as a "natural" part of raising a family, these activities require consistent and continuous planning. In the homes of both black and white townspeople, women are the organizers of family schedules; these schedules – especially during the week – center around children. Women, whether they teach, own their own business, work in a downtown business, or work at home, schedule music lessons for children, practices for athletics events, visits to doctors and dentists, and trips to nearby Alberta for cultural events the entire family will attend. Piano lessons are the most popular choice for music lessons, but there are enough teachers of other instruments, such as the trombone, clarinet, drums, and guitar, that some families choose these. The faculties of local colleges sometimes offer music lessons, and the colleges sometimes schedule recitals for their students. Since life is generally lived in the suburbs or the nearby countryside, and there are no city buses, there is much chauffeuring needed – after school once a week to piano practice, to baseball practice five days a week, Boy Scouts or Indian Guides on another day, or to the city library to get a book needed for a term paper on another. The dentist or orthodontist gets squeezed in periodically with much complaint from the baseball player. There is relatively little time spent in neighborhoods during weekday afternoons. For both children and adults, most of the time out of school or work is spent on the way to or participating in voluntary associations or activities: the YMCA, the church, music lessons, the swimming pool or tennis club, or a nearby stable, where a pony or horse is boarded and weekly riding lessons are offered.

Weekend activities are, in many ways, more of the same, but of a culminating variety: playoffs for the baseball team, tennis matches at the recreation center, music recitals, church on Sunday morning, and either a football game on television in the winter, or the tennis court and swimming pool on summer afternoons. Favorite family vacation spots are the beach, nearby major metropolitan centers, or the nation's capital and historic sights along the way on the two-day drive there and back. Some women sew, often making biannual trips to regional fabric centers to buy up fabric to be used for a wardrobe planned ahead for the coming school year or for the summer. Town women often frequent handicraft shops in the local area or Alberta, making needlepoint covers for pillows, crewel work for dining room chairs, and macrame hangings for the house or patio. They also buy many of their clothes in Alberta or at beach shops during the summer.

For men and women, home maintenance and lawn upkeep provide the major sources of neighborly contact in both black and white suburbs. During spring, summer, and fall, lawnmowers, chain saws, and rototillers hum in each suburban area. Lawns are large, with lots of grass, shrubs, rose gardens, and flower beds of annuals. In addition, many families plant a small backyard vegetable garden. The shrubs require skilled care in pruning and fertilizing on several occasions during the year; males usually take on these tasks and fertilize and mow the grass. Females take care of the rose gardens and flower beds. Children often mow the grass during the summer and rake leaves in the fall. The garden is the major joint family activity: clearing, tilling, and planting involve fathers and sons; weeding, watering, fertilizing, and harvesting are the frequent tasks of women and children. Families freeze most of the excess produce from the garden, and during peach season, they travel to nearby orchards to buy peaches to can and freeze. Canning is an activity of women and children.

Life around and inside the home must be scheduled just like the events and activities beyond the home. All those adults who work outside the home have jobs which run from 8 a.m. until 4 p.m. or 9 a.m. until 5 p.m. Families get up at a regular hour on weekdays and have breakfast together; talk at breakfast invariably includes the day's schedule. All agree on afternoon chauffeuring to baseball games, dance lessons, or the riding ring, and a suitable family dinner hour which can be planned around the afternoon schedule of mother and children and possible evening meetings of mother and/or father at the church, school board, city human relations council, etc. Rarely is the family unable to convene at the dinner table in the evening, even for a hurried meal. The dinner hour is often used to plan weekend activities or to look ahead to summer vacations. A bulletin board or datebook by the telephone and appointment books carried by father, and sometimes mother, are used to check schedules and record decisions.

Before school

Babies are not exempt from the scheduling of townspeople's lives. Many families plan the arrival of the baby to coincide with an appropriate time for the mother to quit her job or the father to have a vacation, so he can be home to help with the newborn or care for the older children. The homes of townspeople are almost always large enough for a baby's room to be possible, and the months before the baby's arrival are spent decorating the room and planning purchases. Parents outfit the room with a crib, playpen, bookshelves, dresser, toy box, and rocker; and infant seat, stroller, and carseat are either bought or borrowed for use in other rooms of the house and for travel. Family members and friends offer the use of some of their furnishings or special articles of clothing, such as snow suits, decorative blankets, etc. A crib, rocking chair, or even a blanket, doll, or christening outfit is closely identified with "the family," and both sides of the family strive to contribute some heirloom, as well as tales associated with it, to the circle of daily activities of the newest family member. Townspeople rarely have baby showers, though the women who work with the mother-to-be may have a luncheon for her and present individual gifts or cooperatively buy one large item for the baby.

Almost all mothers who work outside the home quit their jobs when the baby is expected. Being at home with the children before they start school is an almost universally endorsed ideal among townspeople, and a frequent reality as well. Wives who are teaching school when they become pregnant "drop out of teaching for a while" about halfway through the pregnancy and usually stay at home until their youngest child is in kindergarten. Many of these women remain active in the schools, volunteering as tutors, serving as room mothers, helping out in the library, and planning the annual fund-raising carnivals. Some also become very active on Junior League boards and in church associations, or they take up exercise classes or tennis. They take these activities seriously and carefully schedule these in between preschoolers' naptimes and later playschool attendance, as well as the baseball practice or music lessons of older children.

Many of these women return to the local teacher-training institution to collect credits toward a master's degree. Attending courses in the evenings and on Saturdays, they enlist the cooperation of husbands, parents, or their older children to take care of the preschooler, as they continue their education and prepare for re-entry into the job market at a higher level once their youngest child is in school. Sometimes, husbands accompany their wives to these courses or if their wives have had a successful and enjoyable experience in a course, the husbands may take the course in a subsequent term. Townspeople view continuing education at the advanced-degree level in ways similar to service in a voluntary association: a social occasion which helps one's self and public image. Some of the textile mills encourage their management-level employees to take courses. As the working force of the mills shifted in population during the 1970s, some managers sought social science courses, such as psychology, sociology, and anthropology, in the hope they would gain some practical insights on successful management strategies.

Within their family's scheduling of jobs, self-improvement, and leisure activities, preschoolers learn to fit their routine habits of eating, sleeping, and playing. From their earliest days home from the hospital, they are oriented to "fitting a schedule." As soon as possible, they are put on a routine of eating three times a day, with a nap in the morning and afternoon, and sleeping through the night. Adults consult books on babycare for their first child to obtain confirmation of when these routines should be accomplished as well as when the child should talk, sit, walk, and be toilet-trained. Members of the family and friends compare progress on these activities across children, and grandparents often predict whether or not the child will speak or walk as soon as the parent did.

Talking is of critical importance. Almost from conception, the baby is treated as a potential conversationalist, and mothers and intimate family members often address "that little thing," "that fat butterball," "that kicking monster" in the womb. Mothers, particularly in the final months of pregnancy when the baby is active, sometimes push gently on the stomach and direct comments to the baby: "You've got the longest legs." "Are you all elbows?" A great favorite of families expecting their first child is a book of cartoons in which the unborn child is represented as a wise all-knowing creature, who offers all sorts of humorous comments on life from the protection of the womb.

This view of the child as conversationalist and separate knowing individual is continued after birth. In the hospital, parents and grandparents, and friends talk to the baby through the nursery window. Once home, the baby is addressed, and answered for, by adults and older siblings. Sometimes in these "exchanges," the speaker waits an appropriate time before answering for the baby, as though the speaker actually intends to give the preverbal infant a chance to answer. Adults carry the baby about, pointing out the mobiles, room decorations, family pets, lights, and mirrors, and providing names, descriptions and running commentaries on these items. If there are older children in the household, they follow the same pattern of talking *to* the baby. If an older sibling is still a toddler, parents and other adults often try to teach the toddler to talk to the baby, encouraging the older child to learn to "play" with the baby by handling and talking about his toys. When a toddler seems not to know what to do with the newborn intruder, adults say "Talk to him. Show him your [dollbaby, toy, blanket, etc.]." Within these households, there is a consistent emphasis on the baby as an individual, a separate person, with whom the preferred means of communicating is talk. Nonverbal means are somewhat limited, since townspeople frown on the fondling of babies by any but a very few intimates. A pat or light playful pinch on the arm or leg, or a grasping of hands are about the only nonverbal interactions anyone other than a close family member should initiate. Even mothers and fathers rarely put their face right up to the infant's face, and they confine kissing to the back of the baby's neck or the stomach. Older children often try other means of communicating from a distance: sticking out tongues, making funny faces, or wild waving of hands, but adults make fun of these and encourage the youngsters to "talk" to the baby.

In the homes of preschoolers, most of the contacts babies under two years of age have with other human beings are with their mothers.[3] Even though there may be a maid in the home on certain days of the week to help with household chores, mothers usually take the primary responsibility for their babies until they are about two years of age. When they are toddlers or "terrible twos," they are often left with the maid or taken to a cooperative play-school in either the morning or afternoon. In days past, almost all townspeople had a maid or a cook who came five days a week. Now most homes have a maid only one or two days a week, and her time must be spent on laundry and housework. The toddler is often enlisted to "help" in these chores, and there is little time for the maid to sit and play with the baby or focus attention exclusively on the child, as in years past when white-uniformed maids spent hours pushing baby carriages or walking toddlers along tree-lined streets of Piedmont towns. Mainstream grand-parents often tell stories about how their children came to talk like their maids, either adopting certain terms for things or using their pronunciation and syntax. However, such anecdotes are rare among parents of today's schoolchildren, since both the amount and kind of time maids spend in isolation with preschoolers have changed greatly. Now in the first two years of the infants' lives, their own mothers provide most of the language input. During diaper-changing, bathing, feeding, and other caregiving activities, mothers treat their babies as conversationalists – and as potential literates.

Much of the physical and verbal environment of babies is oriented to literate sources, and from an early age, children are expected to take an interest in books and information derived from books. Their rooms are decorated with murals, mobiles, and stuffed animals which represent characters from books. Many of their toys in the first two years are "educational," and these carry implicit references to books and other kinds of writing. For example, a favorite toy is a wooden mailbox, with slots of different shapes in the top. Blocks of different colors and shapes are to be put into the mailbox in their appropriate slots, and removed from the bottom by lifting a panel. The mailbox is lettered and colored like the real-world item.

In the first six months, the mother's usual position for talking to the baby is face-to-face, either over the child during bathing and diaper-changing or in front of and above the child during bottle-feeding and early spoon-feeding in the reclined infant seat. The mother names items she is handling, talks about their attributes, and makes affective comments on either the item or the baby's interpreted reaction. Mothers assume the baby is attending to their talk, and any response is interpreted in *intentional* and *representational* terms by the mother. If shortly after one interpretation is given, the baby issues a contradictory signal, the mother may even comment on this shift as an attempt on the part of the child to clarify his intentions: "Oh, you *didn't* like that, huh? I'm sorry, Mommy thought you liked that, I didn't mean to scare you." Once the infants are old enough to babble or make other sounds which can be interpreted as having a representational or expressive value, mothers repeat and expand these utterances into well-formed sentences. They restate the infant's utterance as they believe the infant intended it, acknowledging that though the infant is not old enough to say what he intends, he is capable of having intentions which can be interpreted by others. The mother interprets the utterance by assuming the child's intention to express a meaning and to use language to represent something in the environment or situation symbolically.

The negotiation of jointly shared intention in communication between mother and child appears again and again in the numerous question and answer routines these mainstream mothers engage in with their infants. Formulaic exchanges in which mother asks a question, and child responds either verbally or nonverbally mark peek-a-boo games ("Where's Andrew?" "There's Andrew."), responses to strange sounds ("What's that? Who's coming? You hear Daddy's car?"), and book-reading activities. In all of these, the mother coaches the child to attend to a rule-governed event and to share in her way of responding to that event. For example, in book-reading activities, the mother asks a question and supplies the answer, moving from simple requests for labels ("Who's that?") to requests for attributes of these items ("What does the doggie say?").

In these and other exchanges, adults use systematic modifications of their language. They speak more slowly, with a high pitch, and they often vary the pitch. They sometimes offer exaggerated stylized exclamations ("oopsie-daisy," "uh-oh," "whoopsie") or renderings of certain sounds (a dog's bark, a lamb's cry, a horse's neigh) to punctuate their talk and produce peaks of attention from the child. They simplify their utterances to young children by making them shorter than those addressed to other listeners; they often delete verb endings and forms of the verb *to be* ("Daddy sleeping." "Daddy sick now."). They repeat single words, sentences, and accompanying sound effects; they use special words, sometimes known only to family members. Bodily functions, certain foods, toys, and animals, and "special" blankets or dolls are referred to by particular terms, such as "wee wee," "woofie," etc.

Topics of conversations when mothers and children are alone most frequently include: the baby (body parts, expressions of his responses to caregiving, his likes and dislikes); the usual and immediate environment (clothing, room decorations, items on the crib or infant seat, food, and animals); unexpected sounds or events (telephone ring, siren, sibling in Halloween costume); and special items reserved for interaction with the baby (books and toys). Mothers talk about these, point to them, and whenever possible hold them so the child can see them. In book-reading the mother asks *what*-questions about the two-dimensional representations of the three-dimensional real-world objects. Mothers assume children will learn to perceive two-dimensional objects as representations of three-dimensional objects. Using cloth books in which a single object and label appear on each page, mothers read "with" infants as young as six months. Occurring just before bedtime, these episodes are often very short, less than five minutes, and usually end with comments expressing the joint intention to end the activity: "You're gettin' sleepy." "You're too fussy to read, aren't you?"

Mothers continue their question–answer routines when the children begin to talk and add to them running narratives on items and events in the environment. Children are trained to act as conversation partners and information-givers. For example, on rides in the car, the baby is usually put in the car seat in the back seat of the car. Mothers still talk to the child, often looking in the rear view mirror to check on the child's attentiveness and general behavior. A fire truck, dog, broken fire hydrant, or carwash station provide topics of conversation which are often related either to earlier experiences or to materials read in books or seen on television. Between the ages of two and three, children begin to initiate these running commentaries themselves, often interrupting

249

adults or changing the topic of adult talk. These interruptions are rarely condemned when the child is this young, and adults agreeably shift topic or continue the child's topic. Captive-audience times, such as visits to the doctor's office, or periods of waiting in the car for an older sibling to finish baseball practice, are occasions when adults try to have books handy. If books are not present, adults talk about objects in the environment in ways similar to those in which they talk about pictures in books. "Do you see Billy? Can you find him? Maybe he's wearing his red shirt today." Children seem to feel compelled to give answers to adults' questions. When they do not know the answer (or are bored with the usual routine of expected answers), they sometimes invent fantastic answers.

The children's imaginary tales are acknowledged and praised, if they take the form of stories or fantasy and are introduced with appropriate signals of a story. Children are allowed to make up tales about their activities with friends, their future plans, or wild creatures they have seen.[4] These occasions often stimulate adults to model book stories in oral form for children. Some parents make up a story on the spot about their child: "Let's see. What do you think happened to Billy at practice today? I bet he hit a homerun. No, I bet he made a touchdown, and he kicked the football." Some of these are designed to "test" the child's listening ability, to prompt him to say: "No, that not football, Billy play baseball" (Andrew: 2 years, 2 months). Families vary greatly in the degree and kind of use they make of spontaneous fantasy stories to entertain their children. Some mothers make up marvelous stories on almost every trip to the grocery store or drive to the doctor's office, and invite their children to contribute to the story. Other mothers rarely engage in this kind of imaginary story-making with their preschoolers, except in direct connection with book-reading when they ask "Would you have liked to go fishing with Little Bear? What do you think *you* would have caught?"

Throughout the preschool years, questions are the most frequent type of talk addressed to children by mothers.[5] In one home, nearly half of all the utterances (215) directed to Missy (2 years, 3 months) during a forty-eight-hour period were questions (103). Table 7.1 indicates how these questions varied. A majority were Q-I questions in which the questioner has the information being requested of the child; A-I questions are those in which only the

Table 7.1. *Percentages and types of questions directed to Missy (2 years, 3 months) in a 48-hour period*

Type	Examples	Total	Percentage
Q-I	What color is that?	46	44.7
A-I	What do you want?	24	23.3
U-I	Why is it that things can't be simpler than they are?	18	17.5
Others (Such as directives, tag-questions, etc.)	Do you want me to get angry? That's a top. You've never seen one of those, have you?	15	14.5
		103	100.0

Note. Questions were distinguished from nonquestions on a formal basis: Wh-questions, *yes–no*-questions (inversions or sentences with a rising intonation), and tag-questions.

child has the information being requested. Unanswerable questions (U-I) are those for which neither the adult nor the child has the information for an answer.

Most of the Q-I questions were simple in structure: "What's that?" "Where's your nose?" For Missy, most of these were formulaic in nature and repeated again and again on some occasions: book-reading, before-dinner romps with daddy, play with toys. In all of these cases, adults had a set of actions which accompanied the question each time it occurred: "Where's Missy's nose?" was always accompanied by a playful nose pinch and subsequent display of the parent's thumb through the first and second fingers of the hand. A-I questions were rarely repeated verbatim: if the child did not immediately answer, the question was rephrased – "You want chocolate [milk]?" "You want me to put Bosco in?" or the adult answered for the child "No, you've had chocolate once today." Of the A-I questions, 25 percent were requests for clarification, occasions in which the adults did not understand the child and asked the child to clarify, confirm, or repeat what she had said: "Is this what you want?"

Unanswerable questions (U-I) appeared in adults' monologues, occasions when they seemed to be talking aloud to themselves, but Missy was present. On these occasions, adults did not wait for answers from Missy, or pause in their monologue for some other imaginary respondent's reply. These questions were often complex in syntactic structure, including one or more independent clauses and often several dependent clauses. Questions which asked *why* or *how* made up 54 percent of the U-I questions ("Why isn't this coming off like it's supposed to?"). Others asked in more simple utterances *what-* or *yes–no*-questions ("What's this? I don't remember leaving anything on the table." "Do I really need another package of pork chops?"). No claims for answers were made on Missy on these occasions by either her mother or father, and twice when Missy acted as though she thought her mother was talking to her, her mother responded "Oh, never mind." Topics of this type of "self-talk"[6] usually focus on the immediate situation (especially unexpected features – "Who can that be?" in response to a doorbell), replaying of a previous event (a disagreeable encounter with a store clerk), or forecasting of a coming event (planning for supper).

Grouping all the questions addressed to Missy on the basis of formal criteria masks the fact that many of these questions did not serve interrogative functions. Many were, in fact, directives or imperatives, statements of fact, or exclamatory remarks. Many served as reminders to the toddler that her behavior was unacceptable: if Missy began to fuss at dinner, her mother asked "Do you want me to put you to bed?" Missy's mother did not intend this as an A-I question, but as a reminder to Missy that she was getting too fussy. Tag-questions, hooked to the ends of statements, underscored the statements rather than called for a response from the child: "This is chocolate chip ice cream; you had that at Grandma's, didn't you?" These questions-in-form served other functions, and children were usually expected to give no verbal response, but to alter their behavior or attend to the question as a reminder for them to think about or consider a previous event or their background knowledge and experience related to this occasion.

For older children between the ages of two years, six months and four years, questions became increasingly varied in both form and function. Routines for Q-I questions diminished in frequency as toddlers advanced beyond peek-a-boo games and interactive sessions of question–answer routines with familiar books. Adults began to read longer stories to their children and to expect them to sit still and listen until the end of the story. On these occasions, children often became the question-askers. They asked for clarification ("Does he find his dog?"), they initiated mock routines in which they "read" or asked questions of the adults about the pictures or story content, or they asked questions which related the book's content to other situations which were similar ("Is there a witch in *my* closet?"). Adults increased their use of utterances which were questions in form but either directives or statements in function. They used questions as reminders: "Where do those blocks belong?" and expected children to respond with appropriate behavior (removing the blocks to the place where they were usually kept) instead of or in addition to giving a verbal response. Short questions tagged onto statements similarly did not call for verbal responses on all occasions, but they underlined the adult's statement: "You won't forget again, will you?" Many questions were reminders of polite behavior: "What do you say?" (used to remind the child to say "thank you," "excuse me," and the like); "Were you born in a barn?" (used to remind a child to close the door).

By this age, the children were often having experiences in which the mothers or other members of the family did not share. They went to playschool, Sunday School, or took swimming lessons at the YMCA. Thus they were incorporated into family conversations by A-I questions which asked them to share information only they knew. Asked to tell what happened at school, or whether a particular child was at a swimming lesson, the child was expected to produce a narrative account of events or to give a straight answer. Adults often probed children to expand these factual accounts or to recognize their contradictions: "Wait a minute, you didn't go outside to play on the monkeybars today. Miss George told me the playground was too muddy." Children were also coached in appropriate listening behaviors while others gave such accounts. Warned to listen and not interrupt until someone had finished talking, children's interactions around extended talk replayed the listen-and-wait pattern which accompanied bookreading with adults for older preschoolers. Now they were expected to hear the story through, accepting their role as passive listener/spectator, and to wait until the end of the story to ask and answer questions.[7]

Listening and waiting also mark activities of the older preschooler at church, playgroups, or family reunions. For example, before the age of about two and a half, children are simply tended in cribs, playpens, or playrooms during Sunday School and church services. Classes are, however, provided for the toddlers, older two-year-olds, and three- and four-year-olds. Here there is a mixture of listen-and-wait book-reading and story-telling activities, artwork, and free play. Children are given single-page handouts with pictures and labels to exemplify the Bible story of the day or the particular holiday (Easter, Christmas, Mother's Day) being observed. Many of the local churches also run playschools for older preschoolers, and some of the children come to their own churches several hours per day during the week to play with other preschoolers. Activities here are similar to those of Sunday School: listening to and carrying out directions about art, listening to and answering questions about stories, listening to records, and following directions for group games or individual play in specially designated areas of the room or play yard. Some mothers form playgroups on their own, and even those who have an informal arrangement of taking turns at keeping each others' preschoolers in their homes plan some structured activities for the children.

On all of these occasions, children are asked to gather around a story-teller or book-reader. Teachers and mothers expect the children to sit quietly and listen until the reader indicates the children may participate in discussion about the story. Children may talk to each other so long as they do so briefly, quietly, and on the topic of the story; they may talk to the teacher to respond to a question or to contribute general comments in an open discussion of the story or book, so long as they take turns and do not interrupt. The teacher usually acts as a narrator for the text, and she models and questions. She asks questions about the story which directly relate to the story's content most of the time: "Who is this?" "Where does he live?" Often teachers follow up with "How do you know?" questions, in which they ask the children to identify points in the story or, more often, portions of the pictures, which let them know the location, weather, pending action, or other unexplicated events of the story. Teachers mark these story-reading times with many hints to keep the children's attention or to remind them of their need to listen: "What do you think will happen now?" Storytime is often the occasion for discussion of knowledge shared by the children: the word *desert* may provoke one child to tell about a car ride across the desert; a story about a dog may trigger several stories about pets from the children. These usually come at the end of the story-reading, and if children interrupt the story with these, they are asked to "save" their story for another time or until the reading is finished. Throughout the teacher's questions, knowledge from the story and from the child's background are constructed together, but it is the teacher's questions which "scaffold" this knowledge.[8]

The teacher's talk enables preschoolers to show that they can sort out items from both the story and their own experience, designate attributes for these, and manipulate them in a series of settings and situations. At the beginning of such sessions, children are often asked to retell the story heard the day before, if it is one in the same series or on a related topic. Such retellings must follow the structure and sequence of the original story, or be corrected by the general audience of other listeners. In these ways, teachers check up on the listening skills of the children. All of these routines are familiar to the children who attend these playgroups, for they follow predictably the same patterns established in home reading events. The major differences in the playschool settings are waiting for a turn in group sharing, and recognizing that co-listeners can correct one's retelling or challenge one's interpretations. Negotiation of intentions within either evaluations or actual events of the story takes more sharing within a group than in adult–child interactions at home.

Reading and writing

These routines and negotiations of intention and representational meanings surround uses of the written word for the townspeople. Both at home and at work, there is an almost continuous use of written material as a topic or backdrop for talk. Babes in arms learn that it is appropriate for their cribs and walls to be decorated with characters which have no explanation outside a literary reference. A wall plaque showing a cow jumping over the moon takes on meaning only as the child learns to associate that decorative piece with a nursery rhyme. Toys in the shape of mail boxes "make sense" as one comes to know about letters, and the meaning of the postal service. Children's cloth books which feature single items out-of-context are remarkably similar in format and labeling techniques to the parts-identification chart which accompanies the new lawnmower, or the equipment manual for new machinery in the weaving room of the mill.

Children learn in book-reading exchanges to name, hold, and retrieve content from books and other written or printed texts. Labeling procedures and *what*-explanations are used in the classification and construction of knowledge, when children and adults respond to new items in their environment and build running commentaries on old items as they compare their features to new ones. This pattern of linking old and new knowledge occurs in the narratives mothers use to entertain their children during car trips or to keep children attentive in homework sessions. Around the dinner table, mothers and fathers incorporate references to written materials used in their work as they tell stories about the major events of their day.

Both children and adults are producers and consumers of literacy in a consistent, highly redundant, and repetitive pattern of using oral language, and especially dialogue, as a way of learning both from and about written materials. The modes of speaking, reading, and writing are tightly interrelated as children learn to recognize, link, talk about, and "read" the cow jumping over the moon on the bedroom wall decoration and in the nursery rhyme book, *and* to separate this knowledge from the real-world knowledge they might have which suggests cows do not jump over moons. Children learn they should not interpret some oral and written texts literally, for their placement in the frame of a fantasy experience or as part of something which has been written disconnects these texts from a strict adherence to real-world rules. Written materials have a context of their own which disengages them from literal linkages to objects, people, and events of the real world.

As the children of the townspeople learn the distinctions between contextualized first-hand experiences and decontextualized representations of experience, they come to act like literates before they can read. They acquire the habits of talk associated with written materials, and they use appropriate behaviors for either cooperative negotiation of meaning in book-reading episodes or story-creation before they are themselves readers. Missy and all the toddlers in her playgroup tell stories about themselves which incorporate some facts and portions of fantasy from television, movies, or stories read to them at home or school. They dialogue with adults about the names of things in books and from books, and they talk about the sizes, shapes, colors, and other features of these items when asked to do so. Gradually, they recognize how certain contexts assert the priority of meanings. The question "What did the cow do?" asked by a parent looking at the wall decoration calls for an answer which is very different in content from that given to the same question after a visit to a farm animal zoo.

At home, children see adults and older siblings reading for various purposes and in different ways. There are occasions when adults read for pleasure or instruction as individuals and do not share the contents of what they read with others: novels, a business report related to the job, or a set of crochet instructions. On other occasions, adults read for guidance of future behavior: movie ads, game rules, instructions on how to put a toy together. This knowledge is often talked over with others who are present, especially if decisions affect them. On yet other occasions, adults read aloud and share the specifics of the written information socially: features from the newspaper, items in the weekly news magazine, and birthday cards or letters from relatives and friends. Townspeople read at home for a variety of purposes, and the types of uses of reading are greatly varied. Table 7.2 illustrates these.[9]

Just as the purposes and occasions for reading are highly varied, so are the rules for the use of talk with each reading activity. Children are coached on these uses and appropriate behaviors around readers: "Don't bother Daddy until he finishes his report." "Now Mommy is reading; we'll play later." "Listen to this; do you think we want to go [to the movie whose review is read aloud]?" By participation and observation, children learn when to interact and participate in the reading of others and how to try to talk with and about the reading of the adults about them.

There are similar rules for using writing and for recognizing the functions it serves family members. In their homes, townspeople have five major types of uses of writing (see Table 7.3). When asked what they wrote, men and women named *letters* first. They wrote personal letters, prepared a newsletter summarizing the family's past year to enclose with their Christmas cards, filed complaints about faulty products, and advised their state and local politicians through direct letters and letters to the editor of the

Table 7.2. *Types of uses of reading in townspeople's homes*

INSTRUMENTAL:	Reading to gain information for meeting practical needs and scheduling daily life (labels, telephone dials, clocks, wattage figures on light bulbs, bills and checks, school, church, and voluntary association notices, directions for repairing or assembling household items or toys).
NEWS-RELATED:	Reading to gain information about third parties or distant events (newspaper items, news magazines, political flyers, reports from local congressmen).
RECREATIONAL:	Reading during leisure time or in planning for recreational events (comics, sports section of newspaper, sports magazines, novels, movie ads, invitations to parties, motel or campground directories).
CRITICAL/ EDUCATIONAL:	Reading to increase one's abilities to consider and/or discuss political, social, aesthetic, or religious knowledge (popular novels and non-fiction books, news magazines and out-of-town newspapers, denominational newsletters and magazines, the Bible, reviews of Broadway plays and ballet or symphony performances in New York or Washington).
SOCIAL- INTERACTIONAL:	Reading to gain information pertinent to social relationships (greeting cards, letters from family and friends, newspaper features, college alumni magazine).
CONFIRMATIONAL:	Reading to check or confirm facts or beliefs often from archival materials stored and retrieved only on special occasions (wills, income tax forms, bills, birth certificates, passports).

Note. Listed in relative order of frequency of occasions when time on these types of tasks exceeded five minutes per day.

state's newspapers. In all of these, they had to explain background information, recount past events, and summon facts to support generalizations, as well as express their opinions. Some of these letters followed or supplemented telephone calls or face-to-face oral exchanges. Writing which reinforced or "stood behind" the spoken word was often referred to as "writing for the record" and included recording minutes of club meetings, signing petitions, or listing delinquent accounts at the church library. Occasionally mainstreamers brought home some of the writing they did on the job: teachers worked on assignments for students, and businessmen completed reports or drafted memos or letters. Conversations

Table 7.3. *Types of uses of writing in townspeople's homes*

MEMORY AIDS:	Writing to serve as a memory aid for both the writer and others (grocery lists, notes in photo albums, lists of things to do, recipes, reminder notes of dues, meetings, chores, lists of telephone numbers).
REINFORCEMENT OR SUBSTITUTES FOR ORAL MESSAGES:	Writing used when direct oral communication was not possible or a written message was needed for legal purposes (notes for tardiness to school, message left by adults for children coming home before parent arrived home and vice versa, business letters related to consumer goods or politics).
SOCIAL-INTERACTIONAL:	Writing to give information pertinent to social relationships or parental role responsibilities (thank you notes, letters, "practice" writing or drawing for and with preschoolers, joint parent – child negotiation of written homework assignments – reports, stories, poems, etc.).
FINANCIAL:	Writing to record numerals and to write out amounts and purposes of expenditures, and for signatures (checks, signing bills and writing check numbers on them, filling out tithe envelopes for church, ordering from mail-order catalogues).
EXPOSITORY:	Occasional tasks brought home from the job or church and civic duties; writing in connected prose to summarize generalizations and back-up specifics for other people; writer envisions or "knows" audience and attempts to include only those definitions and facts believed not to be known to the addressee, often includes numerals (quarterly or annual reports of business operations, summaries of group and individual past actions – accident or quality-control reports, church nominating committee summary).

Note. Listed in relative order of frequency of occasions when time on these types of tasks exceeded five minutes per day.

around the dinner table sometimes included talk about consulting other professionals for help with certain kinds of writing; for example, parents spoke of working with a lawyer to write a contract or a will, or of asking a realtor friend to help them write an amendment to a lease.

The folklore about writing in townspeople's homes focused on the belief that it was often necessary, because the memory was both short and unreliable. Many comments about writing seemed to view writing as a "necessary evil," because one's "brain power" was not great enough to store the information without writing it down: "I better write that down, or I'll never remember it." "If I didn't have this datebook, I'd never remember anything." Children came to recognize that different types of writing demanded different degrees of attention.

Some types of writing were to be preserved and were thus often written and rewritten; earlier versions of the finished product were destroyed as the final version was judged satisfactory for storage and record-keeping. Other types of writing were one-time-only, and consisted of lists of words, abbreviations, or half-sentences noted as reminders. Certain kinds of writing also required particular types of paper and writing instruments: notes and lists could be written on the backs of old envelopes or notebook paper with pencil; party invitations, business letters, and personal letters required pen and ink and special paper. Almost never was it appropriate to sign one's full name in pencil.

Home, school, and work

In their jobs as mill executives, insurance salesmen, real estate salesmen, businessmen, schoolteachers and administrators, the townspeople replay and expand the routines and habits of using oral and written language they and other members of their families practice with their children at home. For a mill executive, a day's job begins when he checks incoming directives on production quotas, changes in machinery, and shifts in names of fibers or processes.[10] Much of the material which comes to him from the central offices of the mill provides samples of new advertising, and old and new labels for fabrics are prominently displayed in the advertising. He reads the summaries, scans the details of directives, and jots notes on a yellow legal pad as he reads. He marks beside certain items on his yellow pad a large question mark; he gets up often to check files behind his desk, and after an hour or so, he asks his secretary to place a long-distance call to the central office. As he waits for the call to go through, he consults his yellow pad, and when the telephone buzzes, he picks up the phone, identifies himself, his mill location, and refers to the memoranda he has just scanned by a brief summary or abstract of their contents. He then asks several definitional or *what*-explanation questions, checking off those items on his yellow pad which were marked with large question marks. As he talks, he jots notes on the pad. He collects those bits of information needed to fill out the content of the mailed materials, and just before he ends the conversation, he asks the party in the central office if he knows why certain changes were made and what his view is of the effects they will have on production quotas. The request for reason- and opinion-sharing initiates only a brief exchange. At the end of the conversation, the mill executive turns to a new sheet of the yellow pad, jots down a dozen or so points which incorporate the bits of information he has accumulated on the phone into a sequence of topics; he then dictates the agenda for a meeting with mill supervisory personnel to take place within a few days. In the afternoon, he calls in several top-level managers for a routine weekly meeting, during which he briefs them on the morning's memoranda from the central office. The managers are not now given the information to read; they are given an oral abstract of the memoranda they will receive later in the day, and asked to be prepared at the next meeting to discuss specific points of action the changes mentioned in the memoranda may make in mill operations. During the meeting, discussion centers on the need for more detailed descriptions of particular jobs, the possible need for a general plant memo on safety rules to be distributed, and the revision of employment interviews.

Though the topics and setting differ, these on-the-job routines of using oral and written language follow patterns used with preschoolers in the homes of the townspeople. The mill executive talks with and from written materials, following habitual ways of taking meaning from written sources and linking and extending it to shared background experiences with conversationalists. In his phone call follow-up to the memoranda, he asks questions about labels, features, reasons, uses, and the affective consequences of the new information. Following the phone call, he reorganizes the information, and in the meeting with supervisors, he extends the knowledge gained from this process into action. He and his managers consider ways to use written descriptions and rules to improve plant operations. As both mill executive and father, he repeatedly moves from labels to discussion of the features of the items labeled, to questions about the reasons for and uses of these. Through preschool, school, and work, these seem natural, "logical" ways of proceeding, and these ways are passed on, in simplified and repetitive patterns, not only to his own children at home, but also in the training and managing of mill workers. When there are breakdowns in production or signs of miscommunication on the job, executives and supervisors plan ways to transmit their "naturally organized" knowledge to the workers in both written and oral form in meetings, workshops, and on-the-job training sessions. Well-meaning and conscientious executives despair that neither white nor black mill workers seem to find these ways of organizing and talking about transferring knowledge into action "natural."

Townspeople carry with them, as an unconscious part of their self-identity, these numerous subtle and covert norms, habits, and values about reading, writing, and speaking about written materials. As children, the townspeople learned the rules for talking about and responding to books and writing tasks; they came to accept retrieval of the structure and information of written texts as critical to the presentation of form and content in their oral texts. In school, they found continuity of these patterns of using oral and written language, as well as an increasing emphasis on expository talk and writing around events or items not physically present, but referred to in written sources. Once on the job, they met these now thoroughly familiar tasks, and they achieved success in their profession by displaying their skills at performing these tasks. In banks, stores, insurance offices, churches, the tennis and swimming clubs, and the mill's executive offices, they found these ways institutionalized. Throughout their home, school, and work life, successful interactions depended on individuals being able to talk from and with pieces of writing which were integral to appropriate interpretation of on-going events.

When their own children are born, they begin to play again the same script they have followed since childhood, secure in their own success with the necessary roles and lines. They believe their ways of talking about what is written and responding to the content of written materials will impart to their young the necessary skills for achieving school and job success.[11] For them, these ways of thinking and behaving are natural, and they expect others to share them. For the children of Trackton and Roadville, however, and for the majority of the millworkers and students in Piedmont schools, the townspeople's ways are far from natural and they seem strange indeed.

"Once upon a time . . ." (Chapter 8, page 299)

"It gave me a beginning; I needed to learn hard work; I was a wild 'un, and when mamma and daddy put me in the mill, I had to learn . . ." (Chapter 2, page 38)

"Back in my day, we stayed home, and the mill tried to make ways for us to do things with our chil'rn. But nowadays, that's all gone." (Chapter 2, page 36)

On Saturdays and Sundays, there is always time for keeping the porch warm and telling stories hour after hour about "The old days – the times in the cotton field or in the mills..." (Chapter 2, page 62)

"Way/Far/Now/It a church bell/Ringin'/Dey singin' – ringin'/You hear it?/I hear it /Far/Now." (Chapter 5, page 170)

Roadville and Trackton parents agreed "it was probably best nowadays . . . to get some 'schoolin' 'fore school.'" (Chapter 2, page 70)

Mrs. Pat's class became known as the "readingest class in school." (Chapter 9, page 333)

"We grew up with a lot of *shoulds* in our house, 'You *oughta* do so and so...'" (Chapter 4, page 142)

"We all read and write a lot of the time, lots of places. School isn't much different . . ." (Chapter 8, page 289)

"Our children learn how it all means . . . I guess what it all means, you'd say." (Chapter 3, page 112)

"They gotta know what works and what don't . . . Whatcha *call* it ain't so important as whatcha *do* with it. That's what things 'n people are for, ain't it?" (Chapter 3, page 112)

"My brother and me had been playing ball alongside my house. One of us hit a ball went right through the window . . ." (Chapter 4, page 142)

"A time for all things and everything in its time; a place for all things and everything in its place." (Chapter 5, note, page 382; see also Chapter 4, page 137)

"Ain't no use me tellin' 'im: 'Learn dis, learn dat. What's dis? What's dat? He just gotta learn, gotta know . . .'" (Chapter 3, pages 84 and 105)

Part II

Ethnographer Doing

8   *Teachers as learners*

A student again

The first chapters of this book have detailed the ways children of Trackton, Roadville, and the townspeople learn to use oral and written language. The ways of the black and white townspeople are different from the ways of either Trackton or Roadville. In businesses, mills, and schools, Roadville and Trackton residents interact with the townspeople, who are the managers of these commercial, workplace, and educational settings. For the children of Roadville and Trackton, school is the first place in which they meet on an extended basis the townspeople's ways of using oral and written language. They have come to school, bearing the high hopes of their parents and believing school can make a difference in whether or not they learn enough to enable them to move beyond their parents' workplaces. Their physical transition from home to kindergarten and the primary grades will eventually be followed by a larger transition to the commercial establishments and institutions of employment controlled by the townspeople. Intuitively, they and their parents feel language is power, and though they may not articulate precisely their reasons for needing to learn to read, write, and speak in the ways the school teaches, they believe that such learning has something to do with moving them up and out of Trackton and Roadville.

Of what use might the detailed ethnographies of communication in Roadville and Trackton be in enabling teachers and students to bridge their different ways? The answer to this question depends on finding ways to make accessible to teachers an understanding of the differences in language and culture their students bring to their classrooms. In the 1970s, the townspeople who studied in graduate courses I taught learned to become ethnographers of their own and others' interactions and to put to use knowledge about the different ways of learning and using language which existed in the communities of their region. These teachers, in taking social science courses, examined their own habits at home and learned to recognize that they carried these home habits into the classroom just as did their students from other communities. This and the next chapter describe how the ethnographies of communication in Roadville and Trackton became instrumental for teachers and students bridging language and culture differences and discovering how to recognize and use language as power.

A common phenomenon in teacher training in the United States is the periodic return of public school teachers to university classrooms. States offer increased pay for advanced degrees and for courses completed beyond the master's degree. In the 1970s, some state departments of education used desegregation as the rationale for teachers to return to graduate school for courses in the social sciences and in the teaching of reading and writing; nationwide, the "crises" flaunted in the public press were race relations in schools and the declining level of literacy skills among public school graduates. For the first time in the South, black and white teachers met together in university classrooms and regional workshops to discuss ways to improve their teaching methods and materials and to help all students increase their academic achievement.

Some of the teachers caught up in this phenomenon in the Piedmont Carolinas came into the graduate courses I was teaching as a part-time instructor in a state teacher-training institution. In each of my courses, these teachers spent the first several weeks learning to act as ethnographers in interactions in their homes and workplaces. They tape recorded, described activities in fieldnotes, and interviewed family and friends – focusing always on ways of learning and using language. With these data, the class as a whole looked for patterns of mainstream behaving and valuing (Chapter 7). Many class members learned to distance themselves from their beliefs about what they did and why, and to see the redundant and overlapping patterns which compelled the nature of their uses of oral and written language. Once this understanding of their own habits was established, they could see that both they and their students brought their home habits into the classroom, and that they had previously judged their students' habits by the norms of the interactions of the townspeople. In addition to trying to act as objective recorders of behaviors, some subjectively reviewed their past evaluations of students and kept journal accounts of their teaching experiences in the 1970s. The continued public furor over desegregation fueled the determination of many to learn enough about themselves and their students to enable them to help make the school a place in which students could begin to fulfill their potential. These teachers had no desire to become heroes or go public with their faith that the school can be a place in which all children are empowered to make choices about how they will handle their future. As these teachers saw their task, they were simply adapting and learning in order to do well a teaching job in which they believed.

Many began this adaptation by reassessing past patterns of success and failure in their classes and re-examining their own evaluations of students. Before desegregation, their classes had been made up of children from either mainstream homes or farm and mill families. Invariably, mainstreamers and a few mill and farm children made up the regular and advanced classes, and the rest of the mill and farm children, and a few mainstream children fell behind in the remedial or basic level classes. For the latter, teachers slowed down the process of presenting material used in the regular and advanced classes, presenting the information in discrete, isolable components, providing numerous occasions for repetition and practice, and coaching the children on ways to move from labels and attributes to integrated outlines of information which had a predictable development of thesis or general point.

With desegregation, and the accompanying radical reordering of classes and class levels, teachers found the older scheme of advanced, regular, and basic classes did not seem to meet the needs of many students. Though most of the black students did end up in basic-level classes, there were those who succeeded in advanced and regular classes, as well as those who exhibited seemingly bizarre patterns of success in mathematics or art and failure in reading or social studies, while others succeeded in the latter and failed in other classes. Many students, both black and white, showed no improvement in the basic classes. In their graduate courses, some teachers reviewed the comments which, in their earliest desegregated classes, they had used to characterize black and white students who seemed unable to adjust to the social and

Table 8.1. *Examples of teachers' evaluations of working-class students having discipline and academic problems*

Black	White
SOCIAL BEHAVIORS	
"verbally & physically aggressive"	"quiet, laconic"
"disrespectful"	"respectful"
"never says he's sorry"	"know how to let me know they're sorry even if they don't always say so"
"girls are more aggressive than boys – especially by 5th grade [ages 11–12]; they're even sexually aggressive toward the boys at that age!"	"girls are always willing to step back and let boys speak out, take turns first, etc."
"leaders shift all the time; respect for their classmates never seems to be based on something I can identify"	"neither boys nor girls want to step out and take the initiative on anything"
"has no respect for private property; thinks anything in the class 'belongs' to him"	"often shy about sharing; wants 'one of her own'"
"young children will almost never tell me who did what; my friends who teach at the jr. and sr. high school levels tell me it's the same way there. They'll never identify who started a fight"	"getting them to talk, especially the boys, is hard, but if I can find a girl who saw what happened, and I talk to her alone, she'll tell me"
"can't respect classroom rules about asking permission to do things – just barges in and does it without asking"	"girls especially will hold back and wait to be sure they understand specific instructions"
"want things repeated again and again. I find myself shouting before they'll listen; if they don't get it from me, they'll flit about the room until they find someone who'll tell 'em"	"expect simple directions such as those in workbooks to be 'spelled out' on an individual to individual basis by me. They won't work under a buddy system where a classmate helps"
ACADEMIC BEHAVIORS	
"responds poorly, if at all, to phonics approach – can't grasp basic decoding skills"	"catch on to phonics, but transfer from teaching session to individual work is very slow"
"doesn't seem to know how to answer a simple, direct question"	"shows no imagination; answers are always minimal"

Table 8.1. (*contd.*)

Black	White
"I would almost think some of them have a hearing problem; it is as though they don't hear me ask a question. I get blank stares to my questions. Yet when I am making statements or telling stories which interest them, they always seem to hear me"	"instructions have to be clear and straightforward; little ability to interpret or go beyond minimal requirements; respond to low-level questions minimally, with little imagination or extension of ideas"
"they'll never tell a story straight – if there ever was a grain of truth in what they say, it's lost when they get through with it. If they only used that imagination in some constructive way . . ."	"needs help in moving beyond the bare essentials of restating reading stories or social studies materials"
"the simplest questions are the ones they can't answer in the classroom; yet on the playground, they can explain a rule for a ballgame or describe a particular kind of bait with no problem. Therefore, I know they can't be as dumb as they seem in my class"	"polite and does adequate work; completes basic homework assignments; rarely asks questions in class, but is always the first to volunteer answers for review questions"
"disorganized and erratic in work habits"	"shows little imagination; we need to encourage her to go beyond the basic assignments"
"fails to stay on topic during class lessons; talks out of turn and interrupts fellow classmates; always wants to relate class discussion to something else instead of lesson"	"attentive and responsive in class; waits her turn"

academic norms of classrooms. Excerpts from student records are given in Table 8.1.[1] Without having been entirely conscious of their patterns of distinguishing social and academic behaviors which differed for the black and white working-class students, teachers found they had recorded primarily attitudes or activities which centered around patterns of responding to and using oral and written language. Their notes indicated that they had found some students had difficulty following a unilinear pattern of development from learning labels and features, to producing running narratives on items and events, and asking and answering questions about these. This seemingly "natural" sequence of habits for them as mainstreamers was "unnatural" for many of their students. Basic-level classes which slowed down and broke into smaller fragments the steps of the mainstream patterns of unilinear skill development had not seemed to enable these students to break their patterns of failure. Many of the black students had achieved only minimal success in the basic-level classes, and of those who had, teachers reflected: "I don't think it was the class that helped him; something else happened. His motivation changed or something. I think a big brother from up-North came home, and that made a difference." Of the white students in these classes, many had succeeded until the class exercises began to call for "what if?" answers and to provide only minimal directions for reading workbook pages and arithmetic problems. Teachers reported that once beyond requests for *what*-explanations, basic questions asking for terms, dates, facts, and repetition of specific information, these children floundered, and basic-level classes did not seem to help them move ahead. By the end of the fourth grade [ages 9–10], a pattern of failure seemed established for most basic-level students, black and white.

These teachers not only reassessed past patterns, but as they became more familiar with the role of teacher–researcher they had begun in their social science classes, they also reflected on what was happening to them as the first years of desegregation passed. For many, seemingly simple insights into their past classroom behaviors and attitudes opened the way for curricular reforms and modified teaching practices. Two white teachers wrote:

June 20, 1974 – The fact that communication is so important to learning points out the need for learning the child's language and also for allowing children to interact and communicate with each other. The very pictures we put on the walls of the schoolroom show our ethnocentric leanings. Boy was that a slap in my face!

March 18, 1976 – I've been here [in the school district] during the transition period, so I know what frustrations we all felt. The thing that none of us realized was that these children were almost like foreigners to us. True, they lived within our communities; we have all associated with and talked with blacks in our homes all our lives, so we thought we understood them. We knew that their spoken language was different, but we always assumed these differences were from ignorance and lack of education.

Some white teachers wrote the script for a play produced in the summer of 1974 by black and white students on language and culture differences. In this play, an adolescent black girl talks to her teacher:

You must bring yourself to understand that there is a systematic basis for black cultures. Your schools have been operating on the theory that everyone is the same beneath the skin. I realize that you were thrust into a new situation too. You have tried, in your way, to do what you thought was best. I'm only asking that you look a little deeper – see me as I am: I'm one of you but yet, I'm still me. My way of communicating may be different from yours but it fills my adaptive and emotional needs as I perform it. Why should my 'at home' way of talking be 'wrong' and your standard version be 'right'? . . . Show me . . . that by adding a fluency in standard dialect, you are adding something to my language and not taking something away from me. Help me retain my identity and self-respect while learning to talk 'your' way.

A black principal recalled his career as teacher in two all-black schools before he was placed in an integrated school as teacher and then as administrator.

During my . . . teaching in all-black . . . schools I discovered . . . facilities were below average and materials and textbooks were scarce. Teachers were forced to rely on all their faculties for any innovative ideas that might be implemented in the classroom. However, to many of my co-workers and me, teaching was primarily a prestigious occupation, and the actual teaching made little difference to us . . . I now believe we were more concerned with our own public image than the kind of pupils we turned out . . . It took me five years of teaching to realize that something was not as it should be . . . We [had to become] dedicated to the idea that if teachers get involved in working with paraprofessionals from the community, interact with parents, and get to know some of their methods of communication and survival, they will begin to re-evaluate their classroom practices and behaviors, and modify them appropriately with the training resources that we [the school administrators] provide. We felt it necessary to treat all the teachers as professionals, who were not told what to do, but who would as individuals grow as a result of the new approach.

In the spirit of increasingly depending on individual teachers' professional contributions, several school districts agreed to encourage new types of testing, to produce and distribute teacher-made units, to help recruit parents for school participation, and to pressure the local press to accentuate the positive aspects of what could happen in Piedmont classrooms.[2]

During the second half of the 1970s, individual teachers exhibited their resourcefulness in a variety of ways. For example, differences between the structures and uses of Southern dialects and Standard English were reported repeatedly in newspaper features and regional magazines, but what these meant for practice in Piedmont classrooms could be interpreted only by teachers. Some teachers began to record carefully the features of their own students' language structures and uses. Having recorded these patterns, the teachers examined reading workbooks and frequently used tests of auditory perception and speech production to identify items which discriminated against children who spoke Southern dialects, black and white. Several teachers wrote and distributed tests to be used regionally to determine the cluster of dialect features individual children exhibited.[3] Groups of science and mathematics teachers wrote specific units using textile mill terms and situations as background for the word problems of district-wide junior high school mathematics classes. Daycare and kindergarten teachers wrote units on cultural differences in the mealtime habits of families in the region. Home economics teachers collected proverbs about childbirth and development and used the analysis of these in the teaching of their health education courses. The beliefs were not held up to derision, but analyzed in terms of how and why they had evolved and whether or not science could provide answers to some of the questions the proverbs raised.[4]

Simply put, many teachers used the challenge of integration to push themselves into organizing and refining many of the intuition-based practices of observation and teaching they had occasionally used with particularly difficult individual students in their past years of teaching. On those occasions, they had observed and participated closely with the child, and tried to note areas of difficulty and success so that they could, to the extent possible, individualize teaching materials and offer supplementary explanations of general classroom activities. Integration meant that there would be more students in each class who might not adapt to the usual ways of managing social interactions and doing schoolwork

272

in a classroom. Thus teachers resolved to use the methods and principles of their social science courses to become more practiced and more skilled in observing patterns of behavior in groups of children, and determining why and how these differed from mainstream school ways. All of this learning was preparation for the next step – adapting materials and methods to help bring all children closer to a realistic chance for school success.

Using space and time in preschool

In the early 1970s daycare centers and kindergartens were available for the first time for the children of Roadville, Trackton, and many similar communities of the Piedmont. Churches, neighborhood centers, and local colleges offered programs for four- and five-year-olds, and by the middle of the decade, there were kindergartens in many of the public elementary schools. Circulars, television, and radio advertisements urged parents to help prepare their children for entry into the first grade by sending them to available preschool programs. All of the programs emphasized the goal of preparing children for success in school. Since these programs were looked upon as transitional from home to school, many emphasized parental participation, frequent home visits by teachers, parent–teacher conferences, and the use of paraprofessionals from the children's communities.[5] The teachers were townspeople, black and white, many of whom had had special training in early childhood education and welcomed this new opportunity for them to put their training into practice.

In the first years of the preschool, teachers set up their classrooms with centers for various activities: block-building, reading, playing with puppets and dolls, painting, and playing with puzzles. Children were to read in the book corner, engage in water play at the sink in the back of the room, and keep the puzzles at the table near the shelf where they were stored. Children from Roadville and similar communities found these rules linking particular functions to special places familiar; adults in their communities also demanded that certain activities take place only in certain areas. Children from Trackton and similar communities were, however, puzzled by the space–function ties the teachers expected them to recognize and obey. When told to "play," they interpreted play as improvisation and creation, and these called

273

for flexibility in the mingling of materials and the mixing of items from different parts of the room. A truck which had detachable parts and was kept in the puzzle corner was to be taken to the sandbox where water and sand could be mixed, the tires changed, and spare truck parts hauled. If a particular piece of a puzzle looked like a wrench or a jack for a truck, or a spoon for feeding a doll, Trackton children went to the puzzle shelf to incorporate it in their play. Teachers despaired when they found what they classified as *puzzles* in the sandbox or the doll corner. They said repeatedly: "Put the puzzle pieces where they *belong*." "When we finish our puzzles, we put them up [or away]." These directives seemed to have no meaning to the Trackton children, and in the first few weeks of school, the most well-intentioned teachers found themselves making invidious comparisons between the Trackton children and those from Roadville who were "so obedient and so neat with their toys."

In time, however, the behaviors of children from both Roadville- and Trackton-like communities puzzled teachers. For example, teachers and other school authorities believed that toys were to be preserved if at all possible for use in subsequent years. They often cautioned the children against losing puzzle pieces, using water when playing with the dolls in the kitchen corner, and "being rough with the toys." For the school, maintenance of equipment depended on children using items for the purposes for which they were intended, returning items to their usual place of storage after each use, and keeping all items clean of mud and any other sticky substances. Roadville children accepted these rules except when they made it impossible to engage in realistic play the way they did at home. In Roadville, girls who played house usually did so either with their mothers in the kitchen or in a playhouse their fathers had made for them outdoors. Roadville homes were too small to accommodate the equipment for playing house in children's bedrooms or the living room. In the outdoors playhouse and in the kitchen, children played with water, mixed real substances for "brewing tea" or "making cookies," and often incorporated real milk, juice, and flour in their play. In the playhouse corner of the preschool, water and such substances could not be used and had to be imaginary. Some of the Roadville children gradually gave up trying to play in those areas of the room where they could not bring their home play habits. Teachers despaired that they would not try new activities, and individuals seemed to develop and maintain preferences for relatively few indoor activities. Trackton children, on the other hand, were accustomed to playing with toys outdoors almost all of the time and they insisted on taking the school's "indoor toys" outside; at home, almost all their toys stayed outside, under the porch, or wherever they were left when play ended. Moreover, at home, they were accustomed to using toys for purposes they created, not necessarily those which the toy manufacturer had envisioned.

The preschool's rules linking particular activities to special times also caused frustration for Trackton youngsters. At school, there was a time to sit down, a time to listen, a time to draw, a time to eat, and a time to nap; once engaged in an activity, one was not bound by the limit of completion of the task, but by the limit of the time allotted for that task. Trackton children had, before their entry to school, lived in a flow of time in which their wants had been met in accordance with the accessibility of individuals who could meet their needs and the availability of provisions. Trackton children from a very early age seemed to initiate a play activity purposefully, almost appearing to have a plan for the task mapped out in their minds before beginning a certain activity. If interrupted before completion, most would complain; some, such as Lem, would protest shrilly. In the preschool, they found it frustrating to have the clay or paints taken away from them before they finished their preconceived project; they resisted having toys put away before they had been able to complete a play strategy in progress. At home there had been few constraints on time; children had not been admonished to sleep, eat, or play within certain blocks of time. At home, there were no timed tasks or time-task links.

Roadville children, on the other hand, had grown up "on schedule," moving through regular nap and bedtimes as well as a fairly regular pattern of family meals at least twice a day. Sunday School and Bible classes followed rules for using time in ways which were very similar to those of the preschool. Roadville children had grown up with proverbs and sayings about time: "Time is on my side." "It's time to —." "We'll make time for that." Trackton children, on the other hand, had little or no experience of Sunday School; they had participated from infancy in church services for which the ending time was never preestablished; the final *Amen* seemed to come in accord with the congregation's sense of completion. Trackton children, unlike their counterparts in Roadville, did not play games that included calls of "time," or "time's up," until they went to school, but Roadville children participated in tag, hide and seek, and commercial games in which there were time limits to their activities. Mealtimes, with most family members seated at the table, took place several times during the week in Roadville, depending on the work schedules of parents. Certain meals began with certain foods and ended with others. In Trackton people ate when they were hungry, and families rarely sat down to the table together. There were few constraints on the sequence of eating certain items before others. Only breakfasts for the children and the family and Sunday dinners (held in the mid-afternoon after church) were designated family activities with particular constraints on when and where they occurred and the sequence of foods to be eaten.

Using talk

In addition to these nonverbal differences between the children of the Roadville- and Trackton-like communities, and between them and their mainstream teachers, there were verbal differences. By the early 1970s, the public media of the Piedmont had begun to report a surprising amount of information on differences between so-called Black English and Standard English. Many teachers of the Piedmont region either read or read about William Labov's "The Logic of Nonstandard English."[6] State departments of education and universities of the region offered workshops on Black English, and in 1970 the South Carolina State Department of Education published a kit of materials on dialect differences in the state. The kit contained a recording of numerous "white dialects" and "black dialects" from across the state, noted differences and similarities between the black and the white, and argued that the language a child brought with him to school should not be eliminated in an attempt to teach him Standard English. Contained in the kit were a booklet, which illustrated how the sound and grammar systems of black dialects and white dialects varied in systematic ways from Standard English, and games and drills for teaching Standard English as a second dialect. By 1972, when Joey Dillard's *Black English: Its history and usage in the United States* appeared, many Piedmont teachers were willing to accept that the non-standard kind of language used by many blacks had distinct rules of its own and was not a mass of random errors. They recognized that some black children brought to school some language forms unfamiliar to them as townspeople, and there were occasions when they could not understand a particular child's talk and would have another child "translate." These individual cases were, however, not as frequent as teachers had been told in regional workshops and newspaper features that they might be.

Many of the black children often "dropped" the final consonant of a consonant cluster or blend that was heard at the end of a word in Standard English: *test* became *tess, build* became *bill.* The past tense ending *-ed* was often not heard at the ends of verbs: *worked* became *work, laughed* was *laugh.* Many of the children did not pronounce the *r* after vowels (*four → foe*) and said *that* as *dat.* But these features rarely obscured meaning for teachers. More troublesome were differences in the grammatical system. For example, the class was participating in "sharing time" on the topic of pets, and the teacher called on Teegie: "What kind of pet do you have?" Teegie answered, "A dog, a big ol' collie dog. He been stay down my grandmamma house." The teacher asked: "Has he run away?" Teegie hesitated and answered, "No, I been had 'im der." Later in the afternoon, the teacher indicated to me that she thought from Teegie's answer that he had not understood her follow-up question, and she was not certain what Teegie had meant. I explained that his use of *been* in the first answer indicated that the taking and keeping of his dog at his grandmother's house happened in the distant past, and Teegie reaffirmed that point in his follow-up answer. Moreover, a common usage among some blacks of the Piedmont was to use *stay* as a synonym for *live*; thus Teegie had indicated in two ways in his first answer that the dog had been gone a long time and that the dog lived at his grandmother's house.

Both Trackton and Roadville children used *ain't,* and the teachers tried consistently to correct them. A teacher asked one day: "Where is Susan? Isn't she here today?" Lem answered "She ain't ride de bus." The teacher responded: "She *doesn't* ride the bus, Lem." Lem answered: "She *do* be ridin' de bus." The teacher frowned at Lem and turned away. Within the system of Black English Lem used, *ain't* was used as equivalent to *didn't,* the negative of the past tense of auxiliary *do*; thus his answer had to be interpreted as "She didn't ride the bus." The teacher heard the *ain't* as equivalent to *doesn't* and corrected Lem accordingly; he rejected this shift of meaning and asserted through his use of *do be ridin'* that Susan did indeed regularly ride the bus. Roadville children, on the other hand, use *ain't* as the negative form of *to be* and *to have* as auxiliary verbs, but not as the negative form of the past tense of *do*.

Roadville children also had several pronunciation features which bothered teachers: they often dropped the unstressed first syllable of words (*across* → *'cross*) or the *d* in the sequence *-ndle* (*bundle* → *bun'l*). The *r* was frequently dropped in unstressed syllables with an *r* elsewhere in the word (*surprise* → *suprise*). Some of the children said *hit's* for *it's*, and many of them added an emphatic *here* or *'n* to demonstrative pronouns: *this here 'n* or *this'n*. From some of the children, teachers noted "peculiar" pronunciations of some compound nouns; the most common examples in the preschool were *hoppergrass* for *grasshopper* and *peckerwood* for *woodpecker*.

Most of these formal differences among the dialects caused relatively little difficulty in communication. More troublesome were differences in the *uses* of language the children brought to school, a topic rarely discussed in the research literature. Some teachers expressed repeatedly that their problems were not in understanding or accepting the forms of the children's language, but in comprehending how and why the children used their language as they did. Such differences were initially noticeable in naming practices, types and uses of politeness formulae, and habits of questioning. Trackton children often did not respond when teachers called them by the name on the roll (which had been taken from a child's birth certificate). When teachers asked the children their nicknames, they gave no response; when teachers learned from parents the nicknames used in the community, they found these (e.g. "Frog," "Red girl") unsatisfactory for classroom use. Among Roadville children, on the other hand, too many children responded to the same name; there were often multiples of *Bobby*, *Robbie*, and *Betty* in the same classroom, since the proper names (Robert, Elizabeth) of these nicknames were especially popular in Roadville. Teachers tried assigning new nicknames or calling children by their real names, but the children objected.

Politeness – how to define it and ways of showing it – caused problems in preschool classrooms. Numerous teachers reported that they felt it extremely important to model polite behavior for very young children. They tried to speak to the children politely, and they expected the children to do the same to them. They believed "good manners" or "discipline" begins in the years before school, and grave problems at the higher grade levels could be alleviated if children learned at an early age rules for behaving appropriately in the classroom. They felt that, ideally, children should come to school knowing many or all of the usual verbal routines of politeness, but after integration, teachers at all levels of the curriculum complained that manners and respect were appallingly absent in their students' behavior. One of the most frequent complaints came from teachers who felt that most of the black students did not have mainstream or "normal" manners, and many of the white children were losing the manners they had brought to school. Preschool teachers soon took up the cause of teaching manners and discipline to their charges, in the hope that they could help eliminate some of the discipline difficulties in the later years. In their homes and professional educations, mainstream teachers had learned unconsciously what to expect of their students so that the classroom could operate in an orderly way. Drawn from class rules posted on bulletin boards, and from a series of essays several teachers wrote on "the good student," the following generalizations express their beliefs. Students must:

recognize and accept rules assigning designated functions to specific spaces;

recognize and accept that blocks of time are to be used for specific purposes, and workers must manage their time on a task to fit allotted time blocks;

behave as though they believe in the value of present tasks – especially those related to competition and evaluation – for future goals; recognize that there is one teacher and many students; it is the right of the teacher to determine rules and standard of talk in school: who talks, when, how, where, and for which purposes;

show respect for generalized "others," usually in the descending order of "school" (the specific school for young children; also schooling in general for older students), school officials, teachers, fellow students.

Yet, these beliefs were rarely explicitly stated or explained in the initial months of the preschool. Teachers tried instead indirect instruction and modeling for the children. They used familiar verbal formulae from their own home experiences:

Is this where the scissors belong?
It's time to put our paints away now.
You want to do your best work today.
Someone else is talking now; we'll all have to wait.
We have visitors coming to the school this afternoon; we want our school to look nice.

Both Roadville and Trackton children had difficulty interpreting these indirect requests for adherence to an unstated set of rules. Roadville children knew what space–function ties meant, and they responded when asked to put a toy "away" or "where it belonged." They were familiar with adults setting the rules for talk when there were several adults, but not when there were only children in a group. Roadville children in preschool showed "proper" respect when a teacher was talking, but in small-group activities, when no adult was around, they negotiated among themselves in loud and boisterous ways, fighting out what they believed to be their right to a toy or to a position on the floor, and sulking when the teacher intervened before the "score" was settled between two children.

Trackton children had had no experience with either space–function ties or time–task ties, and many were exceedingly frustrated in the first months of preschool when it seemed to them that once they had collected the items they wanted and started a task, the teacher intervened, either to remind them to take objects back to their place or to move on to another activity. At storytime or in the times when the teacher gathered the students on the rug about her to talk about the group as a whole, Trackton children interrupted, tried to "take the floor," and chattered freely to their neighbors. After two months, even the most patient teachers found it hard not to question the "kind of homes these students come from" and whether or not they and their parents had the "right" attitude about school.

What seemed absolutely clear in the minds of school administrators and teachers, as well as those parents who participated in the meetings at school, was that they all wanted children to learn how to succeed in school. In asking the help of parents in teaching their children simple routines at home, preschool teachers often explained that on the basis of their own prior experience teaching in the higher grades, they knew preschoolers would have to learn to accept and abide by the school norms of respect, politeness, and discipline. It was only humane to see that they did so as soon as possible, for between the first and the twelfth grades (ages 6 and 18), children had a lot to learn and a great deal of work to be accomplished. For most of those years, one individual at a time – the teacher – would be in charge of controlling the students and guiding their learning. The classroom situation of one-to-many necessitated certain basic rules of cooperation and participation. As one teacher put it, students had to "learn school," meaning its rules and expectations, just as they had to "learn readin', writin', and 'rithmetic." Most parents agreed that they wanted to help. The question was *how?*

Individuals and small groups of teachers suggested different plans. Almost all were entirely voluntary, and only a few had any financial support from the local school districts. Once both teachers and parents felt the need to find a way to enable students to "learn school," the complex task of "learning school" had to be specified for parents and students. Teachers met informally and broke down the rules they felt were most important into small sets of discrete skills and explicit guidelines. They drew up sample lists of rules to post in their rooms; they made videotapes in which they role-played troublesome children breaking the rules; they shared with each other their specific ideas about what "the good student" was. One group of teachers rented a van and went from neighborhood to neighborhood holding regular preschool classes which the parents could observe, and showing videotapes of classes in school. As teacher and a few students moved through a mini-version of the usual activities of the school day, the teacher explained the guidelines most important for success in each activity (sharing talk during and after the oral reading of a story, returning art supplies to their boxes after each activity, etc.). Many parents from the textile mills could not come to the schools during regular times of operation and were often reluctant to ask to do so at any other time; thus many of them had little or no realization of how schools – especially preschools – operated. Now the school van came to them in the late afternoons and on Saturday mornings, giving an opportunity for them to see in action the way the preschool operated and to hear teachers explain both what they wanted children to learn and why these behaviors made sense in school.

A few teachers agreed to pick up several children once a week during the summer and to take them to local libraries for story-reading, short activities of drawing and writing, and selection of library books. Sometimes the children's mothers went along on these trips, often making their first visit to the library, and having the opportunity to hear and see there reading and talking skills which were similar to those needed in the schoolroom. In Roadville, Sue Dobbs decided that if some parents from her neighborhood and others who had children in the preschool worked together on Sunday afternoons at the church, parents could learn how to help their children prepare for school. For several months, mothers from nearby mill communities met together at the church with several teachers to see videotapes of preschool activities and to talk about required behaviors.

These were exceptional responses: most were short-lived, born of the initial wave of enthusiasm for preschool in the area, and usually conceived and executed by the most committed teachers. They did engender some interest and good will in the neighborhoods, but there is no evidence they had any long-term effect on either parents or children. Yet the discussions of discipline and politeness forced many teachers to be explicit for the first time in their teaching careers about their norms for behavior in the classroom. Some major changes in teaching behavior resulted. For example, some teachers began to introduce tasks which did not have to be completed in a specified block of time and found ways to make explicit to the children that other tasks had to be completed in a time-block. Several teachers made a large face of a clock and placed one set of hands of the clock at the beginning hour of the task and another at the ending hour. They talked to the children about how the real clock in the room would look at both these times. Before the activity, they told children how long they would have to work on this occasion, and when and whether they would be able to return to the task again.

A second change in teachers' behaviors came in their ways of expressing directives. Some were more successful at this than others, but in workshops they all agreed to try to express their commands to students in as direct a way as possible. Instead of "Can we get ready on time?" as an indirect directive to tell children to put their toys away and begin lining up for snack time, teachers tried to say: "Put your toys back where you took them from. We have to line up for lunch. Table three will wash hands first." Directives such as "Give me your attention; look at the board." "Choose two books." "Use only red paint" replaced earlier hints and other indirect ways of giving orders: "Someone isn't going to know what to do when the music starts." "I think two books will be enough for you to read today." "We're going to use only the red paint today."[7] Some teachers became accustomed to stating their requests directly as they came to believe the children showed marked improvement in their responses. Not wishing, however, to abandon entirely the more "polite" ways of giving orders, several teachers used story-reading, watching "Sesame Street" on television, and playing with puppets as occasions to talk about and illustrate "polite" ways of giving orders through hints and indirect requests.

By the early 1970s, many joint workshops between preschool and early primary-level teachers helped the two groups share ideas about teaching. Aside from discipline and general classroom management, another frequent topic was how children responded in group discussion and in direct confrontation by school personnel. Teachers complained that some children gave only minimal answers, and others gave either no answers or "smart-alecky" answers, speaking out of turn and interrupting others. Complaints that some black children did not know how to answer what seemed "the simplest kinds of questions" were heard repeatedly. Those townspeople teachers who had analyzed the types of questions used in their own homes with their preschoolers shared their findings with other teachers; several also analyzed the kinds of questions they asked in their classrooms. Teachers in the primary levels came to help other teachers realize how heavily they had been socialized into believing that one teaches by using questions. At home and at school, they asked questions:

to teach children what to attend to in looking at a book;
to label the discrete bits and pieces of parts of the book or environment about them;

to search out pieces of pictures and to talk about these out of context;

to look for recurring examples of items seen in books in the real world;

to participate in building a joint narrative of questions and answers with adults.

As I was able to share with teachers more and more knowledge about the ways language was used in Trackton and Roadville, they recognized the differences between their own uses of questions and those of Trackton and Roadville parents. Some teachers began to come up with ideas of how to alter their teaching methods and materials to accommodate these ways with the mainstream, school-oriented ways of approaching tasks.

In 1972, one teacher, Mrs. Gardner, was given a class of nineteen black first-grade students, all of whom had been designated as "potential failures" on the basis of reading readiness tests. She chose an unusual course of action. Almost all her children were from Trackton, or Trackton-like communities in the town or rural areas. When she agreed to take the class, she asked the principal for several privileges: she wanted a room with a door to the outside of the building, access to the auditorium for two hours a day, the freedom to decorate her room and the outside area of the room as she pleased, and two sets of old hardcover primary-level reading books which had been stored in the textbook storage room for years. She did not want any of the new small soft-cover books until late in the year.

The principal agreed. Before school began, Mrs. Gardner visited the communities from which her children came, made a simple map of each community and noted names of stores, streets, and churches, and whether or not there were telephone poles and street lights in the area. She checked the list of parents of children in her room and found that several fathers worked in garages around the area. She called them and asked if they could get her several old tires for the classroom. She went to the houses to pick up the tires. Curious parents asked what she would do with the tires, and some went back to the school to see. They helped her cut and rope the tires to pieces of wood to make letters of the alphabet, such as B and P. Tires were cut to make C, D, and G. These were scattered on the sand and grass outside the classroom.

Once the year began, Mrs. Gardner introduced letters of the alphabet not only as symbols on paper, but also as structured symbols which appeared all around the children. They were asked to search their neighborhood for big *T*s (telephone poles), for upside-down *L*s (street-light poles), and to search the streets as they rode the bus to school to see which letters they found in varieties of objects in combination as well as in print. The children learned to distinguish *T*s, *E*s, *L*s, *O*s, *A*s, and *I*s in telephone poles, and in their cups and saucers, tires, guy wires for poles etc., as well as on the names of cars and license plates. Gradually Mrs. Gardner shifted the emphasis from recognizing the shape of the letter to hearing its sound, and children with names beginning with certain letters or sounds had special days at school, and points were given for recognizing certain sounds in words heard throughout the day at school. Children cut up advertisements, separated block capital from lower-case letters, and matched the block capital letters from advertisements to lower-case letters given on the alphabet boards which decorated the room. By Christmas, the children were making their own advertisements for events at school and their own birthday cards by pasting parts of commercial advertisements together and providing photographs from magazines. Mrs. Gardner took pictures of the students in activities which illustrated concepts such as *over, under, higher, lower, bigger, smaller*, etc., and these photographs were used in study books each child made. At the end of the year, the first-graders arranged the pictures in new folders for the use of the kindergarten and special education classes.

Mrs. Gardner gave out the old hardback readers the first week of school. The first story was about an elephant who had a bicycle. She took the children to the auditorium and, using an overhead projector, she projected three feet high on the back of the stage the following opener of the story:

Eddie Elephant was very happy. He had on his best clothes. He looked very handsome. He was going to his grandmother's, and he was wearing his red vest, his yellow coat, his new pair of green pants, and his brown stockings. In his pocket he had his best handkerchief. His mamma gave it to him for his birthday.

The shapes of all of the "small" or function words, such as *was, he, had, on, to*, and *and*, were outlined with a dark pencil. After reading the paragraph through with the class several times, Mrs. Gardner projected individual words with notable configurations on the back of the stage (*elephant, grandmother, handkerchief, birthday*), asking the children to call out the words as fast as she flashed them. Once back in the classroom, Mrs. Gardner asked the children to find the story in their readers, look at the pictures, and read. A flannel board, with removable word labels and pictures, at the front of the room had Eddie Elephant in his best clothes, and as the children named each item, Mrs. Gardner asked the children to choose words from the list of words on the board and to put the word on the appropriate place (*vest* on Eddie's vest, *red* on the vest, etc.). Then she talked with the children about what was going to happen in the story: "What could Eddie do next in the story?" The children made up fantastic story-endings and debated in lively fashion the next steps the story might take. They went back in the afternoon to the auditorium to repeat the procedure with the same material. The next morning, they did the same, adding several sentences of a subsequent paragraph. Each day – morning and afternoon – the children read the larger-than-life words and sentences in chorus, separated into reading groups in their rooms and labeled items using the reading words, tape-recorded new endings for the story, and talked about the "shape" words *he, has was, and*, etc. Sometimes, Mrs. Gardner removed these words in a sentence on the word board, leaving only the outline of the word shape, and asked the children to read the sentence filling in the words noted only by shape.

As the year progressed, Mrs. Gardner helped the children learn to attack new words phonetically, and to "sound out" words when they needed to do so. Mrs. Gardner summarized her radical approach with this class as follows:

> I was angry when I learned these children were designated "no chance of success" before entering school. I decided to try methods I had pulled together that had worked with individual children over the years. My three guidelines are: have them read a story that's fun, that can build suspense; have them talk about how what they have read helps them know what will happen; then have them take apart all the pieces of what they've had to use to read for fun.

Throughout the year, Mrs. Gardner's class caused some stir in the school, because they were arrogant about their hardback readers when all the other first-graders had "baby" paperback books. Mrs. Gardner's class went to the library first and actually checked out books. Her class made a book of photographs of themselves. Mrs. Gardner's class played outside their room at odd times during the day. At the end of the year, all but one of the children in Mrs. Gardner's class were reading on at least grade level; eight were at third grade level, six at second grade level, and the rest were at grade level. Only one child, who was later removed to a class for the emotionally handicapped, did not read at grade level. In 1974 Mrs. Gardner's assessment of what she had done with her first all-black class two years earlier was mixed:

I'm sure I'll never do that again; the classes are more mixed now, and there are children who will expect more conventional methods. Also I am not sure that this taste of success was altogether fair for these children; I just hope they learned enough about school to be able to carry on. They proved they could succeed; that should take them a long way, but will it if their future classes are radically different from that first year's experience? The psychological value of building positive self-concepts by having what could easily have become the "lowest reading class" become the school's prestige group is obvious. Carrying hardback readers and having homework each night from the first week of school gave the class an edge over other groups who had paperback primers and were not considered old enough for homework. Students learned to use the environment about them to recognize letters, to hear different kinds of questions and answers, and to talk about stories. In short, they came to see themselves as readers.

Other teachers adopted methods which were neither so drastic in their effects nor so dependent on the use of special props and spaces. One second-grade room was plastered with familiar signs from advertisements, traffic and road signs, political posters, announcements of meetings that had gone on months before, and notices of sales. The room looked as though a strong wind had gathered up the signs of the streets and roads of the nearby area and dumped them there. Two black youngsters were in one corner of the room cutting up some posters, arranging the capital letters in one pile, the small letters in another. Words or letters written in script or fancy type were placed in a pile by themselves. Roadville's Bobby and another youngster were working in an area of the room set up to look like a grocery store. They were talking into a tape recorder as they negotiated "buying" groceries from a fourth-grader sitting behind a table. Behind the "clerk" were shelves of empty boxes, and the "customers" were reading their grocery list as they asked for what they wanted.

Bobby: We gotta get some oats.
Todd: You mean Quaker oats.
                   [
Bobby: Yea, there it is //*pointing to the shelf*//
Todd: Now we gotta get some salad dressing.
Bobby: That's it.
Clerk: //*reaching for the jar to which Bobby pointed*// Here it is.
Bobby: Yea, but last time she tricked us; hit won't no salad dressing, was mayonnaise, they look alike you know.
Todd: How can you tell then?
Bobby: Read, dummy. They ain't gonna be spelt alike. Mayonnaise goes one way, salad dressing don't, uh. Which is this?
Todd: That's mayonnaise, 'cause that's an *m*=
Bobby: =Sure ain't no *s*.

The two customers continued their buying, sorting out look-alike items on the basis of the names written on labels, and the clerk copied down the names of the items they purchased with prices, and added the column of figures. The children counted out play money and paid their bill. They then went to another corner of the room and replayed the tape of their grocery visit. After the replay, they erased the episode by telling a story about their visit into the tape. They put the tape containing the story, their list of items, and their bill into an envelope in their folders. The grocery goods went into the "warehouse" of large boxes marked with the name of each item, but with no other distinguishing mark such as a name brand.

The next morning, on the desks of several of the children, the following story appeared typed on a single sheet:

Bobby and Todd went to the store. Their mamma had made a list. The list said buy oats, salad dressing, bread, eggs, and a bag of coal. They got them all, but the salad dressing looked like the mayonnaise. Bobby didn't want mayonnaise, so they read the label. Mamma said they did a good job.

The teacher had written out the story the boys had recorded after they had worked from their grocery list and replayed the actual tape of the grocery-store visit. Their directions from the teacher told them to use the tape to help them remember the important things.

The teacher explained her classroom's contents and methods of operation:

At the beginning of the year, I tell my students: "Reading and writing are things you do all the time – at home, on the bus, riding your bike, at the barber shop. You can read, and you do every day before you ever come to school. You can also play baseball. Reading and writing are like baseball or football. You play baseball and football at home, at the park, wherever you want to, but when you come to school or go to a summer program at the Neighborhood Center, you get help on techniques, the gloves to buy, the way to throw, and the way to slide. School does that for reading and writing. We all read and write a lot of the time, lots of places. School isn't much different except that here we work on techniques, and we practice a lot – under a coach. I'm the coach."

She emphasized "traditional" teaching methods (basal readers, phonics, lesson worksheets), but she maintained a steady focus on the fact that students already "read to learn" before they came to school. They read price tags, names and instructions for toys, and notices of upcoming events in school and neighborhoods. She specified a time each day for the retelling of information from these types of reading. On these occasions, students were told to tell "a straight story," to recount facts as they happened. When she read to the students after lunch each day, she read fantasy tales, and talked about how fantasy, imagination, play, and pretend allowed things to happen which could never happen in the real world. The children supplied new endings to the stories, and in a group, they developed the ability to hear and produce each other's styles, though, initially, Roadville children excelled in factual recounts, Trackton children were entertaining in their fanciful accounts, and mainstreamer children were competent in telling facts and recounting the read story with several possible endings. The teacher had persuaded the principal and the fourth-grade teacher to let her have several fourth-grade students for parts of each day as models and helpers in the grocery store, and as occasional participants in story-telling sessions.

Other teachers chose to focus on certain particularly troublesome problems for their students. Workbook illustrations were usually two-dimensional line drawings, which were highly stylized, and familiar only to those students who had had extensive experience in labeling these items in books. A particular series of squiggles always cued the reader that the animal was a lamb; a curled tail cued the reader for the label *pig*; long ears and a round tail were the signs of a rabbit, short ears and a long tail, a cat. These teachers pointed out the stylized features of frequently recurring animals to their students and asked them to look for others. Teachers tried to become alert to workbook questions which could be differently interpreted, because of either individual differences or culturally learned differences in behaviors. In an exercise in which the open *o* sound often spelled by *au* was being stressed, the following two question-and-answer selections appeared.

If you were naughty, what would your mother be most likely to do?
  buy you something
  scold you
  pat you on the head
Which of these would be best for hauling heavy boxes?
  a scooter
  a truck
  a tower

In the first question, many children for whom being swatted on the head was a familiar punishment circled the third answer as correct. In the second question, many children answered from their own childhood perspective and circled "a scooter." Frequently, children offered meanings workbook illustrators and writers did not consider in their answers. An addition sum in an arithmetic workbook for the first grade illustrated two train engines in one column, two freight cars in the next, and in the column for the answer, pictured each engine pulling one of the freight cars (see Figure 8.1). The expected answer was 4, but Trackton children and two other individual children from families who happened to live near railroad tracks answered 2. When asked why they gave 2 as an answer, the children usually said "two trains," or "two trains go," indicating that the recombination had for them changed the members of the original sets into a new entity. Similar problems occurred when one hat was added to three hats on a hatrack in the answer column and one fish was added to a fishbowl with two other fish (see Figures 8.2 and 8.3). Trackton children answered 1, not 4 or 3 as the workbook writers

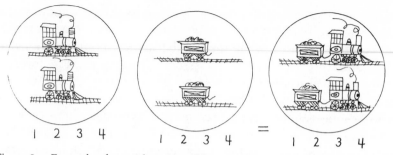

Figure 8.1. Example of an arithmetic problem in a first-grade workbook to which some children answered *2* for each answer

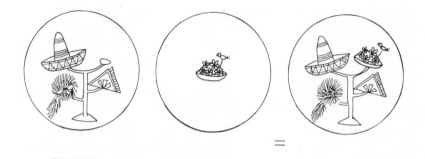

Figure 8.2. Example of an arithmetic problem in a first-grade workbook to which some children answered *1* in each blank

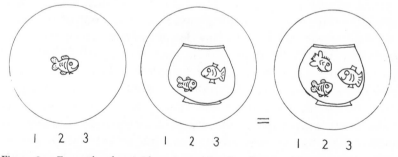

Figure 8.3. Example of an arithmetic problem in a first-grade workbook to which some children answered *1* for each answer

had intended. Most Roadville children, on the other hand, accepted the rule of the page – to add the single objects to a total of several single objects. Trackton children seemed, however, to examine each problem on its own and made no use of the workbook's rule for getting the "right" answer.

291

To accommodate the methods of answering questions the children seemed to prefer, several teachers adapted some materials in accordance with what they had learned about questions in Trackton and Roadville for classroom learning centers. In early units on social studies which focused on "our community," several teachers used actual photographs, and asked questions such as "What's happening here?" "Tell me what you did when you were there and who was with you." "What's this building like?" For specific lessons teachers taped the responses of all children. After class they edited the tapes and added specific questions and statements identifying objects, attributes, etc., for use with a worksheet which showed both the photograph and a simple line drawing of the building naming its parts (door, window, etc.). These teachers sometimes asked children from class to stay after school to tape spontaneously a set of responses to questions about photographs. They then marked these for specific children: a Roadville child's tape of talk about a fire station would be listened to by a Trackton child, who could then tape his own set of questions the next day. Gradually the learning center tapes contained *what-, who-, why-, when*-questions and *yes–no*-questions, such as "Can you climb to the top of that building?" Children from both communities were drawn to these tapes, for they heard themselves and their classmates talking. Children learned to use all types of questions; they learned to articulate carefully; otherwise, their questions were edited out of the tape, and they would not be asked to do tapes after school. Teachers made efforts to talk about talk in class and to label their own question types, and encouraged the children to listen to how their friends asked questions. The students seemed to like to talk about talk, and teachers who had spent time labeling types of questions and preparing tapes in learning centers believed their students had improved in attitude and enthusiasm first and foremost, and in class participation, and that some had transferred their knowledge of certain types of questions in classroom interaction to recognition of these in the exercises and tests in language arts.

Other teachers chose to emphasize language uses in special units and to carry through the learning from that unit to other classroom activities. One male teacher, whose hobby was stock-car racing, made a series of photographs, showing a race in progress and a crash. He used these scene sequences to focus lessons on questions, inferencing strategies, and the kinds of accounts of the race and crash different writers or story-tellers would produce. Some would tell it straight, giving the facts as they happened. Others would begin by building suspense, and only gradually letting the listeners in on the outcome of the crash and identifying the hero of the story. He taped the accounts of the race and crash by several race car drivers and played these for the children, who then decided on the kinds of stories they were, asked questions of the stories and pointed out how certain stories did not tell exactly what happened according to the sequence of scenes in the photographs. Such "fun" tasks which linked home and out-of-school ways of asking and answering questions and telling stories to school ways were not left in isolation in the classrooms, and teachers made great efforts to link the learning displayed in discussions in these special lessons to reading lessons and to the comprehension tasks of textbooks, tests, and the teachers' oral talk.

Many of these teachers' ideas for building school skills on home skills and ways of talking were simply imaginative, intuitive teaching strategies. But many were also backed by some social science theory and descriptive facts about their own and their students' backgrounds and the uses of oral and written language in different communities. The major tasks of the preschool and primary levels of teaching were to enable all children to recognize and to participate successfully in oral and written activities which had the following school features: space–function ties; time–task limits; requests to label, describe, and manipulate items and features apart from the context in which they exist in the real world; and rules of behaving as a member of a group which has a predetermined goal. Beyond the primary years, usually by the fourth grade, adaptation to school began to require successful grasp of more than these attitudes and behaviors. Children had to participate intensively in tasks which depended heavily on the ability to write extended prose and to do more than recognize stylized objects and label parts and features. There were expectations that students would synthesize book and real-world knowledge, and bring skills and facts learned in one class to another. In many ways, success in meeting these new expectations depended on gradual adaptations in methods of telling short stories and building meaning out of the facts and knowledge one had collected in and out of school and across curricular areas.

The story in school

When Trackton and Roadville children go to school, they meet very different notions of truth, style, and language appropriate to a "story" from those they have known at home. They must learn a different taxonomy and new definitions of stories. They must come to recognize when a story is expected to be true, when to stick to the facts, and when to use their imaginations. In the primary grades, the term "story" is used to refer to several types of written and oral discourse. When the first-grade teacher says in introducing a social studies unit on community helpers, "Now we all know some story about the job of the policeman," she conjures up for the children different images of policemen and stories about them, but the concept of story which holds in this school context is one which refers to factual narratives of events in which policemen are habitually engaged. Following their home model, Roadville children might conceive of such a story as "telling on" a policeman or recounting his failure to follow certain rules. Trackton children would expect stories of a policeman to exaggerate the facts and to entertain with witticisms and verbal play. During rest time after lunch, the primary teacher may read to the students the "story" of "Curious George," a monkey who talks, gets involved in a wide range of antics, and always comes out the victor. Roadville children have had little experience with such wild fantasy stories, and Trackton children have not heard stories about such animals read to them from books. Neither group of children has had the experience of helping negotiate with an adult the meaning of the story: "Isn't he crazy?" "Do you think they'll catch him?" "What would have happened if . . .?"

On one occasion when they were in the third grade, Roadville's Sally and Wendy expressed their understanding of the distinctions between "stories" at home and at school. On the school bus on the way home from school, Wendy had regaled her friends with a tale about how she was going to bring her dog to the end-of-school party. When they got off the bus, Sally, somewhat outdone by the story, decided to invoke home knowledge on her friend.

Sally: That story, you just told, you know that ain't so.
Wendy: I'm not tellin' no story, uh-er-ah, no I'm tellin' the kind Miss Wash [her teacher] talks about.

Table 8.2. *Content and interactional feature of most highly valued stories*

	School		Roadville nonfictive only	Trackton modified nonfictive
	fictive	nonfictive		
Content features				
1. Story-teller introduces himself	±	−	−	+
2. Story-teller summarizes story with moral	−	−	+	−
3. Story-teller summarizes story with factual recapitulation	−	+	−	−
4. Story must adhere to actual experience or written text	−	+	+	−
5. Conversation in story reported verbatim	−	−	+	+
6. Story-teller evaluates story	−	−	−	+
Interactional features				
1. Adult must request story	+	+	+	−
2. Audience directly evaluates story	+	+	+	−
3. Two or more story-tellers collaborate on story	−	−	−	+
4. Audience questions elements of story	±	+	+	−
5. Adults preconceive story, and structure it through questions	−	+	+	−

+ = trait is valued.
− = trait is not valued.
± = variation in evaluation of trait.

Sally: Mamma won't let you get away with that kinda excuse. You know better.

Wendy: What are you so, uh, excited about. We got one kinda story mamma knows about, and a whole 'nother one we do at school. They're different //*looking at Sally*// and you know it=

Sally: =You better hope mamma knows it, if she catches you making up stuff like that.

Here the girls took up the differences between story-telling, an event accepted and promoted in school, and tellin'-a-story, an event equated with lying and exaggerating at home. This exchange was a rare description of how the girls recognized the differing conventions and moral values home and school attached to stories.

Table 8.2 outlines the major interactional and content features which mark preschoolers' stories in Roadville and Trackton and those of the earliest grades of the elementary schools they attended. The features are marked for only those stories most highly valued in each context. For the school, features are marked as they are judged by the teacher for school performance. In all three contexts – Roadville, Trackton, and the classroom – there may be occasions in which the features noted here do not appear or other features are present. This variability is particularly true of the school, where individual differences in teacher style and in providing alternatives to usual lesson practices may cause a teacher to deviate from her normal expectations of story conventions. On occasion, she may question whether or not there is a moral to a story or ask that a child introduce himself before he tells a story.

For Roadville children, their community's ways of learning and talking about what one knows both parallel and contradict the school's approach to stories. In the classroom, occasions for story-telling between adults and children are established by adult request, just as they are in Roadville at home. Teachers sometimes politely listen to very young children's spontaneous stories (for example, those volunteered during a reading lesson), but these are not valued as highly as those specifically requested by adults as part of a preplanned lesson. Unsolicited stories are often seen as digressions. When teachers ask children to "make up" a story or to put themselves "in the shoes of a character" in a story from their reading book, they prefer fanciful, creative, and imaginative accounts. In Roadville, such stories told by children would bring punishment or a charge of lying. The summary of one story can be related to the summary of another, and the moral of one story can be linked with another, but extension of the facts of a story by hyperbole without qualification, and the transfer of characters, times, and places would be unacceptable features of stories in Roadville.

For Trackton children entering school, the problems presented by the school's conventions and expectations for story-telling are somewhat different. Questions which ask for a strict recounting of facts based on a lesson and formulated in the teacher's mind before she asks the question are unfamiliar. The request for a story which simply recounts facts accurately has no parallel in their community. Their fictive stories in response to assignments which ask them to make up a story often fail to set the scene or introduce characters, and often the point of their stories is not clear to either teachers or other students.[8] Inside the classroom, their language play, incorporation of commercial characters, and many of their themes are unacceptable. The close personal network which gives Trackton stories their context and their meaning at home has no counterpart in the school. For each community, the story whose features are marked here are only those produced and recognized as "a story" by community residents – modified nonfictive for Trackton and nonfictive for Roadville. "Story" in the school context, however, is noted as fictive or nonfictive – the fictive being the type most often used in language arts contexts (reading and writing lessons) and the nonfictive that most frequently used in social studies and science lessons. Table 8.2 indicates that for Trackton, the features marked here are those of the "true story," not retellings, formulaic, or factual accounts they recognize as stories external to their ways of judging stories in their own community.

Roadville differs from the school's requirements for the content of fictive stories in three ways, and may sometimes differ on the requirement calling for introduction of the story-teller. Trackton differs from the school's requirements for content of a fictive story on only two features, and on the question of introduction of story-teller only sometimes. However, Trackton's nonfictive stories differ in content features from all but one – summarizing a story with a moral – of those of the school. For nonfictive stories, Trackton's interactional features also differ from all those required in school contexts; Trackton differs from the school in all but two of the interactional features of fictive stories; one of these – the asking of questions – is highly variable in the school context, since if teachers do not understand a child's fictive story they will often ask for clarification. Interactional features of Roadville's nonfictive stories differ from those of the school on no features and on only two features of the fictive stories. One of these differs only occasionally – the matter of whether or not teachers ask for clarification of fictive stories.

Such a checklist of similarities and differences does not capture ways in which Roadville and Trackton children's conceptions of stories affect their response to and performance of stories in school. Trackton students enjoy and respond enthusiastically to stories read aloud to them, especially when the central characters are animals or fanciful human characters. After teachers finish reading a book aloud to the class, Trackton students seek out these books, read through them again and again, and when they have heard them often enough, they are able to say from memory portions of particular pages. They pick up chunks of the language from the stories – the formulaic openings, the direct quotations, and long-running passages of word play, such as those in Dr. Seuss books. In the latter, rhyme and nonsense are the major features of the story, and Trackton children can recite portions of these rhymes. Dr. Seuss characters and portions of text find their way into playsongs.

Their response to straightforward factual accounts in a social studies lesson, science class, or explanation of discipline rules depends on the content of the story. If the stories feature a person they know or a situation with which they are familiar, they remember and retell these stories with elaboration. In their earliest years of school, Trackton children fasten intently on details of the personal lives of their teachers, the principal, or student teachers. For example, an explanation of a school rule stays with Trackton children and may become the topic of some of their conversations, if it has been given along with personal anecdote or illustration. They hang on to representative anecdotes and often repeat them on the school grounds to remind offenders of rules. Straight-forward accounts which are not personalized often do not stay with them, and they either do not answer questions about these materials, or they give answers which seem to the teacher to bear little relevance to the account given.

Roadville children, especially girls, excel in class when they are requested to recall a straightforward account or to retell a lesson. They can answer questions which call for bits and pieces of information, and they can often reconstruct a particular lesson almost verbatim. When substitute teachers come, Roadville girls can give them the particulars of the day's routine, the components of the lesson, and the ways in which orders are given in the class. They listen to, and many take enthusiastic part in, storytime, when their teachers read aloud to them. However, only certain individuals seek out on their own those books which have been read to them. When they do, they "read" and recite formulaic openings and direct quotations. They also enjoy naming the characters in the book.

Several teachers began in the primary grades to have children tell stories into the tape recorder. The teachers would then type up these stories, and ask the children to edit them and dictate changes they wanted made to produce a story the entire class could read. The telling of such stories into the recorder often drew a small audience; some stories were told by two or more students; some were cut off by listeners, because they did not fit the listeners' notion of what a story should be. In general the practice of recording, typing, editing, and reading their own stories revealed that the children from Roadville and Trackton brought with them numerous features of story-telling from home, but gradually began to add to their stories the kinds of features that school stories carried. When Nellie was in the first grade, near the end of the year, she told the following story.

Once upon a time, uh-er-ah, I, uh, I saw a monster
'n my mamma (pause) said
'n my mamma (pause) said
'n my, my mamma had a cockroach in her bed
//laughter//
'n she kicked 'im outta de bed
'n then it was a big giant mice in my mamma's room
'n then I hadda kill 'im
I got a big giant mice 'n then I kilt 'im
We chop 'im 'til he was bleedin'

By this time in the year, Nellie had learned the traditional opening formula of a "made-up" story: "Once upon a time." After opening her story with this, however, she paused, presumably to collect the story's plot, and then she began by claiming to have seen a monster. Following this false start, she went into a pattern familiar from exchanges of "my mamma" insults, perhaps to fill a gap in the story with a familiar chunk of language until she could collect her thoughts about where the story was going. On the fourth start, she moved into the story by recounting a tale of a cockroach in her house. Such subjects are fairly common in insults exchanged among older children ("my mamma eat steak, yo' mamma eat cockroaches"). The two-line unit on the cockroach ended with her mother kicking the roach out of bed; she then began her own story of victory over a "big giant mice." She exaggerated the size of the mouse, and, no doubt, the method of killing, and her own role in the killing. The story ended with no summary or evaluation on her part, but the death of the mouse and her victory were fitting material to mark for the audience the end of this major episode. At this stage Nellie had not begun to use the formulaic "The End" for her stories, which Trackton children usually began to use in the second grade. She also did not use extensive evaluation of the deeds, or report actual dialogue.

By the time she was ready to enter the third grade, Nellie and others from Trackton had begun to incorporate in their oral stories (told in school) numerous features of the written stories they read in their reading books and heard read to them. They usually introduced characters, began and ended the story with a formula, and followed a right chronological order. Exaggeration of detail was far less common than it had been in the early school months, and sentences were often much shorter than those of their non-story-telling discourse. They also recognized and explained details which might not be familiar to the listener, using flashbacks or parenthetical-like comments. They gave their own view of events of the story. In the third grade, Nellie told the story given in Table 8.3 in response to the teacher's request that she tell a story on the tape recorder. The story has one episode – her dog's fight and injury, and the resolution of the conflict the injury created. Nellie had by the third grade acquired a number of story-telling strategies highly valued by the school. She abstracted her story and adhered to the temporal order and details of the actual experience being recounted. She provided enough evaluation through adjectives to help the listeners visualize the events of the story. She also structured her story according to those features of stories usually called for in school: she provided an opening, oriented the listener to the setting and characters, gave the necessary details for understanding the set-up of the conflict, and moved to a climax or point in her story. She used either or both formulaic openings and closings.

The following story (Table 8.4) told by Sissy, Nellie's older sister, in the fourth grade, is in response to her teacher's request that she tell about something that happened to her at home. Here she has not organized a central episode, but there are three episodes, each one vaguely related to the other. She ends the story abruptly with a formula; other students were getting restless, since her story was longer than usual. She begins the story by introducing herself, orienting the listeners to the characters, and establishing the time and setting. The breaks between the episodes are marked by hesitations and occasional false starts. She repeatedly talks about how mad she gets, as she outlines the numerous conflicts she is involved in with her pup and brothers and sisters, and finally her trials as she is punished by her mother. She cannot win; there seems no resolution, and her classmates cut her off. This story presents the story-teller in a no-win situation, and those who listen to it condemn it for not "gettin' to the point" and tell the teacher: "Don't bother to type that one."

Roadville students, in contrast to Trackton students, excel in the early grades in recounting brief highly specific recapitulations of lesson pieces, actual events, and stories read to them. Teachers' requests for repetition and recall of previous lessons fit the requests of Roadville parents for stories. In both cases, adults have preconceived ideas about the stories they want the children to tell; they then coach children to produce these specific stories and to make them adhere to the facts or to the earlier telling. Roadville children remember slogans, proverbs, and single-utterance pre-scriptions for behavior. However, when asked to create fictive stories, Roadville children have little success. They either retell stories read to them at school or repeatedly quiz the teacher on what she wants them to do. If the teacher says simply "Tell about something that happened to you, or make up a story about a pet," they choose a specific incident and repeat it with a tight adherence to chronicity. The following story was told by Jed when he was in the fourth grade.

One day I was outside, and my dog was hiding in the bushes
and I walked by the bushes and he jumped on me
and I had to fight to get up
I went in, and my mother yelled at me
so I had to change my clothes

Before he told the story, Jed had spent several minutes thinking quietly. He had seemingly rehearsed the story in his head, so that his oral performance was a neatly balanced series of three compound sentences, including the high point of action, the culmination of the action, and a coda of a simple sentence. He orients the reader by his opening "One day I was outside" and sets up the potential for action by describing his dog's location and

Table 8.3. *Organization of orally recounted story by Nellie (third grade) (Trackton text XIII*)*

I'm Nellie	Story-teller introduction	Here Nellie introduces herself and claims the floor, establishing that she has a story she will tell. This is especially important in the classroom situation in which these stories are elicited, because the teacher issues a general invitation to the group. Unsuccessful story-tellers announce themselves, and perhaps even their desire to tell a story, but if they fail to "get to the point" – to tell what their story is about in a brief abstract – their place will be taken away from them. They must have the story's characters, episodes, and outcomes preconceived before they begin, in order to continue to hold the floor, in this story-telling free-for-all. If they pause in these first few moments, their place is taken.
'n I'm gonna tell, I wanna tell 'bout my dog		
my dog	Topic introduction	
he a big German Shepherd	Report of main character's major attributes	
he stay down my granmamma's house	Orientation of story and explanation of detail critical to determining setting of story	Here Nellie orients the listeners to the story by establishing its setting. She explains the setting briefly: the dog is Nellie's, yet it lives at her grandmother's house, which is not where Nellie lives. Had the dog not been at her grandmother's house, the major episode of the story could not have taken place.
he, uh-er-ah	False start	
my mamma don't like dogs	Explanation of background relevant to particular setting	Before moving into the story's main episode, Nellie explains, almost parenthetically, why her dog stays with her grandmother: her mother dislikes dogs, and her
'n he big too		

he, my granmamma got 'nother ol' dog, 'n they fight	Reminder of central character; set-up of conflict, introduction of protagonist; first temporal event	Here Nellie introduces the source of the story's conflict – her grandmother's other dog. She simply dispatches with the fight between the two animals – a part she did not participate in – and moves on to something she did participate in – the outcome of the conflict and its resolution.
my dog, he got a big hole in his shoulder	Second and critical event	Nellie repeats the topic, provides the build-up of events which will lead to the climax. Nellie does not attempt to detail the fight which led up to the injury, but she evaluates its outcome by the use of both the adjective *big* and the exaggerated label *hole*.
we hadda take 'im to a ol' man	Third temporal event of episode	Nellie points out the conflict, the problem to be overcome, and the resolution of the problem with both an outside agent – the old man – and her own family's initiative – taking the dog to the man. She then gives the details of how the helpful agent took care of the problem by using the "white stuff."
he put some white stuff on it	Climax and resolution of events in episode	
'n dat's all	Formulaic ending	This ending, a modification of the movie industry's "That's all Folks," was adopted instead of "The End" by many of the children by the time they were in the third grade. Nellie never goes to movies, so she has no idea of its original usage, but has learned it in school from the other children who picked it up from movies and brought it into their story-telling.

action. A majority of stories told by Roadville boys follow a similar pattern:

My dog and I play a lot
when I get home, I let him out
his name is Rocky
Rocky likes to go out
he plays with my cat
my cat's name is Miss Kitty

Repeatedly, the central character in boys' stories is their dog; the girls usually tell about their activities with their friends. These stories are similar in their simple plot and major characters to those of their preschool books which feature boys and girls at play with their pets and friends. The children's stories very rarely contain any expression of their own evaluation of the story's events or any indication of emotional involvement by any of the story's characters. There are few expressions of causal connections or links between dependent and independent clauses in the primary-level stories. In an attempt to encourage some elaboration, some teachers asked students to illustrate their stories. The following story was told and then written by Martin in response to such a request by his fourth-grade teacher. Above the story, he drew a red car with a crushed front fender, a police car, and a wrecker; a young boy was standing beside the car, as other people stood by to watch the episode.

Here is a red Camaro, 1978. He ran into a telephone pole. He was going kind of fast. He broke his leg. The policeman is getting out to come check it, make sure he has not got any liquor or pot. He has got the siren and the lights on. He did not find anything. The wrecker will pull the car up off the ground. They will fix the car. The boy is mad because a dog ran out in front of him and made him wreck.

Martin's story is somewhat exceptional in its expression of protagonist's emotions and its indication of the hidden cause of the accident in the final sentence.

In the primary grades, teachers used these oral story-telling activities for several purposes. After typing out the stories just as they were told into the tape recorder, some teachers found that a few students would reject their oral version in written form. Since the written versions of stories were often distributed on the desks of class members when they came into language arts class, students began to develop sensitivities about what their classmates liked to read. These student-authored stories were only supplements to numerous other types of reading, but they generated considerable class involvement. Some teachers went over each student's written version with the individual student, using it to point out punctuation problems, spelling errors, and to encourage use of the dictionary. When individual students scored poorly on specific skills worksheets (for example, use of *before, after, then, next*), some teachers illustrated in the students' own stories their knowledge of these terms when they had recounted experiences known to them. Teachers reported that a major advantage of these oral story-telling sessions was that they gave children opportunities to contribute long stretches of speech, or extended discourse, in the classroom. Most class recitation and even small-group work gave children only short turns at talking. The oral stories and recountings of past events enabled teachers to look carefully at children's ways of connecting ideas, sequencing events, and providing evaluations of events, individuals, and ideas.

At the sixth grade level, teachers in several classes not only continued to give students an opportunity to practice recounting accounts of events which occurred to them, but also expanded uses of these stories. Language arts classes used the tape recording, original typed version, and edited version for discussion of graphic representation of emphasis and meaning through punctuation, choice of words, sequencing of narrative events, building of compound–complex sentences, and increasing skills of supporting generalizations with facts. Social studies teachers emphasized that the children's stories of events which had happened to them could be used as models for social studies questions which asked them to imagine themselves as a character in history. As one teacher put it, "I see sixth grade as the time I better teach 'em to marshal some facts and get them put down on paper in some order. Then they can see what generalizations and topic sentences mean." In the following edited version of a story she told in the sixth grade, Nellie uses direct quotation, summarizes the feelings of those involved, and details graphically what transpired in the key event of the story. The editing – placement of capitals, punctuation marks, title, and author – was done by Nellie.

305

Table 8.4. *Organization of orally recounted story by Sissy (fourth grade) (Trackton text XIV*)*

My name Sissy	Story-teller introduction
me 'n my brother 'n my sister	Introduction of main characters
'n I was in de bed 'sleep, 'n every Sat'day mornin'	Establishment of setting
dey, dey, dey come to my room	Build-up to episode one
'n dey be up early	Background situation for episode
early in de morning 'fore me 'n my mamma my sister, dey be up early in de mornin', 'fore we do	
'n dey be comin' sneakin' up on me	Conflict
scarin' me, ticklin' my feet	
'n I get mad	Attempt at conflict resolution
'n git up	
'n start fussin'	
den so	
I git back in de bed 'n go back to sleep	Conflict resolution
I git in de bed wid my mamma some-time	Beginning of episode two; orientation by *sometime* indicates new and different episode
'n when dey be fussin'	
when I be fussin'	
'n den some hour	
den when I go back sleep I git up early in de mornin'	
'n I clean up 'n dey make me mad again	False starts to build-up of conflict
dey have to	
'n de puppy	
I've got a pup	Introduction of new character
'n it make me mad sometimes too	
have to put 'im outside	
'n den so dey, dey	Attempt to pick up episode two's action and original characters again
'n den so dey, dey git up so early	

306

ۇ pageۇ

Table 8.4 (*cont'd.*)

I hate to wake dem up	
'n me 'n my brother	
sometime we stay sleep so late	Dropping of episode two without conflict and resolution
'n den so my sister	
she came in at my room	Orientation to episode three
'n my bicycle	
fell on me	Explanation of background for conflict
'n I hurt my leg	
'n my mamma she start fussin'	Conflict
'n I had to clean up de house	
'n when my mamma make me wash dishes	
I git mad at her	Attempt at resolution
I 'on't 'on't 'on't hardly do it right	
when I wanna do it right	Parenthetical explanation of main character's behavior
I do it right	
'n she make me, make me, make, make up de beds	
I'd make 'em up	
'n den go, she make me clean up de whole house	Further conflict and response
I git so mad	
'n fold up clothes	
'n I hate to fold up clothes	Triple repetition of conflict ("'n I hate . . .")
'n I hate to go out der 'n hang 'em on de line	
'n I hate to go out der 'n take 'em off	
'n dat's de end	Formulaic ending

Ethnographer doing

A True Story[9]

Last week I was an usher at church, and my Uncle Red was in church too. He was asleep in the back of the church while the preacher was preaching. My uncle started dreaming he hit on the ball tickets [won on a football or baseball pool]. He started hollering "YAHOO! The ten with the five!" He kept on hollering, and you couldn't even hear the preacher preaching. He had to stop. Everybody was laughing. Reverend Jones had to come and wake him up. My Grandmamma was mad at my uncle but he was happy because he really did hit the next day!

Nellie

The teacher who collected this story used it to illustrate not only ways Nellie's use of punctuation added emphasis, but also how Nellie created suspense and humor through placement of events. On occasion, the classes looked at two stories and compared them, rewriting each into another style. For example, Nellie's story was contrasted with Randy's story below. Randy was a friend to Jed and several other Roadville children.

My name is Randy, My Daddy's name is Rob, and my cousin's name is Luke. We went out the boat landing Saturday, and we had gone out there to fish. We were out on the water, and the boat started to sink. The water came up to the back seat. We were going back to the pier, and we were paddling our boat. There was another man paddling his boat too. This motor boat came by and swished a bunch of water into our boat. The man in the other boat asked us if we needed any help. My daddy said no. We got up to the pier and my daddy told me to throw the stopper (whatever you call it) out. Then we went to the dam and fished and caught a catfish and four brim. Then they opened the gate so we went up to the top of the dam. We caught two catfish. Then it was 7:50 and we left and went home.

By Randy
Sixth grade

Randy very straightforwardly sets out the characters, the time, and place of the story. He then moves through a recital of events, following a strict chronological order and recounting specific details. He uses only one piece of direct quotation, his father's "no," which he does not instruct the teacher to mark graphically in any way. He does not comment on or evaluate the feelings of anyone in the story. The sixth graders talked about the emotions Randy and his dad must have felt and rewrote Randy's story to fit the model of Nellie's tale. They asked Randy to supply dialogue, comments on how he felt in the boat and when he reached shore. Nellie's account was rewritten as a straight chronological rehearsal of events, drawing on details Nellie supplied about what occurred after church and before the "hit" on Monday.

Several weeks later, Randy wrote the following story, in which he altered his earlier style somewhat and more openly expressed his feelings about the event.

The other day I went to the disco. I was dancing with this really pretty girl. They were playing Kiss's new album. If You Think I'm Sexy was on, and then I started dancing with the other girls. My mama came in. She embarrassed me! My cousin was up there and a big pile of kids. My mama said, "Does anybody know Randy Bocker?" My cousin said, "Yeah, I know him." My mama said, "I didn't even KNOW you!" She said, "Boy, when I get you home, I'm going to tear your tail up!" Then she took me home. See, I forgot to tell her where I was going, and this happened at about 11:00 p.m. Saturday night.

The story carries a lesson – "bad deeds are punished" – as most oral tales told in Roadville did, and Randy suggests that lesson in his final sentence. One language arts teacher used stories similar to Randy's above and the following true story from Lisa to illustrate the meanings of "lesson," and "moral," and to introduce the class to fables.

Another True Story

I was riding down the road on my bicycle, and I did not see this car coming, and it hit me, and I fell off my bicycle on top of the car. This woman came and got me. I was running up the hill trying to get away. I was trying to go home. This lady caught me. She went in the house and got a chair and made me sit down in it. She called the ambulance. I went into the Emergency Room at the hospital. They put a cast on my leg. I stayed up there one day. My mother came up there to see me. I came home and had to lay on the couch. My sister hit me on my broken leg! Then I was able to walk after a while, and soon I was able to dance and play again. But I want to tell all of you to please be careful when you are on your bike.

Lisa's tale clearly carries a moral or a lesson, and her story was used as a build-up and introduction to some of Aesop's fables. The students tried to rewrite some of their own stories as well as those in their reading books to make them come out with morals. There was much joking about the fact that many of the stories could not be interpreted to have a "good" direct lesson or moral about human behavior; sometimes the "bad guys" did win.

When, near the end of the 1970s, federal and state efforts to bring students with physical handicaps into the regular classrooms began, several teachers were asked to volunteer with the initial transitions. One teacher interested in writing offered to have her students help orient a blind student to the building and its classrooms. Student volunteers had to agree to wear a tape recorder as they guided the new student, orienting him to the scene ahead, providing specific details, guiding him through the halls, lunchroom, library, etc., and concluding with a summary of the territory covered. Following these sessions, groups in the class listened to the tapes, paying special attention to the questions the blind student asked. The teacher typed out the opening scene description or generalizations about what was to come, supporting details the student gave the newcomer as he led him through a specific area of the school, and the concluding comments of each session. These lessons continued for several weeks, while the students built skills for preparing a two-page expository essay on other topics, in which they had to explain a generalization and support it with details and a conclusion. At the end of the "experiment," the teacher reported her own joy in discovering how easily this class had come to understanding terms such as "topic sentence," "generalization," and "conclusion" in comparison to classes she had taught in years past: "When the students' own words out of their own mouths do what it is I try to get them to put on paper, they can hardly miss getting it right when they do try to write." This view summarized in general the opinions of those teachers who used the stories of students in the first through sixth grades to build their skills for writing and reading.

The question of relevance

During the 1970s there were numerous working-class black and white students who were in remedial reading and language arts classes in the junior and senior high schools. Many, such as Jed and the Turner girls, were waiting until they were sixteen and could quit school. Others had reached sixteen, but were still trying to stay in school; many had already begun work on the mills' second shift and were helping support families. In the Piedmont region in the 1970s there was a strong push toward making vocational skills available in the public schools, and an increasing number of language arts and reading teachers tried to determine their role in preparing students who were headed for jobs in the textile mills, or as construction workers, mechanics, nursing assistants, and food services workers. Teachers had always felt secure in urging students to learn to read and write in order to increase their job skills and to improve their chances for employment at higher levels. However, reports from the vocational education teachers that their students needed different kinds of skills than those of college-bound students made sense to many teachers, and they welcomed the impetus to learn more about the kinds of reading and writing which took place in different kinds of jobs.

Several teachers asked mill foremen, carpenters, plumbers, and mechanics to provide them with types of reading and writing they did on the job, and some agreed to come talk to classes about the skills they needed in their work. It soon became clear that there were few occasions for writing or reading extended prose in these jobs; instead, workers had to read bits and pieces of prose, usually combined with numerals, and make quick decisions for action. Instead of writing reports, they usually filled out forms or summarized orally to someone else who "wrote up" the "final" report. Teachers took note of the fact that skills at oral recapitulation of a task or series of events were generally viewed as highly desirable by the workers who came to talk to classes. Moreover, during one period of the 1970s the textile mills tested this skill in their interviews of potential employees. For a brief period in the mid 1970s, there were far more potential employees for jobs in the textile mills than there were jobs, and the mills changed their method of evaluating workers in the hope of finding better ways of identifying good workers. Prospective employees were taken through the section of the mill in which they might work and asked to watch the operations. They did not interact directly with those who were operating the machines, but they observed and had opportunities to ask questions of foremen. The potential employees then returned to the personnel office and were asked to describe how to run a particular machine and what they had seen in different parts of the mill. Employees were selected on the basis of the adequacy of their oral descriptions of the jobs they would be doing. When employment conditions returned to normal, the mills dropped this method of interviewing applicants, reportedly because it was more time-consuming than other methods, and it had not proven more satisfactory in choosing good employees than their usual methods.

Teachers' questions about the kinds of reading and writing used in real job settings had convinced many of the need to probe further into students' future uses of reading and writing. The next question teachers asked was: If extensive reading and writing are not needed in vocational settings, are they needed in the home lives of these students? My ethnographic work in Trackton and Roadville had revealed that there were few situations in which adults individually wrote extended prose, and that patterns of individual and group reading varied greatly across communities. We then looked at the social networks of the students. There we found that pool halls and other local gathering places bore some evidence of writing of various types and purposes by the students themselves. They used their recreational centers for posting protest messages (usually by modifying previously posted commercial posters), advertisements for parts of cars and musical instruments, or calls for participation in local sports or musical events scheduled by their social networks.[10] But this writing once again usually consisted of short passages or phrases and did not call for extended discourse.

Those teachers most concerned about the linkage of their teaching of reading and writing to the vocational goals of working-class students decided to ask students to talk about the writing of others which created problems for them or their parents. Immediately – and with considerable sarcasm – the students pointed out that most of the information about social services, warranties and guarantees, and regulations from the city offices were "too tough" to read. Often their parents or elderly individuals known to the students asked for help at the offices of these agencies, but their employees explained the meaning of the regulations in language which was only slightly more understandable than the written language. Many residents depended on their children to help them, and students were concerned that they would be able to take on this task in the future.

Asked by their teachers to be "researchers" in their own communities, students brought in numerous types of writing that came into their own lives or the lives of their parents: traffic tickets, housing regulations, warranties, advertising, directions for appliances, income tax forms, etc. The students grouped themselves and began to try to make sense of each of the documents, recording the questions they asked in these attempts to get clarification. The students decided that for the documents to be accessible to their parents, they would have to be rewritten at about fourth to sixth grade level. As the students began to do this rewriting, they were introduced to readability tests and basic word lists, and they examined high-interest/low-level readers to determine their features. They asked "What makes reading easy?" – words or length of sentences, construction of longer units, printing format, or illustrations, or all of these?[11] Teachers used student interest in documents from their communities as the stimulus to lead them to numerous other kinds of reading during the term: newspaper accounts of problems caused by complicated language, short stories about people in different kinds of jobs, and brochures on job training and employment possibilities. Occasionally the teachers asked outsiders to come in and offer advice: a lawyer talked to classes about legal language, what it was like and why it had to have certain characteristics that "normal" language did not have. One student who had been caught speeding tried to remember and later to write the talk between him and the police officer at the time of the incident; he later recorded his interaction with the officer at the courthouse. He compared, to the delight of the class, the oral accounts on the two occasions and the written accounts of the incident.

The active senior citizen groups in the area seemed appropriate audiences for sharing some discussion of the tasks the students accomplished in language arts and reading classes. Some students recorded a videotape program for the senior citizens. Teachers proposed that a written version of the videotape be prepared, in case the tape was ever accidentally erased. When the students saw in print what they had said on the tape, they were uneasy; several recognized that their choice of words and ways of talking "didn't look right." They decided to write a summary of the tape's contents, and to keep the script on file, but not to share it outside the class. Several weeks were spent in summarizing in report-like form what had happened on the tape, why and how they had come to do the tape, and what they hoped to accomplish. The students began to generate other types of writing. Local radio stations were enlisted to accept spots written by students on reports of local events and how-to accounts; students wrote for their own social centers "how-to-do-it" manuals. Many were "turned on" to writing in ways which surprised themselves, but this writing was their own, generated by them for purposes which both met their needs and allowed teachers to emphasize school skills of spelling, punctuation, and requirements of style for different purposes. They wrote now for a readership of young and old in their own communities – a readership which trusted these students to translate public documents into common-sense language and was entertained by their frequent interjections of personal stories.

At the junior and senior high levels, teachers found they drew more and more on what the students could bring to class to teach the teachers about their reading and writing needs and habits. With imagination, initiative, and the help of some outsiders, teachers were able to create interest and motivation in the students and to involve them in not only reading and writing tasks, but also research tasks which led them to feel the need for basic word lists, dictionaries, and outside experts. Spelling, punctuation, clarity in writing, and general neatness of presentation became increasingly monitored by class members themselves as students began to gain a sense of producing a class project. When being right, neat, clear, and not appearing "dumb" mattered to them in environments they cared about – with the elderly at the senior citizens center and in their own communities – they were not hesitant to be rough judges on themselves and others.

From these efforts to re-examine their roles in teaching reading and writing for students who would not be going into college immediately after high school, teachers came to new definitions of relevance. In finding ways to make reading and writing make sense to these students they had to alter their methods of teaching, but not their standards of judging the mechanics of writing and clarity of writing. They learned to believe that their students could learn, and that they could learn from their students. One teacher summarized this feeling: "The needs are many, the motivation is amazing; and the goal of learning from students is for us to know what they have, not to tell us what they lack."

Becoming science "translators"

The fifth-grade science classroom was a mess. One corner was piled high with seed catalogues; the window sills were filled with cups and containers of dirt. Pumpkins and squash were piled in one corner of a low bookshelf, and dead geranium plants hung from the ceiling over the storage shelves. The work tables were filled with hoes and trowels of different sizes and shapes, and photographs of larger tools. A bulletin board was plastered with news clippings. The warm sun of a late November afternoon brightened this untidy classroom of a school just outside Gateway.

Children were clustered in small groups about the room, some working with poster board and magic markers, others with tape recorders, and some poring over science books, almanacs, dictionaries, and how-to-garden books. Four boys on one side of the room were involved in intensive debate:

Terry: What'd you get?
Tony: Wait 'til you hear ol' Mr. Feld.
Paul: We gonna do the old informant or the new one first?=
Tony: =The old – I talk to him a long time 'fore he tol' me 'bout gardenin'. Then he start 'memberin' 'bout how to cut the potato eyes, how to hill 'em up.
                    [
Terry: You get drawings?
Tony: Yea, //*pulls pencil sketches out of folder and passes them around*// 'n he checked 'em.
Terry: Did he say when he planted, why the sprout come from the eye?
      [
Tony: Yea, wanna hear the tape?
Mike: But we gotta hear Mr. Purcey tape too. Ol' Mr. Feld 'll be different from somebody young as Mr. Purcey.
Tony: All that's gotta go on the informant chart.

As the boys listened to the two tapes, one of an eighty-six-year-old retired farmer, another of a thirty-five-year-old part-time farmer, they gathered art materials on the floor around them and doodled on piles of scratch paper. They frequently stopped the tape to talk about what had been said, to ask the boy who had interviewed the farmer what a word meant or how the farmer used a certain tool. After the tapes, they made several "scratch lists": terms used by each informant for the potatoes (*rooter, spongy, big-eye*), folkways of growing "good potatoes," and names of tools, fertilizers, or other substances used by the farmers. The boys argued about the different ways each man stressed certain aspects of the planting process: Mr. Feld had insisted on planting by the moon; Mr. Purcey had stressed buying potatoes for planting at the feed store instead of using sprouted potatoes from the grocery store. Once the boys went to the teacher to ask for help in identifying the meaning of something an informant had said.

Before the end of the class period, the boys had agreed to interview the younger informant again; he had not answered some questions well enough for them to fill a comparative chart with information given by Mr. Feld. For example, they did not know whether Mr. Purcey planted by the moon or by some other timing method. They wondered too, if he did plant by the moon, whether or not he would share this fact with them. They planned the direct questions they would have to ask and find answers for to make a chart explaining in scientific terms the farmers' folk concepts. They decided to interview the feed store owner to ask him how his potatoes were different from grocery store potatoes which sprouted under the kitchen sink or in the back of the pantry. As the bell rang, and they scurried to clear their mess, Tony pointed to a newspaper clipping on the bulletin board which pictured an elderly black man standing beside a pile of huge pumpkins. A king-sized one of just over 100 lbs had set the county record.

Ol' man Feld can grow big pumpkins too, he doin' sumpin' right, science or no science.

This fifth-grade science class in 1974 was made up almost entirely of black boys who were reading at second-grade level or below; their class was designated the lowest track of science in their grade. The unit on plant life had begun with my talking with them about the research of anthropologists and a film on life in a Latin American village in which I had done research. The students were intrigued by the food habits of the people, how I had learned about these, and how I had managed to live in the area. By prior agreement with the science teacher, I suggested to the class that the methods of an ethnographer were no different from those which could be used in their own communities to answer questions about foodstuffs, how to grow them, and how to prepare them for eating. Caught up with the "fun" idea of becoming ethnographers, the students were launched into their science unit on plant life. The teacher (who had taken several courses in ethnographic field methods) and I agreed on ways I could help the students learn how ethnographers ask questions, collect data, identify folk concepts, and relate informants' data to other sources for a comparative perspective. During the eight weeks of the unit, I visited the class occasionally to check on the students' progress as ethnographers and to offer suggestions on field methods.

Armed with some basics of ethnographic techniques, the students were told to imagine they had just been set down as strangers in their own community. They were scouts or early arrivals of a group which would set up an agricultural resource center in the area. Most of the children were familiar with this idea, since there had recently been several highly publicized research projects in the area promoting new approaches to soybean production and the substitution of soy products for meats. As employees of the imaginary center, they were to have the task of learning as much as possible about the ways of growing foodstuffs currently used by the local people. They had only the local residents to learn from as they participated, observed, interviewed, collected documents and artifacts, took photographs, and collected life histories in the area. At the end of their preliminary stay, their task would be to advise the agricultural resource center on ways in which the local people's folk concepts were like or different from "scientific" approaches. In other words, for their bosses, they would have to translate folk knowledge into scientific knowledge and answer the question of whether or not science could explain why the local folk methods either worked or did not work.

The boys decided to focus on a minimal number of initial questions in their ethnographic work.

What were the foodstuffs most commonly grown in the area?
Who were considered the best farmers and what were their
methods?

In an effort to have students recognize that spoken and written
sources sometimes reinforced and sometimes contradicted each
other, the science teacher and I stipulated that answers to each of
these questions had to come from at least two sources, one oral
and one written. Otherwise, their data could not be accepted as
reliable. To answer the first question, some students suggested
grocery store ads; others protested that grocery stores sold foods
which were raised elsewhere and not just in their own region.
Finally, the boys agreed they would "ask around" in their
neighborhoods to see who was most frequently named as a good
farmer, and they could then ask those individuals about the most
commonly grown plants. Numerous selections of the same person
would also clinch that choice as someone to be interviewed on
gardening methods. Verifying either the most common foodstuffs
or the "best farmer" by written sources was more difficult. On the
third day of class discussion, a triumphant Tony brought in a
clipping from the local newspaper. Pictured was an old man who
had grown a pumpkin exceeding 100 lbs; the article said he often
grew vegetables of immense size, and he was widely known for the
good garden he produced year after year. Written verification of
one of the best farmers (and perhaps of one commonly grown
plant) had been found. After this first breakthrough, the boys
collected back issues of the weekly newspapers distributed in the
textile mills in which their parents worked. These carried local
features, many of which focused on gardening or cooking talents.
The class also asked the local newspaper for back issues of
October and November editions, many of which featured harvest-
time articles, recipes, etc. Good readers paired with lower-level
readers in searching the newspaper to identify more "good
farmers."

To provide written verification of foodstuffs that were most
frequently grown in the area, the boys – at the suggestion of a local
minister's wife – checked through recipe books produced by local
church groups. The recipes often depended on local vegetables and
seasonings, and the vegetables for which the greatest number of
recipes were offered were sure to be those grown locally. The six

foodstuffs the boys identified for focus in their interviews on gardening methods were: potatoes, string beans, okra, corn, tomatoes, and greens. The local folk category *greens* opened up unexpected areas in the lesson, for there were greens which were cultivated – spinach, kale, turnips, mustard, collards – but there were also highly prized greens which could not be cultivated. These grew only in certain places at certain times of the year. There were numerous myths surrounding these greens: which portions were poisonous, when they should be picked, why they grew, etc.

The boys collected life histories and artifacts, and they scoured newspapers and recipe books. Word spread quickly of their interests in gardening and farmers, and their classroom received numerous contributions from their communities. Many community members were not restrained by the request for information on foodstuffs only; growing flowers was an important part of community life as well. Dead geraniums were donated for the children to hang upside down inside the room until spring, when they could be planted anew. Teacher and students agreed that one unit in the spring would have to incorporate their newly found sources on raising flowers.

The life histories of the "best farmers" were summarized by the boys. They listened to the tapes over and over until they could write a brief summary of a particular life history. The teacher typed this and placed it in the "science book" along with photographs of the informant. Comparative charts translating and/or explaining folk concepts through scientific reasons were placed about the room. As the boys prepared these, they drew information from science books available in class and in the library. For example, to explain the folk concept that feed store potatoes were better for planting than those which sprouted under the sink at home, the boys experimented by planting some of each kind. Through their experiment and interviews, they discovered that grocery store potatoes were not treated with chemicals to make them resistant to pests which might attack them once they were planted. Thus the feed store potatoes produced more pest-free potatoes. Shorter versions of comparative charts were prepared by the teacher for the "science book." In essence, the culmination of the unit's work was a "book" written by the class. Similar to a chapter on gardening in a traditional ethnography, the class book also contained "translations" of the knowledge of the local folk into scientific concepts presented in textbooks, films, and commercially prepared materials on plant life. At the end of the unit, the boys had learned some of the vocabulary of ethnographic fieldwork: *interview, bias, folk culture, artifact, life history*, etc., as well as terms such as *photosynthesis, chlorophyll, osmosis, pesticide.*

By the end of the eight weeks, the standard unit test of the textbook was given: twelve boys scored above 90 percent, eight scored in the 80s, and three in the 70s. Of the twenty-three boys in the class, none failed the test. Their cumulative folders indicated that none of these boys had ever passed a standardized unit science test in his school career. Average attendance during earlier units of the year which had been approached through traditional teaching methods had been 68 percent; average attendance during the two months of this unit was 92 percent. Six parents visited the school, sharing information or demonstrating techniques of gardening; eleven family members sent information or artifacts to the school. Prior to this unit, only two family members had contacted the teacher regarding any matters other than discipline or failing grades.

Learners in this science classroom had become ethnographers of a sort; in so doing, they had improved their knowledge of science. In addition, they had learned to talk about ways of obtaining and verifying information; terms such as *sources, check out* (in the sense of *verify*), *summarize*, and *translate* had become part of their vocabulary. They had come to recognize, use, and produce knowledge about the skills of inquiring, compiling, sorting, and refining information. They had not only made use of "inquiry" and "discovery method" skills discussed in science and social studies methods texts;[1] they had acquired the language to talk about these skills. They had not liked many of their tasks: rewriting the summaries for the "science book," producing explanatory charts, writing descriptions of sizes, shapes, and uses for each of the artifacts photographed and placed in the "science book." However, they had been motivated to push ahead with these tasks to provide a permanent record of their knowledge for next year's class, and to "announce" in a school-accepted format all that they had learned. Their world of science uses had expanded far beyond the classroom, as they and members of their community had been caught up in their inquiry. Many had, for the first time in their lives, carried on conversations with feed store owners, nurserymen, and local agricultural agents. They had been forced into situations in which they had to formulate specific questions to obtain particular bits of information needed to fill in a particular space on a chart or to complete definitions of a term. Traditionally, these boys and their families in Trackton and similar communities preferred giving a story in narrative form in answer to a generalized query; they noticed this trait in their informants and came to laugh about the fact that they "couldn't get ol' Mr. Feld to answer a question directly." They had come to pay attention to the kinds of questions people in different situations in life asked and answered directly. When the unit test time drew near, they joked about the fact that they knew they would be asked direct questions; on that kind of test they could not get by with telling a generalized story. Without direct formulation, but with guidance by the teacher on ways in which vocabulary, styles of language use, and features of discourse differ across situations, the students had come to these conclusions and had, through the structure of the unit, begun to articulate these differences. When boys listened to their tapes repeatedly, they pulled out vocabulary items they had to define – both in informants' terms and in scientific terms.

A key objective of their two-way manipulation of knowledge about plant life from community to school and from school to community was to learn to translate the knowledge familiar in one domain into the other. Table 9.1 illustrates schematically how students moved between the personalized, contextualized, orally expressed knowledge of home to the depersonalized, decontextualized, primarily written knowledge of the classroom. They labeled folk terms, identified bits and pieces of processes which had parallels in the science domain, and specified gaps in information between the two domains. In the classroom, the scientific paradigm and third person objective accounts of knowledge had to be used as filters for the information from folk concepts.

Nonverbal knowledge or experience in daily home life differed from laboratory experience, instructor demonstration, or the accounts of the behaviors of scientists. The latter often specified sequenced steps or stages, identified factors or conditions which could disturb a pattern predicted from past experience, and stipulated these factors and conditions. In short, the highly

Table 9.1. *Translation of the social reality of the familiar community domain into the unfamiliar school domain*

Familiar community domain features	Translation process	Unfamiliar school domain features
Personalized, contextualized verbal knowledge – chiefly oral		Depersonalized, decontextualized verbal knowledge – largely written
opinions narratives with evaluations sayings, proverbs recipes, newspaper items	identify and define folk terms, folk concepts specify elements and processes from folk domain which have parallels in unfamiliar domains identify gaps in information between two domains formulate specific questions for obtaining missing information determine methods of testing occurrence of events against known principles of operation	statements of fact written accounts of principles as borne out in experiments, demonstrations, third person objective narratives without evaluation from a personal perspective explanation and demonstration of scientific method defense of scientific method, need for testing of hypotheses, facilitating replication,

knowledge

observation of others
trial and error attempts
repeated participation without
articulation of processes

specify sequenced steps of stages
of activity
segment continuum into episodes
if process does not work, specify
trouble sources and conditions
in environment which could
aggravate problems
identify in unfamiliar domain
possible explanations of problems

identify in unfamiliar domain
principles which may help predict outcomes under given conditions

Depersonalized behavioral
knowledge

pictorial illustration, instructor
demonstration according to
formalized procedures
written accounts of trial and
error of others
narrative biographical accounts
of individual scientists,
groups, or institutions involved in scientific research

context-specific, and personalized statements of causation ("My greens ain't sweet this year – not enough water") had to be translated into scientific statements using concrete terminology and drawing from general theories stated in the abstract.

The first step in the translation process was learning skills for collecting and reporting such knowledge; the second step was engaging collectively in a process of translating this knowledge into the format and categories of the unfamiliar domain. The end result was realization by students that participation in *both* domains is viable for the individual, and features of one domain can be used in the other. The translation process was bidirectional; by trying to translate the folk into the scientific, students learned to interpret or latch the scientific system into a familiar folk system. There were definite relations – equivalence, contradiction, complementation, and generalization – between the two systems. Learners, under the guidance of teachers and fellow students, decontextualized their knowledge from home and community grids and reconstructed their learning into categories and abstractions valued in academic settings. Other students helped them recognize gaps in their knowledge and forced them to make explicit knowledge which had previously been only implicit in their daily experiences. For example, implicitly the students knew greens were eaten more frequently than other vegetables; ethnographic investigation raised the question of *why* and made explicit the fact that other green vegetables have only one growing season, cultivated greens have two seasons, and some wild greens are available year-round. Thus, expanded knowledge helped fill in and extend the background underlying daily customary events.

Talk about language

What happened to the teacher's role as the learners became ethnographers, as the students became the basic suppliers of information for the unit? Clearly, she was responsible for keeping the boys' learning oriented to the specific textbook unit and test on plant life. But in this task she also became a resource in the same sense in which informants and other community members were resources. She had to provide sources of information of various types: science books with units on plant life; poster boards and suggestions on ways of setting up charts; examples of formats for depicting tools and their uses. One major traditional role left to the teacher in this unit was determination of the objectives for the unit: what were the students to learn? what skills should they display upon completion of the unit? About halfway through the unit, I sat down with the teacher and asked her what she hoped the tangible and intangible results of our "experiment" with this unit of science might be. Among her tangible outcomes, she included:

improved scores on the standardized unit tests;
the "science book" for use by other classes;
an increased number and variety of written materials done by students;
posters in acceptable form for use with other classes;
a selection of artifacts to retain for next year's unit.

Intangible products were less restricted to the subject of science *per se* and included general intellectual and social benefits:

enthusiasm and motivation for school work, and for science in particular;
parent involvement;
an improved self image for the boys (several of whom were leaders on the playground, but previously had been self-acknowledged failures inside the classroom);
increased awareness of the types of sources which could verify information;
an increased diversity of opportunities for displaying knowledge and skills (talking to people, reading public information, seeking out oral ways of getting knowledge, and using people as resources).

These intangible products allowed methods of showing off abilities which students could rarely display through traditional classroom measures of ability. In addition to these subject-matter and attitudinal goals, the teacher wanted specific goals of language use to result from participation in the unit.

If the students were to be able to convince others they had gained scientific knowledge from this experience, they had to be able to use the language of science and to produce acceptable scientific statements. In the teacher's terms, students displaying

325

these specific language skills should be able to:

1. make statements and back them up with an acceptable source or authority recognized in the science world;
2. ask and answer questions briefly and precisely: be direct;
3. know the vocabulary of science used in textbooks and by teachers of science;
4. avoid telling stories about their knowledge: be able to discuss an item or event for its own sake, not in terms of their direct experiences with it.

The teacher therefore constructed the objectives of the unit and made particular requirements in the unit to insure that the students would not get lost in the "good stories" of their informants: the discursive, redundant, and sometimes entertaining but often irrelevant stories individuals told to express their views of how they grew "good tomatoes." In class, the teacher and those students who were not part of the immediate context of a particular interview or life history asked repeatedly "How?" "Why?" "What does that mean?" The situation, therefore, not teacher authority, forced students to provide answers to these questions. They had to seek information having to do with the transmission of food and water through plant cells to answer questions related to why tomatoes should be tied up, why the foliage died as potatoes formed in the ground, why greens picked before turnips formed were "sweeter" than those picked after turnips formed. For these students, the necessity of scientific discourse evolved out of the opportunity *to contrast the familiar,* their own community's ways of speaking and ways of living, *with the unfamiliar,* those of science texts and teachers.

The ethnographic experiences of the students had enabled them to focus their attention on a variety of features of knowledge and information collected in their own communities and in their personal repertoires. The experience had, however, also forced them to compare these methods with those of the classroom. The unit requirements set up by the teacher and, more importantly, the questions of fellow students not present during collection of interviews or life histories, led students to identify elements and processes in both domains: the folk and the scientific. For each activity – tying up tomatoes, planting by the moon, or picking greens – the students had to identify and manipulate elements and processes to seek parallels and correspondences in classroom science. They had to begin to develop the habit of translation, to link activities dependent on one type of knowledge in their community domain to elements and processes specifiable by science across the generalized domain of plant biology. Particularly important in this classroom were: (1) the emphasis on the role of imitation and guidance, and (2) absence of reliance on individual learning. Throughout the unit, the students were imitating me as the ethnographer and each other as they sought new ways of finding information; they were guided by the questions of their peers, the teacher, and the need to make themselves clear in material prepared for use by next year's classes. Opportunities to return to sources of information with different methods of inquiring and organizing facts were possible. The collectiveness of student–community–teacher knowledge in this unit was a radical deviation from the formerly independent individual-student and teacher-dominated approaches to learning. Though the students were tested at the end of the unit, their collective product was also "tested"; that is, it had to meet the requirements of teacher and students for preservation and use in the future.

The newly acquired language skills of the fifth-grade science class were side effects of their role as ethnographers in a unit on plant life. Language learning can, however, be a direct product of ethnographic activities adapted for other grade levels. Mrs. Pat, a second-grade teacher, developed numerous ways of having students become ethnographers or "detectives" focusing on language, looking for the ways in which language, written and spoken, differed across contexts. Her school, which included kindergarten through twelfth grade (ages 5–18), was set in a rural area twenty miles from Laurenceville. Sixty-five percent of the students were white, 35 percent black. Many of the local residents worked in the Laurence textile mill, and most of their daily life away from their job centered around their community's two "country" stores, hardware store, department store, fire station, and several small churches. All students attending the school were from farming families, many of whom had one or more family members working in the textile mill as well. A majority of the school's population qualified for social services under the federal government's definition of poverty level. Of twenty-four students entering the second-grade class, eighteen scored below grade level (six

327

of these had repeated the first grade twice); six had scored at grade level in standardized tests at the end of the first grade. Roadville's Sue Dobbs had had Mrs. Pat as her second-grade teacher, and when Lisa was in the second grade, she sent her to live with a cousin whose home was in Mrs. Pat's school district.

During the first week of school, Mrs. Pat asked visitors from the community into the class to talk about their ways of talking, and to explain what they read and wrote, when they used reading and writing, with whom, and why; they brought samples of their writing and of materials they read. Over the summer, she had visited with these individuals telling them of her concern for the low reading scores of children in the early grades and suggesting that reading and writing could become meaningful to children only if they saw these skills used by their families. In addition to parents and community members, the principal, lunchroom workers, custodian, and several other members of the school also came into the classroom to share their oral language and uses of reading and writing during the early weeks of school. Eighth-grade students brought favorite stories they had read or heard; they spent two class periods of each week reading to the second-graders and helping them choose books of their own from the library. The teacher had prepared the second-graders for these visits, giving them practice in acting as "detectives" by listening for answers to four questions:

> What sounds do you hear when — talks?
> What did — say about how he talked?
> What did — write?
> What did — read?

During the early weeks of the year, Mrs. Pat began working on sound–symbol relationships, introduced the basal readers in which she would start the children, and read a variety of types of literature to them: dialect poetry, pieces of scripts from radio and TV, comic books, biographies of favorite baseball heroes in which there was much lively conversation. Traditional workbook exercises, reading circle activities, basal reader instruction, and administration of sequenced skill tests were maintained throughout the year in conjunction with the linguistic-detective approach. Extra practice came during an hour or so each day, when children listened to the radio and practiced the detective work they would later try with classroom visitors.

All of these sources provided Mrs. Pat and her students with language data, descriptions of situations for language use, and assessments of attitudes toward language. Following each visit by community residents, story-reading by an eighth-grader, or poetry-reading by the teacher, class discussion focused on the kinds of language used. Children identified the differences between formal and informal speech, and the dialect of their visitors and that used on radio news broadcasts. They noted:

> sounds that did not match those discussed in reading lessons (the diphthong /æh/ seemed "longer" in the speech of visitors than in the discussion of the sound for "long *i*" in phonics lessons);
> sounds that were discussed in reading lessons, but were not heard in some casual talk (final *ng*, final *s*);
> expressions not found in reading materials (*ain't, yonder*);
> words used in school written materials, but rarely used in talk (*notice*, instead of *pay attention*, *this evening* instead of *tonight*).

The teacher introduced terms to describe those features the children noticed: *dialect, casual, formal, conversational, standard.* Oral talk defined as formal was that used by Mrs. Pat during lessons and when talking to visitors, by radio and TV news broadcasters, by the principal in formal announcements and talks made to the school or class, and by adults in service encounters with clerks, waitresses, and garagemen when they did not know each other. Through the discussions evolved a series of charts for the students' notebooks. Such a chart was made for each visitor and for certain radio announcers. Each reading period contained time for students to listen to tapes and to discuss jointly and mark those features they heard most frequently. Mrs. Pat's goal was identification of the most frequent and most noticeable features, not a thorough description of dialect features (Table 9.2). Work-sheets listing different sounds were introduced during the year. The students described themselves as "writing up" someone's speech.

At the end of the sixth week, Mrs. Pat began to help students focus their attention not only on the ways people talked, but on

Ethnographer doing

Table 9.2. *Worksheet for oral language study – grade two*

Tape number *10*
Write up for the talk of <u>Mr. Morris (principal)</u>. Date: March 6, 1972

Your name:_____	Casual	Formal
Were you able to hear:		
the beginning /m/ sound in words?	×	×
the beginning /s/ sound in words?	×	×
the beginning /t/ sound in words?	×	×
the beginning /b/ sound in words?	×	×
the beginning /r/ sound in words?	×	×
the beginning hard *c* sound in words?		
the beginning /l/ sound in words?	×	×
the beginning /d/ sound in words?	×	×
the beginning /st/ sound in words?	×	×
the beginning /br/ sound in words?		
the beginning *ch* sound in words?		
the beginning *sh* sound in words?	×	×
the beginning *str* sound in words?		
the middle vowels:		
long *o*?	×	×
long *e*?		
long *a*?	×	×
long *u*?		
long *i* as /æh/?	×	×
the final /t/ sound in words?	×	×
the final /p/ sound in words?	×	×
the final /d/ sound in words?		×
the final /s/ sound in words?		
the final *ng* sound in words?		×
the final *st* sound in words?	×	×

what people said about how they used reading and writing in their daily lives. Together the class listened to several tapes, and she helped them complete lists of what and why people read and wrote (Table 9.3). She asked a tenth-grade art student to visit the class, listen to the discussions, and draw up a series of cartoons depicting uses of reading and writing. The thumb print with stick-figure-like appendages was the central character of the cartoons, and the second graders soon began to imitate these to depict ways they themselves used reading and writing.

Throughout the year, the entire focus of the classroom was on language, its "building blocks" in sound and in print, the ways its building blocks were put together, and how these varied in accordance with speaker and use in print or speech. Reading materials included not only the basal readers, but also pieces of writing used in the school. The principal, custodian, lunchroom workers, and other students contributed forms, receipts, blank report cards, store notices, etc. Teachers and students began to "play" language in its many variations as an instrument, sometimes sounding formal or classical, at other times informal or disco-like. Students called attention to shifts of style, picked out expressions characteristic only of speech, and laughed about the various meanings the same combinations of words could carry. "We're not all here today, are we?" carried a different meaning during calling of the roll than it did when said to a confused student who had left his mittens and hat under a tree at recess.

Throughout the spring term, the students were encouraged to read and write for others whenever possible, both in and out of school. When students read or wrote for someone else, they reported that event to the teacher who donated a penny (cent) to the class bank. The money was used for occasional treats. For example, if Lisa went to the local country store and asked the clerk if she could read labels for him, that event was reported by Lisa to the teacher. If students made a list for parents at home or wrote a note to be left for other family members, they could report that event for a penny donation. Several teachers in the school developed numerous ways in which students could read and write for the sake of their classroom as a community – thanking the cooks for a good lunch, etc.[2] Public notices sent from the office were read orally by students. Each day contained a free writing period, when students could write notes to the teacher and to each other; these were placed in the mail box and distributed after lunch each day. Public notices of school events were not sent home to parents in only their formal, coldly impersonal mimeographed form; the information was rewritten by some members of the class for distribution to parents. Birthday and get well cards were made by students for distribution to others in the school as well as to family members. Mrs. Pat kept a record of birthdays of school personnel (from principal to cafeteria workers) and a list of birthdays of family members of the children. These were checked weekly, and those who wished to use their free writing time in this way could provide birthday cards from the class as a whole or

Table 9.3. *Worksheet for reading and writing study – grade two*

Reading and Writing for: <u>Mr. Morris (principal)</u>

	Reading	Writing
For fun	sports magazines paperback books ads for TV/movies, social events	letters to friends cards to friends jokes on the office joke bulletin board
For news	newspaper *Time* memos from school district, state Dept. of Education, community groups church bulletin church newsletter	school newsletter memos to teachers, school districts, parents notes to parents news items for local newspaper about school
In buying and selling things	ads contracts warranties directions on putting things together or using things	checks filling out order forms letters to order things receipts
To get through daily work routine	telephone dial clocks traffic signs names of roads and buildings signs on doors brand names of items used (pencils, stapler, car, foods)	reports to school district, state Dept. of Education federal forms permission forms for field trips, away-games for athletic teams
In religious activities	Bible Sunday School lesson church bulletin	checks for church tithe

individually. Children increasingly developed their own ideas of what they wanted to write during their free writing periods.

During the final two months of the second grade, students were asked to keep a record for one week of occasions and types of reading and writing they did in their own communities and to bring in samples of these. They analyzed the many levels and types of reading and writing in which they were engaged. They matched their lists to those made for visitors earlier to see which types of reading adults engaged in that they themselves did not.

By the end of the year, the children had produced a staggering amount of written material, and their records of what they had read during those weeks when they were asked to keep records were equally impressive. For example, on a given day in the second term, each child read an average of 600 different message tokens (ranging from the number of the bus he rode home on, to television commercials, to library books). A notice was placed outside the classroom door each day of this experiment giving the total number of pieces of information read by the class on the previous *day*: "Mrs. Pat's class read 15,528 different messages today." The class became known as the "readingest" class in school.

The children had, by the end of the year, developed a special "metalinguistic" vocabulary and ways of talking about their language and that of others.[3] They could point out different levels of reading beyond those levels traditionally presented through reading books; they knew different styles of writing and speaking were used by different individuals on various occasions. They were able to identify and label, and talk about the whys of dialect features, elements of formal and informal style, casual speech. They had developed a definition of literature which included dialect poetry, stories told them by eighth-graders, their own stories, as well as the literature the teacher chose to read to them or the librarian suggested they read. On reading tests given at the end of the year, fourteen students were reading on grade level, eight above grade level, and two below grade level.

The children had learned to observe, record, categorize, and analyze ways in which people spoke and the ways in which they used their language for writing and reading. Gathering information from familiar community members, they had contextualized reading and writing in their community life and in their own daily existence at home and in the school. They had come to look on school reading and writing as attached to that done in the wider world. Learning to read and write in school was now linked to reading and writing labels and bills in the country store, the cafeteria worker's set of recipes, the church bulletin, or a notice of a local baseball game. Perhaps most important, the second-graders now defined themselves as readers and writers. As they had become observers of their own participation in reading and writing, they had verified skills of theirs which were not being measured by school tests. Their development of analytic concepts to describe and explain their experiences and the social behavior of those around them had increased their vocabulary of scientific terms about language, enabled them to recognize and label discrete features of language such as sounds, endings, and styles, and to apply these concepts in listening to dialect poetry, conversations, radio and TV programs, and oral story-telling. In short, their central lesson had been: it is important for a person to know what he is doing when he uses language. If one uses a dialect form, one should know why. If one uses a casual style, one does so in relation to the occasion and the listener. The principal made his announcements over the loudspeaker using Standard English and a formalized style of talking; in the hall, he greeted the clown of the football team by using a different dialect and style of talking. There were reasons why he made this shift; the students in Mrs. Pat's second-grade class could understand them.

Keeping journals

In several junior and senior high school classes of basic-level students, many of whom were old enough to be working second or third shifts in the mills and raising families, English and mathematics teachers introduced the idea of keeping journals. At the beginning of the academic year, English teachers introduced the idea by reading portions of autobiographies to their students and asking them to imagine how they would write such stories about themselves. Several students in class suggested that they would have forgotten much of their earlier life, and they would have to ask others about those years. One teacher pushed this idea by asking, "But what if you had to write an autobiography of yourself several months or years from now? What could you do now that would help you then?" The students suggested that daily accounts of their lives written now could be used as a way of remembering. I visited the class and shared with them portions of my journals and notes from fieldwork in Mexico, showing slides and artifacts. We talked about portions of the notes which expressed how I felt during the fieldwork, where I was, and when and what happened. The teacher asked the students to keep journals or fieldnotes during the school term, to interview people who had known them in their childhood, and to write their autobiographies at the end of the term.[4]

Each week they were to read with a class partner of their choice portions of their fieldnotes and interviews. This was a time for reading each other's notes and asking questions about the meaning of incidents, expressions of feelings, and generally talking about each other's writing. The teacher and I moved among the students, joining discussions when it seemed appropriate and reading particular entries in notebooks when asked to do so. Students were asked to talk to each other about how they would reword certain entries for the autobiography, and partner discussions often centered on how to express "what I mean," and how "saying it" in an autobiography would be different from writing it in a journal. Several weeks before the end of the term, the partners began submitting portions of their autobiographies to each other for discussion, and by the end of the term, each student had produced an essay which was an autobiography of himself, plus a journal or set of fieldnotes used for the autobiography.

Zinnia Mae, the daughter of Mrs. Green who lived in Trackton, became pregnant during the term, and her journal took on an intense meaning for her. She completed several hundred entries about herself and her family, and with the teacher's help, she bound these into three books she planned to save for her children. Most of her writings centered on comparing the childhood of oldtimers, her own life, and that projected for children nowadays and in the future.

Now day's childrens are so hardheaded and bad. In the old day's children's had to stay from school pick cotton, plow the farm, but now day's you better not tell no child to go out their and pick no cotton or plow no field. Childrens back in those day's got a lots of education and didn't go to school much. But we go to school nine months and still don't learn too much. Like my cousins that stay right side me, they are the baddest things I have every seen, their ages are, one-9, one eight, and one seven, they have light colored skin. They curse back at their mother, they tell her I ain't going to do this or that, and she don't do nothing about it. Back when I was that age, I better not curse my mother or tell her ain't. Because I knowed what was good for me than. Don't care how you beat my cousins they still bad.

This and her other early journal entries were generally marked by correct spelling, but a seemingly random use of apostrophes and other punctuation marks. Only on occasion did she add tense markers to her verbs. Her partner was Rosie, a black girl who did not have the "tough" reputation of Zinnia Mae, and in the first weeks of class she seemed unwilling to offer comment on Zinnia's journal entries, while Zinnia Mae chattered on about what Rosie should include in her writing. Rosie was a shy girl who wrote very little, but her knowledge of the mechanics of writing was far superior to Zinnia Mae's. The teacher noticed the one-sided exchange and asked Rosie after school one day what she intended to do about it; Rosie shrugged and said "Nut'n, I guess." The teacher suggested that since Zinnia Mae had said she wanted to save these entries for her children, and she wanted her children to learn more in school than she had, Rosie might use these ideas in offering some help toward the autobiography. The next week, Rosie suggested to Zinnia Mae that the final writing of her autobiography would be easier if she could write only "the necessary and best parts" from her journal entries. Zinnia Mae asked quizzically what Rosie meant, and together they went through several entries removing unnecessary apostrophes, commas, and conjunctions, and adding semi-colons or commas. They talked about some words, such as contractions, which would have to be written another way in the final essay. Zinnia Mae asked Rosie, "Anything else I oughta do?" opening the way for future improvement of the mechanics of her writing.

During one week of the term, one English teacher asked her students to select some portions of their journals which might serve as the script and stage directions for a scene of a skit. Several offered suggestions, and other members of the class tried to stage what was described in a particular journal entry. But the class soon realized that most of their entries were not detailed enough, nor were they written to show sequence of actions. During the next week, the students were asked to choose a few incidents to describe in such detail that they could be reenacted the next week in class. Roadville's Jed wrote about being in a store when a robbery took place.

First this man with a stocking on comes into the ice cream store. Then he walks up and down looking. He is thinking about what he will do next. Now he takes a number. He has to wait his turn, you see. When his turn comes, he tells the boy he wants Bubble Gum and the cash. The boy gets the bubble gum. It's pink like that. Now he gives it to the man. The man says CASH. After that the boy looks scared and looks at me. He takes the money out and and gives it to the man. The man wipes his mouth with a napkin. He leaves out the door.

With little trouble, three students re-enacted this event, adding to it their own versions of how each character reflected his feelings. On the first assignment of this type, Roadville students provided better scripts than Trackton students; but within a few days, Trackton students wrote acceptable scripts as well. They reacted, however, to these written versions of events as "boring," and said they did not want their autobiographies "to sound like that." Subsequent class discussion centered around occasions when details in sequence are needed and for which purposes, and ways to write leading the reader to share the writer's fear, excitement, sadness, or joy.

Another use of journals emerged in a consumer mathematics class, designed to help students handle their daily buying and selling needs. The teacher, whose hobby was photography and film making, asked permission from several local merchants to film their transactions with customers who also agreed to partici-pate in the filming. Initially, students watched these films and wrote mathematics word problems to describe the numerical transactions in the films.[5] Within several weeks, however, the teacher realized that students were not comprehending some basic aspects of the transactions; in class he asked them how they would ask questions on the scene to clear up their confusion. Many had no idea how to clarify their understanding of what was happening or how to verify a particular viewpoint they developed about the scene. Day after day, the class watched scenes and talked about how to extract and clarify meaning from the films. For example, in one transaction, a customer's bill was $3.61; the customer gave the clerk four one-dollar bills and a penny (cent). The clerk gave the customer 39 cents, and the customer protested, saying: "No, that's why I gave you the penny." Both the clerk and many members of the class were confused. The class talked about the assumptions of the interaction and the questions the clerk had to ask to clear up his confusion. Students were then asked to go out and record in journals confusing transactions in which either they or others in their family were involved, noting causes of confusion and writing out questions which could have been used for clarification in the situation. Some students moved away from purely numerical transactions and recorded exchanges with nurses at the doctor's office or the employment bureau.

For a week or so, the class focused on communication and not mathematics. Class discussion of these incidents helped students from both Roadville- and Trackton-like communities identify when and where breakdowns in communication occurred, enabled them to recognize points at which they could ask clarification questions, and gave them practice in initiating strategies at confusing points in transactions. The initial use of scenes they could view, and later uses of scenes in which they had taken part and/or recorded enabled them to understand the latching of details to the main idea, juxtaposition of facts and opinions, and the necessary sequence for incorporating critical details, numerical and otherwise, in word problems or any other recounting of an event. Both teacher and students reported satisfaction with the new journal approach to learning arithmetic. In class evaluations at the end of the year, students wrote of their teacher and his methods: "A teacher that helped us learn what is necessary." "Someone who had good assignments." "A teacher that takes us places to see different kinds of experiences." Many of these students were already breadwinners and/or parents; they responded to the class problems and journal assignments as necessary to making sense in their daily lives.

The next term an English teacher devoted one unit of her class to a similar experiment, using films the math teacher agreed to make of interviews in employment offices and courtrooms, at the scene of accidents, etc. She used the films first to have the students pick out the "main idea," identify the sequence of the action, and name details which supported the main idea or purpose of the interaction. The class took apart the arguments of each party in the films, pointed out how interpretation of events at an accident shifted both from person to person and from time to time. Many of the students were unfamiliar with extended interviews, and the study of these films helped them prepare for job interviews, interactions with loan officers in banks, and medical histories to be given to doctors or dentists. Lists of the types of questions used in interviews, occasions for restatement, and ways of accounting for what one had done were drawn up from films shown in class, and studied in conjunction with the written forms used on these occasions.[6] Near the end of the term, the students took turns interviewing and filling out forms with each other and analyzing these to identify ways of asking for clarification and restating information politely, and forming questions which did not seem overly aggressive. The teacher's goal was to enable students to learn ways of disentangling meaning from types of written and oral information prevalent in their daily lives.

From the familiar to the unfamiliar

Teachers in the classes described here captured for schooling purposes their students' natural abilities and daily habits as participant observers, hypothesis builders, and information synthesizers. These teachers saw nothing particularly mystical or forbidding about participant observation as practiced by the ethnographer. In the words of several teachers: "We do that every day, and so do our students." What these teachers did with these everyday habits, however, was to help their students learn to see their daily actions in new terms: as the recording of events, discovering of patterns, and figuring out of options in making decisions. Then teachers helped students transfer these ways of investigating and analyzing information to the content areas of science, language arts, social studies, English, and mathematics. Within class work, the stress was on making linkages between how the students learned information in their daily lives, and ways they could talk about these ways of knowing at a "meta" level. The talking about these skills was one step removed from the actual doing of the task, and teachers tried to help students link these ways of looking at the familiar to ways of learning the unfamiliar content information of the classroom. The second-grade teacher who enlisted community and school adults, and turned her students into young sociologists of language, believed what she did was no more than what students did on the playground as they learned to play new games by watching other children:

Second-graders play games I can't begin to understand. To learn to do that, they've got to use certain intuitive knowledge about how to figure out how those games work. Nobody tells them how to play; they watch the other kids, learn enough to try, and in *doing*, they soon learn how to correct any mistakes they've made in figuring out how it works. All I had to do was figure out how I could get them to try out their intuitive know-how on learning to talk about language.

She and other teachers constructed curricula from the world of the home to enable students to move to the curricular content of the school.

The goal of these teachers was not a focus on the collection of cultural materials from an ethnic perspective. During the ethnic heritage revival movements of the 1970s, there were many efforts to collect folk songs, tales, and music from ethnic communities for incorporation into classroom routines and published materials. The methods and materials described here had no focus on ethnic heritage, and the purpose of the ethnographic efforts of the students was not to bring their folk culture back into the class-room for memorization and study by all of the class. Instead, teachers' goals were: (1) to provide a foundation of familiar knowledge to serve as context for classroom information; (2) to engage students in collecting and analyzing familiar ways of knowing and translating these into scientific or school-accepted labels, concepts, and generalizations; and (3) to provide students with meaningful opportunities to learn ways of talking about using language to organize and express information. Through their roles as participant observers moving from the familiar to the unfamiliar, the students improved their textbook unit test scores, standardized test results, attendance records, and attitudes toward school; positive teacher–parent contacts increased. These teachers felt they did not change the basic core of the content taught in their classes, nor did they believe the increased student involvement replaced some of their more "traditional" classroom methods (such as the use of the textbooks, basal readers, films, worksheets, etc.). They did see themselves as engaging students in an *inter-active* process in which students learned to share the goals and methods of the classroom as a result of their activities as "ethno-graphers." The mutual peer excitement in the process brought peer pressure to bear on their learning experiences in a positive way, as classmates challenged and questioned each other on information collected in their communities and offered for analysis and translation in classroom terms.

The success of these teachers' promotion of ethnographic methods for students was heavily dependent on the individual style of each teacher and the geographic location of these schools. The settings described here contributed in each case significantly to the successful use of these teachers' approaches to using students as junior ethnographers. For example, the boys of the fifth-grade science classroom came from Trackton and two other black communities in close proximity; the boys lived in an area where they could easily walk to feed stores, and get their information in their own communities. They were not dependent on adults to transport them to other locations for their interviews. The geographic region in which the school was located is highly oriented to agriculture, and many adults of the communities spend much of their time in a variety of agricultural pursuits, even though such pursuits are not their primary means of making a living. Thus, the boys' topic was one of considerable interest to a majority of adults in the communities and obtaining information was no problem.

The second-grade classroom that studied speaking, reading, and writing habits was located in a unique school and community. The school was itself a tightly knit community, in which students from upper grades often served as teacher aides in lower-level classes or offered their particular talents – artistic, musical, etc. – for use in teacher planning. The principal was an "oldtimer," a well-loved member of the community, and a family metaphor was often used to refer to his school. Teachers within the school were part of "the family" and their efforts on behalf of students were not likely to be viewed with suspicion in either the school or the community. The country stores, gas station, etc. were local social centers, and merchants or garagemen knew their customers, young and old. Thus, a student's request that he be allowed to read the labels or directions on products because of a school assignment was likely to be viewed with tolerance. In short, it was relatively easy for a teacher like Mrs. Pat to enlist the community to help promote a goal in line with members' views of the school's purpose: to improve reading and writing and to teach basic subject-matter content.

In the cases reported here, many of the students involved were not succeeding in the standard curriculum, and traditional methods of presenting knowledge were not reaching them. Their teachers' new ways of linking familiar strategies of knowing to unfamiliar classroom content and tasks resulted in success at a variety of levels: test scores, self-concept, interest in attending school, interaction with adults in their own communities, and attitudes toward what it was that school was all about. But perhaps most important, the emphasis in these classrooms on talking about "how we come to know" gave students a meta-language based on descriptions of their own daily activities. They now had the language to talk about acquiring, integrating, and controlling knowledge in school.

An additional goal of these teachers was to improve school and community relations. Knowledge in their classrooms moved on a two-way path, from the community to the school and from the school to the community. There was positive value orientation toward involving the communities and families in the learning experiences of the students. These teachers chose neither to ignore community influences on students nor to try to replace these with the standard or scientific norms of the school. They did not want parents to judge themselves or their children as failures because they did not succeed by school standards. They hoped their methods would enable students to be effective in school as well as to continue to deal with the values and ways of living of their own families.

Parents, merchants, oldtimers, and the students themselves became valued sources of information. What happened at home did not seem totally divorced from what happened at school as it had in some of the past education of students and their parents.[7] Students began to accept adults other than teachers as sources of information they could use in school. Socialization with a wide range of adults became the core of their learning process, and students learned how to interact in new ways with new adults, and in new ways with their teachers. Students now provided information for the teacher to question – the reverse of the usual classroom practice of the teacher presenting the information and questioning students on their knowledge. Teachers' impressions that their students talked more than ever before matched those of students whose assessments of these classes ranged from: "I hated this class at first 'cause she made us talk all the time," to "The teacher got away from the books for a change; all of this made me and others happy."

Epilogue

This book has been about how children of two culturally different communities in the Piedmont Carolinas learned to use language in their homes and communities. This book has also been about how teachers' knowledge of children's ways with words enabled them to bring these ways into their classrooms.

The patterns of language use of the children of Roadville and Trackton before they go to school stand in sharp contrast to each other and to those of the youngsters from townspeople families. Though parents in all three communities want to "get ahead," their constructions of the social activities the children must engage in for access to language, oral and written, vary greatly. The sequence of habits Trackton children develop in learning language, telling stories, making metaphors, and seeing patterns across items and events do not fit the developmental patterns of either linguistic or cognitive growth reported in the research literature on mainstream children. Roadville children, on the other hand, seem to have developed many of the cognitive and linguistic patterns equated with readiness for school, yet they seem not to move outward from these basics to the integrative types of skills necessary for sustained academic success.

The townspeople teachers described in the final two chapters of this book used knowledge about ethnography as an approach to *learning* to move to new ways of *doing* in their classrooms. The townspeople adapted materials and methods by using their ethnographies of interactions in their own homes and classrooms in combination with ethnographies of communication done in their students' communities. Their interactive approach to incorporating these communities' ways of talking, knowing, and expressing knowledge with those of the school enabled some Roadville and Trackton children to understand how to make choices among uses of languages and to link these choices to life chances.

Epilogue

From ethnographies of communication

From ethnographies of communication in Roadville and Trackton which detail the ways with words into which each community socializes its children, three general points stand out:

> *First*, patterns of language use in any community are in accord with and mutually reinforce other cultural patterns, such as space and time orderings, problem-solving techniques, group loyalties, and preferred patterns of recreation. In each of these communities, space and time usage and the role of the individual in the community condition the interactional rules for occasions of language use. The boundaries of the physical and social communities, and the extent and density of interactions within these influence such seemingly culturally remote language habits as the relative extent to which babies are talked to or about.

> *Second*, factors involved in preparing children for school-oriented, mainstream success are deeper than differences in formal structures of language, amount of parent–child interaction, and the like. The language socialization process in all its complexity is more powerful than such single-factor explanations in accounting for academic success.

> *Third*, the patterns of interactions between oral and written uses of language are varied and complex, and the traditional oral–literate dichotomy does not capture the ways other cultural patterns in each community affect the uses of oral and written language. In the communities described here, occasions for writing and reading of extended prose occur far less frequently than occasions for extended oral discourse around written materials.

The communities into which Roadville and Trackton children are socialized as talkers, readers, and writers are only a few miles apart. Both are tied commercially, politically, and educationally to the townspeople – mainstream blacks and whites of the region. Yet, the *community* for young Roadville and Trackton children is geographically based and spatially limited until they go to school. With the exception of church and a few commercial establishments, there are no other locales in which the children under four years of age interact with either adults or children in primary

344

face-to-face relationships. Children of the townspeople, however, grow up in a community which is socially based through the voluntary associations of their parents, and their primary network extends far beyond their immediate neighborhoods.

Yet within the closed physical boundaries of Roadville and Trackton, the paths covered by preschoolers make them different sorts of travelers. Roadville parents keep their young children "close to home," inside the house with their mothers or accompanying them on a visit to a friend or relative's house, usually within Roadville. The threshold of a Roadville home marks the boundary between a family's private castle and the public world. Within Roadville, there are numerous other boundaries, and once outside the house with a parent, the toddler is expected to conform to the communication norms established for these territorial and social boundaries. Some kinds of talk are for inside the house, others for outside. Stories from children told in the presence of adults follow coaching cues from adults. Only in play among themselves do children invoke different sets of rules for framing their pretense, flights of fantasy, and performance options for their cooperative, yet often overlapping, dialogues. The most obvious social boundaries are those of age: Mrs. Dee as the oldest member of the community commands extensive politeness norms in speech and listening behaviors. Toddlers must learn that all adults and even older children are to be addressed with appropriate politeness formulae, especially for opening and closing encounters and for gift or service exchanges. Appropriate time and space usage rules set further boundaries within Roadville. There are only certain times of day when any but the closest of relatives or friends can be visited without prior notice. In Roadville only front doors are open to visitors; the back door is used only by family members coming and going from the house to the yard or out of the community. Everything in Roadville homes ideally has its place; from the huge pressure cooker on the back porch to the placement of toys on the bookshelves in the baby's room, there is an attempt to order space–function ties.

Trackton children travel freely in their neighborhood without rules putting boundaries around time, space, or social interactions. Neither times nor places in Trackton are protected from neighbors' visits, though most visiting is done outdoors in the plaza. It is there on the plaza that the major portion of the drama of life is played out, and on this stage, children hear multiple streams of communication. Radios, stereos, conversations, jump-rope games, and fussing flow together in the open arena. There are few boundaries between public and private in Trackton, and space, like time, takes on multiple functions which shift according to need, the social composition of the group, and the availability of certain props. The unbounded flow of time is broken only by exits for work and by weekend rituals – Friday afternoon sharings, the wide option of activities Saturdays offer, and the extension of the community to the church on Sundays. During the week, there are no set occasions for visits either among community members or from outsiders. Gas meter readers, social workers, transients, respectables, and no-counts come and go, forming a partially shifting cast of players who interact with the youngsters on the plaza.

The size of the physical area of the communities in which preschoolers play out their roles in their years before school is about the same in Roadville and Trackton. Yet the scenes and casts of characters with whom they perform their scripts are vastly different. Roadville children are given a limited number of roles. They are seemingly tutored into pre-scripted performances, in which their parents "hold book" for them as they learn their parts for labeling, describing, and answering questions. Except on those occasions when Roadville children are among other children only, their parts are scripted by adults. Their stories cannot be improvisations, but instead they must be tales which come more out of adults' structural schemes of organization and views of reality than out of their own. Roadville children are prepared for, tended, encouraged, played with, talked to, and as they grow older, they share in family plans for fishing, gardening, using the camper, and going to Alberta. Fathers and mothers help show them how to make a batch of cookies, dress a doll, mow a lawn, fix a bicycle, or repair a broken screen door. Roadville parents bring up their children in the drama of life by carefully scripting and rehearsing them for the parts they expect them to play.

In the drama of Trackton life, new babies are seen as potential players who will grow up to take on a variety of roles. Their repertoires will depend on how they discover roles for themselves in the multiple scenes with different players on the Trackton stage. There, children will experience numerous shifts of scene and cast, and players will take on different roles on different occasions. Exempted from no part of the on-going drama, children grow up hearing the multiple channels of communication about them and seem to sort out chunks of words with patterns of intonation to repeat and vary as they practice for their parts. During their first year they are carried about by most of the members of the community of players, and they feel the variety of nonverbal responses of anger, fear, joy, and sadness the Trackton cast can display. Children come to respond to unspoken signals of emotion and states of preparedness for action. As they become conversationalists, they draw from their viewing of others' performances on the plaza, and they imitate motions, facial expressions, and extraneous sounds to set the background for their discourses. They are encouraged to tease, taunt, fuss at or with, curse, and challenge any and all in the community in a wide range of teasing interactions. There are few limits on the toddlers' role playing, and they prepare and practice for multiple adult roles in this preschool apprenticeship. Trackton children grow up developing their own styles of playing roles in the community and watching and feeling how to do the tasks available to them. As they accompany older siblings to Mr. Dogan's store, the stage directions they hear warn the children to watch prices and not squeeze or eat the bread on the way home. They hear their siblings play the scene with Mr. Dogan, and once home again, they share in their parents' evaluations of how well the children have played their part. In their stories and in those they hear about them, the ordinary is made fantastic, and the playsongs of older sisters, insulting rhymes of older brothers and sisters, and the stream of adult tales, boasts, and quarrels give them numerous models for playing with rhyme, characterizations, and dialogue.

For Roadville and Trackton children, the what, how, and why of patterns of choice they can exercise in their uses of language prepare them in very different ways for what lies ahead in school and in work or other institutional settings. The socialization of Roadville children into a world of lines, time blocks, and limits on space usage emphasizes the structuring, lessoning, and boundedness of knowledge, and the selected roles individuals of different sexes and ages may play. When they enter school, their home world and that of the school seem to match well. There is a lulling sense of a familiar continuity of past experiences in the new setting of school. Parents turn over to the school their child's education, believing in the school's ability to make a difference and to build on the orchestrated preparation they have given their pre-schoolers. To try to reinforce or extend the school's academic activities and to bring these back again into the children's homes is not considered. Theirs is a faith that hard work, a will to get ahead, and strong parental and family models of the "good life" will inspire their children to move ahead in school.

The preschool years of Trackton youngsters are a series of minor discontinuities – a thing being one thing one time, something else the next. The children listen, observe, practice, and finally participate, getting their encouragement often in unpredictable and uneven doses. Trackton parents believe that when their children go to school, they will continue to learn the same way, the only way they have known how – by watching, listening, and trying. For the children, however, the school is a sudden flood of discontinuities in the ways people talk, the values they hold, and the consistency with which the rewards go to some and not others. Some Trackton children and parents continue to believe in school, and some take on new roles for the drama of school. Others resist having someone else deciding on their performances and trying to coach them into parts which they are not sure they wish to play. Still others grow increasingly restless in the uncertainties of a system in which there seems to be no possibility for playing the multiple roles they have learned at home.

The different types of uses of reading and writing of Roadville and Trackton have prepared the children in different ways for negotiating the meaning of the printed word and the production of a written text. Children from neither community have had experience in seeing their parents read or write extended pieces of prose. Both have concepts of print. Roadville's children have been coached in book-reading at bedtime and in sessions around the kitchen table over coloring books. Trackton's concepts are un-articulated and unrehearsed. The children hold onto some perceptual antecedents of shape and style in the print on signs, cans, and newspapers. Roadville children come to school imbued with oral testimonies about the values of reading, but with few models of reading and writing behavior. Trackton children have not heard the activity extolled, but have seen numerous group debates over what letters, notices, and bills mean. Children of both communities have heard preachers and their adult friends and relatives speak from the written word in church, and they have come to know the limits of oral interpretation of these words. In Roadville, extension from the authority of the written text is bounded, in terms of situations which may be used as parallel examples, and in terms of those who may make such interpretations publicly. Only men, and occasionally older women, may talk about applications or extensions of the meaning of written materials in public. The young may not interpret the written word in the presence of adults; theirs is to be a passive spectator role in which they may memorize materials or answer specific questions. Trackton children have learned through their long hours in the laps of adults and on the hard church benches, that in the free flow of time, there are multiple types of talk and song about the written word. Written words shaped on paper are recomposed in each time and space, created anew in each performance.

The significance of these different patterns of language socialization for success in school soon becomes clear. After initial years of success, Roadville children fall behind, and by junior high, most are simply waiting out school's end or their sixteenth birthday, the legal age for leaving school. They want to get on with family life and count on getting a high school diploma when and if they need it in the future. Trackton students fall quickly into a pattern of failure, yet all about them they hear that they can never get ahead without a high school diploma. Some begin their families and their work in the mills while they are in school. But their mood is that of those who have accepted responsibilities in life outside the classroom, and that mood is easily interpreted negatively by school authorities who still measure students' abilities by their scores on standardized tests. Trackton students often drift through the school, hoping to escape with the valued piece of paper which they know will add much to their parents' and grandparents' pride, although little to their paychecks.

The detailed ethnographies of communication of Trackton and Roadville children must inevitably be compared with what we know about the boundaries of the physical and social networks of the townspeople. There are profound differences across the three communities in the limits and features of those situations in which communication by and to children occurs, and the patterns of choice children can exercise in their uses of oral and written language. The townspeople, like parents in Roadville and Trackton, have a strong ethos of wanting their children to get ahead and of depending on the school to play a critical role in plans for their children's future. Townspeople, like Roadvillers, prepare for, tend, talk to, and play with their children. They teach them to label items and events, to describe their features, to read books, and to play with educational toys. But beyond these aspects of language socialization, townspeople also immerse their children in an environment of repetitive, redundant, and internally consistent running narratives on items and events. They draw from fantasy books and their own imagination to read, perform, and create stories with their children. They link items in one setting to items in another, naming the points of similarity in labels, attributes, uses, and functions. Once their children enter school, they continue the early pattern of stress on individual achievement – in sports, extracurricular activities, and academic work. They draw school activities and values back into the home and into the voluntary association network in which their children share. Perhaps most important, they expect events of the moment to bear on the outcome of future events. They assume that what happens at school and at home are linked, and they make possible a variety of activities, resources, and authorities to support these links. A family outing to an air show may be primarily for entertainment, but the next science project at school may well incorporate an extended prose account of the air show, photographs from the air show, and a detailing of the features of a particular airplane on display there. When children do not initiate these links, parents suggest them, and when too many weeks go by without direct and extended talk of what is going on at school, parents begin looking for ways to build anew some connections. Most children from townspeople families succeed in school. All are not top scholars, but most go through the system without questioning its usefulness and its critical role in their future. Discontinuities between out-of-school activities and in-school lessons occur for individuals, but not for the group as a whole.

On the surface, these summaries of the language socialization of the children in the three groups support a widespread common notion about links between language at home and at school: the more parents talk to their children, the more likely the children are to succeed in school. Yet when we look closely at the details of how such a correlation is played out in the lives of the children of townspeople, Trackton, and Roadville, we recognize the limited way such ideas apply. Trackton children hear and take part in far more of the talk around them than the children of either the townspeople or Roadville families. Yet in their case, *more* talk does not have a positive transfer value to the existing primary-level practices of the school. Townspeople, on the other hand, consciously create on-going social activities in which their children participate, and they also specifically focus children's attention in these social activities. It is as though in the drama of life, townspeople parents freeze scenes and parts of scenes at certain points along the way. Within the single frame of a scene, they focus the child's attention on objects or events in the frame, sort out referents for the child to name, give the child ordered turns for sharing talk about this referent, and then narrate a description of the scene. Through their focused language, adults make the potential stimuli in the child's environment stand still for a cooperative examination and narration between parent and child. The child learns to focus attention on a preselected referent, masters the relationships between signifier and the signified, develops turn-taking skills in a focused conversation on the referent, and is subsequently expected to listen to, benefit from, and eventually to create narratives placing the referent in different contextual situations. Townspeople children learn a referent in some particular domain, and later occurrences of the referent are monitored by adults who declare the two occurrences "the same" by naming the referent and describing features found in both the previous and the current instance. The child is not left on his own to see the relations between the two occurrences or to explore the ways the integration of the referent in a new context may alter its meaning. He is held initially to a literal meaning for many objects and events of the world; of those which are not sorted out and expressed in terms of labels and features for him, he may learn on his own some relational meanings not seen by adults. Thus he may sometimes surprise adults by comparing two items or naming one item as another, without any rational basis in adults' terms. In short, townspeople adults see to it that children acquire labels for items and features which are then established as long-term memory information, so that on future occasions they can retrieve this information to mediate the relations between the categories of membership and structural or attributional features of items or events. In essence, this process enables the child to view each new referent out of its context, and to approach it with decontextualized labels of identification and attribution, rather than only with contextualized responses which link it to specific dated events or situations.

Thus it is the *kind* of talk, not the *quantity* of talk that sets townspeople children on their way in school. They come with the skills of labeling, naming features, and providing narratives on items out of their contexts. In addition, their home life has also given them extensive exposure to stories and situations in which they and adults manipulate environments imaginatively and talk about the effects of changing one aspect of a context while holding all others constant ("What do you think would happen if we didn't put the candles on the birthday cake?"). Children hear questions and are coached to give answers which enable them to express the fact that a cake at a birthday party has the same name and some of the same features as any other cake, but the context of the special occasion, and the addition of some features or their replacement by others make it become a new entity – a birthday cake and not some other kind of cake.

The talk to Roadville children differs in quantity and kind from that of the townspeople. The social activities in which they participate are constructed to make them focus for the most part on labels and features, and they are given few occasions for extended narratives, imaginative flights of establishing new contexts, or manipulating features of an event or item. Thus their readiness for school is a limited readiness – and not a preparedness for the types of tasks necessary for higher-level school work. To understand the success of a specific military leader in a particular battle of the American Revolution requires more than the naming of generals, or the detailing of the numbers of soldiers and supplies. It demands setting events within a full background or framework and recognizing, for example, that a shift in one or another aspect of the battle could have caused the victory to go another way. Academic success beyond the basis of readiness depends on becoming a contextualist who can predict and maneuver the scenes and situations by understanding the relatedness of parts to the outcome or the identity of the whole.

Trackton children have not had their perception of items and events monitored by a schema in adults' heads of what and when they should learn. They have had to find their own schemata in the complex, multi-channeled stream of stimuli about them, for neither talk, time, nor space is set aside especially for them. Their intense nonverbal learning during their first year of almost constant body contact can be viewed only as a flow pattern, in which no one explicates the components of the emotions that surround them or the objects with which they come in contact. As they learn to talk, they again pick and choose among lexical items and practice in repetition, and repetition with variation, until they can productively handle the rules of the language. This initial learning to use language is then spurred and prodded in public performances in which there are few predictable outcomes. Saliency in the fast-moving drama of which they are a part is a shifting matter dependent on the combination of contextual clues. Trackton children may initially assume a resemblance among episodes, but they must then search for the critical cues which will enable them to interpret the space about them in the most appropriate way, for such interpretation is critical not only to meeting their immediate needs (getting a bag of goodies at the Friday afternoon sharing) but also to maintaining relationships with those upon whom they depend for stimulation, resources, and emotional reinforcement. No one lifts labels and features out of their contexts for explication; no one requests repetitions from Trackton children. Thus their entry into a classroom which depends on responses based on lifting items and events out of context is a shock. Their abilities to contextualize, to remember what may seem to the teacher to be an unrelated event as similar to another, to link seemingly disparate factors in their explanations, and to create highly imaginative stories are suppressed in the classroom. The school's approach to reading and learning establishes decontextualized skills as foundational in the hierarchy of academic skills. The creative embedding of items and events in unexpected settings is reserved in the primary grades for the brief occasions of creative writing and art. Thus the Trackton children receive little encouragement to maintain until the upper grades, when they will be needed, their abilities for contextualization. They fail in the initial sequences of the school-defined hierarchy of skills, and when they reach the upper grades, the social demands and habits of failing are too strong to allow them to renew for school use the habits they brought to their first-grade classroom.

Teachers and students building bridges

The teachers of this book are portrayed as learning researchers, who used knowledge from ethnographies of communication to build a two-way channel between communities and their classrooms. They came to see the tools of ethnographic research as highly compatible with their own intuitive strategies for observing children, looking for patterns of behavior, and trying to understand how the children define themselves as children in their own communities. The crisis of desegregation in the late 1960s became for these teachers a challenge. At that time, the educational system allowed teachers as professionals to develop many of their own solutions to the crisis.

The challenges of desegregation led many teachers – far more than were ever noticed in any public way – to accept the challenge of working with students whose preparation for schooling differed markedly from their own children's. The opportunities for black and white teachers to meet in social science courses of universities and regional workshops guided many to shift some of their classroom habits and materials to accommodate group differences in language and culture. They studied their own ways of talking to their preschoolers at home and the extent to which they carried these home habits into the school. They tried to recognize and accommodate group differences among students without stereotyping behaviors according to race or class membership. They brought into their classrooms the people, ideas, and practices of the communities of their students. They believed their altered ways of teaching allowed some children to succeed who might not otherwise have done so. Dogged by the constant cries to improve standards, they were determined that their new ways would not lead to lowered standards, but to success by different routes.

Through their experience in becoming, and leading their students to become, ethnographers of a sort, they saw themselves helping to develop the special potentials and skills of children from Trackton, Roadville, and townspeople homes. Their central role was to pass on to all groups certain traditional tools and ways of using language. A critical component in the process was allowing

354

children to articulate how what they knew related to what the school wanted them to know. School was a new context in which Roadville, Trackton, and townspeople children had to reformulate to different degrees their home habits of handling knowledge and their ways of talking about knowledge. They had to integrate new content from school into a reformulated organizational pattern. The tightly interwoven nature of language and context made it especially necessary for teachers to tease apart and make as specific as possible aspects of the language and context of both home and school domains. Critical in the thinking of these teachers was that their approach was not a remedial one designed for poor learners. Instead, they felt that the attention given to different ways of talking and knowing, and the manipulation of contexts and language benefited all students.

In different grade levels and subject areas, these learning researchers embedded class materials in the lives of the students. Teachers enabled students to translate and expand knowledge gained in activities outside the classroom to focus on different aspects of the curriculum and school skills. Throughout these efforts, language was the focus. Students could not escape recognizing and having to articulate the differences in language structures, uses of language, and types of interactional cooperation which existed between their familiar domains and the unfamiliar domains of the classroom and other institutions calling for formal language use and special types of speech events, such as interviews.

These students as ethnographers of their own home habits and those of the classroom became, in a sense, analogues of the two systems in which they operated daily as students – the classroom and their own communities. They learned to accept the possibility of reacting according to the rules of either of these two systems, or in accord with the uses of language of other communities. In a sense, students had to learn to "code switch" between systems. Making explicit the rules of each system became possible through active involvement in experiencing how facts are known and how they can be built from bits of information into structures carrying more information. Probing their own ways of organizing information and talking, they learned to build upon these to construct the school's details, concepts, and generalizations. Also, facility in articulating the ways their own home communities used language, and comparing these with the ways of the school, weakened the boundary between the systems. Students became engaged individually and as a group in translating and organizing community knowledge into the classroom and classroom knowledge into the community. They learned to recognize where and how the materials and methods fit in either context, and where they could be latched on to familiar concepts for comparison and contrast. Students engaged in a process of self-awareness by which they, in a sense, *re*constructed a social and cognitive system of meanings. In this reconstruction, however, they neither reserved classroom ways of learning for school only nor did they destroy or replace the community habits of knowing and using language they had brought to school.

The future of home, school, and work

In the Piedmont today, the methods used by these teachers have all but disappeared. Some of these teachers have left public-school teaching; those still in the public schools look back on the decade of the 1970s as a creative high point in their careers. In a series of interviews held in late 1981 with many of the teachers whose classrooms are described in this book, they explained to me their view of the future of bringing classrooms and communities together. Most agreed that ethnographic methods were very effective as tools for discovering the language use patterns of communities served by the school. They agreed also that they believed they had successfully used ethnographic methods in their teaching, and they had enabled their students to use ethnographic methods in ways which had benefited them academically and socially. In short, their productive innovations in philosophies, methods, and materials had helped them meet the challenge of the crisis of integration in the 1970s.

These teachers, were, however, quick to point out that both the crises in education and the structures of schools are radically different in the 1980s. The major crisis of today is, in their words, "a lack of faith in schools," and the response has been a decrease in the autonomy of teachers as competent professionals and an increase in the bureaucratization of teaching and testing. One teacher explained that his district required him to give criterion-referenced tests to his students and then teach each student on the basis of the profile of needed subsets of skills which came back to him on a computer printout. "At that point, I figured they could put a robot in my classroom. No longer was there any way for *me* to decide how to meet the needs of those kids – the computer had done it. I'm teaching now only markin' time until I can retire."

Other teachers jokingly referred to teaching to the results of criterion-referenced tests as "individualized" teaching: "They run every kid through the same hierarchy of learning; it's as though everyone developed along the same pattern, and school's gonna make 'em all fit that pattern, like it or not." Following the test, the sequence of skills the child had to master to move up another level was set according to a standard skill hierarchy. The time required to administer and follow up these diagnoses and keep subsequent records allowed little time for the creative projects teachers such as Mrs. Pat had initiated in their classrooms a decade earlier. Teachers beyond the primary grades gave other reasons why their innovations of the 1970s had not remained with them. They felt that the concrete realities of the new experience of facing black and white students in their classes had been a crisis impelling creative output from teachers and students alike. The crises of today seemed to them more abstract and embroiled in distant legal controversies. For example, minimum competency testing worried many teachers, but they saw no way for their classroom practices to affect the broad legal and social consequences they expected these tests to have in the future.

Many teachers also pointed to the catalytic effect my presence in the communities and schools had for their behavior and attitude changes in the 1970s. Every anthropologist involved in long-term fieldwork has to recognize that his presence affects in some ways the on-going stream of behavior of those with whom he has a long-term association. These teachers tried to identify how they thought my presence in the communities and classrooms had affected them. For these teachers, I was:

someone outside the "system" to talk to – not an administrator, teacher, or parent of a child in my classroom; I knew I could blow off steam and you would listen.

a fellow teacher. Because you once were a public school teacher, I never felt I had to hide those "little problems" of daily life in the classroom, which end up becoming a massive "big problem."

someone who knew something solid about the kids in my classroom –

black and white kids. Knowing you had direct knowledge of what their community life was like made what you said count for me. I used to go home and think for a long time about things you told us – like their story-telling habits – and I knew there were ways I could use that knowledge in my teaching.

someone who did not tell me what to do. Workshops, in-service training, and even our regional meetings of the reading association, seem to be times when outsiders lecture at us and tell us what to do. I used to go to those things to see my friends, but I never expected to do anything any expert told me to do. I remember feeling when desegregation was for real that if one more Yankee university person told me how to get along with the kids in *my* classroom, I'd throw something at 'im.

a sounding board for my ideas. I remember how the fieldnote idea put me off at first, but reading and rereading those made me come up with new ideas, and comparing my fieldnotes and ideas with other teachers' gave us something solid to talk about when we wanted to make changes in materials or methods. Your presence in my classroom and the chance to compare my fieldnotes with yours made me talk and think a lot more about my teaching than I had ever done before.

The most frequent observation teachers made about how my presence had affected them was the special structural relationship I had to them and to their schools. Any positive force my presence played in their implementation of innovations seemed in their view to be possible because I was both insider and outsider. As a former classroom teacher and a sometime-aide or co-teacher in their classrooms, I was a knowledgeable insider, a "member of the club of teachers"; yet I was also an outsider who had no institutional links or powers in their schools. The second most frequent theme in their comments was that the fieldnotes and model of ethnographer-at-work forced them to describe and then examine their own practices and beliefs. With my fieldnotes and analyses of life in the communities from which their students came, they could compare their data on their ways of believing, behaving, and valuing in the classroom. The evidence from which they could work toward innovations was solid and specific and reflective of common patterns across individuals and groups.

These teacher-researchers generally agreed that neither the current crises nor the existing structures in schools could inspire the kind of imaginative innovations they had implemented in the past decade. The most outspoken of those still teaching argued that given the tight reins the school districts now hold over instruction and testing, teachers have become "only lackeys in a system over which we have no control." Some teachers recalled with sarcastic humor their enthusiasm in the projects of the 1970s when they had been "excited" over new discoveries about their own behaviors and those of the Roadville and Trackton children. One teacher summarized her current feelings: "There's no joy left in teaching now. Everyone has decided teachers are the scapegoats for the ills of society, and I'm tired of being the goat on a salary of $14,000 a year."

Many teachers pointed out what they believed to be the effects of the loss of many college-bound students to private schools. They recalled their use of upper-level academically successful students as models, aides, and tutors in their classrooms. Without these human resources, in a general climate of decreasing support systems for classroom teachers, some teachers feared a general settling into "mediocrity." They wistfully remembered their role in the past as professional creator and critic. In retrospect, many agreed that by using the human resources available to them, they had, behind the closed doors of their classrooms, helped schooling make a difference – at least at that point in time – for some youngsters. They had grave doubts that handing over the solution of the current crisis to governmental controls and external standards would be at all satisfactory. They spoke with a sense of urgency for restoring some teacher autonomy and for building a public confidence in teachers as professionals. Their pasts had prepared these townspeople to see themselves as decision-makers, who could and should have a part in determining how and when they would use the skills and knowledge they had grown up expecting to use in schools, offices, and other professional settings. They have now come to see school teaching as increasingly inappropriate for either their vocational futures or those of their children. Talk of the road ahead for the children of current schoolteachers does not include planning for a career in teaching.

But what of changes in Trackton and Roadville today? In 1982, Trackton is a quiet place. There are no young children to take the place on the plaza of those described here. Zinnia Mae and her sister, who have had babies in the past year, moved away. Their blind mother was no longer able to pay the rent, and all moved in

359

with the oldest daughter across town. Teegie and Lem are finishing their early primary years of school, and in the past two years they have settled in to being "bad boys" at school. Lem has failed the second grade once. Gary, Gary B., Nellie, and Benjy are finishing elementary school. Gary has had a succession of teachers who found inventive ways of harnessing his energy to his studies. Gary B. is in special education classes. Nellie has blossomed, and the community regards her now as "the brightest of 'em all." Her inability to compete with her Trackton peers on the plaza and to build fanciful stories has apparently left her ready for accepting the slow, methodical, step-by-step teaching of reading and arithmetic in the primary-grade classes. She is floundering in the sixth grade, but her quiet, polite way has thus far carried her through without a serious failure. Her twin, Benjy, is a year behind her, having failed a grade along the way. He was in Mrs. Gardner's first grade, and there he excelled, but the power of initial success in her class faded under a new teacher who chose to judge him by step-by-step skill performances in the second grade. Even under imaginative and caring teachers since the second grade, he has not recovered the enthusiasm and imagination he had at the end of the first grade. Sissy is in her middle years of high school, enjoying social studies and science, and struggling with basic English and arithmetic. Tony is in his first year in a small college in his state in which only 10 percent of the student body is black. His athletic prowess, tenacity in his work, and individual drive to move ahead did not waver throughout high school, and though he is struggling in his first year of college, he says he will become an accountant.

The quiet community now has several cars which clog the plaza. Ol' Frank is dead, burned in a fire his smoldering cigarette started in his bed one evening. Annie Mae's Bub has toned down his life style, and he and Annie Mae take pleasure in the progress of Marcy who has completed the nursing course at a hospital in Alberta. They keep Teegie, except on weekends when he goes to visit his mother. The mayor and his wife still live in the top house on the hill, but the mayor is much more subdued now since a heart attack a few months back. Miss Lula's Darett has gone to Alberta to live, and her other son is now living with her and working in the mill.

These days the oldtimers talk little of the future. No one speculates about a dream house, and the blankets and towels stored under the beds in anticipation of the move have been used. Trackton students remember nothing of the days in the rundown houses on the outskirts of Gateway. They listen to tales of cotton fields with much less involvement than to tales of recent car wrecks. They hear of hardships in the past mostly from preachers who equate the new-found black freedoms to the Biblical exodus. They find, as do their white classmates, stories of the Depression, Reconstruction, and the days of slavery as fictional as any other facts of history from the remote past. Their church experiences, their preferences in dress and music, and their uses of certain words and slogans are today the only ways they consciously assert their identity with a generalized black-is-good-powerful-and-able image. For them, however, this image is not born of a past with which they associate themselves. Their sights are on the future, getting on at jobs in the textile mills, and "gettin' on outta Trackton" to the new future they so often heard their parents wish for.

In Roadville, Rob Macken has retired from the mill. He now putters around his house and garden and works part-time at a local Ford dealer's service center. Mrs. Macken is still teaching and watching over Kim's progress as she prepares to enter junior high school. Mrs. Dee died and her daughter gave up the old Roadville house to go to live with a cousin in a town above Alberta. Jed has married his girl from Gateway, and they moved into Mrs. Dee's old house now that they are expecting their first child. Jed is enrolled in night classes now, planning to earn his high school diploma and to go on to get a license as an electrician. Lisa is planning to be married in the next year, but Sue is hoping the fact that Lisa's boyfriend is attending a community college in Alberta will keep her in school until she finishes. Sally and Wendy enter high school next year, and both are looking forward to the freedoms the big consolidated school will give them. Wendy hopes to be a cheerleader, Sally wants to learn to play in the band. Martin, now in his second year at a nearby state university, comes home several times a year, and Peggy and Lee wonder about the life of books and fraternity parties he jokes about. He plans to go on to law school, and Peggy still shakes her head and says "Where that boy got his brains, I'll never know." Danny is a stocky junior high student, who has already set his sights on playing on the varsity football team in high school. He has gone to football

Epilogue

camps the past two summers, and his parents feel confident he will make the team if he can keep his grades up. He is enrolling in the business education courses, hoping that the English classes there will be easy enough for him to make the grades needed to play on the varsity team. Bobby, who is of a slighter and lankier build than Danny, started playing for the YMCA soccer team when he was in the fourth grade, and is now on a locally sponsored team. His baby brother is now in third grade, still carrying with him the talents at naming, reading, and writing that Betty worked so hard to develop before he started school. The Turner children have left Roadville: one is married; another lives with a friend in Alberta and is enrolling in a nurse's aide program at the community college.

Today memories of their families' origins in Appalachia and their rural roots, their moves in the early twentieth century from mill village to mill village, and their settlement beside the gully below Laurence Mill in Roadville are fading rapidly. Few youngsters in school know the history of their ancestors' association with the textile mills of the Piedmont. Unions, Brown Lung disease, and the competition from the foreign textile industry are far away from these youngsters' thoughts. They do remember vivid stories they have heard about the years of segregation from blacks their families practised, and they have not been allowed to forget that their parents did not come face-to-face with blacks in the mills, schools, or in their home communities until this past decade. Part of their urgency to move ahead and away from any association with the textile mills is their desire to find jobs in which they will not have to compete with blacks. They wish for ways to avoid conflicts in competition over housing, city and county political issues, and educational and recreational institutions.

In both Trackton and Roadville, the promise of good living and getting ahead helps guide the young people's ways of seeing school in their children's futures. Jed is already talking about how he will make his child work harder in school than he did. Tony says he plans to get an accounting job in Alberta, so his children can go to better schools. The young of both communities are slowly moving into paths which will, no doubt, take them away from many of the customs of the worlds of their past.

An ethnographer of communication has no more talent for

accurately predicting the future than any other social scientist. However, our examination here of the maintenance of patterns of language use and their mutually reinforcing cultural patterns leave us with ample possibilities for speculation. Through the numerous geographic and economic moves of this century, both Roadville's and Trackton's forefathers maintained habits which were forged in the social, regional, and economic milieux of preceding centuries. In the 1920s, the schools of the Piedmont began to articulate their mission as preachers of culture to the mill people, the poor whites, and the mountain folks who had come to the mill villages. Through the decades, the schools maintained this goal while mill people kept their faith in the power of schools to help them get ahead. When blacks came to school with whites in the late 1960s, most people saw no need for a change of mission or methods. Only a few teachers used the difficult decade of the 1970s to teach themselves and their students with some new methods and materials.

Will the road ahead be altered for the students from Trackton and Roadville who have, through the efforts of some of their teachers, learned to add to their ways of using language learned at home? Will their school-acquired habits of talking about ways of knowing, reporting on uses of language, and reading and writing for a variety of functions and audiences be transmitted to their children? Will these habits influence the vocational choices and chances of the next generation? Internalization and extension of these habits depend on opportunities for practice as well as on a consciousness that these ways may have some relevance to future vocational goals. Maintenance of these habits depends on both sustained motivation for entrance into some vocation in which they are seen as relevant, and exposure as adults to multiple situations in which the habits can be repeatedly practiced. Moreover, concepts of parenthood and roles in teaching and modeling these language uses must stand behind both a recognition and a drive to use language as a source of power for access to and maintenance of expanded types and places of work. In short, the orientation toward uses of language must include not only the interactions of the present, but also the needs of the future.

Thus, parents in Roadville and Trackton will initiate changes in their cultures only when they see it as their responsibility to provide opportunities for their children to practice or to extend the ways the school teaches. Early in the century, the millowners had planned schools as places which preached the culture of the townspeople to make millworkers docile and receptive. Through several decades, each new generation replaced its parents in the mill, in spite of increased schooling. In earlier decades, black leaders had pushed movements such as vocational education for young blacks. These earlier educational reforms had led black and white working-class members to put their faith in the school as the agent which would change their chances for moving up. Today, Roadville and Trackton adults still see their children's successes and failures at school as primarily the responsibility of the school, and though they care a great deal, parents do not see themselves as interveners in the process of expanding on or applying school habits for their children. It is a given that the children will have to try to make it on their own as their parents did, and though residents of both Trackton and Roadville believe their children have better times and more opportunities than they did, they accept that ultimately each individual will make his own way. They rarely ask their young: "What will you be?" "What do you want to do when you grow up?" Once the young reach their early teens, the answers to these questions depend on the individual child, and not on the parents' guidance, teaching, or exhortations. Parents, if asked, say they know they cannot determine the direction of the road ahead for their children; the specifics of the journey ahead depend on a mixture of "just what comes" and the application of talent and will by the young person. For some Roadville and Trackton parents, there is some faith that what lies ahead depends on the will of God, but working out one's destiny within that will is up to the individual. Some few families recognize that townspeople set specific vocational goals for their children and link these to current schooling habits, but few Roadville and Trackton parents move beyond believing that schooling ought to make a difference in their children's futures to specifying how that difference can be made. Since they themselves reached their occupations not through schooling, but through combinations of historical accident, family history, and luck, they have little experience from which to draw road maps for the future paths of their children.

Moreover, in their jobs, they do not find that schooling has made or can make a difference for them. With almost no opportunities to write, few chances to read, and almost no occasions when their uses of oral language are critical for success in their current jobs, most live out their days and nights at work making few instrumental or heuristic uses of language. Most are told what to do by a foreman or job supervisor, and once routines are established, changes in this routine are the only occasions for further instrumental uses of language. There are occasional assessments by supervisors, and confusion about tasks is usually clarified by demonstration. Locked into routines in which there is little variation in decision-making, workers do not ask questions about the labels for items which surround the job; these are given in descriptions of the tasks to be done. Unable to make changes in the procedures for accomplishing a task, and often not privileged to know the ultimate outcome of a project in which their task is only a small part, the workers look for no reasons for the task, nor do they give their opinion of the role of their task in the whole. On the job, they socialize with fellow workers, sharing news and opinions and telling stories, but the topics of their talk rarely include their work. Their talk on the job focuses on both the social organization created among workers at work and on those portions of their life off the job which they are willing to share with co-workers who may not be members of the same community.

Roadville parents, like most white mill workers, talk little at home about their work, and then only of their social relations or unusual events. The young of Roadville-like communities see no links between their parents' jobs and their home lives, and since they themselves have no plans to work in the mill, there are no inquiries linking vocation and home. In any talk of the future, girls speak of nursing, teaching, becoming secretaries, or getting a job in the city. Boys speak of adventuresome occupations such as flying, becoming professional athletes, and finding work which involves travel. All implicitly plan to move away, to join their cousins and friends who have found varieties of different types of training and work available in the urban areas of the South. Most agree they will enroll in "some kind of technical training" to enter the jobs for which they feel neither schooling nor their parents' experiences prepare them. They look forward to having families, brick homes in the suburbs, and clothes bought from the city department stores' seasonal displays.

The children of black mill workers are divided about the future role of the textile mills in their lives. Some who have completed high school have gone North to try to find work and returned to the South, seemingly satisfied that the pay of the mills and the relatively lower cost of living make the quality of life better in the South. They seek, instead of different kinds of jobs, housing and recreation opportunities commensurate with their new incomes; and yet few of the locales in which the mills are found provide such opportunities. Many males and females begin work in the mills before they finish high school, and they like mill and construction jobs because they offer "good pay." The younger blacks who are not yet in high school speak of adventuresome "far away" jobs, but they do not openly spurn the mills.

Increasingly, there is no single black experience, for the differentials of individual initiative, assessments of incentives to work in school and on the job, and willingness to break away from extended family responsibilities determine the future of young blacks. Today there is less and less mill and construction work for those who want such jobs. The chances for getting the kinds of housing and leisure time activities many young blacks would like to have are more limited, in spite of money earned. In the next decades, the families of young blacks will, no doubt, speak more and more of jobs other than mill work and of moving to places where opportunities for their children are greater. Their children may aspire to becoming teachers, nurses, secretaries, pilots, electricians, and business owners. They will leave their places in the weaving and spinning rooms of the Piedmont mills to others who have not yet found mill work as a way up and out of their past.

The young couples of Roadville and Trackton, as they build their families, will move away from some of their parents' habits and ties to the past. But because the home patterns of language use are inextricably linked to other cultural features, changes in those language uses which so powerfully determine a child's success in school and future vocational orientation will come very slowly, and only in concert with numerous other types of change. The ways with words, transmitted across generations, and covertly embedded and intertwined with other cultural patterns, will not change rapidly. The next generation of Roadville and Trackton parents will socialize children who will follow many of the language habits of their parents and grandparents before them.

Many of these ways with words will continue to be in accord

with and to reinforce other cultural patterns, such as space and time orderings, problem-solving techniques, group loyalties, and preferred patterns of recreation. For Trackton's young families, life in apartment complexes or homes without a plaza or open space for gathering will vary the cast of characters from whom preschoolers take their cues and the breadth of roles the preschoolers have an opportunity to perform. Marriage with partners who prefer town churches or no church at all will remove a long-standing institutional niche which reinforced uses of oral and written language and social interactions stretching over unbounded time periods. For Roadville's young families, new kinds of jobs will inevitably bring moves to larger towns and life among young couples who do not share the values of hard work, rules of bounded space and time, and do-it-yourself attitudes with which the children of Roadville grew up. City churches may either prove entirely unsatisfying, or they may envelop young couples in more wide-ranging uses of testimonies and lay participation than their home churches did. Nevertheless, ways of talking around and about written materials are deeply ingrained in both Trackton and Roadville, and proverbs, stories, morals, talking junk, and group negotiation of the meaning of written materials will not pass rapidly.

The deep and wide-reaching complexities of uses of language, time, and space are far more resistant to change than are single-factor activities traditionally associated with preparation for school. The amount of parent–child interaction time, the habit of reading bedtime stories, and early promotion of increased talk between parents and children depend for their establishment in these young families' homes on how they can fit in a network of other cultural patterns, such as problem-solving techniques, role relations and shared functions across sex and age, and favorite ways of interacting with others and spending one's leisure time. It is through these ways of living, believing, and valuing that the descendants of today's Roadville and Trackton will unconsciously pass on their knowledge and skills in the symbolic manipulation of language.

The school is not a neutral objective arena; it is an institution which has the goal of changing people's values, skills, and knowledge bases. Yet some portions of the population, such as the townspeople, bring with them to school linguistic and cultural capital accumulated through hundreds of thousands of occasions for practicing the skills and espousing the values the schools transmit. Long before reaching school, children of the townspeople have made the transition from home to the larger societal institutions which share the values, skills, and knowledge bases of the school. Their eventual positions of power in the school and the workplace are foredestined in the conceptual structures which they have learned at home and which are reinforced in school and numerous other associations. Long before school, their language and culture at home has structured for them the meanings which will give shape to their experiences in classrooms and beyond. Their families have embedded them in contexts that reflected the systemic relationships between education and production. From their baby books to their guide books for participation in league soccer, the townspeople's children have been motivated towards seeing their current activities as relating to their future achievements. Their socially determined habits and values have created for them an ideology in which all that they do makes sense to their current identity and their preparation for the achievements which will frame their future.

The teachers described here learned to bring some of the ways Trackton and Roadville children shaped experience and expressed knowledge into classrooms. They worked to enable the children to elaborate the similarities and differences among different cultural groups, and times, places, and styles. The cultural patterns of all involved expanded, and as this book is completed, some of Roadville's and Trackton's young adults are using that expanded knowledge to make life choices. But structural and institutional changes in the schools and patterns of control from external sources, such as the federal and state governments, have forced many of the teachers described here to choose either to leave the classroom or to revert to transmitting only mainstream language and culture patterns. In the first decade of desegregation, when the focus of external forces was primarily on population shifts and structural changes within the schools, the individual teacher was given enough professional autonomy to search out and use information to change what happened in individual classrooms. Neither the degree nor the direction of focus of external forces on schools in the 1980s is clear; possibilities include either reinstatement of a relative autonomy of teachers over decision-making in their own classrooms, or a structured dictating of curricular and discipline matters by either the power of the state or the public at large.

In any case, unless the boundaries between classrooms and communities can be broken, and the flow of cultural patterns between them encouraged, the schools will continue to legitimate and reproduce communities of townspeople who control and limit the potential progress of other communities and who themselves remain untouched by other values and ways of life. The story of this book gives a single example of how such changes can come about. The challenge of a structural change imposed by law, in conjunction with community confidence in teachers and schools, and the availability of applicable social science training, led to pedagogical innovations that were effective at least on a small scale. But in different times and places, the challenges are different and the resources and possibilities not the same.

It is easy to claim that a radical restructuring of society or the system of education is needed for the kind of cultural bridging reported in this book to be large scale and continuous. I have chosen to focus on the information and bridging skills needed for teachers and students as individuals to make changes which were for them radical, and to point to ways these cultural brokers between communities and classrooms can perhaps be the beginning of larger changes. It is only ventures like those of the teachers and students of these Piedmont communities in the 1970s and careful studies of such ventures that can lead to the knowledge educators and community members must have to break past patterns of ways in which language and schooling have been linked to the ways one gets on at home, school, and work.

Notes

Chapter 1

1 Gilman 1956: 32. For a detailed description of the physical and human geography of the Piedmont region, see Gilman 1956: Chapter II. Klein 1979 describes the shift in cultural habits and land use patterns which the inland spread of cotton brought yeomen farmers between 1767 and 1808. Odum 1936 and Robertson 1942 describe the style of life possible in the "red hills" in the late nineteenth and early twentieth centuries. Wertenbaker 1963: Chapter IV provides a picture of the independence of the life of up-country planters, farmers, artisans, and craftsmen in the colonial and early national periods.

2 The question of the role and extent of cotton manufacturing in the antebellum South has been taken up by numerous historians; the classic work is Mitchell 1968. Other studies report in detail aspects of the antebellum history (e.g. Kohn 1907; Lander 1969), or the influence of manufacturing activities of the South on the rise of industrialization after the Civil War (Lemert 1933).

3 Potwin 1927 gives an historical and sociological account of ways in which agriculture was "supplemented rather than supplanted by industry in the Piedmont" (p. 18). This source also provides a detailed case study of one Piedmont cotton mill from 1899 to 1925. For a statistical analysis of the migration from the Southern Appalachians to the Piedmont mills, see Brown and Hillery 1962. Oates 1975 traces the economic development of the textile mills and discusses the effects of the textile mills on the surrounding economy. A wide range of participants and outside observers assess the family-like character of the mills during the days of local ownership. The story of Louis Harrell in Conway 1979 provides an insider's view; Odum 1930: Chapter XVII gives an outsider's perspective. Pope 1971 traces the relationships of churchmen and millowners and workers in Gaston County, North Carolina, and portrays how the church did not challenge the ways that millowners' profit motives controlled workers' lives.

4 Camek 1960: 19. The growing distinctions between mill and town during the late nineteenth and early twentieth centuries are most objectively summarized by Carlton 1977. This work traces the townspeople's support of key measures of progressive reform movements, such as child labor laws and compulsory school attendance, and the responses of the mill people to them. Contemporary accounts of the early decades of the twentieth century are numerous, and vary greatly in both the extent and objectivity of information presented. Potwin 1927 is a "sociological" study by a recreational leader who went to live in the heart of the Piedmont textile region in 1916. Though this is a somewhat romanticized description of both mill and town people, the study details the actions and attitudes taken by members of this community on

education and other social legislation. Rich in descriptions of the daily life of mill and town interactions, Potwin looks at child labor in the mills, uses of parks and playgrounds, celebrations of holidays, and the effects of locally established compulsory attendance rules. Potwin also comments on the language habits of the millworkers, characterizing that of the oldest residents as marked by *a*-prefixing (*a-sitting, a-working*), and strong forms of the past tense of such verbs as help (*helped = holped*). She put many of the comments on current events in the words of the millworkers themselves. Another primary source which is especially rich in detail is Camek 1960, an autobiographical account of a preacher/teacher who opened a school for millworkers in 1911. Initially called the Textile Technical Institute, this school continued operation until 1941 when it became Spartanburg Junior College. The Will Lou Gray collection of the Caroliniana library, local curricular materials (e.g. Lyon 1937), and newspapers, such as the *Spartanburg Herald,* of the mill towns describe both regional and local efforts at social reform during the early decades of the twentieth century. Will Lou Gray was the major figure in adult education, and throughout South Carolina, she promoted literacy programs and other adult educational opportunities. Barnwell 1939 is a photographic record of life in North Carolina mills, sponsored by the Southern Combed Yarn Spinners Association. MacDonald 1928 and Rhyne 1930 are secondary sources which also offer useful interpretations of the mill people's lives. Numerous local histories (e.g. Brown 1953) integrate sources on mill life.

5 The life of blacks in the Piedmont during the first three decades of the twentieth century is difficult to reconstruct. Accounts by whites are either condemning or patronizing. Gordon 1929, written by a black, reflects his "double consciousness" and aspirations to mainstream status, but it includes numerous surveys and vignettes which are a rich supplement to Census data and state statistical surveys. A rich source on the life of white millworkers is their proverbs and songs. The latter illustrate particular aspects of their shifting views of the mill: patriarch, protector, demon, lover, master, etc.; see, for example, Smith 1928, Odum 1930, and Bradley 1937. Cook 1925 and Herring 1929 describe the educational and social programs of mill companies in the early twentieth century. Coe 1939 provides an account of the unionism movement in the South during the 1920s and 1930s. Lahne 1944 supplements this account. A detailed description of the most infamous strike – that in Gastonia, North Carolina in 1929 – is given in Pope 1971. Simpson 1943 gives one of the few accounts of mill life in the 1940s. Miller 1980 is a collection of accounts of mill life during the sometimes stormy decades from the 1930s to the 1960s.

6 In South Carolina between 1960 and 1966, the proportion of black workers in the textile wage force rose from 5.7 percent to 10 percent. Their exclusion in the earlier part of the century from all but the most menial jobs in textile mills is discussed in Newby 1973.

7 The struggle for unionism in the Southern textile industry in the 1970s is most frequently told through the stories of individual millworkers such as "Crystal Lee" (Leifermann 1975; cf. Conway 1979) who have become local heroes in their support of unions and improved working conditions. These accounts illustrate the ambivalence some long-time mill families still have about leaving the mill for other jobs.

8 The classic participant observation studies of a black community (Lewis 1955) and a white mill community (Morland 1958) in the Southeastern

United States were carried out in an area close in both geographic location and historical background to the two communities described in this volume. These earlier studies point to the pervasive changes blacks and whites linked to the textile mills were undergoing in the late 1940s and early 1950s, as a result of unionism, educational emphases, residential shifts, and the evolving role of religion in their lives. One participant observation study (Newman 1978, 1980) of blacks and whites in textile mills describes work and community life in a Piedmont North Carolina county between 1971 and 1977. Extensive interviews detail the relative cultural and social independence blacks had earlier in the century, in comparison with white textile workers. Newman 1978 also describes differences in schooling and work patterns for blacks and whites and relates these to aspirations for education on the part of the two groups in the late 1970s.

Chapter 2

1 An oral history collection of such stories taken from the oldtimers in one of the few remaining mill villages appears in volumes 1 and 2 of *The Old Mill Stream*, published in Lando, South Carolina in 1975 and 1976 under the editorship of Charles and Judy Inabinet.
2 There are numerous similarities between the lives of Roadville men and women and the working-class families described by Rubin 1976: the division of male–female roles, disillusionment with current jobs, continual financial struggles, and educational and vocational aspirations which seem to have little relationship to the skills and experiences their children obtain in school.
3 Lewis 1955 uses the terms *respectable* and *nonrespectable* to refer to the two distinctive styles of life he describes for Kent Negroes; he points out that these categories are "recognized and designated by Negro and White Kentians" (pp. 3–4). Similarly, in Trackton, "respectables" termed themselves such and believed there were clear distinctions between their behaviors and those of others. Rodman 1963, Stack 1974 and others have maintained that respectable blacks stretch their own values to adjust to their life circumstances, since they are unable to meet the conduct and achievement demands of the larger society. Trackton residents do this to some extent, especially in their expressions of ideals regarding housing, independence, etc.; however, they also maintain certain behaviors in religious and social life created by their historical circumstances.
4 For a description of the sharing-for-survival routines of inner-city black families, see Stack 1974. In the community Stack described, individuals in kin-based household groupings who married and wanted to get ahead as husband and wife had to move out of the community. They tried to break off their links to the old community network, so they could get ahead on their own. See the account of Ruby Banks' life history (Stack 1974: 114–17, 129).
5 The matrifocality of black households has been considerably stressed in the sociological and anthropological literature (Rainwater 1970; Stack 1970, 1974). However, in Trackton and similar surrounding communities, the pattern of mother plus son(s) is a common and important complementary pattern to the matrifocal unit of elderly matriarch and daughters. The mother–son pattern is, however, rarely acknowledged or discussed in the research literature.
6 The description here of Trackton's plaza as stage for community theatre is similar to that of Gregor 1977 which portrays a Brazilian Indian village as a

village theatre. The script and stage directions which accompany performances the children give on the plaza prepare them for the varied roles they
must play elsewhere; there are rare places in Trackton where one is not
on-stage. The dramaturgical metaphor developed by Goffman 1959, 1974 to
describe the scripting of social status is best illustrated in Trackton through
the conspicuous and redundant opportunities life on the plaza gives for the
practice of verbal and nonverbal enactments of different identities.

Chapter 3

1 Anthropologists, in describing ways babies are carried in some cultures so
   that they maintain continuous body contact with another human, have often
   suggested the possible effects of this contact on later behaviors of the
   children. Mead's classic study of Balinese children, reported through photographs and text, indicates that for the first two years "the usual life of a
   Balinese child is in arms . . . So the child learns life within human arms" (Mead
   and Macgregor 1951: 42–3). In such cultures in which the very young child is
   "like one of the adult's own limbs, and needing no continuous attention" (p.
   142), there may be no need for early specially directed conversational
   attempts by the mother to the child. Snow 1979 tentatively speculates on the
   possible effects constant contact in the early years in some cultures may have
   on adults' responses to children's early utterances.
2 Practices such as identifying early babbling vocalizations as "words" and
   expanding these into well-formed sentences are extensively reported in the
   child language literature (cf. Cazden 1965; Brown, Cazden and Bellugi 1968;
   Bloom 1973; Newport 1976). Extensive reports of such expansions and the
   mainstream mother–child behaviors which surround them are usually of
   first-born children reared in homes in which mother and child have only each
   other as a communicative partner for a large portion of the day. Almost all
   verbal interactions are dyadic, and the mother often expands the child's
   vocalization into a sentence which is in turn responded to by the mother in a
   conversational frame of alternating turns at talking. For summaries of this
   literature, see Snow 1977b, Bruner 1978, and Gleason and Weintraub 1978.
   A contrast to this pattern is reported by Schieffelin, for Kaluli mothers who
   regard babbling as "bird talk" and stop older siblings from engaging in
   babble-like language play (Schieffelin 1979b).
3 For similar descriptions of the interactions of babies and adults in rural
   Southern black families, see Young 1970 and Ward 1971.
4 For discussion of third person substitutes for first and second person
   references and other types of pronoun shift in talk addressed to children, see
   Ferguson 1964, 1982, and Wills 1977.
5 The naming pattern in this community, which seems to be typical of black
   rural Southern culture, differs in major ways from other naming patterns in
   American society. The distinction between the "real name" and an ordinary
   name and the use of numerous transitory nicknames are comparable to
   practices in other societies. For general discussion of nicknaming, see
   Morgan, O'Neill, and Harré 1979; for discussion of certain aspects of
   Afro-American naming, see Dillard 1976.
6 Ward 1970 provides a description of similar teasing practices in a Chinese
   village where the adults emphasize nonverbal communication in early childhood.
7 Other observers of child language have noted individual cases of the

phenomenon of "favorites," where the child fastens on favorite words or sounds and persists in saying them in a wide range of uses for a considerable period of time. Labov and Labov 1978 reports Jessie's use of *cat* and *mama*; Farwell 1976 discusses a child's preference for fricatives. Halliday 1975 discusses how Nigel gradually learned to attach multiple functions to single words. Observers have also noted cases of the phenomenon of "chunking," where the child makes active use of unanalyzed whole units before proceeding to segmentation, identification of the constituents, and control of the combinatorial possibilities (Fillmore 1976; Vihman 1982). Both these phenomena – and in part at least they overlap or may be considered the same – have generally been regarded as possible individual strategies, in first and second language acquisition. In Trackton, however, the behavior described here is the normal pattern of all young children in the community.

8 Though the anthropological literature describes numerous types of teasing in various cultures (cf. Radcliffe-Brown 1952; Ward 1970), little attention has been given to its role in the socialization of children (but see Mead and Macgregor 1951; Loudon 1970). Schieffelin 1979b, relates a kind of teasing in Kaluli society to children's development of communicative competence. Miller 1982a,b indicates teasing challenge routines were differentially responded to by each of the three white working-class children of her study. For a summary of research on teasing as a stimulus for language learning, see Heath 1981a.

9 This requirement on Trackton children adds perspective to the discussion of the ability to decenter in Donaldson 1978. Though Trackton children's final goal is ego-centered – to provoke the most pleasant kind of interaction – they must get a sense of the other person's perspective to reach this goal. Trackton children, therefore, have to become their own strategists in these interactions, testing reactions to their actions on an almost continual basis in their human environment. Halliday 1975 makes a similar argument for Nigel's becoming his own strategist in learning language, though Nigel does so in the context of a much more language-focused and consistently responsive verbal environment than that of the children of Trackton.

10 For similar descriptions of the wide personal network into which babies of working-class black families are taken, see Stack 1974 and Young 1970.

11 Compare this unreliability of expectations in response to politeness formulae, for example, with the predictable responses and contexts of learning politeness formulae reported by Gleason and Weintraub 1976 for mainstream middle-class children. Ferguson 1976 raises the general issue of how children acquire politeness exchanges in different speech communities.

12 For an example of the detailed fine adjustments necessary to anticipate and respond correctly to varieties of handshakes used in black communities, see Cooke 1972 and Baugh 1979. Erickson and Schultz 1981 provides an extended discussion of how the learning of ways to coordinate and synchronize body movements in politeness gestures in one's own cultural group breaks down in cross-cultural situations.

13 Teaching by example and demonstration rather than by analytic description and questions related to specific steps of the process is a topic much debated by psychologists and anthropologists; see, for example, reports of research by Childs and Greenfield 1981 and Greenfield and Lave 1982.

14 Snow 1979 offers a summary of the work of linguists on the role of repetitions in child–adult interactions. This summary points out that the inclusion of children in discourse is a predominant feature of caregiver–child

interactions. Trackton children, however, uninvited into adult discourse, seem to practice by repeating pieces of the discourse, then varying these pieces, and finally breaking into adult conversation with their own discourse topic. This process is strikingly similar to the language play reported in various sources; Weir 1962 on a child's presleep monologues and Keenan 1974 on the dialogues of a pair of twins are the most commonly cited; Ferguson and Macken 1980 provides an overview of the literature on children's language play.

15 In the literature on language learning, there are scattered reports of such chunking of language for repetition by children. These are usually viewed as invariant forms, stock phrases, which the children sometimes imitate in intonation contours before they articulate the separate words of the phrases clearly. Cazden 1968 pointed out that the Harvard children had these stored fragments of speech which they seemingly used from memory and only later separated into pieces for production. Peters 1977 pointed out two similar strategies in the child she described. The first to appear was that in which the child repeated combinations, imitating intonation contours of whole phrases and providing the proper number of syllables and accurate stress in imitation of whole phrases or sentences. A later strategy was the use of one-word utterances which presumably resulted from the child's application of productive rules. Nelson 1973, 1981 and other studies of individual children (usually of the mainstream middle class) (see Peters 1983 for a comprehensive review of this literature) suggest that the extent and pattern of use of both strategies may be a matter of individual differences. However the consistency of this pattern of repetition and repetition with variation among Trackton children suggests that the chunking strategy may be more widespread in certain speech communities than in others.

16 Prior to this stage, Trackton children often engage in pretend play while modifying the talk of adults around them. These modifications come first in monologues, in which the children seem to superimpose a story on their activities: Lem makes the shoe "walk" and play the part of Miss Lula. Between twenty-two and twenty-four months, children, especially girls, appear to begin to practice for the participation stage. The toddlers begin to use dialogue in their pretend play, giving their doll babies or toy soldiers parts to play and taking on roles themselves. Themes of this pretend play are variations on the talk picked up from adults about them. For a discussion of the role of monologue and dialogue in pretend play in mainstream middle-class children, see Sachs 1980. When Trackton children finally break into adult discourse, they do so by engaging the attention of the speakers and providing specific nonverbal and verbal cues linking their topic to a situation familiar to both child and addressee; see Keenan and Schieffelin 1976 for a discussion of other children's strategies of introducing discourse topics.

17 From time to time, Trackton children in the early years of school bring home baby talk and use it for several weeks, sometimes influencing younger members of the family. Adults fuss at the children when they hear this talk, often choosing to do so on occasions when there are numerous other children around, thus maximizing the embarrassment of having their babyish talk pointed out. Sissy, in the second half of the third grade, went through several weeks of saying "Me want," "Me read," and whining as she talked. Lillie Mae fussed at Sissy very severely, reminding her of her baby brother and asking: "You want him to talk like dat?"

18 Baby talk (Ferguson 1964) is simplified language directed to children in

cultures around the world as they are learning their first language. Ferguson 1978 proposed universals of talking to children. Characteristics of such talk include high pitch, exaggerated contours, a slow rate of speaking, short sentences, repetition, use of special lexical items (for kin terms and body parts, etc.). Phonological simplification includes the reduction of consonant clusters, reduplication and substitution of sounds, and the use of special sounds. Discourse with children is marked by special features, such as the use of questions, pronoun shift and frequent repetition of the topic of the discourse. Much of the work in language input to children describes ways in which baby talk is structured and used and tries to explain how this talk relates to the actual language production of the child at various stages (cf. Snow and Ferguson 1977). The analysis of a baby talk register into simplifying, clarifying, and expressive features is introduced in Ferguson 1977 and taken up in Brown 1977 and elsewhere. It seems clear that baby talk is not universal; it is almost completely absent in Trackton and in several other communities investigated recently by linguists (e.g. Schieffelin 1979b), including the extreme case of the Ik (Turnbull 1972). However it probably occurs in a majority of cultures, and features of simplification in this talk are similar to those of other simplified registers such as foreigner talk, and of pidgins and creoles.

19 This strategy is similar to *elema*, the practice of Kaluli mothers in Papua New Guinea who tell their young children what to say to others in teasing encounters (Schieffelin 1979b).

20 For a detailed analysis of this phenomenon, see Whatley 1981.

21 This table is presented primarily for the purpose of comparing the types and rank ordering of playsongs performed in each setting. Playsongs collected at schools were performed by both black and white students, and collection took place over three spring months at numerous schools which both Trackton children and children from other neighborhoods attended. The determination of topic was made on the basis of the primary content of the song. For example, many playsongs, such as the following, included both body parts and number content.

> Dr. Knickebóck, you're the óne
> You sure got búmp by bumpty búmp
> Now lét's gét the rhýthm of the hánds
> Now you got the rhýthm of the hands
> Now lét's gét the rhýthm of the féet
> Now lét's gét the rhýthm of the whíp o will will [name and cry of a local
> bird]
> Now you got the rhýthm of the whíp
> Now lét's gét the rhýthm of the éyes
> Now lét's gét the rhýthm of the number fíve . . .
> [song can continue – up to 100]

When both types of content occurred, the topic of body parts was chosen as primary, since the number content was optional and often shortened. Numbers were seen as topics only when numbers and counting always constituted the major focus of content in the playsong. Thus, no playsong was classified in two categories.

22 The general pattern of these songs was familiar across communities in the region, but the specific words varied not only from school to community, but from community to community and from time to time. Though the girls in

Trackton maintained this playsong "didn't mean nut'n" and its nonsense sounds were "just for fun," girls in a nearby community consistently performed the playsong as follows.

Miss Súe, Miss Súe
Miss Súe from Alabáma
Lét's máke a móvié
Chick-a-bóom, Chick-a-bóom, bóom bóom
Your mámma got the méasles
Your dáddy got the flú
I don't cáre and neither do yóu
[girl's name], somebódy's calling your náme
——, somebody's pláying a gáme
——, somebódy wánt you on the télephone
If it's nót my báby, I'm nót at hóme
Síttin' at the táble, péeling white potátoes
Lísten to the clóck go
Tick Tóck Ta Wally Táh
Tick Tóck Ta Wally Wáh Bóom

It is possible that nonsense renderings and new rhyming patterns developed as a result of repeated misinterpretations, and some girls in each community simply chose to let their hearings of the playsong and moods of the movement guide them to new renderings.

23 Trackton adults' ideas of questions and their uses with children differ markedly from those of mainstream school-oriented parents; see, for example, Holzman 1972, 1974. Some studies suggest that questions have an important role in children's acquisition of communicative competence, especially in their learning of conversational skills (Ervin-Tripp and Miller 1977 and Snow 1977a). Yet cross-cultural studies of language socialization have pointed out how the use of questions varies across cultures and raises doubts about the universality of the critical role of questions in language development; see, for example, Goody 1977; Harkness 1977; Schieffelin 1979a; Heath 1982b; Philips 1983.

24 The literature on metaphorical uses of language by black children is summarized by Taylor and Ortony 1980 and illustrated with discussions of signifying, marking, and sounding. In all of these uses of speech, meaning is not literal, but conveyed through innuendo, suggestion, and comparison. It is important, however, to look beyond these sometimes stereotyped language uses to the patterning within the child's home environment which could promote adroitness in metaphorical and conveyed cognitive and linguistic generalizations; see, for example, Paivio 1979.

25 There are numerous studies of the differences in the types of questions (and answers) used by mothers of different classes with their children; see, for example, Robinson and Rackstraw 1972. A majority of these suggest that *why* and *how* questions are not used as frequently by working-class mothers as by mainstream middle-class mothers; see especially Blank 1975.

26 This kind of question as well as others such as "You know what?" "Guess what?" are described for mainstream school-oriented children as rhetorical questions, through which children seek acknowledgment to continue their talk (Dore 1978). However, in Trackton, they are important in establishing a conversational frame for story-telling among both adults and children.

27 Compare this use of A-I questions for bringing a misunderstanding to the

attention of people in the conversation with the uses described for mainstream children. Corsaro 1977 examines "clarification episodes" between
mother and child; Garvey 1977a shows that children of three and a half often
seek clarification in their "contingent queries" with their peers; Cherry 1978,
1979 classifies adults' use of clarification into two types: "repetition" and
"confirmation."

28 Abrahams 1964, Kochman 1970, Labov 1972, 1973, Smitherman 1977, Folb
1980, and numerous other studies provide accounts of playing the dozens,
toasting, rapping, and other highly skilled verbal performances which have
come to characterize black language use in urban settings. Chapter 5 points
out ways in which Trackton's forms of these speech events vary from those
described for urban environments.

Chapter 4

1 The details of a stork shower which took place in the mill village of Kent in
the late 1940s (Morland 1958: 162–3) parallel those given here down to such
specifics as the scrambled word puzzles and the type of talk engaged in during
refreshments. The stork shower is one of the few social activities aside from
some aspects of religious life which do not now differ greatly from those
found in the mill community described in Morland's study.

2 Ethnographic accounts of childrearing in a variety of cultures give only bits
and pieces of information about the assumptions of mothers regarding the
early "noises" of children. Snow 1979 summarizes the available cross-cultural
data on the expectations of response to crying, babbling, cooing, etc.; see also
Schieffelin 1979b.

3 The baby talk of most Roadville adults carries a majority of the features listed
by Ferguson 1978 as possible universals of this simplified register. They
modify their prosody, syntax, lexicon, phonology, and discourse features to
adjust their talk to infants and young children, and on occasion to household
pets.

4 The classic study of children's language play in monologues is Weir 1962. In
that study, the author analyzed the monologues her child produced in his crib
just before and after nap times. The child's monologues resembled pattern
practice drills used in language teaching, in that he actively produced new
versions of combinations he had heard around him and repeated these again
and again. Subsequent studies report similar types of language play in
monologues; see, for example, Black's (1979) analysis of her child who often
"replayed" pieces of mother–child dialogue when he was alone.

5 The psychological literature stresses ways in which adults present opportunities for youg children to focus their attention, to center their perceptual and
linguistic attention for a sustained period on an item which has been selected
out of a range of stimuli by an adult. See, for example, Bruner and Sherwood
1976; Ninio and Bruner 1978. These studies emphasize attention-focusing as
a critical aspect of cognitive and linguistic development.

6 For extended discussions of cross-cultural patterns of socializing children into
book-reading, see Scollon and Scollon 1979 (especially Chapter IV), 1981;
Heath 1982c, and Chapter 6 of this book.

7 Sutton-Smith 1979b summarizes the role of girls' play and toys in developing the behaviors and values mainstream girls are expected to have as adults.
Schwartzman 1979 contrasts these findings with the limited cross-cultural

data on play and sex roles, and suggests the influence of objects or toys on children's play.

8 Bruner and Sherwood 1976 emphasizes that peek-a-boo games teach the child to engage cooperatively in a social interaction with shared rules. Children learn to recognize and play by the basic rules of the game – initial contact, disappearance, reappearance, and re-established contact – and to respond to acceptable variations of these rules. One developmental variant Roadville mothers offered was that disappearance of an object in its entirety was unacceptable in the game when it was played with very young children.

9 There is an abundant literature on play and its functions and forms; see, for example, Herron and Sutton-Smith 1971; Bruner, Jolly, and Sylva 1976; Garvey 1977b; Schwartzman 1979; and The Newsletter of the Association for the Anthropological Study of Play. Much of the literature on mainstream or "Western" children reports the "object orientation" of adults, who structure their play with very young children around objects and with older children around games (Sutton-Smith 1979a). There are rare reports of adults' engaging in sociodrama with children (but see Kelly-Byrne and Sutton-Smith forthcoming) or children spontaneously initiating play without objects among themselves.

10 Morland's descriptions of the mill villagers' faith in the Bible and its acceptance as the "ultimate authority in all religious matters, and to some extent in secular matters as well" (1958: 131) are also applicable to Roadville. Many of the church activities and secular practices Morland describes contain the rote recitations and acceptance of "the Word" found in Roadville. Morland notes: "No higher praise can be given a minister than to say, 'He preaches the Bible,' or 'He sure knows his Scripture' . . . Not only the preachers, but anyone who has knowledge of the Bible is highly respected . . ." (p. 132). "Quotations are relied upon when one wants to make a point, for support from the Bible lends strength to any argument . . ." (p. 135). Morland recounts an humorous incident in which a Church of God preacher in the mill village shows he is "a Man of the Book" by proving to a snakehandler that a passage the latter had quoted was *not* in the Bible (1958: 130–2). The question of the understanding of "literalness" in religious language and the links between this understanding and behavior is much debated by philosophers. See, for example, Holmer 1968 and Santoni 1968 for discussion of the cognitive nature of religious propositions. Holmer argues that belief in the truth of descriptions of possibilities and historical claims is a necessary condition for religious faith, but faith itself is the "becoming of a possibility."

Chapter 5

1 Morland 1958 provides several descriptions of such testimonials in Chapter 9. These testimonials are typically confession of sinful behavior or recitation of a state or event for which God is to be thanked. They reflect the community-shared knowledge of human behavior in relation to religious precepts, and they evoke responses based on personal experiences that reconfirm this knowledge (Fawcett 1971).

2 Numerous studies of gossip in different cultures attest to the ways in which evaluative reporting confirms certain roles in the social group (e.g. Gluckman 1963; Abrahams 1970; Rosnow 1976). Haviland 1977 is an ethnography of communication which focuses on gossip in a Mexican community.

3 The Hebrew *mashal* originally meant a comparison of one thing with another and referred to similes, proverbs, and parables. (The English word *parable* is derived from the Greek word used to translate *mashal* in a number of Biblical passages.) Jesus used proverbs and parables in his teaching, much in the manner of the rabbis of his day and later centuries; for discussion of the characteristics of New Testament parables and their Jewish backgrounds, see Dodd 1961; Jeremias 1963; Fawcett 1971. Some of these scholars particularly emphasize the role of metaphor in religious thought and experience: "Metaphor unites us and our world at a level below subject–object, mind–body; it is the nexus of 'man in the being of the world'" (TeSelle 1975: 56). The positive valuation of metaphor, parable, and allegory by religious scholars is generally shared by philosophers, and more recently by linguists (e.g. Lakoff and Johnson 1980) and psychologists (e.g. Ortony 1979). However, a negative valuation of the use of illustrative stories, parables, and proverbs appears repeatedly in discussions contrasting literate and oral traditions. For example, Bourdieu characterizes working-class language as manifesting itself "in the tendency to move from particular case to particular case, from illustration to parable" (1967: 377).

4 In spite of numerous functional descriptions of proverbs in different cultures, there seem to be no studies of how members of a culture learn to link proverbs to situations (but see Wagner, Winner, Cicchetti, and Gardner 1981). Developmental studies of children's abilities to interpret proverbs verbally (e.g. Richardson and Church 1959; Billow 1975) indicate children younger than eight cannot restate the metaphorical sense of a proverb. However, Roadville preschoolers know what proverbs mean in terms of how they themselves should act, and their altered behaviors suggest they can compare the situation of the story behind the proverb to their current experiences or narratives. Petrie 1979 suggests methods of explicating the cognitive skills involved in the collective understanding of comparisons between the message of a proverb (and/or parable) and the situations to which it may be applied. Manzo 1981 presents ways of using proverbs in elementary reading classes to extend cognitive skills, and Cambourne 1981 provides a naturalistic study of the use of metaphor among first-graders.

The culturally sensitive position that metaphor is not primarily a matter of language, but is instead "primarily a matter of thought and action" (Lakoff and Johnson 1980: 153) is based on the view that the only similarities relevant for metaphor are those similarities which people have experienced. It is the sharing of this experience which enables metaphor to provide a partial understanding of one kind of experience in terms of another kind of experience. Many of Roadville's metaphors make sense only if one has shared the cultural experiences upon which the expression of thought and action is based. For example, the experiential correlations in the following proverbs are not immediately evident to those who have not shared the experience or folklore of rural Southern ways:

It takes a piece of bread to show what's in some folks.	(Only a low-down person will quarrel over his share of available food.)
I don't chew my tobacco but once.	(I will repeat a remark only one time.)

The interpretation of other proverbs depends on linking them to their Biblical source which gives them additional authority.

A time for all things and	(The first part is an adaptation
everything in its time; a	of Ecclesiastes 3:1; the second a
place for all things and	parallel formation which does not
everything in its place.	exist in the Bible.)
A soft answer turneth away	(Proverbs 15:1)
wrath.	

5 Cultural constraints on the use of fantasy by children are rarely reported in the literature on children's story-telling. If children in school settings do not create fantasy stories or engage in imaginative play, their abilities are judged deficient in relation to those of children who do. For example, Feitelson and Ross 1973 reports that children in "rural communities" do not engage in role-playing or elaboration of themes, because there are few props or toys for play and adults do not model pretend play. However, the absence in any community of those aspects of socialization believed to promote imaginative play and creative stories in mainstream middle-class homes should not lead researchers to the conclusions that children in that community do not engage in thematic play activities or creative story-making. Sutton-Smith and Heath 1981 suggests that the "paradigms of pretense" underlying most current research in play and story-telling are not applicable cross-culturally.

Roadville's stories as coached by adults make especially apparent the story-grammars or story-schemata children learn in those situations in which adults ask them to tell about an experience. In the head of the adult coaching the story, the plot has been sheared to its bare relevancies, and the flow of events is from beginning to end. This naturally occurring request for story-recall bears many similarities to the recall tasks experimental psychologists have given children and adults in laboratory settings. There children are read or told a story and then asked to recall the narrative. Researchers have then derived models of story structures from these recalls. For example, Rumelhart's (1975) proposal of a story-grammar, as developed in the research of Mandler and Johnson 1977, Stein 1978, and Stein and Glenn 1979, includes a setting episode, initial development, reaction, and outcome in the structure of children's recall of fantasy stories. Botvin and Sutton-Smith 1977 applies Propp's (1968) structural analysis of fairy tales to children's fantasy narratives and sketches a developmental pattern of plot and form complexity (see also Sutton-Smith, Botvin, and Mahony 1976). Applebee 1978 analyzes the plot-structure, content, and evolution of the stories of children aged two to five years. The stories of Roadville children from a very early age fit, with two exceptions, the characteristics of story-grammars based on story-recall in laboratory experiments. First, as Roadville children grow older, their plots do not develop the complexity described for children of their age by Botvin and Sutton-Smith 1977 and Sutton-Smith 1980b. Their plots are bound by both chronology and the "real" experience as conceived by an adult coaching the narrative. Second, Roadville children rarely tell fanciful stories. See note 11 of this chapter and Chapter 6 for further discussion.

6 Recent research in story-reading practices includes diary accounts of individual children's experiences with their parents in book-reading activities (e.g. Crago 1975; Lowe 1975; Graetz 1976), or experimental investigations of the relationship between story-grammars and comprehension for groups of children (e.g. Brown 1975; Rumelhart 1975; Mandler and Johnson 1977; Stein and Glenn 1979). A recent focus uses the methods of ethnography of

communication to describe story-reading in a mainstream middle-class nursery school – Cochran-Smith 1983. This work makes explicit many of the practices nursery school teachers use to prepare children for the expectations of print they must have for school success. This study also points out the links the nursery school makes between creative story-telling and play as story-framing activities. The effect of play, and especially the role of frames in the development of the creativity in children, is well-documented across cultures (e.g. Garvey 1977b; Sutton-Smith 1979a). Sutton-Smith 1980a, b summarizes the major positions psychologists have taken on this issue since Piaget's *Play, Dreams and Imitation in Childhood* (1951).

Recently, not only psychologists interested in play, but also literary critics, discourse analysts, and other scholars focusing on language performance have given considerable attention to the power of framing (see, for example, Barthes 1974; Leondar 1977; Scollon and Scollon 1981). Barthes asserts the frame as a critical aspect of literary description: "To describe is thus to place the empty frame which the realistic author always carries with him (more important than his easel) before a collection or continuum of objects which cannot be put into words without this obsessive operation . . . in order to speak about it, the writer, through this initial rite, first transforms the 'real' into a depicted (framed) object; having done this, he can take down this object, remove it from his picture: in short: de-depict it . . ." (1974: 54–5). Roadville children's departures from reality in stories in play situations illustrate Barthes' point.

7 Suggestions from play theory that play is imitative of and preparatory for adult activity (e.g. Sutton-Smith 1979b) also include arguments that play, on occasion, may defy or challenge the usual social norms (Sutton-Smith 1974, 1975). Roadville children's sociodramas seem to be of both types – reinforcing and contradicting adult norms. They frame their fictive sociodramas in "let's pretend" routines and then take on a variety of identities through their conversation, assumption of character parts, narration of fictive events surrounding the conversation, and designation of props and even time lapses. Much more work on the complex linguistic, social, and cognitive learning which goes on in such pretend play is needed; see Garvey 1977b; Sachs 1980; and Kelly-Byrne and Sutton-Smith forthcoming.

8 The uses of these toasts among urban blacks as described in Abrahams 1964, Kochman 1970, Labov 1972, and Folb 1980 differ from the practices of Trackton. Unlike the urban blacks, only middle-aged men in Trackton know about such toasts, and they do not value them highly in their own interactions. The majority of young men and adolescent males in Trackton know nothing about them, although those who have contacts in Alberta or have visited up-North can sometimes recite parts of such classic toasts as "Stagger Lee."

9 The conceptualization of these early stories of Trackton children as poems benefited greatly from discussions with Brian Sutton-Smith at the University of Pennsylvania during 1979. His view of the stories of very young children as a kind of music, with a theme and variation structure and some elements of verse, is presented in his introduction to Sutton-Smith 1980b.

10 Compare Lem's spontaneous story-telling with the story-episodes described by Umiker-Sebeok 1979 for a group of mainstream middle-class children aged three to five years. See also Scollon and Scollon 1981 for the story-telling strategies of a two-year-old mainstream school-oriented girl.

11 The story-poems of Trackton's preschoolers match Labov's definition of

narrative as "one method of recapitulating past experience by matching a verbal sequence of clauses to the sequence of events which (it is inferred) actually occurred" (1972: 359–60). Labov's description of the overall structure of narrative is not based on story recall in an experimental setting, but on actual stories told in East Harlem. The structure of these stories is, however, somewhat similar to the story-grammars proposed by Rumelhart 1975 and adapted by others. Labov's analysis includes: abstract, or summary of the story; orientation which establishes actors, time, and place of story; complicating action(s); resolution; coda, or signal of finish; and evaluation, which he defines as the way in which the narrator indicates the point of the narrative (1972).

12 A now classic treatment of ritual insults among black preadolescents and adolescents is Labov 1972. He suggests that the use of ritual insults is gradually "moving down in the age range" (p. 308). This is certainly true in Trackton, where even older preschoolers begin using prototypes of ritual insults. Few young people over eighteen years use these at all, although older men in the community remember using such verbal "wargames" in their late teens and early twenties. Folb 1980 contextualizes teenager talk in the culture of urban black teenagers and provides extensive examples of types, uses, and functions of ritual insults.

13 Burling 1966 and 1970 points out that the majority of English nursery rhymes have sixteen beats divided into four lines of four beats each. Burling 1966 provides numerous references to treatments of children's verse and goes far toward suggesting the four-beat rhythm of children's verse as a universal.

14 Labov 1972 has pointed out that the underlying structure of ritualized insults is: "your mother (or other relative of the addressee) is so — that —." The attributes which follow *so* usually focus on age, ugliness, blackness, standard of living, or sexual prowess. Thus, it is possible to understand Benjy's "yo' daddy have false teef" as a ritual insult, with the underlying structure: "Your daddy so old he has false teeth." However, since false teeth were common among the middle-aged and were seen in the community as a source of pride and not a negative feature, we view Benjy's one-liner as reflecting an immature understanding of what constituted a ritual insult. The same line delivered by a school-age child who had learned in school the typical negative valuations associated with false teeth could be understood as a ritualized insult. The other example given here from Benjy's early efforts, "Yo' daddy name Brer," is simply a statement of fact – the addressee's father's nickname to many in the community was "Brer" and this was not an insult or mockery at all.

15 Mastery of the forms of verbal routines, such as riddles, before mastery of their appropriate content and juxtaposition of ideas is well-documented for children in other cultural settings as well; see for example Bauman's description of the development of knock-knock joking routines by children in Texas (1977).

16 Swanson 1981 examines the cheers of black and white cheerleaders in South Carolina, and describes features of body control and rhythmic display as they co-occur with certain verbal routines. Such analysis indicates how defensive actions of the cheerleaders often signal meanings to the audience which are counter to verbal content; such actions are occasionally interpreted as offensive by the sports crowds. Gilmore 1982 analyzes playsongs used by preadolescent girls in Philadelphia to defy adult conventions; both verbal and nonverbal messages are ambiguous, always carrying double meanings.

The shifting combinations of neutral verbal message, suggestive action, loaded verbal message, and neutral actions display the complex dramatic skills of the girls.

17 In Trackton, there was a series of "ghost tales" about "Miss Maggie," now told occasionally to children to keep them away from a certain part of town, and remembered by their parents as having been told to them when they first moved to Gateway. Some children identified an elderly woman who currently lived in that section of town as *the* Miss Maggie, and they often told tales about her blood-curdling deeds, their own bravery confronting her, and their narrow escapes. A high school student from a community near Trackton reported, in confidence, to me one day that he had actually talked to the presumed Miss Maggie, and he had the "true story" about why she was so scary. She had recounted to him a night of horror in her own life when she and her husband were attacked in their home by two strangers. Her husband put up a valiant fight, but he was killed. Since that time, she had tried to scare off strangers. The student paused after telling the story, as though expecting a response from me. Then he laughed and said, "Where is the 'true story'?" See Chapter 6 for discussion of the Trackton children's use of the term "true story" in school settings.

Chapter 6

1 These game-like tasks under natural conditions carried purposes similar to those of experimental psychologists who have investigated the effects of the perceived context on children's referential description. It seems clear that the script Kellogg's was easily distinguished or highly encodable on the cereal box, in part, because it differed in both position and style from the printed words on the box. (Cf. Watson's (1977) discussion of the influence of context on referential description by children.) What is much less clear is how and why the Trackton children's apparent strong tendency to remember what I call the "scene and staging" of *print* was also manifest in their linkage of text *illustrations* to a story – either that of the printed text or one they made up. When we went to the library together, the children preferred books with photographs or realistic color pictures to books with flat-line drawings. Often before they heard the book read to them or they had read the book themselves, they could "read" the illustrations. In doing so, their stories were much longer, and more inclusive of fine details given in the illustrations, than the actual text of the book. They would also often use the occasion to branch off into another story, making up stories about themselves on the basis of hints from the book's illustrations. Once they heard the printed text's version, they often voluntarily identified pieces of the illustration which related to details of the story. Samuels 1970 and Concannon 1975 report that there is little evidence that pictures aid reading comprehension or that children can take the integrated simultaneous information of pictures and relate it to the sequential presentation in the written text. Schallert 1980 reports, however, that pictures aid both comprehension and recall of stories. Trackton pre-schoolers and primary-level children seemed to extend and integrate the text best when its story was staged and set in a scene they could visualize either through illustration in the book or dramatization. For example, often in the community when children were doing homework and asked what a portion of printed text meant, I would suggest an imaginary scene and drama to play out the text. They entered into this "play" eagerly and often extended the

text's interpretation in ways similar to Trackton adults' group reading habits (see note 3, this chapter). Paley 1981 gives numerous examples of the effects of dramatization by children of their stories on extended discourse around the text. Much careful research is needed to enable scholars to link levels of comprehension with different types of illustrations and dramatizations. Answers must be sought in the perceptual antecedents that contexts, such as graphic design and layout, illustrations, and dramatizations, have for pre-schoolers from different communities and cultural backgrounds. Chipman 1977 and Chipman and Mendelson 1979 summarize the debate in psychology over the memorial representations of visually perceived patterns.

2 Those occasions in which the talk revolves around a piece of writing have been termed *literacy events*. Anderson, Teale, and Estrada 1980 defines a literacy event as "any action sequence, involving one or more persons, in which the production and/or comprehension of print plays a role" (p. 59). They break literacy events into two types. The first are reading events in which an individual either comprehends or attempts to comprehend a message which is encoded graphically. The second are writing events in which an individual attempts to produce these graphic signs. Heath 1982a suggests that literacy events have social interactional rules which regulate the type and amount of *talk* about what is written, and define ways in which *oral language* reinforces, denies, extends, or sets aside the written material. Just as speech events occur in certain speech situations and contain speech acts (Hymes 1972a,b), so literacy events are rule-governed, and their different situations of occurrence determine their internal rules for talking – and interpreting and interacting – around the piece of writing. Jenny Cook-Gumperz, in her proposal of the "situated meaning" (1977) of any verbal message, was perhaps the first to recognize the importance of knowing the rules for talking around written materials in school:

> After the achievement of literacy, the child's communicative ability is judged not only by criteria of effectiveness – do the requisite actions get performed? – but by whether the communication meets adult criteria of contextually relevant and appropriate speech. We suggest that the acquisition and use of these appropriate and relevant speech strategies depend not only on acquiring the strategies, but also on acquiring the adults' rules (perhaps we should call these meta-rules) for the recognition of speech contexts. Contextualizing rules chunk the stream of events into speech activities, which then provide the context for the choice of appropriate strategies from the range of known or possible speech acts. (1977: 110)

The child must know not only how to read but also how and when to talk about what he or someone else has read. Compare this description with Philips' (1972) discussion of participant structures.

3 Current research in reading suggests three ways or levels of extracting meaning from print: attending to the text itself, bringing in experiences or knowledge related to the text, and interpreting beyond the text into a creative/imaginative realm or to achieve a new synthesis of information from the text and reader experience (Rumelhart and Ortony 1977; Adams 1980; Fillmore 1981). Trackton residents *as a group* use these methods of extracting meaning from print on some occasions. In the case illustrated here, Lillie Mae decodes the letter, and that information is taken as the basis for the move to the next level in which the group members relate the text's meaning to their own experiences. The third level is achieved by Lillie Mae, after her

own text decoding and sharing of experiences from the group. Though these levels match those described in the research literature for school-successful readers, there are some important differences. First, Trackton individuals have relatively few occasions to focus on specific decoding skills such as letter–sound relationships. Weak readers can always find someone else to read aloud, so that the negotiation of text meaning can take place in the group. Second, since reading is a social activity of the group, there are few opportunities when individuals practice extracting meaning and achieving the final synthesis or reintegration of meaning on the basis of only their own experiences.

4 A detailed social historical analysis of the Mt. Zion A.M.E. Church at Promised Land, South Carolina (Bethel 1979) chronicles the history of this Piedmont "back country" church from its establishment in 1868 to the present. In the rural countryside, in the midst of a white-dominated region, the church created a firm identity for the black community which emerged during Reconstruction. Bethel writes: "Readily apparent are a distinct level of bureaucratization and rationalization in church structure, a governing body maintained through the principles of participatory democracy, a commitment to the principles and fact of education, and an articulated social responsibility to those in the community unable to meet their own needs" (p. 2). Bethel drew these conclusions on the basis of a content analysis of the ledger books containing church records. For example, in the ledger book covering the period from September 1, 1889 through March 13, 1898, of 177 entries, she found 111 entries recording Sunday School proceedings, 34 recording meetings of the Sunday School Board, 8 detailing special church services, 7 giving financial reports, 3 stating formal resolutions of church policy, and 4 miscellaneous reports. Bethel's analysis of these records illustrates the formality and authoritative chain of command with which the elected church officials kept records and implemented policies. In 1894, the church received a gift of religious books from their minister. The Sunday School Board's resolution thanking the minister read as follows:

> ... wher as we have received through the agency of our pastor Rev. N. Chiles Such a beautiful lot of Bibles, Testemon & other periodical to the amt of Twenty five ($25.00) wish, for the small sum of $3 25/100 to cover the cost of packing & Transportation. ... And whereas the School wer greatly in need of said Bibles etc, And is herby greatly bennefitted by the reception of them. Resolved 1st That we do herby tender to Rev. N. Chiles for those most highly appreciated from a rising vote of thanks ...

> Signed Respectfully For the fishers of men
> R. H. Marshall Teacher

As Bethel points out, both the content and form of Marshall's oratorical excesses illustrate the extent to which the congregation held education and formality in writing for such occasions in esteem. The library's holdings of nineteen volumes included books about the Bible, the standard hymnal catechism, and "how to talk books." Bethel's linguistic analysis of the records indicated that the most distinguishable features of their written language were not those commonly associated with Black English syntax or morphology. Though lacking the careful and precise analysis of documents of Bethel's research, earlier studies of the central role of the black church in building a black community cohesiveness (Kiser 1932; Hunter 1953) also provide evidence of the group cooperation these churches depended on in tasks ranging from maintaining the church building to keeping official records.

5 Mitchell 1970 is a sensitive, informed account for seminarians by a black preacher–scholar of the history and structure of black preaching. Mitchell characterizes black preachers of today as coming from a tradition in which preachers in black churches have lacked extensive formal training, but have developed two principles: (1) declare the gospel in the language and culture of the people, and (2) speak to the contemporary man and his needs.

6 The stability of these practices is evidenced in regional church records, which report the "order of service" for Sunday School and preaching Sundays. These documents indicate that the routines of Sunday School services, held by congregation members without a minister, were similar in order and form to the preaching services which took place when a pastor was available. For example, in 1894 the Promised Land Sunday School opened with a hymn, followed with a prayer and/or a responsive reading, a calling of the roll, reading of the minutes of the Sunday School Board, reading of the lesson text, and the singing of a hymn. The congregation then subdivided for Sunday School classes to discuss the Bible reading and collect offerings. Following this period of instruction, the members reconvened to hear a report of attendance and collection for each class. A third hymn, announcements, and "talks" by church members (on topics such as Our Educational Money, Does God divinely bless the education? True womanhood. What has the niggro done to envelop America?) preceded the benediction (Bethel 1979).

7 The following are excerpts from a brochure for such a service held in 1975 near Gateway: "Music will be rendered by Misses Louisa and Myrtle Jones, accompanied at the piano by Mr. Roger Brown." "The Missionary Society of Mt. Hope Baptist Church and Mrs. [name of person being honored] are deeply appreciative of your presence and patronage. May God Bless Each of you." The brochure was six pages long and included lists of "patrons" who had supported the testimonial honoring the elderly community member. The events of the testimonial were subdivided into "family harbor, religious harbors, educational harbors, and civic and community harbors." Prominent figures in the life of the honored person spoke, and the testimonies were interlaced with instrumental and vocal music.

8 The literature on styles of black preaching and types of music in the worship of black churches is extensive. A comprehensive summary of this research given by Levine 1977, Chapters 3 and 4, emphasizes how the changing patterns of worship since slavery affected the forms and uses of language in public oratory and in music. Mitchell 1970 and Rosenberg 1970 provide detailed analyses of the feeling current black ministers report they try to inspire in their congregations. Rosenberg holds black sermons up for analysis by the Parry–Lord theories of oral composition (Parry 1930, Lord 1965), and concludes that the American folk preacher's art does not fit many of the principles Lord used in his analysis of the spontaneous productions of Yugoslavian folk singers. The sermon is ultimately narrative, but it is narrative based on literate sources. Lord argued that it was the illiteracy of his oral singers which determined "the particular form that their composition takes and which distinguishes them from the literary poet" (p. 20). Rosenberg points out that for his oral performers, literacy is not a critical issue, since all were literate, wrote out a prepared text, and based their sermons on Biblical Scriptures. Rosenberg suggests that preachers may have "catalogues of themes" for performance, and they may store in their memory gestures and

expressions linked to these themes which facilitate their rapid spontaneous creation and performance. Both Rosenberg and Mitchell suggest that the dialogic nature of call and response between preacher and worshipers may also facilitate rapid spontaneous creation and manipulation of sermon passages.

9 Mitchell describes these unique combinations as "a blessed unpredictability that keeps Black preachers at least a little humble and keeps their audiences in a state of expectancy, always wondering which way the truth will unfold and which direction the winds of the spirit will blow" (1970: 105–6).

10 For this alternation of raised hymn and chant, inspired by a prayer, I have not attempted to indicate intonation patterns, rises and falls of pitch, or pace. I leave aside such an attempt on the advice of a black preacher who said, having seen his own sermon and accompanying chants in transcribed form: "It's dead. You can't do that." Mitchell as a black preacher confirms this reaction and recommendation. Of the preparation of black church services for reading by an academic audience, Mitchell writes:

"the content of each could easily be heavied up for the intellectual expectations of a reader rather than a hearer. But before one yields to such a temptation, he must ask himself how the 'improved' version would fare in Black dialogue, which is the heart of the matter. For this reason, among others, I chose to cite only actual homiletic dialogue rather than to project what a dialogue might become. Otherwise, all one can possibly do is guess. A free Black dialogue cannot be written until it has taken place, and reduced to writing, it loses the essence of what it was. Anything else must be classified as 'written for reading'" (1970: 16).

11 Features of this chanted prayer are similar to those Mitchell 1970 lists for black sermons. He details (Chapter 6) the most common features of Black English in black sermons, but he gives much more attention to the "performance" aspects of the "Black dialogue." To initiate and maintain this dialogue, the black preacher must use the familiar "as a model for understanding the unfamiliar . . ." (p. 98), a notion which Mitchell suggests "squares with the best educational concepts, both in starting where people are and in keeping them directly involved in the process as God's truth unfolds" (p. 100). Mitchell describes (Chapters 7 and 8) eight ways in which preachers achieve this personal dialogue with worshippers: (1) variation in pace and intonation patterns; (2) use of rhythm, especially in setting the audience up for the call and response pattern (pauses for breath are timed for those points at which the audience is most likely to respond); (3) repetition of portions of the written texts, aphorisms, and significant statements; (4) good story-telling techniques, which include introduction of the speaker and launching of the text or story through role-playing and spontaneous dramatization; (5) highlighting of conflicts between the powerless and the powerful; (6) use of language play such as poetic language, and well-turned phrases; (7) slow rate of delivery measured to maximize comprehension and influence, as the preacher judges displays of these in the audience; (8) expression of a humbleness and identification with the lowly worshipper at different points throughout the sermon. Mitchell's descriptions of sermons of black preachers, and the analysis offered here of the interplay between prepared written texts and spontaneous delivery, illustrate the potential of Hymes' (1973) recommendation that scholars be willing "to augment analyses of the structure of written codes with analyses of their manifest and latent functions

in particular sociocultural settings." Hymes urges this combination of analyses, because: "it is only on the basis of a comparative study of writing that we can begin to generalize about its effects on the development and organization of cultural systems (and vice versa) as well as its influence upon the lives of individuals" (p. 432).

12 Since Basso 1974 proposed ethnography of writing as "a grammar of rules for code use together with a description of the types of social contexts in which particular rules (or rule subsets) are selected and deemed appropriate" (p. 428), few researchers have written such ethnographies. A comparison of Basso's description of letter-writing by faculty and graduate students at an American university (and that given in Chapter 7, this volume, for townspeople) with Roadville's letter-writing points out the nature of the "restricted" uses (Goody 1968) in Roadville. The primary difference is the absence in Roadville of "open" written communicative exchanges in which background information must be given, and the particular expertise of the audience considered by the writer. Moreover, as Szwed 1982 suggests may occur in many communities, the types of uses of writing as well as of reading decrease in Roadville as an individual grows older and differ markedly along sex lines.

13 Britton closed his *Language and Learning* (1970) with the statement: "We cannot afford to underestimate the value of language as a means of organizing and consolidating our accumulated experience, or its value as a means of interacting with people and objects to create experience; nor can we, on the other hand, afford to ignore *the limits of its role* in the total pattern of human behavior" (p. 278, my emphasis). In the past decade, as social scientists have attempted to describe uses of written and oral language, they have made evident the limits of the role of each in the daily life of adults and children in different communities. Hall and Carlton 1977 details the basic skills of written English language use in a community in Canada. Kirsch and Guthrie 1977–8 describes tests of functional literacy used in the United States. Anderson, Teale, and Estrada 1980 characterizes the preschool literacy experiences of children from low-income families and communities in southern California. Scollon and Scollon 1979, on the basis of comparative research in a Northern Athabaskan community and their own mainstream home, suggests at least three kinds of literacy. The most widely discussed is essayist literacy, "which involves the ability to read and write decontextualized material" (see also Olson 1977). Less often discussed are "pragmatically grounded literacies," which are heavily bound to the situation and depend on a prior relationship between writer and reader. A third kind is that in which the material involves the understanding of the religious or inherent truth within sacred texts. The latter two types prevail in Roadville; the first rarely occurs in either the community or its work settings.

14 Numerous researchers emphasize that the literacy experiences of young children should be viewed as an extension of their oral language development. Platt 1977 has shown how some children's control of graphic images grows with their language abilities. Platt sequences the stages of "grapholinguistic" abilities into (1) scribbling, (2) controlled scribbling, (3) the development of an early scheme, and (4) the advanced scheme. Controlled scribbling is seen by Platt as similar to the transition from babbling to naming objects, because at this second stage, the child shows that he understands the representational function of scribbling: a round circle is the sun, a triangle is a tree, etc. As the child develops an early scheme, he adds additional marks within or around the early figures of circle or triangle, etc. The advanced

scheme stage is one in which drawings have recognizable images, and the child grounds the pieces of the drawing in a setting. (See also Lindstrom 1970 for a description of the development of children's "writing" in early art.) Roadville mothers allow children to use pencils or crayons only under supervision, and preschoolers considered too young for coloring or work-books are not encouraged "to just scribble." In their use of workbooks and coloring books, children are encouraged to follow the same sort of system of labeling and naming of attributes of objects ("the sun is yellow, not purple," etc.) which they have become familiar with in book-reading.

15 Harste, Burke, and Woodward 1981 reports research on the knowledge preschoolers from several cultural groups have with written language and their expectations of print in books, letters, and other written materials. Many of the preschoolers in their study could read labels, read and dictate a story, pretend to write a story or letter themselves, and pretend-read either a story or letter they had written. Their findings underscore the fact that learning to read and write develop in concert with the deliberate, conscious training practices of adults and other children around the preschoolers, and that young children often come to comprehend and construct meaning from the written word as a result of its setting and co-occurring familiar events. Their research and that of Anderson, Teale, and Estrada 1980 also illustrate the vast differences in degree and kind of ways in which parents verbalize for their children the links between early book-reading and drawing tasks and school tasks.

Chapter 7

1 Data for analyses and interpretations in this chapter were collected by myself and by students in my courses in Anthropology and Language and Culture at the regional teacher training institution. These townspeople students took fieldnotes and wrote papers on a wide variety of patterns they identified as *mainstream*, and these data, in addition to my own fieldwork in homes and institutions in which they and their families and friends lived and worked, are the bases for interpretations offered here. The purpose of this chapter is to provide background on the school practices and values of the townspeople – teachers and students – and a full ethnographic account is therefore not given. Some sense of the patterns of oral and written language uses, in particular, is however necessary for an appreciation of the shifts in behaviors and values described for these teachers in Chapters 8 and 9. The reader will find that the description of the townspeople given here differs from stratifica-tional analyses of southern towns which speak of upper-, middle-, and lower-class members (see Davis, Gardner, and Gardner 1941; Dollard 1949; Feagin 1979: Chapter III). The emphasis here is on self-identification by the adoption of behaviors and values through which these townspeople announce themselves as part of the mainstream of American society. For an ethnographic account of another mainstream group, see Fischer and Fischer 1963.

2 Terms such as *mainstream* or *middle class* are frequently used in both popular and scholarly writings without careful definition. Useful descriptions of some of the ways of life associated with these terms and their effects on schools are in Charnofsky 1971 and Chanan and Gilchrist 1974. Charnofsky sees most of these cultural norms as covert and deeply ingrained in individual and institutional habits: for example, habits and attitudes of time and space

usage, conformity and neatness, and competition for individual achievement. Yet these habits are rarely specified in ethnographic detail, and numerous accounts of life in these homes portray these behaviors and values as universal and "natural" rather than as the learned and shared habits of a particular social group. Groups may be found in many societies around the world who share a significant number of the characteristics of these mainstreamers, in spite of substantial linguistic and cultural differences.

Mainstreamers exist in societies around the world that rely on formal educational systems to prepare children for participation in settings involving literacy. Cross-national descriptions characterize these groups as literate, school-oriented, aspiring to upward mobility through success in formal institutions, and looking beyond the primary networks of family and community for behavioral models and value orientations. See, for example, the description of middle-class families in Cohen 1981. Uses of space and time, standards of childcare and lawn and household maintenance, and aspirations for the children of this British middle-class suburb parallel in numerous ways those described here for the Piedmont townspeople.

3 The data presented here on preschoolers' interactions with adults come from a group of fifteen primary-level school teachers whose families lived in suburbs around Gateway and are referred to as Maintown residents elsewhere (Heath 1982c). These families, all of whom identified themselves as "typical," "middle-class," and "mainstream," had preschool children, and the mother in each family was either teaching in a local public school at the time of the research, or had taught in the preceding academic year. Through a research-dyad approach, these teacher–mothers and I audiorecorded and analyzed their interactions with their preschoolers in their primary network. For details on the research-dyad approach, see Heath 1982b. With some training in anthropological and linguistic field methods, these teacher–mothers audiotaped their children and made fieldnotes on the context of the verbal interactions. Specific quotations are taken from these recordings, and the ages of the children are noted.

4 The stories of these mainstream children were comparable in content, structure, and occasions of occurrence with those described by Sutton-Smith 1980b for other mainstream children.

5 The role of questions in early mother–child interactions in mainstream homes is well-attested, and numerous studies point out that a large percentage of the utterances middle-class mothers direct to their preschoolers is made up of clearly stated, simply structured questions (cf. Newport, Gleitman, and Gleitman 1977; Snow 1977b). There is a consensus in the literature that caretakers believe questions should be used for "training" or "teaching" children, for directing their attention to what it is they should learn (Holzman 1972, 1974; Snow, Arlman-Rup, Hassing, Jobse, Joosten, and Vorster 1976; Goody 1977), and to appropriate behavior as conversational partners (Ervin-Tripp and Miller 1977; Snow 1977a).

6 Goffman 1978, 1981 first termed the solitary talk in which "we kibitz our own undertakings, rehearse or relive a run-in with someone, speak to ourselves judgmentally about our own doing . . ., and verbally mark junctures in our physical doings" (1981: 79) as "self-talk." He noted what Missy and other preschoolers of townspeople have to learn: self-talk provides for no exchange of speaker–hearer roles. Missy's mother, when listening with me to the tapes of her talk, was particularly embarrassed about these utterances.

Each time they appeared in our replayings of the tape, she made self-denigrating comment ("There I go again!" "Why do I do that?" "I know she can't answer me."). She expressed some amazement at herself for doing this. In her evaluation of her general performance on the tape, she admitted to being conscious of the tape much of the time, and said she felt she did not talk as much to Missy during those two days of taping as she usually did. There were long periods of silence on the tape as well as chatter by Missy – seemingly to herself – in her pretend play.

7 Scollon and Scollon 1979, 1981 provide a detailed account of a mainstream preschooler's literacy socialization. They describe their daughter Rachel's "incipient literacy," and claim that in terms of her responses to books and to what one does orally to display literacy, Rachel was "literate before she learned to read" (1979: 6). Before the age of two, Rachel had learned at least six critical behaviors and values about book-reading and displaying knowledge learned from reading. The townspeople of the Piedmont Carolinas provided their children "lessons" in all of these: (1) books are a natural and "good" part of homes; (2) books involve writing; (3) the reading aloud of books or the retelling of what is in books requires a particular kind of prosody which is different from regular conversational prosody; (4) reading is in many ways like play: it suspends reality, and is so framed, either through verbal or prop-type cues, that everyone knows immediately that it is not normal conversation; (5) reading as a dyadic interaction carries with it the understanding that there is one person who is exhibitor and questioner and another who is spectator and respondent; (6) the respondent is expected to display knowledge of literacy in prescribed ritualistic ways; he should not provide a full knowledge of the text, but rather give responses to specific questions about the text addressed to him by the exhibitor/questioner. Cook-Gumperz 1977 illustrates the numerous ways in which early school tasks and teacher expectations are based on such literacy socialization behaviors and values. Michaels and Cook-Gumperz 1979 and Michaels 1981, studies of the narratives of black and white six-year-olds illustrate the importance, for example, of numbers (3) and (4) above. If children did not mark their narrative with appropriate formulaic beginnings and intonation contours, the teacher effectively rejected the narrative by interrupting and asking questions which showed that she did not view the narrative as either topic-centered or structurally appropriate.

8 Bruner 1978 and Ninio and Bruner 1978 use the term "scaffold" to refer to adult–children interactions which are pre-scripted by the adult, and involve the adult playing out the script initially, but gradually allowing the child to assume a bigger part in the performance of the script. In these interactions, there is assumed to be a close relationship between (1) what the adult believes the child can currently do and what the child can now actually do; as well as between (2) what the actual current performance or developmental level of the child is, and what it is that the adult believes the child can next potentially do (or learn to do). Some researchers have investigated parental sensitivity to the child's current capabilities in language (Levelt 1975; Gleason and Weintraub 1976; Gleason, Greif, Weintraub, and Fardella 1977), but there has not yet been much systematic investigation of teachers' sensitivity to students' language use. The role of adult–child language interactions and the concept of "zone of proximal development" (Vygotsky 1962, 1978) – the second relationship noted above – is developed by Wertsch (1978 and forthcoming, a, b). Chapter 9 in this volume provides examples of teachers'

verbal scaffolding in problem-solving and its effects on guiding students to comprehend mature tasks.

9 The summaries of the occasions, uses, and types of reading and writing in townspeople's homes are based on the fieldnotes of students in my university classes and on my own participation and observation in these homes. Data were collected using methods and objectives outlined in Heath 1978a. The types of letters written by townspeople (personal, business, etc.) compare with those in Basso's (1974) taxonomy of letters written by faculty and graduate students of an American university.

10 Data on the daily job routines of mill executives, supervisors, foremen, and workers were collected on numerous visits to the mills, in which I followed the various personnel through their daily activities, recording oral and written language uses and noting the contexts of usage. This strategy was also used in Wolcott 1973, a study by an ethnographer of the daily activities of a school principal throughout the year. Recent research on the ethnography of writing emphasizes the recording of writing practices of individuals in different job settings and compares these with types and occasions of writing in the home and the school (see Basso 1974, Heath 1981b and Szwed 1982, for programmatic discussions of the ethnography of writing; and Goswami and Odell 1981 and Scribner forthcoming for specific case studies).

11 Scribner and Cole 1981 provides the most comprehensive summary of research on the cognitive and behavioral consequences of school literacy; see especially Chapter 14. Scribner and Cole 1973 and Olson 1977 outline in detail the major features of literacy tasks in the school. Numerous treatments of "class language" (Bourdieu 1967; Bourdieu and Passeron 1977, 1979; Bisseret 1979) emphasize the institutionalization of the "dominating" class's uses of oral and written language.

Chapter 8

1 These excerpts are drawn from the journals of teachers in my courses at Winthrop College, the University of North Carolina at Charlotte, and workshops in six Piedmont counties of the Carolinas in the period between 1969 and 1977. In these journals, they recorded and reacted to assessments of their students which they had given in the past such as those in Table 8.1; they also subjectively evaluated their own sense of being teachers caught up in a period of rapid and multiple changes in education. Many of these journals are now located in the archives of Winthrop College. They exceed 3,000 pages written by approximately 200 teachers, and include records of special activities, such as dramas, library programs, public speaking engagements, and workshops, which teachers developed and directed in their own school districts.

2 Many of these articles linked home and community habits and traditions to curricular units in the schools and to the teaching styles of specific individuals. For example, a public symposium on "Heritage and Progress: Must there be a contradiction?" held in a Piedmont city in January, 1974 brought together over 100 black teachers, administrators, and community members to meet with local college instructors. Over a period of several weeks, the integrated group discussed ways in which resources within black communities could be used to identify and encourage the cooperation of community members and teachers in curricular development, civic programs, and fine arts performances. Press coverage in the region included such news features

Notes to Chapter 8

as interviews with story-tellers, a simple guide to basic techniques of oral history for high school students, capsule careers of black teachers and administrators, and critiques by black and white educators of social studies and language arts textbooks. Other types of press coverage included extended interviews with individual teachers (see, for example, the full-page coverage of an interview with Henrietta Massey, a black business education teacher, in the *Rock Hill Evening Herald*, June 21, 1976). Other news articles emphasized alternative styles of teaching and the involvement of individuals beyond the public school in educational projects. For example, in March, 1979 a Piedmont paper with a circulation in excess of 50,000 devoted two full pages to a preschool program designed and run by inmates at the state correctional institution. Inmates, including several from the Piedmont region, built a child-care center and developed a weekend preschool program for the children visiting their family members at the correctional institution. The story emphasized ways in which the inmates, black and white, incorporated their childhood ways of learning into their teaching in the correctional institution's preschool program.

3 In 1970, the South Carolina State Department of Education sponsored the preparation of a kit of materials on dialect differences in classrooms of the state (see p. 276 of this chapter). Bringing together classroom teachers, reading supervisors, and university professors of reading, English, and linguistics, the project emphasized the teaching of Standard English as a second dialect. The kit was designed to make teachers aware of differences in the sounds and grammars of "nonstandard black" and "nonstandard white" dialects and Standard English and to provide ways in which teachers could recognize those occasions when students used clusters of features of one or the other of these dialects. In numerous counties of the Carolinas, speech therapists prepared analyses of auditory perception and speech production tests used widely in their districts. For example, the Ruth K. Webb Nonstandard Black English Test, developed in 1976, was field-tested in three Piedmont counties before development for use by the school districts' speech therapists and reading teachers.

4 Approximately sixty of these curricular units developed by Piedmont teachers during the period between 1975 and 1979 are collected in the archives of Winthrop College. The format and topical coverage of these vary greatly. For example, "Using the Language Experience in Reading for Teaching Standard English" is a detailed analysis of features of the structures and uses of the language of a ten-year-old black girl. The project also includes the design for a learning center and a sample language arts unit for children exhibiting similar features of language use; a collection of standard worksheets is modified to eliminate discriminatory items for such children. Another curricular unit is designed to teach the metric system to ninth-graders (ages 14–15) by a series of lessons which constitute a story that can be followed only if the metric system is understood. Grade levels and subject areas of the units range from kindergarten through high school courses such as Home Economics, English, Science, and Vocational Education.

5 Several Piedmont teachers and administrators reviewed the literature on the links between home activities and reading success in the first and second grades. In parent meetings and in home visits, they offered examples from these studies of the types of parental activities which helped students' school achievement. For example, they encouraged freedom of exploration for the child (Flint 1977), maternal warmth and use of praise (Barton, Dielman, and

395

Cattell 1974), and books in the home and visits to the library (Napoli 1968; Miller 1969, 1975). Other teachers were concerned that they not seem to be "preaching" mainstream values, and they questioned the benefits of any program taken from school authorities to parents in different communities. They found that the research literature (e.g. Hoskisson, Sherman, and Smith 1974; Thurston 1977) reported that programs were successful in fostering earlier reading and increased gains in word attack skills. However, several key leaders among the teachers were still not convinced that what they viewed as the "missionary" spirit of teaching "poor parents" how to help their children was the right approach; these teachers preferred involving parents in the school itself and allowing them the opportunity to acquire the widest possible range of school-linked habits for modeling at home (see Hess 1980 for an expression of similar concerns). In the Piedmont, the use of paraprofessionals and volunteers in daycare centers, kindergartens, and the primary grades evolved as the more popular and less controversial way of trying to ensure that parents knew the habits which the school expected; but see the discussion on pp. 281–2 of this chapter.

Many of these habits include what has been described as part of the "hidden agenda" or the "hidden persuasion" of the school. The ordering of time and space and submission to authority are among those aspects of carefully structured learning which are not, on the surface, readily identifiable as components of the curriculum. Graff 1979 illustrates the historical tenacity of the organization of the school to transmit the ordering of space and time. The long-standing general association of such rules of personal conduct with the "educated" or the "modern man" is further evident in Dreeben 1968, Inkeles 1969, and Inkeles and Smith 1974. Numerous recent critics of education criticize the school as a "hidden persuader" of the values necessary to maintain the existing class arrangement and socioeconomic order (Charnofsky 1971; Carnoy 1974; Bowles and Gintis 1975).

6 First published in the *Georgetown Round Table on Languages and Linguistics* (1969) and later reprinted in *The Atlantic Monthly*, this article received widespread publicity. Local papers excerpted the article and summarized its central argument that neither were the language habits of children speaking black dialect impoverished nor were their abilities to form concepts and convey logical thoughts impaired.

7 Ervin-Tripp 1977 lists six types of adult directives which have the apparent intention of eliciting goods or services or regulating the behavior of others: personal need or desire statements ("I need a helper"), imperatives ("Give me your paper"), imbedded imperatives ("Could you sit still?"), permission directives ("May I have all eyes looking my way?"), question directives ("Have you finished your work?"), hints ("We'll have to wait for someone to stop talking"). Illustrations of these types of directives in teacher talk in classrooms are given in Heath 1978b, and re-examined by Cazden 1979 in terms of the universals of negative and positive politeness strategies posited by Brown and Levinson 1978.

8 The problems of building a story in a manner which is predictable to the teacher and mainstream classmates are best illustrated in Michaels and Cook-Gumperz 1979 and Michaels 1981. The latter gives an account of Deena, a black child, as she attempts to tell a story at her teacher's request and fails, because she does not follow the discourse style, intonation patterns, and collaborative interaction rules her teacher expected. The teacher's efforts to get Deena back "on the track" in what appeared to be a tale full of

irrelevant digressions were, for Deena, interruptions which eventually caused her to give up on her tale. The extensive work of Steven Boggs (forthcoming), Kathryn Hu-pei Au (e.g. 1980; Au and Jordan 1981), and others on the research staff of the Kamehameha Early Education Program in Hawaii also illustrates the importance of children's prior experiences with highly specific discourse strategies for their eventual success in pre-scripted lessons in school. Much of this research builds on the concept of "participation structures," proposed by Philips 1972 and 1983 to describe the different aspects of interactional rules the children of the Warm Springs Indian Reservation brought to school.

9 The students' uses of titles for their dictated and edited stories supplement some findings of recent research on the effects of titles on student reading and writing. Bock 1978 found that the choice of title affected the selection of content words judged important. Other researchers have found that titles stated as propositions were more frequently remembered by students than other titles (see Kintsch 1972, 1974, Thorndyke 1977, Kintsch and Van Dijk 1978, and Bock 1980 for discussions of the influence of titles on information processing of various types of texts). Trackton children almost always titled their dictated stories as they dictated them. They paid special attention to the graphics of these titles in their editing. However, they rarely included a proposition in a title. Roadville children did not name their stories when dictating them, but they did give them descriptive labels when they edited the teachers' first typed versions. Teachers, who asked students to modify their stories for different occasions and styles, found that a change of style more often than not led to a change of title. Nellie's rewritten story was titled by her "Making it rich." Randy's new story was titled by him "The Day I almost Drowned."

10 Research in these community settings is more extensively reported in Heath 1981b.

11 See Heath forthcoming for further discussion of similar projects. The Document Design Project (DDP) of the American Institutes of Research, Washington, DC, was not in operation at the time of these teachers' efforts. This project now has the goal of fostering clear and simple writing and design of public documents and of "making forms, regulations, brochures, and other written materials easier for people to read, to understand, and to use" (Felker 1980: n.p.). The DDP has now produced numerous materials appropriate for adaptation by teachers in secondary school classrooms. See, for example, Charrow 1979, Redish and Racette 1979, Goswami, Felker, and Redish 1981, and the newsletter *Simply Stated* of DDP, edited by Robin Battison.

Chapter 9

1 Numerous inquiry or discovery textbooks, units, and games are available to social science and science teachers. These include many of the types of tasks used in this classroom; see, for example, Diesing 1971. A major difference between these inquiry approaches and the learners-as-ethnographers approaches described in this chapter is the emphasis on types of language uses. In the classrooms described here, the children had to focus on different ways in which they and others asked questions, formulated answers, and used vocabulary in order to make their inquiries into the folk domain translate into the school domain. A second aspect of the emphasis on ethnography is that it enables students to see how two apparently dissimilar activities – for

example, learning to live in a Latin American village, and collecting information for a science unit on plant life – are similar. In these students' science
activities, they made the metaphor between these two events interactive. In
the words of Petrie (1979: 442), these activities provided "the bridge between
a student's earlier conceptual and representational schemes and the later
scheme of the totally unfamiliar subject to be learned by the students."

This type of bridging across contexts and language practices ("codes")
used for expressing knowledge can be a first step in helping students explain
and analyze what is variously termed "educational knowledge codes,"
"public language," "elaborated code" (Bernstein 1975), "cultural capital"
and "linguistic capital" (Bourdieu and Passeron 1977, 1979; Bisseret 1979).
Critics of education, such as Basil Bernstein, Ivan Illich, and Pierre Bourdieu
point out that schooling reproduces a class society. Repeatedly – and with
more abstractions than linguistic or cultural data – these critics argue that the
preschool language socialization patterns of the middle class ensure their
preparedness in the knowledge and skills of symbolic manipulation of
language required for school success. Critical in these discussions is the need
to open up closed systems of knowing (see Douglas 1970).

2 The idea of students seeing their classroom and school as a community in
which writing can be meaningful is perhaps best developed by Florio 1978.
Graves 1982 contains descriptions of numerous similar writing programs for
young children.

3 Cazden 1974 first proposed the importance of enabling children to talk about
language and to use their metalinguistic awareness to enhance their performance in school. The success of Mrs. Pat in helping second-graders carry out a
wide range of activities to develop their metalinguistic awareness parallels in
several ways the kinds of thinking kindergarteners in Paley 1981 exhibit in
their discussions of classroom rules, forces controlling the unexplainable, and
reasons why some children are "bad." Paley 1981 is a kindergarten teacher's
account of the tales of Wally and his classmates told primarily through their
words, as they debate the principles by which rulers (used for measurement),
pulleys, fairies, and wishes work.

4 Using journals to encourage student writing has been frequently reported in
Language Arts, The English Journal, and *College English* in the past decade.
See, for example, Staton, Shuy, Kreeft, and Mrs. R. 1982.

5 See Noddings, Chaffe, and Enright 1981 for a discussion of the difficulties
some students have in understanding word problems in mathematics classes.
The deeper and more widespread problem of being unable to ask for
clarification from authoritative figures in public institutions and settings is
richly reported for the British working-class, counter-school culture by Willis
1977. Willis' long interviews with working-class boys who reject the school
culture include numerous examples of rationalizations the boys offer for
using aggression instead of verbal means of getting clarification, seeking
necessary information, or defending themselves. Similar difficulties in seeking
clarification, especially when speakers are from different ethnic backgrounds,
are reported in Erickson 1975, Erickson and Schultz 1981, and Gumperz and
Cook-Gumperz 1981.

6 For an extended discussion of ways in which teachers can use such
videotaped interviews for teaching composition, see Heath forthcoming.

7 It is important to note that on several occasions parents from Roadville or
Roadville-like communities did question individual teachers on their practices of asking children to collect information from their homes and

communities. Teachers tried to predict when certain assignments might cause difficulty, and in several schools, they telephoned some parents to ask for their help before the assignment was given. Inclusion of the Roadville parents in classroom activities of various types helped break down some long-standing barriers between these communities and the school. Each year, teachers in several districts asked Mrs. Dee of Roadville and the elderly women of nearby communities to come to junior-high classes studying mathematics. The community members' discussions of their quilting patterns, and ways of measuring and placing pieces of the designs were used as the kick-off for units on geometry. Numerous personal testimonies from students and teachers in the Foxfire project started by Eliot Wiggington in 1966 (and in projects spawned from his work) indicate a similar willingness on the part of community members to accept teaching practices, if their purposes are explained, and if parents are not excluded from the school's network of adults who are authoritative sources and models for students. A long-term perspective on making "classrooms and communities one" is given by Wiggington in the introduction to *Foxfire 5:* "teaching is best as a two-way proposition. We teach, and at the same time allow ourselves to be taught by those we teach. We talk, and at the same time, listen. We experience the world anew through another's eyes. And therein lies a part of the secret of renewal" (1979: 7).

Bibliography

Abrahams, R. 1964. *Deep Down in the Jungle: Negro narrative folklore from the streets of Philadelphia.* Chicago: Aldine.

Abrahams, R. 1970. A Performance-centered Approach to Gossip. *Man* 5: 290–301.

Adams, M. J. 1980. Failures to Comprehend and Levels of Processing in Reading. In *Theoretical Issues in Reading Comprehension.* R. J. Spiro, B. C. Bruce, and W. F. Brever (eds.). Hillsdale, NJ: Erlbaum.

Anderson, A. B., W. B. Teale, and E. Estrada. 1980. Low-income Children's Preschool Literacy Experience: Some naturalistic observations. *The Quarterly Newsletter of the Laboratory of Comparative Human Cognition* 2(3): 59–65.

Applebee, A. 1978. *The Child's Concept of Story: Ages two to seventeen.* Chicago: University of Chicago Press.

Au, K. 1980. Participation Structures in a Reading Lesson with Hawaiian Children. *Anthropology and Education Quarterly* 11: 91–115.

Au, K. H. and C. Jordan. 1981. Teaching Reading to Hawaiian Children: Finding a culturally appropriate solution. In *Culture and the Bilingual Classroom.* H. Trueba, G. Guthrie, and K. Au (eds.). Rawley, MA: Newbury House.

Barnwell, M. 1939. *Faces We See.* Gastonia, NC: Southern Combed Yarn Spinners Association.

Barthes, R. 1974. *S/Z.* New York: Hill and Wang. Translated by R. Miller.

Barton, K., T. E. Dielman, and R. B. Cattell. 1974. Child Rearing Practices and Achievement in School. *Journal of Genetic Psychology* 124: 155–65.

Basso, K. 1974. The Ethnography of Writing. In *Explorations in the Ethnography of Speaking.* R. Bauman and J. Sherzer (eds.). Cambridge: Cambridge University Press.

Baugh, J. G., Jr. 1979. Linguistic Style-shifting in Black English. PhD Dissertation, University of Pennsylvania.

Bauman, R. 1977. Linguistics, Anthropology, and Verbal Art: Toward a unified perspective. In *Georgetown University Round Table on Languages and Linguistics.* M. Saville-Troike (ed.). Washington, DC: Georgetown University Press.

Bernstein, B. 1975. *Class, Codes and Control,* Volume 3: *Toward a Theory of Educational Transmission.* 2nd ed. London: Routledge & Kegan Paul.

Bethel, E. 1979. *Social and Linguistic Trends in a Black Community.* Department of Sociology, Lander College, Greenwood, SC.

Billow, R. M. 1975. A Cognitive Developmental Study of Metaphor Comprehension. *Developmental Psychology* 11: 415–23.

Bisseret, N. 1979. *Education, Class Language and Ideology.* London: Routledge & Kegan Paul.

Black, R. 1979. Crib Talk and Mother–child Interaction: A comparison of form and function. *Papers and Reports on Child Language Development* 17: 90–7.

Bibliography

Blank, M. 1975. Mastering the Intangible through Language. In *Developmental Psycholinguistics and Communication Disorders*. D. Aaronson and R. W. Rieber (eds.). New York: New York Academy of Sciences.

Bloom, L. 1973. *One Word at a Time*. The Hague: Mouton.

Bock, M. 1978. Überschriftsspezifische Selektionsprozesse bei der Textverarbeitung. *Archiv für Psychologie* 131: 77–93.

Bock, M. 1980. Some Effects of Titles on Building and Recalling Text Structures. *Discourse Processes* 4(3): 301–12.

Boggs, S. T. Forthcoming. *Learning to Communicate Hawaiian Style*. Washington, DC: Center for Applied Linguistics.

Botvin, G. and B. Sutton-Smith. 1977. The Development of Structural Complexity in Children's Fantasy Narratives. *Developmental Psychology* 13(4): 377–88.

Bourdieu, P. 1967. Systems of Education and Systems of Thought. *International Social Science Journal* 3(19): 338–58.

Bourdieu, P. and J. C. Passeron. 1977. *Reproduction in Education, Society and Culture*. Beverly Hills, CA: Sage. Translation of *La Réproduction: Eléments pour une théorie du système d'enseignement* by Richard Nice.

Bourdieu, P. and J. C. Passeron. 1979. *The Inheritors*. Chicago: University of Chicago Press.

Bowles, S. and H. Gintis. 1975. *Schooling in Capitalist America*. New York: Basic Books.

Bradley, F. W. 1937. South Carolina Proverbs. *Southern Folklore Quarterly* 1(1): 57–101.

Britton, J. 1970. *Language and Learning*. Harmondsworth, England: Penguin Books.

Brown, A. 1975. Recognition, Reconstruction, and Recall of Narrative Sequence by Preoperational Children. *Child Development* 46(1): 156–66.

Brown, D. S. 1953. *A City without Cobwebs: A history of Rock Hill, South Carolina*. Columbia, SC: University of South Carolina Press.

Brown, J. and G. A. Hillery, Jr. 1962. The Great Migration, 1940–1960. In *The Southern Appalachian Region: A survey*. Thomas R. Ford (ed.). Lexington: University of Kentucky Press.

Brown, P. and S. Levinson. 1978. Universals in Language Usage: Politeness phenomena. In *Questions and Politeness: Strategies in social interaction*. E. N. Goody (ed.). Cambridge: Cambridge University Press.

Brown, R. 1973. *A First Language: The early stages*. London: George Allen & Unwin.

Brown, R. 1977. Introduction. In *Talking to Children: Language input and acquisition*. C. E. Snow and C. A. Ferguson (eds.). Cambridge: Cambridge University Press.

Brown, R., C. Cazden, and U. Bellugi. 1968. The Child's Grammar from 1 to 3. In *Minnesota Symposium on Child Development*. J. P. Hill (ed.). Minneapolis: University of Minnesota Press.

Bruner, J. 1978. The Role of Dialogue in Language Acquisition. In *The Child's Conception of Language*. A Sinclair, R. J. Jarvella, and W. J. M. Levelt (eds.). Berlin: Springer-Verlag.

Bruner, J. and V. Sherwood. 1976. Peekaboo and the Learning of Rule Structures. In *Play: Its role in development and evolution*. J. Bruner, A. Jolly, and K. Sylva (eds.). Harmondsworth: Penguin Books.

Bruner, J., A. Jolly and K. Sylva (eds.). 1976. *Play: Its role in development and evolution*. Harmondsworth: Penguin Books.

Burling, R. 1966. The Metrics of Children's Verse: A cross-linguistic study. *American Anthropologist* 68(4): 1418–41.

Burling, R. 1970. *Man's Many Voices: Language in its cultural context.* New York: Holt, Rinehart & Winston.

Cambourne, B. 1981. A Naturalistic Study of Metaphor in the Linguistic Environments of Grade 1 Children. Unpublished technical report, Riverina College of Advanced Education, NSW, Australia.

Camek, D. E. 1960. *Human Gold from Southern Hills.* Greer, SC: Published by the author.

Carlton, D. L. 1977. Mill and Town: The cotton mill workers and the middle class in South Carolina, 1880–1920. PhD dissertation, Yale University.

Carnoy, M. 1974. *Education as Cultural Imperialism.* New York: Longman.

Cazden, C. 1965. Environmental Assistance to the Child's Acquisition of Grammar. PhD Dissertation, Harvard University.

Cazden, C. 1968. The Acquisition of Noun and Verb Inflections. *Child Development* 39: 435–48.

Cazden, C. 1974. Play and Metalinguistic Awareness: One dimension of language experience. *The Urban Review* 7: 23–39.

Cazden, C. 1979. Language in Education: Variation in the teacher-talk register. In *Georgetown Round Table on Languages and Linguistics.* J. E. Alatis and R. Tucker (eds.). Washington, DC: Georgetown University Press.

Chanan, G. and L. Gilchrist. 1974. *What School is For.* New York: Praeger.

Charnofsky, S. 1971. *Educating the Powerless.* Belmont, CA: Wadsworth Publishing Co.

Charrow, V. 1979. *Let the Rewriter Beware.* Washington, DC: American Institutes for Research.

Cherry, L. 1978. A Sociocognitive Approach to Language Development and its Implications for Education. In *Language, Children, and Society.* O. Garnica and M. King (eds.). New York: Pergamon Press.

Cherry, L. 1979. The Role of Adults' Requests for Clarification in the Language Development of Children. In *New Directions in Discourse Processing*, Volume 2. R. O. Freedle (ed.). Norwood, NJ: Ablex.

Childs, C. and P. Greenfield. 1981. Informal Modes of Learning and Teaching: The case of Zinacanteco weaving. In *Advances in Cross-cultural Psychology*, Volume 2. N. Warren (ed.). New York: Academic Press.

Chipman, S. 1977. Complexity and Structure in Visual Patterns. *Journal of Experimental Psychology* 106(3): 269–301.

Chipman, S. and M. J. Mendelson. 1979. Influence of Six Types of Visual Structure on Complexity Judgments in Children and Adults. *Journal of Experimental Psychology* 5(2): 365–78.

Cochran-Smith, M. 1983. *The Making of a Reader.* Norwood, NJ: Ablex.

Coe, R. 1939. *The Textile Industry in South Carolina: A vocational guidance study.* Columbia, SC: National Youth Administration for South Carolina.

Cohen, G. 1981. Culture and Educational Achievement. *Harvard Educational Review* 51(2): 270–85.

Concannon, S. J. 1975. Illustrations in Books for Children: Review of research. *The Reading Teacher* 29: 254–6.

Conway, M. 1979. *Rise, Gonna Rise: A portrait of Southern textile workers.* Garden City, NY: Anchor/Doubleday.

Cook, J. H. 1925. *A Study of the Mill Schools of North Carolina.* New York: Teachers College, Columbia University.

Bibliography

Cook-Gumperz, J. 1977. Situated Instructions: Language socialization of school-age children. In *Child Discourse*. S. Ervin-Tripp and C. Mitchell-Kernan (eds.). New York: Academic Press.

Cooke, B. 1972. Nonverbal Communication among Afro-Americans: An initial classification. In *Rappin' and Stylin' Out: Communication in urban Black America*. T. Kochman (ed.). Urbana, IL: University of Illinois Press.

Corsaro, W. 1977. The Clarification Request as a Feature of Adult Interactive Styles with Young Children. *Language in Society* 6(2): 183–207.

Crago, M. 1975. One Child and Her Books: A case study, 11–24 months. *Children's Libraries Newsletter* 11(1): 3–8.

Davis, A., B. B. Gardner and M. R. Gardner. 1941. *Deep South: A social anthropological study of caste and class*. Chicago: University of Chicago Press. Abridged edition, 1965. Directed by W. L. Gardner.

Diesing, P. 1971. *Patterns of Discovery in the Social Sciences*. Chicago, IL: Aldine-Atherton.

Dillard, J. 1972. *Black English: Its history and usage in the United States*. New York: Random House.

Dillard, J. 1976. *Black Names*. The Hague: Mouton.

Dodd, C. H. 1961. *The Parables of the Kingdom*. New York: Charles Scribner's Sons.

Dollard, J. 1949. *Caste and Class in a Southern Town*. 3rd edition. New York: Anchor/Doubleday.

Donaldson, M. 1978. *Children's Minds*. London: Croom Helm.

Dore, J. 1978. Variation in Preschool Children's Conversational Performances. In *Children's Language*, Volume 1. K. E. Nelson (ed.). New York: Gardner Press.

Douglas, M. 1970. *Natural Symbols: Explorations in cosmology*. London: Barrie & Jenkins.

Dreeben, R. 1968. *On What is Learned in School*. Reading, MA: Addison-Wesley.

Erickson, F. 1975. Gatekeeping and the Melting Pot: Interaction in counseling encounters. *Harvard Educational Review* 45(1): 44–70.

Erickson, F. and J. Schultz. 1981. *The Counselor as Gatekeeper: Social interaction in interviews*. New York: Academic Press.

Ervin-Tripp, S. 1977. Wait for Me, Roller Skate! In *Child Discourse*. S. Ervin-Tripp and C. Mitchell-Kernan (eds.). New York: Academic Press.

Ervin-Tripp, S. and W. Miller. 1977. Early Discourse: Some questions about questions. In *Interaction, Conversation, and the Development of Language*. M. Lewis and L. A. Rosenblum (eds.). New York: John Wiley.

Farwell, C. 1976. Some Strategies in the Early Production of Fricatives. *Papers and Reports on Child Language Development* 12: 97–104.

Fawcett, T. 1971. *The Symbolic Language of Religion*. Minneapolis, MN: Augsburg Publishing House.

Feagin, C. 1979. *Variation and Change in Alabama English: A sociolinguistic study of the white community*. Washington, DC: Georgetown University Press.

Feitelson, D. and G. S. Ross. 1973. The Neglected Factor – Play. *Human Development* 16: 202–23.

Felker, D. B. (ed.). 1980. *Document Design: A review of the relevant research*. Washington, DC: American Institutes for Research.

Ferguson, C. A. 1964. Baby Talk in Six Languages Part 2. *American Anthropologist* 66(6): 103–14.

Ferguson, C. A. 1976. The Structure and Use of Politeness Formulas. *Language in Society* 5(2): 137–51.

Ferguson, C. A. 1977. Baby Talk as a Simplified Register. In *Talking to Children: Language input and acquisition*. C. E. Snow and C. A. Ferguson (eds.). Cambridge: Cambridge University Press.

Ferguson, C. A. 1978. Talking to Children: A search for universals. In *Universals of Human Language*, Volume 1, *Method and Theory*. J. H. Greenberg, C. A. Ferguson, and E. A. Moravcsik (eds.). Stanford, CA: Stanford University Press.

Ferguson, C. A. 1982. Simplified Registers and Linguistic Theory. In *Exceptional Language and Linguistics*. L. Obler and L. Menn (eds.). London and New York: Academic Press.

Ferguson, C. A. and M. Macken. 1980. Phonological Development in Children: Play and cognition. *Papers and Reports in Child Language Development* 18(2): 19–27. To appear in *Children's Language*, Volume 4. K. E. Nelson (ed.). Gardner Press: New York.

Fillmore, C. J. 1981. Ideal Readers and Real Readers. In *Georgetown University Round Table on Languages and Linguistics*. Washington, DC: Georgetown University Press.

Fillmore, L. W. 1976. The Second Time Around: Cognitive and social strategies in second language acquisition. PhD Dissertation, Stanford University.

Fischer, J. and A. Fischer. 1963. The New Englanders of Orchard Town, USA. In *Six Cultures: Studies of child rearing*. J. Whiting and B. Whiting (eds.). New York: John Wiley.

Flint, D. 1977. Some Relationships Between Maternal Variables, Reading Achievement, and IQ for Low SES Black First Graders. Master's Thesis, Rutgers University.

Florio, S. 1978. Learning How to Go to School: An ethnography of interaction in a kindergarten/first grade classroom. PhD Dissertation, School of Education, Harvard University.

Folb, E. A. 1980. *Runnin' Down Some Lines: The language and culture of Black teenagers*. Cambridge, MA: Harvard University Press.

Garvey, C. 1977a. Contingent Queries. In *Interaction, Conversation, and the Development of Language: The origins of behavior*, Volume 5. M. Lewis and L. Rosenblum (eds.). New York: John Wiley.

Garvey, C. 1977b. *Play*. Cambridge, MA: Harvard University Press.

Gilman, G. 1956. *Human Relations in the Industrial Southeast*. Chapel Hill, NC: University of North Carolina Press.

Gilmore, P. 1982. The Right to Read: Attitudes and admission to literacy. PhD Dissertation, University of Pennsylvania.

Gleason, J. B. and S. Weintraub. 1976. The Acquisition of Routines in Child Language. *Language in Society* 5: 129–36.

Gleason, J. B. and S. Weintraub. 1978. Input Language and the Acquisition of Communicative Competence. In *Children's Language*, Volume 1. K. E. Nelson (ed.). New York: Gardner Press.

Gleason, J. B., E. B. Greif, S. Weintraub, and J. Fardella. 1977. Father Doesn't Know Best: Parents' awareness of their children's linguistic, cognitive, and affective development. Paper presented at the meeting of the Society for Research in Child Development.

Gluckman, M. 1963. Gossip and Scandal. *Current Anthropology* 4: 307–16.

Goffman, E. 1959. *The Presentation of Self in Everyday Life*. Garden City, NY: Anchor Books.

Goffman, E. 1974. *Frame Analysis: An essay on the organization of experience*. New York: Harper and Row.

Bibliography

Goffman, E. 1978. Response Cries. *Language* 54(4): 787–815. Also in Goffman 1981.

Goffman, E. 1981. *Forms of Talk*. Philadelphia, PA: University of Pennsylvania Press.

Goody, E. N. 1977. Towards a Theory of Questions. In *Questions and Politeness: Strategies in social interaction*. E. N. Goody (ed.). Cambridge: Cambridge University Press.

Goody, J. 1968. Introduction. In *Literacy in Traditional Societies*. J. Goody, (ed.). Cambridge: Cambridge University Press.

Gordon, A. H. 1929. *Sketches of Negro Life and History in South Carolina*. Columbia, SC: University of South Carolina Press. Reprinted 1971.

Goswami, D. and L. Odell. 1981. *Writing in Non-academic settings. Final report* (NIE-78-g-0224).

Goswami, D., D. Felker, and J. Redish. 1981. *Writing in the Professions*. Washington, DC: Document Design Center, American Institutes for Research.

Graetz, M. 1976. From Picture Books to Illustrated Stories: How children understand all those words. *Children's Libraries Newsletter* 12(3 & 4): 79–87, 122–6.

Graff, H. 1979. *The Literacy Myth: Literacy and social structure in the nineteenth-century city*. New York: Academic Press.

Graves, D. H. 1982. *Writing: Teachers and children at work*. Exeter, NH: Heinemann Educational Books.

Greenfield, P. and J. Lave. 1982. Cognitive Aspects of Informal Education. In *Cultural Perspectives on Child Development*. D. A. Wagner and H. W. Stevenson (eds.). San Francisco: W. H. Freeman.

Gregor, T. 1977. *Mehinaku: The drama of daily life in a Brazilian Indian village*. Chicago: University of Chicago Press.

Gumperz, J. and J. Cook-Gumperz. 1981. Ethnic Differences in Communicative Style. In *Language in the USA*. C. A. Ferguson and S. B. Heath (eds.). Cambridge: Cambridge University Press.

Hall, O. and R. Carlton. 1977. *Basic Skills at School and Work: The study of Albertown, Toronto*. Toronto: Ontario Economic Council.

Halliday, M. A. K. 1975. *Learning How to Mean: Explorations in the development of language*. New York: Elsevier North-Holland.

Harkness, S. 1977. Aspects of Social Environment and First Language Acquisition in Rural Africa. In *Talking to Children: Language input and acquisition*. C. E. Snow and C. A. Ferguson (eds.). Cambridge: Cambridge University Press.

Harste, J. C., C. L. Burke, and V. A. Woodward. 1981. *Children, their Language and World: Initial encounters with print. Final report* (NIE-79-g-0132). Bloomington, IN: Language Education Department.

Haviland, J. 1977. *Gossip, Reputation, and Knowledge in Zinacantan*. Chicago: University of Chicago Press.

Heath, S. B. 1978a. *Outline Guide for the Ethnographic Study of Literacy and Oral Language from Schools to Communities*. Working Papers in Language and Education 2. Philadelphia: Graduate School of Education, University of Pennsylvania.

Heath, S. B. 1978b. *Teacher Talk: Language in the classroom*. Language in Education: Theory and Practice 9. Washington, DC: Center for Applied Linguistics.

Heath, S. B. 1981a. Teasing Talk: Strategies for language learning. Paper presented at the 1981 meeting of the American Anthropological Association.

Heath, S. B. 1981b. Toward an Ethnohistory of Writing in American Education.

In *Variation in Writing: Functional and linguistic cultural differences.* M. F. Whiteman (ed.). Baltimore, MD: Lawrence Erlbaum.

Heath, S. B. 1982a. Protean Shapes in Literacy Events: Ever-shifting oral and literate traditions. In *Spoken and Written Language: Exploring orality and literacy.* D. Tannen (ed.). Norwood, NJ: Ablex.

Heath, S. B. 1982b. Questioning at Home and at School: A comparative study. In *Doing the Ethnography of Schooling: Educational anthropology in action.* G. Spindler (ed.). New York: Holt, Rinehart & Winston.

Heath, S. B. 1982c. What No Bedtime Story Means: Narrative skills at home and school. *Language in Society* 11(2): 49–76.

Heath, S. B. Forthcoming. Language Beyond the Classroom. In *Symposium on Language Studies.* R. DiPietro (ed.). Newark, DL: University of Delaware.

Herring, H. L. 1929. *Welfare Work in Mill Villages.* Chapel Hill, NC: University of North Carolina Press.

Herron, R. and B. Sutton-Smith. 1971. *Child's Play.* New York: John Wiley.

Hess, R. D. 1980. Experts and Amateurs: Some unintended consequences of parent education. In *Parenting in a Multicultural Society.* M. D. Fantini and R. Cardenas (eds.). New York: Longmans.

Hoffman, M. 1976. *Reading, Writing and Relevance.* London: Hodder & Stoughton.

Holmer, P. 1968. The Nature of Religious Propositions. In *Religious Language and the Problem of Religious Knowledge.* R. E. Santoni (ed.). Bloomington, IN: Indiana University Press.

Holzman, M. 1972. The Use of Interrogative Forms in the Verbal Interaction of Three Mothers and Their Children. *Journal of Psycholinguistic Research* 1: 311–36.

Holzman, M. 1974. The Verbal Environment Provided by Mothers for their Very Young Children. *Merrill-Palmer Quarterly* 20: 31–42.

Hoskisson, K., T. Sherman, and L. Smith. 1974. Assisted Reading and Parent Involvement. *The Reading Teacher* 27: 710–16.

Hunter, F. 1953. *Community Power Structure.* Chapel Hill, NC: University of North Carolina Press.

Hymes, D. H. 1972a. Models of the Interactions of Language and Social Life. In *Directions in Sociolinguistics: The ethnography of communication.* J. J. Gumperz and D. H. Hymes (eds.). New York: Holt, Rinehart.

Hymes, D. H. 1972b. Speech and Language: On the origins and foundations of inequality among speakers. In *Directions in Sociolinguistics: The ethnography of communication.* J. J. Gumperz and D. H. Hymes (eds.). New York: Holt, Rinehart.

Hymes, D. H. 1973. Speech and Language: On the origins and foundations of inequality among speakers. *Daedalus* 102 (3): 59–85.

Inabinet, J. G. and C. R. Inabinet. 1975–6. *The Old Mill Stream.* Published in Lando, South Carolina.

Inkeles, A. 1969. Making Men Modern. *American Journal of Sociology* 75: 208–225.

Inkeles, A. and D. H. Smith. 1974. *Becoming Modern.* Cambridge, MA: Harvard University Press.

Jeremias, J. 1963. *The Parables of Jesus.* Revised edition. New York: Charles Scribner's Sons.

Keenan, E. O. 1974. Conversational Competence in Children. *Journal of Child Language* 1(2): 163–83.

Keenan, E. O. and B. Schieffelin. 1976. Topic as a Discourse Notion: A study of topic in the conversations of children and adults. In *Subject and Topic*. C. Li (ed.). New York: Academic Press.

Kelly-Byrne, D. and B. Sutton-Smith. Forthcoming. *Intimate Play*.

Kintsch, W. 1972. Notes on the Structure of Semantic Memory. In *The Organization of Memory*. E. Tulving and W. Donaldson (eds.). New York: Academic Press.

Kintsch, W. 1974. *The Representation of Meaning in Memory*. Hillsdale, NJ: Lawrence Erlbaum.

Kintsch, W. and T. Van Dijk. 1978. Toward a Model of Text Comprehension and Production. *Psychological Review* 85: 363–94.

Kirsch, I. and J. T. Guthrie. 1977–8. The Concept and Measurement of Functional Literacy. *Reading Research Quarterly* 13(4): 485–507.

Kiser, C. V. 1932. *From Sea Island to City*. New York: Columbia University Press.

Klein, R. 1979. The Rise of the Planters in the South Carolina Backcountry 1767–1808. PhD Dissertation, Yale University.

Kochman, T. 1970. Toward an Ethnography of Black American Speech Behavior. In *Afro-American Anthropology: Contemporary perspectives*. N. E. Whitten, Jr. and J. F. Szwed (eds.). New York: Free Press.

Kohn, A. 1907. *The Cotton Mills of South Carolina*. Columbia, SC: Privately published.

Labov, W. 1969. The Logic of Nonstandard English. In *Georgetown Round Table on Languages and Linguistics*. Washington, DC: Georgetown University Press. Reprinted in Labov 1972.

Labov, W. 1972. *Language in the Inner City*. Philadelphia: University of Pennsylvania Press.

Labov, W. 1973. The Linguistic Consequences of Being a Lame. *Language in Society* 2(1): 81–115.

Labov, W. and T. Labov. 1978. The Phonetics of Cat and Mama. *Language* 54(4): 816–52.

Lahne, H. J. 1944. *The Cotton Mill Worker: Labor in twentieth century America*. New York: Farrar & Rinehart.

Lakoff, G. and M. Johnson. 1980. *Metaphors We Live By*. Chicago: University of Chicago Press.

Lander, E. M. 1969. *The Textile Industry in Antebellum South Carolina*. Baton Rouge, LA: Louisiana State Press.

Leifermann, H. P. 1975. *Crystal Lee: A woman of inheritance*. New York: Macmillan.

Lemert, B. F. 1933. *The Cotton Textile Industry of the Southern Appalachian Piedmont*. Chapel Hill, NC: University of North Carolina Press.

Leondar, B. 1977. Hatching Plots: Genesis of storymaking. In *Arts and Cognition*. D. Perkins and B. Leondar (eds.). Baltimore, MD: Johns Hopkins University Press.

Levelt, W. J. M. 1975. *What Became of LAD?* Lisse, Netherlands: Peter de Ridder Press.

Levine, L. W. 1977. *Black Culture and Black Consciousness: Afro-American folk thought from slavery to freedom*. New York: Oxford University Press.

Lewis, H. 1955. *Blackways of Kent*. Chapel Hill, NC: University of North Carolina Press.

Lindstrom, M. 1970. *Children's Art*. Berkeley: University of California Press.

Lord, A. B. 1965. *The Singer of Tales*. Cambridge, MA: Harvard University Press.

Loudon, J. B. 1970. Teasing and Socialization on Tristan da Cunha. In *Socialization: The approach from social anthropology.* P. Mayer (ed.). London: Tavistock Publications.

Lowe, V. 1975. Books and a Preverbal Child: 3–28 months. *Children's Libraries Newsletter* 11(3): 73–9, (4) 108–13.

Lyon, R. M. 1937. *The Basis for Constructing Curricular Materials in Adult Education for Carolina Cotton Mill Workers.* New York: Teachers College.

MacDonald, L. 1928. *Southern Mill Hills: A study of social and economic forces in certain textile mill villages.* New York: A. L. Hillman.

Mandler, J. M. and N. S. Johnson. 1977. Remembrance of Things Parsed: Story structure and recall. *Cognitive Psychology* (9): 111–51.

Manzo, A. V. 1981. Using Proverbs to Teach Reading and Thinking. *The Reading Teacher* 34(4): 411–16.

Mead, M. and F. C. Macgregor. 1951. *Growth and Culture: A photographic study of Balinese childhood.* Photographs by Gregory Bateson. New York: G. P. Putnam's Sons.

Michaels, S. 1981. "Sharing time:" Children's narrative styles and differential access to literacy. *Language in Society* 10(3): 423–42.

Michaels, S. and J. Cook-Gumperz. 1979. A Study of Sharing Time with First-grade Students: Discourse narratives in the classroom. In *Proceedings of the Fifth Annual Meetings of Berkeley Linguistics Society.* University of California.

Miller, M. S. (ed.) 1980. *Working Lives; The Southern Exposure: History of labor in the South.* New York: Pantheon.

Miller, P. J. 1982a. *Amy, Wendy, and Beth: Language learning in South Baltimore.* Austin: University of Texas Press.

Miller, P. J. 1982b. A Case Study in Language Socialization and Verbal Play. *The Quarterly Newsletter of the Laboratory for Comparative Human Cognition.*

Miller, W. H. 1969. An Examination of Children's Daily Schedules in Three Social Classes and their Relation to First-grade Reading Achievement. *California Journal of Educational Research* 21: 100–10.

Miller, W. H. 1975. Longitudinal Study of Home Factors and Reading Achievement. *California Journal of Educational Research* 26: 130–6.

Mitchell, B. 1968. *The Rise of Cotton Mills in the South.* New York: Da Capo Press. (With a new introduction by the author.) (Originally published Baltimore, MD: Johns Hopkins Press, 1921.)

Mitchell, H. H. 1970. *Black Preaching.* Philadelphia: Lippincott.

Morgan, J., C. O'Neill, and R. Harré. 1979. *Nicknames: Their origins and social consequences.* London: Routledge & Kegan Paul.

Morland, J. K. 1958. *Millways of Kent.* Chapel Hill, NC: University of North Carolina Press.

Napoli, J. 1968. Environmental Factors and Reading Ability. *The Reading Teacher* 21: 552–8.

Nelson, K. E. 1973. *Structure and Strategy in Learning to Talk.* Monographs of the Society for Research in Child Development 39(1–2) (Serial No. 149).

Nelson, K. E. 1981. Individual Differences in Language Development: Implications for development and language. *Developmental Psychology* 17: 170–87.

Newby, I. A. 1973. *Black Carolinians: A history of Blacks in South Carolina from 1895 to 1968.* Columbia, SC: University of South Carolina Press.

Newman, D. 1978. Work and Community Life in a Southern Textile Town. *Journal of Labor History* 19(2): 204–25.

Newman, D. 1980. Textile Workers in a Tobacco County: A comparison between yarn and weave mill villages. In *The Southern Common People: Studies in nineteenth-century social history.* E. Magdol and J. L. Wakelyn (eds.). Nestport, CN: Greenwood Press.

Newport, E. 1976. Motherese: The speech of mothers to young children. In *Cognitive Theory*, Volume 2. N. Castellan, D. Pisoni and G. Potts (eds.). Hillsdale, NJ: Lawrence Erlbaum.

Newport, E. L., H. Gleitman and L. R. Gleitman. 1977. Mother, I'd Rather Do it Myself: Some effects and non-effects of maternal speech style. In *Talking to Children: Language input and acquisition.* C. E. Snow and C. A. Ferguson (eds.). Cambridge: Cambridge University Press.

Ninio, A. and J. Bruner. 1978. The Achievement and Antecedents of Labelling. *Journal of Child Language* 5: 1–15.

Noddings, N., P. Chaffe, and D. S. Enright. 1981. How Children Approach Mathematical Word Problems. Unpublished paper presented at the American Educational Research Association Meetings.

Oates, M. J. 1975. *The Role of the Cotton Textile Industry in the Economic Development of the American Southeast: 1900–1940.* New York: Arno Press.

Odum, H. 1930. *An American Epoch: Southern Portraiture in the National Picture.* New York: Henry Holt.

Odum, H. 1936. *Southern Regions of the United States.* Chapel Hill, NC: University of North Carolina Press.

Olson, D. R. 1977. From Utterance to Text: The bias of language in speech and writing. *Harvard Educational Review* 47(3): 257–81.

Ortony, A. (ed.) 1979. *Metaphor and Thought.* Cambridge: Cambridge University Press.

Paivio, A. 1979. Psychological Processes in the Comprehension of Metaphor. In *Metaphor and Thought.* A. Ortony (ed.). Cambridge: Cambridge University Press.

Paley, V. G. 1981. *Wally's Stories.* Cambridge, MA: Harvard University Press.

Parry, M. 1930. Studies in the Epic Tradition of Oral Verse-making. 1. Homer and Homeric style. *Harvard Studies in Classical Philosophy* 41: 73–147.

Peters, A. 1977. Language Learning Strategies. *Language* 53: 560–73.

Peters, A. 1983. *The Units of Language Acquisition.* Cambridge: Cambridge University Press.

Petrie, H. G. 1979. Metaphor and Learning. In *Metaphor and Thought.* A Ortony (ed.). Cambridge: Cambridge University Press.

Philips, S. 1972. Participation Structures and Communicative Competence: Warm Springs children in community and classroom. In *Functions of Language in the Classroom.* C. Cazden, V. P. John, and D. H. Hymes (eds.). New York: Teachers College Press.

Philips, S. 1983. *The Invisible Culture: Communication in classroom and community on the Warm Springs Indian Reservation.* New York: Longman.

Piaget, J. 1951. *Play, Dreams and Imitation in Childhood.* London: Routledge & Kegan Paul.

Platt, P. 1977. Grapho-linguistics: Children's drawings in relation to reading and writing skills. *The Reading Teacher* 31(3): 262–8.

Pope, L. 1971. *Millhands and Preachers, A Study of Gastonia.* New York: Oxford University Press.

Potwin, M. A. 1927. *Cotton Mill People of the Piedmont: A study in social change.* New York: Columbia University Press.

Propp, V. 1968. *The Morphology of the Folk-tale*. 2nd edition. Austin: University of Texas Press.

Radcliffe-Brown, A. R. 1952. *Structure and Function in Primitive Society*. London: Cohen & West.

Rainwater, L. 1970. *Behind Ghetto Walls: Black families in a federal slum*. Chicago: Aldine.

Redish, J. and K. Racette. 1979. *Teaching College Students How to Write*. Washington, DC: American Institutes for Research.

Rhyne, J. J. 1930. *Some Southern Cotton Mill Workers and their Villages*. Chapel Hill, NC: University of North Carolina Press.

Richardson, C. and J. Church. 1959. A Developmental Analysis of Proverb Interpretations. *Journal of Genetic Psychology* 94: 169–79.

Robertson, B. 1942. *Red Hills and Cotton*. New York: Alfred A. Knopf.

Robinson, W. P. and S. J. Rackstraw. 1972. *A Question of Answers*. 2 volumes. London: Routledge & Kegan Paul.

Rodman, H. 1963. The Lower Class Value Stretch. *Social Forces* 42(2): 205–15.

Rosenberg, B. A. 1970. *The Art of the American Folk Preacher*. New York: Oxford University Press.

Rosnow, R. L. 1976. *Rumor and Gossip: The social psychology of hearsay*. New York: Elsevier.

Rubin, L. B. 1976. *Worlds of Pain: Life in the working-class family*. New York: Basic Books.

Rumelhart, D. E. 1975. Notes on a Schema for Stories. In *Representation and Understanding*. D. G. Bobrow and A. Collins (eds.). New York: Academic Press.

Rumelhart, D. E. and A. Ortony. 1977. The Representation of Knowledge in Memory. In *Schooling and the Acquisition of Knowledge*. R. C. Anderson, R. J. Spiro, and W. E. Montague (eds.). Hillsdale, NJ: Lawrence Erlbaum.

Sachs, J. 1980. The Role of Adult–child Play in Language Development. *New Directions for Child Development* 9: 33–48.

Samuels, S. J. 1970. Effects of Pictures on Learning to Read, Comprehension, and Attitudes. *Review of Educational Research* 40: 397–407.

Santoni, R. E. (ed.) 1968. *Religious Language and the Problem of Religious Knowledge*. Bloomington, IN: Indiana University Press.

Schallert, D. L. 1980. The Role of Illustrations in Reading Comprehension. In *Theoretical Issues in Reading Comprehension*. R. J. Spiro, B. C. Bruce, and W. F. Brewer (eds.). Hillsdale, NJ: Lawrence Erlbaum.

Schieffelin, B. B. 1979a. Getting It Together: An ethnographic approach to the study of the development of communicative competence. In *Developmental Pragmatics*. E. Ochs and B. B. Schieffelin (eds.). New York: Academic Press.

Schieffelin, B. B. 1979b. How Kaluli Children Learn What to Say, What to Do, and How to Feel: An ethnographic study of the development of communicative competence. PhD Dissertation, Columbia University.

Schwartzman, H. 1979. *Transformations: The anthropology of children's play*. New York: Plenum.

Scollon, R. and S. Scollon. 1979. *Linguistic Convergence: An ethnography of speaking at Fort Chipewyan, Alberta*. New York: Academic Press.

Scollon, R. and S. Scollon. 1981. *Narrative, Literacy, and Face in Interethnic Communication*. Norwood, NJ: Ablex.

Scribner, S. Forthcoming. Studying Working Intelligence. To appear in *Everyday Cognition: Its development in social context*. B. Rogoff and J. Lave (eds.). Cambridge, MA: Harvard University Press.

Bibliography

Scribner, S. and M. Cole. 1973. Cognitive Consequences of Formal and Informal Education. *Science* 182(1): 553–9.

Scribner, S. and M. Cole. 1981. *The Psychology of Literacy.* Cambridge, MA: Harvard University Press.

Simpson, W. H. 1943. *Life in Mill Communities.* Clinton, SC: The Presbyterian College Press.

Smith, R. 1928. *South Carolina Ballads.* Cambridge, MA: Harvard University Press.

Smitherman, G. 1977. *Talkin' and Testifyin': The language of Black America.* Boston: Houghton Mifflin.

Snow, C. E. 1977a. The development of conversation between mothers and babies. *Journal of Child Language* 4: 1–22.

Snow, C. E. 1977b. Mother's Speech Research: From input to interaction. In *Talking to Children: Language input and acquisition.* C. E. Snow and C. A. Ferguson (eds.). Cambridge: Cambridge University Press.

Snow, C. E. 1979. The Role of Social Interaction in Language Acquisition. In *Children's Language and Communication.* The Minnesota Symposia on Child Psychology, Volume 12. Hillsdale, NJ: Lawrence Erlbaum.

Snow, C. E. and C. A. Ferguson (eds.) 1977. *Talking to Children: Language input and acquisition.* Cambridge: Cambridge University Press.

Snow, C. E., A. Arlman-Rup, Y. Hassing, J. Jobse, J. Joosten, and J. Vorster. 1976. Mother's Speech in Three Social Classes. *Journal of Psycholinguistic Research* 5: 1–20.

Stack, C. B. 1970. The Kindred of Viola Jackson: Residence and family organization of an urban Black American family. In *Afro-American Anthropology: Contemporary perspectives.* N. E. Whitten and J. F. Szwed (eds.). New York: The Free Press.

Stack, C. B. 1974. *All our Kin: Strategies for survival in a Black community.* New York: Harper & Row.

Staton, J., R. Shuy, J. Kreeft, and Mrs. R. 1982. *Dialogue Writing as a Communicative Event.* Washington, DC: Center for Applied Linguistics.

Stein, N. L. 1978. *How Children Understand Stories: A development analysis.* Technical Report No. 69. Urbana, IL: Center for the Study of Reading, University of Illinois.

Stein, N. L. and C. G. Glenn. 1979. An Analysis of Story Comprehension in Elementary School Children. In *New Directions in Discourse Processing,* Volume 2. R. Freedle (ed.). Norwood, NJ: Ablex.

Sutton-Smith, B. 1974. Toward an Anthropology of Play. *The Association for the Anthropological Study of Play Newsletter* 1: 8–15.

Sutton-Smith, B. 1975. The Importance of the Storytaker: An investigation of the imaginative life. *The Urban Review* 8(2): 82–96.

Sutton-Smith, B. (ed.) 1979a. *Play and Learning.* New York: Gardner Press.

Sutton-Smith, B. 1979b. The Play of Girls. In *Becoming Female: Perspectives on development.* C. B. Kopp and M. Kirkpatrick (eds.). New York: Plenum.

Sutton-Smith, B. 1980a. Piaget, Play and Cognition, Revisited. In *The Relationship between Social and Cognitive Development.* W. Overton (ed.). New York: Lawrence Erlbaum.

Sutton-Smith, B. 1980b. *The Folkstories of Children.* Philadelphia: University of Pennsylvania Press.

Sutton-Smith, B. and S. B. Heath. 1981. Paradigms of Pretense. *The Quarterly Newsletter of the Laboratory of Comparative Human Cognition* 3(3): 41–5.

Sutton-Smith, B., G. Botvin, and D. Mahony. 1976. Developmental Structures in Fantasy Narratives. *Human Development* 19: 1–13.

Swanson, C. 1981. High-school Cheerleading in South Carolina: Movement and the pursuit of status. Unpublished paper presented at Language and Culture Symposium, University of South Carolina.

Szwed, J. F. 1981. The Ethnography of Literacy. In *Writing: The nature, development, and teaching of written communication*, Volume 1: *Variation in Writing: Functional and linguistic cultural differences*. M. F. Whiteman (ed.) Baltimore, MD: Lawrence Erlbaum.

Taylor, M. and A. Ortony. 1980. Rhetorical Devices in Black English: Some psycholinguistic and educational observations. *The Quarterly Newsletter of the Laboratory of Comparative Human Cognition* 2(2): 21–6.

TeSelle, S. M. 1975. *Speaking in Parables: A study in metaphor and theology*. Philadelphia, PA: Fortress Press.

Thorndyke, P. W. 1977. Cognitive Structures in Comprehension and Memory of Narrative Discourse. *Cognitive Psychology* 9: 77–110.

Thurston, L. 1977. The Experimental Analysis of a Parent-tutoring Program to Increase Reading Enjoyment, and Oral Reading, and Comprehension Skills of Urban Elementary School Children. PhD Dissertation, University of Kansas.

Turnbull, C. M. 1972. *The Mountain People*. New York: Simon & Schuster.

Umiker-Sebeok, D. J. 1979. Preschool Children's Intraconversational Narratives. *Journal of Child Language* 6(1): 91–109.

Vihman, M. M. 1982. Formulas in First and Second Language Acquisition. In *Exceptional Language and Linguistics*. L. Obler and L. Menn (eds.). New York: Academic Press.

Vygotsky, L. S. 1962. *Thought and Language*. Cambridge, MA: MIT Press.

Vygotsky, L. S. 1978. *Mind in Society: The development of higher psychological processes*. Translated by M. Cole, V. John-Steiner, S. Scribner, and E. Souberman. Cambridge, MA: Harvard University Press.

Wagner, S., E. Winner, D. Cicchetti, and H. Gardner. 1981. "Metaphorical" Mapping in Human Infants. *Child Development* 52(2): 728–31.

Ward, B. E. 1970. Temper Tantrums in Kau Sai: Some speculations upon their effects. In *Socialization: The approach from social anthropology*. P. Mayer (ed.). London: Tavistock Publications.

Ward, M. C. 1971. *Them Children: A Study in Language Learning*. New York: Holt, Rinehart & Winston.

Watson, J. M. 1977. The Influence of Context on Referential Description in Children. *British Journal of Educational Psychology* 47: 33–9.

Weir, R. H. 1962. *Language in the Crib*. The Hague: Mouton.

Wertenbaker, T. J. 1963. *The Old South: The Founding of American Civilization*. New York: Cooper Square.

Wertsch, J. V. 1978. Adult–child Interaction and the Roots of Meta-cognition. *The Quarterly Newsletter of the Laboratory of Comparative Human Cognition* 2(1): 15–18.

Wertsch, J. V. Forthcoming a. *Cognitive Developmental Theory: A Vygotskian approach*. Cambridge, MA: Harvard University Press.

Wertsch, J. V. Forthcoming b. From Social Interaction to Higher Psychological Processes. *Human Development*.

Whatley, E. 1981. Language among Black Americans. In *Language in the USA*. C. A. Ferguson and S. B. Heath (eds.). Cambridge: Cambridge University Press.

Whiting, J. and B. Whiting (eds.). 1963. *Six Cultures: Studies of child rearing*. New York: John Wiley.

Bibliography

Wiggington, E. 1979. *Foxfire 5*. Garden City, NY: Anchor Books.

Willis, P. 1977. *Learning to Labour*. Westmead, England: Saxon House.

Wills, D. D. 1977. Participant Deixis in English and Baby Talk. In *Talking to Children: Language input and acquisition*. C. E. Snow and C. A. Ferguson (eds.). Cambridge: Cambridge University Press.

Wolcott, H. 1973. *The Man in the Principal's Office: An ethnography*. New York: Holt, Rinehart & Winston.

Young, V. H. 1970. Family and Childhood in a Southern Negro Community. *American Anthropologist* 72(2): 269–88.

Index

Index

stories (cont'd)
300; factual (nonfictive), R, 152, 158,
164–6; fictive, M, 250, 256, 289; R,
160–6; T, 161–3, 289; formulaic, T,
188–9; ghost, T, 188–9, 385; opening
and ending formulae in, R, 298–9; T, 171,
185, 299–300, 302–3, 306–7;
orientations in, 384; T, 171–2; 300, 302–
3, 306–7; R, **149–66, 222–30**, 294, 295,
296–310, 352; retold, T, 188; in school,
160–6, 189, 253–5, 281, 294–310, 295,
302–3, 326; story-poems, T, 170–4,
383–4; story-starter questions, T, 104,
109–10; T, 109–10, **166–89**, 295, **296–
310**, 347, 376; "tellin' a story" (lie), R,
149–51, 157–60, 189, 295; "true story",
R, 158; T, 183, 186–9; titles of, 397
Sunday School and church schools, 387–8;
M, 253; R, 41, 42, 139–40, 147, 157,
216, 222–3, 226, 275; Sunday School
lessons, R, 32, 220, 220

taboo words, 123, 163, 177
"talkin' junk", **166–74**, 189; learning,
174–84
tape recording: as research method, 8–9,
266, 392; as teaching technique, 281,
287–9, 292–3, 299–310, 313, **316–24**,
337–8, **339–42**
teachers as researchers, 1–4, 12–13, **265–
314**, 324–32, 339–43, 354–9, 363, 394,
395, 399
teacher training, 1–4, **265–73**, 354–9, 394,
395; advanced degrees in, 245, 266
teasing: R, 115, 146; T, 71, 79–86, 110–
11, 347, 374, 375, 377
television: M, 243; R, 41, 161–2, 216, 221,
222, 228, 229, 273; in school, 328–9,
334; "Sesame Street", 134, 223, 228,
283; T, 55, 78, 169, 170, 186, 189, 190,
199, 273
testimonials, 153, 187, 203–5, 380, 399
tests and testing: minimum competency
testing, 357; standardized tests, 7, 8, 239,
272, 340, 349, 390, 395; unit tests, 293,
320, 321, 325, 340
time, see space–time functions
townspeople, **236–62**; comparison with R
and T, 3–4, **343–54**; cultural description
of, 236–44; defined, **1–4**, 9–12, 61, 236–
7, 265, 391–2; history of, 22–4, 371–2;
language learning among, 245–53, 351–
2; reading and writing among, 255–62,
351–2; story-telling among, 249–55; as
teachers, **266–343**, 354–69, 394–6
toys, 379–80, 382; educational, 133–4,

136, 138; M, 246–7, 249, 255, 257, 258;
R, 37, 41, 42, 114–16, **133–8**, 146,
160–2, 164–5, 229, 232, 280, 346; T,
53–5, 71, 76–7, 86, 96, 173–4, 231, 350,
376
Trackton (black mill community), 48;
children of, in school, 265–70, 273–6;
comparison of, with M and R, 3–4, **343–
54**; comparison of, with R, **28–9, 144–8,
184–9, 230–5, 294–310**; cultural
description of, **47–72**; future of, 359–67;
language of, 276–81, 315–24; language
learning in, **73–112**; reading and writing
in, **190–211**, 284–93, 315–24, 335,
336–9; as site of fieldwork, 1, 3, 5–7,
9–11, 28, 29; story-telling in, **166–84**,
294–310
transcription, **15–16**, 389

unions and unionization, 25, 27–9, 57,
362, 372–3
urban redevelopment, housing projects of,
49, 62, 236; see also houses

voluntary associations, 1, 42, 46, 240–1,
242, 245; YMCA, 238, 241–2, 253, 362

welfare payments, 52–4, 57, 60, 62
whites, 9; attitudes of, toward education,
22–5, 242, 262, **268–9**, 365; children of
working-class 267–70, 310, 363;
churches of, 22, 138–41, 144; in mills,
20–8, 260, 365–9, 371–3; in Piedmont
history, 20, 371–3; as teachers, 1–3, 5,
23, 240, 265–7, 270–3, 354–69, 394–6,
398–9; townspeople, 1, 10, 22–5, 236–
41, 265, 270, 391–2; "white trash", 22;
see also Roadville, townspeople
work, 10–11, 20; aspirations, of M, 236–8,
240–2, 359; of R, 33–44, 348, 361–7; of
T, 53–4, 57–69, 360–7; children's, of M,
243; of R, 33, 40–1; of T, 59, 63–5, 68; in
agriculture, 21–2, 25–7, 32–3, 61, 341;
on house maintenance of, M, 243; of R,
40–1; of T, 54–7, 68; language at, 233–4,
260–2, 328–9, 365, 394; men's, of M,
243–4, 260–2; of R, 40–1, 365; of T, 57,
59, 66–9, 72, 366; in mills, 5, 21–9,
33–7, 198, 234, 260–7, 365–6, 371–3;
relations between school and, 46–7, 57,
310–11, 329, 364–5; women's, of M,
242–5; of R, 40–1, 116–18, 365; of T,
59, **63–8**, 95, 366
writing, 390–1, 393–4; adults', M, 237,
244, 257–62, 259; R, 212–19, 218, 231;
T, 198–201, 199; adults', with children,